T4-ALD-999

LABOUR MARKET CONTRACTS AND INSTITUTIONS

A Cross-National Comparison

CONTRIBUTIONS TO ECONOMIC ANALYSIS

218

NORTH-HOLLAND
AMSTERDAM • LONDON • NEW YORK • TOKYO

LABOUR MARKET CONTRACTS AND INSTITUTIONS

A Cross-National Comparison

Papers presented at the International Workshop for
Labour Market Contracts and Institutions
at the Netherlands Institute for Advanced Studies (NIAS)
Wassenaar, The Netherlands

Edited by

Joop HARTOG
University of Amsterdam
Amsterdam, The Netherlands

Jules THEEUWES
University of Leiden
Leiden, The Netherlands

1993

NORTH-HOLLAND
AMSTERDAM • LONDON • NEW YORK • TOKYO

ELSEVIER SCIENCE PUBLISHERS B.V.
Sara Burgerhartstraat 25
P.O. Box 211, 1000 AE Amsterdam, The Netherlands

ISBN: 0-444-89927-8

This book is printed on acid-free paper.

PRINTED IN THE NETHERLANDS

INTRODUCTION TO THE SERIES

This series consists of a number of hitherto unpublished studies, which are introduced by the editors in the belief that they represent fresh contributions to economic science.

The term "economic analysis" as used in the title of the series has been adopted because it covers both the activities of the theoretical economist and the research worker.

Although the analytical methods used by the various contributors are not the same, they are nevertheless conditioned by the common origin of their studies, namely theoretical problems encountered in practical research. Since for this reason, business cycle research and national accounting, research work on behalf of economic policy, and problems of planning are the main sources of the subjects dealt with, they necessarily determine the manner of approach adopted by the authors. Their methods tend to be "practical" in the sense of not being too far remote from application to actual economic conditions. In additon they are quantitative.

It is the hope of the editors that the publication of these studies will help to stimulate the exchange of scientific information and to reinforce international cooperation in the field of economics.

The Editors

CONTENTS

PREFACE

Joop Hartog*
Jules Theeuwes**

A. The Problem

In our survey of the development of labour economics (Hartog and Theeuwes (1990)), we conjectured that some decades ago, research on labour markets could be classified into three research programs: the highly aggregated view of macro-economics, the richly detailed approach of the institutionalists studying "industrial and labour relations" and the smooth highly abstract world of neoclassical economics. Since then neoclassical labour economics has moved from the smooth auction market view of the labour market, which was assumed always to arrive swiftly at equilibrium through a perfectly flexible wage rate, to more complex theoretical models that take account of the institutional idiosyncrasies of the labour market stressed by the institutional school (see e.g. D.O. Parsons (1986)).

Crucial among these developments is the new view on the role of labour market institutions and on the specification of labour contracts. It is clearly realized that labour contracts specify more than a wage rate and the number of hours and that the wage structure serves more functions than the optimal allocation of labour in a fully competitive market. It is also obvious that labour market institutions such as unions, employers' associations, and collective bargaining are essential to the functioning of labour markets. Some key words in this new theoretical development are optimal remuneration and incentive schemes, asymmetric information, risk allocation, internal labour markets.

An obvious research program would thus be to take up these new theoretical developments on labour market institutions and contracts and to relate them to the actual content of labour contracts and to the specific characteristics of the institutional environment in different labour markets. As a first step in such a research program we have organized an international conference of labour market specialists presenting a careful description of selected characteristics of labour contracts and

---

* University of Amsterdam.

** University of Leiden.

traits of the institutional environment and a discussion of their national emergence. This description is a preliminary step for a theoretical analysis of why these differences emerge and of the consequences they have for the efficient performance of the labour market.

What we ultimately want to achieve with this research program is an integrated approach of practical specification of labour contracts and theoretical analysis based on economic principles of efficiency. We want to use existing contract theory in labour economics and if necessary extend it so that we can explain the occurrence of certain contract clauses, the division between legal and private arrangements, the role and function of institutions in the labour market etc.

In order to do that well one should first of all pay close attention to the details of existing contracts, some historical perspective and the relevant institutional environment. As far as we know, the international literature does not provide an accessible, internationally comparable description of the typical contents of labour contracts and the institutional structure of the labour markets in individual countries. This is certainly disturbing for students of labour markets. However, it has also important policy implications, as in the public debate one often points to pro's and con's in other countries ("the greater flexibility of the US labour market", "lifetime contracts in Japan", "the success of the Swedish model"), without providing easy recourse to reliable descriptions. Providing such a source is the first objective of this volume. It contains the description of twelve OECD countries according to guidelines, discussed in this introduction.

The perspective of the research project is an assessment of the relative efficiency of various institutional arrangements of labour markets. At the present stage of the research this is only a far goal at the horizon. Yet some reflection on the concept of efficiency is inevitable even at the outset of the project. Since Pareto efficiency is the standard concept of economic theory which also features prominently in the new contract literature, we will discuss its merits in Chapter 1. We will also present a small sample of results from applying the Pareto criterion to labour markets. We conclude that chapter by briefly considering alternative measures for evaluating labour market performance and comparing them with the Pareto-efficiency criterion. In Chapter 14, after the separate chapters describing the national labour markets, we will return to our general problem and present a tentative analysis of emergence and effects of the international variations in labour market organization and institutions. Hence, we will sandwich the country chapters between reflection on the efficiency concept and speculations about the role of institutions.

Of course, this is not the first study to deal with an international comparison of flexibility and efficiency of labour markets. Especially the rise and persistence of unemployment in Europe has stimulated such studies, such as those by Bean, Layard and Nickell (1987), Lawrence and Schultze (1987) and most recently, Layard, Nickell and Jackman (1991). Calmfors and Horn (1986) have studied trade union behaviour in different countries. Also related is Abraham and McKersie (1990), Boyer (1989) and Emerson (1988a, 1988b). At the present, mostly descriptive stage we will not attempt to integrate these studies with the work reported here, as it would better fit the analytical stage of the research project.

B. The Country Studies

Actual labour markets differ from the highly stylized model of perfect competition. Analytically, the world of perfect competition is well known, but the effects of many deviations have not been properly analyzed. Analysis of cause and effect needs careful description of actual labour contracts, labour market structures and institutions. Such descriptions will be given in the next chapters for twelve OECD-countries and we will now introduce the guidelines imposed on these country studies.

Labour contracts usually have many paragraphs and can deal with many other subjects. To name only a few:

- length of working day and working week, number of holidays;
- procedures for contract termination;
- procedures for promotion;
- grievance procedures;
- pension plans and retirement schemes;
- working conditions;
- training facilities and reimbursement of training costs;
- unemployment compensation;
- health and disability programs;
- maternity leave, child care facilities.

What is or is not stipulated in a contract, depends to a large extent on what is already taken care of by labour law or legal social insurance provisions. In some countries there exist binding legal rules which restrict arrangements between employers and employees whereas in other countries much more is left to private negotiations e.g. safety standards, firing rules, health and retirement plans etc. Casual observation suggests large differences among countries in the balance between public regulations and private arrangements. In fact, it has often been suggested (and studied) that the inflexibility of public regulations in European labour markets is the main cause of European labour market problems that developed during the seventies and the eighties ("Euro-sclerosis").

With respect to institutional differences between countries one can point to differences in the status of trade unions and to the structure of bargaining. There are large differences between countries in the stipulation of laws concerning the legal status of unions, the rights of representation, the extent of coverage of negotiated contracts, the right to strike or lock-out, the possibility of exclusive union contracts, the legal position of union representatives etc. Bargaining over the labour contract can be individual or collective. Collective bargaining can differ by type of bargaining unit: plant-, firm-, industry-level or even the national level. The composition of the parties at the bargaining table can vary from one employer against one union to a large number of employers organizations and trade unions. The role of the mediator can vary from country to country. The situation of public sector employees has peculiar features in most countries.

The combination of different public regulations and private contractual arrangements, of the legal status of unions and of institutional aspects in bargaining gives rise to large differences in the actual content of labour contracts across countries. Of course it is impossible to tackle all these aspects at once. One has to select and concentrate on a few topics only.

To guide the selection, and to make the papers comparable across countries, we asked the authors to observe the following structure:

Section A: Introduction
The chapter should start with a general characterization of the national labour market and, if relevant, some typical historical features.

Section B: The institutional and legal environment
This section aims at a description of the importance of labour unions, employers' organizations and collective bargaining, and requires delineation of what is normally convened in collective bargaining, to contrast it with what is left for private arrangements or already taken care of by law. Where possible, the description should be quantitative: union density, size and structure of organizations. But also rules and regulations should be outlined, such as on unions right to represent and legal provisions for conflict handling.

Section C: Outcomes
This section should focus on the actual results of bargaining and statutory provisions in terms of working time, wages and wage structure, fringe benefits and the termination of labour contracts.

Section D: Conclusion/evaluation
This final section presents an opportunity for the national author(s) to give some assessment of the specific institutional characteristics of the labour market.

The distinguishing feature of the present study is the common framework imposed on all the country studies. With the minimum contract and the minimal institutions of perfect competition as a starting point, the country papers should indicate the important features that describe the actual national labour markets. The information on unionization and the bargaining environment should give an indication of market structures. Bargaining institutions and the legal environment should give an indication of the balance between private and public influences on the labour contract. And the outcomes should give some information on the differences between countries in terms of actual content of the labour contract, such as hours of work, fringe benefits, termination provisions, etc. The analytical work, to explain the emergence and to evaluate the effects of the cross-country variations in the institutional details, should take it from here. In the final chapter of this book we make a modest start, by trying to discover similarities and differences in the national labour market structures, and by relating them loosely to received theory. But that, even more than the descriptive part of this book, is only a beginning.

C. The Workshop

On January 24 to 26, 1991, an international workshop was held at the Netherlands Institute for Advanced Studies (NIAS) in Wassenaar, a retreat for academic contemplation in the Dutch dunes, near The Hague. The workshop was part of an extensive research project aiming at intensifying the explanation and evaluation of institutions in actual labour markets. A proposal was first submitted to NIAS, who accepted it as a nucleus for inviting scholars to spend (part of) an academic year at its premises. Under these terms, Richard Burkhauser (Syracuse), Pierre Cahuc (Paris), Bob Flanagan (Stanford), Aldi Hagenaars (Rotterdam), Philip de Jong (Leiden), Ronald Schettkat (Berlin) and Günther Schmid (Berlin) stayed at NIAS between September 1990 and June 1991.

The workshop was made possible by funding from the European Community's SPES program (Contract No. SPES CT91-50001), from the Royal Dutch Academy of Sciences (KNAW) and from the Organisation for Strategic Labour Market Research (OSA). In preparing the NIAS project and the workshop we got invaluable support from a Program Committee which is listed below.

This volume presents the papers that were initially written for the workshop and revised after the discussion in Wassenaar and after complying with our editorial demands which we submitted to realize the goal of the volume: an easily accessible description of relevant institutional features of twelve developed labour markets, following the same outline for each country. At the workshop, there was a discussant for each paper. We have chosen not to publish the comments, but rather ask the authors to use them in their final version. Hence, this is the place to thank the otherwise invisible discussants for their contribution: Richard Burkhauser (commenting on the paper for the US), Jean-Paul Vosse (Australia), Sol Polachek (New Zealand), Wouter van Ginneken (Japan), Günther Schmid (Austria), Ronald Schettkat (Germany), Philip de Jong (Sweden), Guy Caire (France), Hessel Oosterbeek (Spain), Robert Boyer (Italy), Rob Janssen (United Kingdom) and Aldi Hagenaars (the Netherlands).

The organization of the workshops was greatly facilitated by the help of our secretaries, Hedy Braun and Milada Gadourek, and by the staff of NIAS. We are very grateful for their efforts. On top of that we specifically want to thank Hedy Braun for her invaluable help preparing this volume and for a meticulous editing job.

The project is certainly not finished. The descriptions of labour markets collected in this volume will serve as an input in the next stage of research, that of explaining and evaluating the differences in institutional arrangements among nations. We are organizing international cooperation and another workshop to advance economic analysis in that direction. We hope that results will reach the scientific community before too long, and that they will improve understanding of the rich variety of labour market institutions and contracts.

D. Program Committee

P.A. Boot, Ministry of Economic Affairs, The Netherlands
R. Boyer, CEPREMAP, France
M. Emerson, Commission of the European Communities, Belgium
L. Fina, Commission of the European Communities, Belgium
W. van Ginneken, International Labor Organization, Switzerland
J. Hartog, University of Amsterdam, The Netherlands
S. Polachek, State University of New York, Binghamton, U.S.A.
P. Scherer, OECD-ESD, France
R. Soltwedel, OECD-ESD, France
F. Spinnewyn, Catholic University of Leuven, Belgium
J.J.M. Theeuwes, Leiden University, The Netherlands
J.P. Vosse, Organization for Strategic Labour Market Research (OSA), The Netherlands
H. van Zonneveld, Commission of the European Communities, Belgium

REFERENCES

Abraham, K.G. and R.B. McKersie (1990), *New Developments in the Labor Market: Toward a new institution paradigm*, Cambridge: MIT Press.

Bean, C., R. Layard and S. Nickell (1987), *The Rise in Unemployment*, Oxford: Basil Blackwell.

Boyer, M. (1989), *The Search for Labour Market Flexibility*, Oxford: Oxford University Press.

Calmfors, L. and H. Horn (1986), *Trade-Unions, Wage Formation and Macroeconomic Stability*, London: Macmillan.

Emerson, M. (1988a), *What model for Europe*, Cambridge: MIT Press.

Emerson, M. (1988b), Regulation or Deregulation of the Labour Market: Policy Regimes for the Recruitment and Dismissal of Employees in Industrialised Countries, *European Economic Review*, 32, pp. 775-818.

Hartog J. and J.J.M. Theeuwes (1990), Post-war Developments in Labour Economics, in: *Advanced Lectures in Quantitative Economics*, F. van der Ploeg (ed.), London: Academic Press, pp. 313-348.

Lawrence, Z. and C. Schultze (1987), *Barriers to European Growth*, Washington: Brookings.

Layard, R., S. Nickell and R. Jackman (1991), *Unemployment*, Oxford: Oxford University Press.

Parsons, D.O. (1986), The Employment Relationship: Job Attachment, Work Effort, and the Nature of Contracts, in: *Handbook of Labor Economics*, P.R.G. Layard and O. Ashenfelter (eds.), Amsterdam: North Holland, pp. 789-848.

Labour Market Contracts and Institutions
J. Hartog and J. Theeuwes (Editors)

CHAPTER 1

EVALUATING LABOUR MARKET PERFORMANCE*

Joop Hartog**
Solomon Polachek***
Jules Theeuwes****

A. Introduction

Throughout the world, country labour markets are similar to each other in many ways yet at the same time very different in others. For example, in all developed countries female labour force participation is increasing, agricultural employment is decreasing and gender differentials in pay and occupational structure are relatively comparable. In these same developed economies despite these similarities, unions have very different roles. Union membership varies greatly and there are wide differences in wage, fringe benefits and employer-employee work contract provisions. In addition, the degree of government intervention regarding labour market policies varies, as well.

At least several questions come to mind based on these labour market patterns: Why do some labour market institutions differ across countries? What effects do these differing institutions have on country economies? And finally how can one evaluate which country economies are more efficient? In this essay we deal mostly with the latter question because if one can determine efficiency, then one can isolate which labour programs are efficient. Clearly this knowledge can be helpful to government policy makers.

To begin, some criteria to evaluate efficiency must be identified. Since most neoclassical economic analyses use Pareto efficiency as a criterion we begin with the concept of Pareto efficiency (hereafter abbreviated P), which we discuss in Section 2 along with results that can be obtained by applying the P criterion to the labour market. However as shall be illustrated in Section 3 the Pareto criterion is not without fault, and is especially hard to apply to large economies. Thus section 4 deals with alternative frontier estimation measures that can be used for assessing labour

---

* Comments by Coen Teulings on an earlier draft are gratefully acknowledged.

** University of Amsterdam.

*** State University of New York, Binghamton.

**** University of Leiden.

market performance. In section 5 we conclude by describing the circumstances under which each of the criteria can be applied, and the type of conclusions that can be reached.

B. Pareto Efficiency and the Labour Market

To set the stage, we invoke the First Theorem of Welfare Economics (Arrow and Hahn, 1971; Arrow and Debreu, 1954): if a competitive equilibrium exists, it is Pareto efficient. Welfare is maximized and any changes in resource allocation necessarily make at least some participants worse off. This P optimality also holds intertemporarily, even under uncertainty, provided there is a complete set of markets for all goods no matter what probability or date of delivery. Labour markets would obviously be included and thus in this framework allocate efficiently as well.

Invoking the Arrow-Hahn/Arrow-Debreu world is like starting in heaven. In the real world, there is neither perfect competition nor a complete set of markets. The ArrowDebreu world is an ideal theoretical standard for equilibrium and efficiency, but it serves more as a general framework than as a beacon for actual policies.

Clearly markets are not complete. Because of uncertainty – the inability to use a probability distribution to define a set of possible outcomes – states of the world cannot be identified making it impossible to write contracts conditional on them. Perhaps for this reason there are futures markets for very few goods. Since money and securities are very imperfect substitutes (Gravelle and Rees, 1981, chapter 20), appropriate control cannot be made for future vagaries in the smooth way envisaged by the Arrow-Debreu framework.

Further, perfect competition, even if it existed for a while, would be vulnerable to the deliberate actions of participants to get away from it. Monopoly rent seeking would lead to attempts by individuals and by firms (either individually or through collusion) to protect themselves from competitive pressure on their income.

Incentives for participants to move away from perfect competition and imperfect solutions for uncertainty make the perfectly competitive model one to use only initially. One should be clearly cognizant that both financial incentives and the desire to deal adequately with uncertainty lead to deviations from perfect competition. Deviation can take many forms. For example, workers may organize themselves in unions to seek contracts that are more attractive for them. Firms may merge to gain market share and hence monopoly power. Finally special interest groups seek to influence or manipulate the government to obtain support and protection. It may well be that these rent seeking motives for creating market imperfections generate inefficiencies (as is suggested by standard theory). On the other hand a risk aversion motive may lead to improvements in efficiency as is perhaps hinted in the newly developing contract theory. But this is, at the present stage, mere speculation.

To study efficiency, then, it makes sense to define the conditions for pure competition, then see how efficiency is affected as these prerequisites for competition are eliminated. Thus in this section, we will summarize some results on the efficiency of labour markets and indicate the nature of the conclusions we ultimately seek. It provides at the same time a background for the selection of characteristics that we imposed as guidelines for the country papers.

Taking perfect competition as our point of reference, we assume labour markets to satisfy the following conditions:

a. there are many profit maximizing firms and many utility maximizing individuals of any given labour quality, all devoid of individual market power
b. production technologies, capital stocks and worker qualities are given
c. firms have fixed location, worker mobility is costless
d. all actors have perfect information, available at zero cost
e. there is no uncertainty: technologies and product demands are non-stochastic
f. the government guarantees property rights, but abstains from any intervention in markets.

In this set of markets, under appropriate conditions on supply and demand functions, there will be equilibrium with one wage rate for each type of worker. Equilibrium wage rates will be equal to marginal revenue products for the marginal worker, and compensate the marginal worker for the disutility of work in that particular job. Inframarginal workers will receive a rent. The allocation will be P in all respects: efficiency in the use of resources, in checking who works and how workers are distributed to occupations and to firms.

We may now look at some consequences of changes in these assumptions.

a'. Labour market power

If (some) firms are monopsonists, wages will fall below competitive levels thereby distorting the allocation of workers to firms, and P will be destroyed. On the other hand, if such monopsonistic firms are unionized deviations from P will depend on the assumptions about the bargaining process. If unions are powerful enough to essentially dictate wages (the union monopoly model), the labour market outcome is not P. On the other hand if there is union-firm negotiations as in an efficient bargaining model, the result can be P at least for the parties involved in the contract. Here the outcome is on a contract curve shaped by the firm's isoprofit curves and the indifference curve of the union defining union preferences for union-employment trade-offs. Though this is partial efficiency (efficiency for outsiders, i.e. other suppliers of labour, never enters the picture), it's an old proposition in labour economics that negotiations may hit upon the wage-employment level that perfect competition would have established: unions as a successful countervailing power to monopsony (cf. Hartog, 1990). In this case the partial equilibrium would also be general.

A complication in these models is the relation between preferences of individual union members and the union utility function. Under reasonable conditions, it is possible to derive a union utility function where the utility of the wage and of unemployment are weighed by the proportions of employed and unemployed members. But clearly, this only applies if membership exceeds employment. Even in Europe with nationwide bargaining this is reasonable if abnormally high union wages leads to lay-offs of previously employed unionized workers. Though not formally union members, these unemployed and discouraged workers would work if they could.

Changing the assumptions regarding worker-firm bargaining can alter the results. For example the standard model of efficient bargaining implicitly assumes that employers cannot hire non-union labour at an alternative wage. This may be part of the contract: unions negotiate for a closed shop. On the other hand right-to-work laws prevalent in many countries require firms not to discriminate between members and non-members. This would add weight to the necessity of analyzing the decision to join a union. Here one must consider the free rider problem since membership decisions are not based strictly on individual financial benefits. Clearly, efficiency must be compared across different regimes. Considering the closed shop and the open shop may be simple compared to what happens when there are internal requirements on union representatives and elections , as well as what happens when laws extend collective agreements to every worker in the industry, or when there is competition among different unions in different legal environments, i.e. exclusive union rights versus simultaneous multi-union bargaining.

b'. Endogenous technology

Production technology and working conditions are not necessarily fixed. Firms can often choose such working conditions, as exposure to noise, dirt, toxic conditions, speed of a production process, etc. Given a firm's working conditions there is a collective good problem. Yet the preferences for these conditions vary, workers face the same working conditions despite their diverse preferences. Assuming insufficient degrees of freedom (i.e. no perfect sorting of worker types to firms) and barring the Lindahl solution (different individual "prices" for the collective good), the question is how an optimum can be reached. A perfect market will not be P in this case. Unions may be an instrument for negotiating an optimal solution with the firm. Freeman and Medoff (1984) calculate substantial benefits for such a union voice mechanism to improve working conditions and reduce quit rates. But here also, the government may enter by imposing safety standards (as is the case in many countries), or prescribing consultation and negotiation (as is the case in the Netherlands), for example by prescribing works councils (with a partially set agenda) at the firm or plant level.

A similar story holds for job requirements, i.e. required worker qualities for adequate job performance. Again, collective good properties emerge, and it seems one cannot rely on a free market to generate P. Moreover, it is not clear what arrangements could remedy this.

b''. Human capital investment

Worker qualities can be changed through human capital investment. Strictly speaking, this can be analyzed in a dynamic, multi-period setting with no great complications. Given perfect information, no uncertainty, perfect capital markets, and no external effects there will be optimal human capital investment. Firm-specific human capital creates no special problems since specific investments may be protected by binding long-term contracts. On the other hand, government support for investments (subsidies, free schooling) can lead to overinvestment. Often equity arguments are used to justify these subsidies. If innate worker qualities could be observed, lump sum redistribution could equalize the opportunities of non-competing groups without disturbing efficiency. If capital market imperfection were the problem, the government could restore efficiency by supplying loans at an appropriate interest rate. External effects may be a further motive for such government intervention as compulsory education or subsidies, but in this case such laws need not imply inefficiencies.

b'''. Physical capital investment

Investments in physical capital are the vehicle for introducing technological change. Both job content and the volume of employment will generally be affected and this gives workers an interest in the process. In the efficient union-firm bargaining model, the opportunity set may change, and hence, there may be reason to extend the negotiations to the introduction of new technology. In fact, this may well be the most important theme when decisions on job content and job requirements can be taken. Union involvement in these "technological agreements" may affect efficiency, but not necessarily negatively, since it is quite conceivable that a legal compulsion to consult or negotiate improves efficiency, by replacing one-sided by two-sided decision making. But once again, the concept of efficient bargaining only guarantees (predicts, actually) efficiency for the bargaining partners and not necessarily for others, such as consumers. The issues are not frequently studied. An exception is Ulph and Ulph (1989).

c'. Positive mobility cost

Even with non-zero labour mobility costs, whether they be direct cost or disutility of mobility, labour market outcomes will be P as long as markets are open. If capital is mobile again even at non-zero cost, the market will find an efficient combination of capital and worker mobility. Policy issues arise if workers receive income support (unemployment benefits, welfare, etc.) subsidizing immobility. Such subsidies are inefficient, but often are justified on equity grounds. Restrictions on entering an occupation, such as those set up by professional organizations (associations of medical specialists or plumbers), are inefficient at first sight, but when the restrictions take the form of minimum training requirements it is harder to assess the outcome, as it depends on firms' ability to judge (expected) worker quality. Similarly regional capital subsidies might be efficient given high costs of factor mobility.

d'. Costly information

Imperfect information arises if information on job offers and worker reservation wages is costly to collect. Here one might distinguish information on market conditions (vacancies, job seekers, wage rates, for jobs and workers of given known quality) and on characteristics of workers and jobs. Since, just like with mobility collecting information involves real costs, full information will not be P: this would entail overproduction of information.

Among others Mortensen (1986) discusses the question of optimal production of information in his survey of search theory. He starts his discussion with an "island economy": employment is located on islands, workers are identical and live forever, but they may loose their job because the employment on their island ceases to exist. Once unemployed, they have to search for a new job, an island where they want to work. Productivity is a draw from the match specific productivity distribution, the same for every worker on every island. In this context, unemployed workers, searching to maximize average net income per period over the indefinite future (a strategy that has the reservation wage property), behave socially optimal: the private reservation wage is equal to the socially optimal reservation wage. However, externalities may arise to hurt this social efficiency. The model just outlined assumes that any number of workers can be hired on every island at the realized match specific productivity. However, since the number of jobs at a given island is fixed, and individuals do not know where the vacancies are, they randomly search among the islands. This implies an externality: returns to search depend on the vacancy rate which in turn depends on individuals' reservation wage. Conversely, an individual's reservation wage affects the returns to search for other unemployed workers. This external effect is not considered in determining an individual's reservation wage. Consequently, from a social point of view, the reservation wage is too low as is the volume of search unemployment.

Interestingly, the external effect disappears if information technology improves. If unemployed workers have access to a listing of vacant job openings and their location, the conditions of the original model are restored, and social efficiency reappears. This implies that a government employment agency, up-to-date newspaper want ads, or private labour market brokers may correct the market failure.

Such an easy correction is not available if the islands are reduced to single employers. In that case the employer's monopsony power will push the wage rate below marginal productivity so that if workers do the searching, there will again be too little search unemployment with the private return to search below the social return .

What one assumes about productivity is important for the results. Both models assume that productivity is match specific, i.e. depends on both the worker and the job. But if productivity is job specific, and identical for all workers, search is only privately beneficial. Through search, a particular individual may find a job with high productivity and hence, high wage. But the search is socially useless: for output, it does not matter who occupies a particular job. Search is just a game of musical chairs.

The question on the optimal production of information can be approached from a different angle than Mortensen did. If the government fully abstains from any intervention, private labour market brokers may enter the information business, providing actors the choice between collecting information themselves or buying services from a broker. This might lead to optimal investment in information. On the other hand monopolies such as a labour market brokerage will most likely hurt efficiency.

Optimal information on characteristics of jobs and workers is a complicated matter. Workers may not fully understand the requirements of a job before they have actually occupied it (jobs as "experience goods"), firms may not fully know the qualities of workers they intend to hire. Given the inevitability of such information problems, the relevant question is once again: what is the relative performance of different structures? Workers themselves will try to collect information on the spectre of potential jobs. Firms will try to collect information on workers. In addition there may evolve entrepreneurs specializing in the production of information. Hence, one way to phrase an optimum question is: will there be an efficient supply of information producing firms (occupational counselling, head hunters, outplacement services, testing agencies, etc.)? This involves an evaluation of the optimum mix of information collecting by labour market actors and by specialized firms. This also involves evaluating firms' own attempts, through personnel departments. So, to some extent it boils down to a question of (optimal) industrial organization: internal versus external (market) transactions. It may boil down to evaluating information handling by relevant agencies. Using observable characteristics (age, education, sex, ethnicity) as signals, these agencies homogenize a heterogeneous population. As Spence (1974) has shown, the formation of coalitions to promote the use of such signals may affect Pareto optimality.

e'. Uncertainty

In the search models discussed above, workers do not know where their good job opportunities are, but in a given match output would be fixed. They have imperfect information about productivity that by itself is not uncertain. Now, allowing for uncertainty, we acknowledge that productivity itself may be stochastic. In this situation, with actors differing in degree of risk aversion, and with risk independent of actors' behaviour, it is optimal for the less risk averse to insure the more risk averse. If one actor is risk-neutral, it will be optimal to sell full insurance to the risk averse individual. This idea has also been applied to the labour market. Risk-neutral firms, with easier access to the capital market than workers, could provide insurance against the wage fluctuations that an auction market would generate (under fluctuating demand conditions), in exchange for a lower wage level. The basic notion is that the contract between firm and worker is set up to deal with the allocation of risk. This is the heart of implicit contract theory. The topic has become complicated because it is not just one issue that is being treated, but rather involves a different perspective on many related issues: allocation, mobility, reward systems, control of worker effort, hours and timing of work, etc. The field is too complex and too much in development to summarize here.

A very important observation of implicit contract theory is that the labour contract is derived assuming Pareto optimality for the contracting parties. The negotiations result in a bargain on the contract curve, which is *locally* efficient by assumption. Of course, this need not hold socially and this indeed is precisely the issue at stake.

Contract theory adds a third task to the wage mechanism in a private market economy: it should guide the allocation of labour, generate optimal investment in (specific) human capital and allocate risk in a stochastically fluctuating environment. Contract theory is most interesting when information is asymmetric. With perfect (symmetric) information on the stochastic event's realizations contracts could attain first-best allocation of risk, i.e. the risk-neutral party could fully insure the risk-averse party. To maintain desirable incentives asymmetric information generally implies incomplete insurance.

Indeed, rather than attempting a survey of results, we give a simple example of how our problem fits in with this approach. Consider the model presented by Rosen (1985). A given number of individuals contracts with a firm. Output depends on labour and a stochastic (product demand) shock, with known distribution. The contract between workers and the firm seeks to maximize worker utility (dependent on leisure and income), subject to the firm's profit constraint. In equilibrium, the following results hold: the wage rate will be constant and independent of the stochastic fluctuations. Marginal productivity will also be held constant, by adjusting the size of the labour force, and laying off people in slack demand conditions. If unemployment compensation is ruled out, there will be socially excessive employment, with marginal productivity below the reservation wage which occurs because individuals can only match the lack of insurance by working more. If workers and the firm include unemployment compensation, efficient allocation of risk will be paired with efficient employment levels: marginal productivity will equal the reservation wage, utility when working will equal utility when unemployed. These are standard results in the contract literature, under the given assumptions. A compulsory unemployment insurance, imposed by the government, would have no effect at all on these outcomes. Premiums and benefits would be fully integrated in the contract, and the results would be exactly identical (Hartog and Theeuwes, 1990).

Of course, these results are derived in a very simple world, with no moral hazard and no mobility, i.e. workers are tied to the firm forever. But the equivalence of the private contract and the compulsory government arrangement is interesting, and precisely the sort of conclusion we aim for. It would be valuable to see if the result can be upheld in a model such as that developed by Arnott, Hosios and Stiglitz (1988) that does allow for worker mobility.

f'. Government intervention

Governments do more than just defining and guaranteeing property rights, and this generates two questions: why, and with what effects? Analyzing the effect of government interventions is one well-developed activity of economists. Explaining the interventions is a newer activity. Of course the questions are related, in the sense that the (presumed) effects may motivate intervention. Government intervention has a central role in our research project. Why does the government intervene, why do actors in the labour market turn to the government (and to law makers) in some countries, and to private action in other countries? For example, why do unions sometimes turn to the government for worker protection (e.g. legislation on lay-offs, severance pay) and sometimes directly to employers in collective bargaining? What explains the different balance in different countries? In the final chapter of this book, after all the country-specific chapters, we will speculate on these matters, but it is only a very modest start.

The small sample of labour market efficiency results illustrates the sort of knowledge we would like to have available. The illustrations deal with the effect of altering assumptions in moving away from perfect competition. In the examples, there is only limited attention of the effects of different institutions, of government regulation and of the trade-off between government regulation and regulation through collective bargaining. This is due to a lack of results in the literature which we would like to see filled.

C. Pareto Efficiency as a Criterion

Pareto efficiency is obtained if it is impossible to improve the welfare of any one individual without reducing the welfare of someone else. Theorists use it and indeed seem to like it, as illustrated by the results in section 2. Practical labour market watchers (policy makers, employers, union leaders, commentators, people interested in day-to-day labour market performance) are less fond of it. In their discussions, the criterion never shows up explicitly, and perhaps for good reason since it is probably impossible to have a Pareto optimal situation given the size of the economy. Surely there are very few policies, even good policies, that do not make at least someone worse off. Thus from a policy perspective one probably wants to weigh whether a sufficient number of people are better off to compensate those made worse off. Thus from a policy perspective Pareto optimality may just be too strong. Perhaps for this reason policy makers focus on directly measurable variables like the rate of unemployment, the level and growth rate of per capita real income, labour productivity growth, the ability to adjust to structural change, the speed of adoption of innovations on the workfloor, etc. In this section, we will try to assess the merits and demerits of the Pareto criterion and its relation to the "practical" measures that are in use. To highlight the nature of the gap, we will discuss main characteristics of the P criterion and problems encountered in practical applications.

P is individualistic

The Pareto criterion is individualistic and squarely based on consumer sovereignty. It is individuals' welfare, in their own assessment, that serves as the basis for evaluation. The individuals are considered the best judge of their own situation and paternalism is not admitted. But paternalism may very well be a motive in actual government interventions (compulsory old age pensions, disability insurance, workplace safety regulation).

The motive of paternalism is closely related to what Tobin (1970) calls "specific egalitarian preferences". Policy makers may consider some goods so important for an individual's welfare as not to leave the provision of that good to private decisions or to market allocation. Compulsory education and social housing programs are examples of such "merit goods". An example in the labour market would be safety regulation. Under specific egalitarian preferences ("nobody should be exposed to such dangers"), one must consider the externality. Unsafe working conditions though leading to higher wages may cost society great sums in health care. To alleviate such costs these laws are often passed under "egalitarian preferences", but minimizing society 's cost may be the prime motivation. Moreover, with such preferences the conflict between equity and efficiency disappears. If social welfare is determined in terms of the distribution of specific goods, rather than the distribution of individual welfare, providing the goods might be the most efficient approach. Of course, the conflict between an individual's own preferences and those imposed on him/her remains, as the key problem of paternalism itself.

Usually, the P criterion is applied to the case where individuals have welfare functions defined only over their own position in the allocation: the goods and leisure at their disposal. In such a situation nobody feels deprived if some other individual's welfare improves. However, there are compelling arguments in favour of relative individual evaluations: an individual's welfare is also determined by consumption, leisure or welfare of other individuals (relatives, neighbours, reference group, etc.). Nothing prevents us from allowing for individual utility functions with such external effects. But analytically, this is quite complicated, and immediately implies that there will be "market failure" even in a competitive world: there is no market for such external effects (cf. Hochman and Rodgers, 1969).

P is normative

P is usually viewed as a normative criterion (cf. Blaug, 1980, p. 143: "avowedly and unashamedly normative"). But there have always been authors who deny this. Hennipman (1981) is a clear example. He argues that welfare economics may be put to a normative use, if writers conclude from their analyses that particular measures *should* be adopted. But such conclusions are in no way the substance of welfare economics. Welfare theory and its outcomes (such as that monopolies generate welfare losses) are positive statements, right or wrong, independent of ethical values. Or, as Hennipman cites Randomysler who argued in 1946, "the task of welfare economics is to study the causes of welfare ..." (p. 220). "It is a study, it is true, of sensations and feeling ... But a study of subjective feelings is not the same thing as a subjective study" (p. 200). Ng's (1979) approach is similar. He takes social welfare as the vector of individual utilities, without aggregating. Then, welfare comparison involves vector comparison, which indeed fits in with the P criterion. The claim that one institutional arrangement leads to higher social welfare than another arrangement is a positive statement that is in principle amenable to empirical testing.

Yet, this leaves one big question unanswered: how to go about this testing? Absence of an operational measurement method of welfare does not make the approach normative. But if the method for testing "positive" statements is not outlined, i.e. if it is not clear how they can be falsified, at least there is a methodological flaw. For example, one could calculate the deadweight welfare loss from monopsony in a labour market, compared to perfect competition. Given the measure that is used, the welfare loss is undeniable. But it is no proof of the proposition that individuals are worse off, as long as the welfare measure is not convincingly related to individuals' evaluation of the situations. Without such a link, it is at least uncomfortably close to a normative statement that individuals are worse off if the triangle under the demand curve has non-zero surface.

The problem emerges because of the lack of an accepted direct measure of individual welfare. Individual welfare and aggregate welfare losses are interpretations derived from observed choices. Hence, the validity of a proposition of welfare gain from a policy measure or an institutional change depends on the validity of the entire underlying theory. And the critical element is the link with the latent, unobserved concept of individual welfare.

Obviously, evaluations would be much easier with a direct measure of individual utility, cardinal and interpersonally comparable. The impossibility claim of such measurement is rather sterile and prevents valuable developments. It may be noted that there have always been "pockets of resistance" to this impossibility. Tinbergen usually proceeded on the notion of cardinal measurability. Van Praag built an entire school on the notion of a cardinally measurable individual welfare function of income (see Hartog, 1988, for a review), and there have been many applications, both explicitly (e.g. the literature on optimal income taxation) and implicitly (as in actual policy decisions). Why should not economists aim at developing actual measures of individual welfare, if that concept is so central to our theorizing? One might then distinguish observability from the scale of measurement. At present, even ordinal individual utilities are usually considered latent variables, apparently in no way directly observable. But why should for example direct interview methods be depicted as useless *in principle* to elicit information on individual preferences? Even without assuming cardinality, one could attempt direct measurement. What now mostly is an article of faith, could then be turned into an empirical question, which seems much more fruitful. Perhaps, the tide is already turning?

Why bother about P efficiency?

Returning to the present situation, with welfare interpretation rather than welfare measurement, there are some other problems worth discussing. An important question is the separability of equity and efficiency. If equity is important so that the distribution of welfare is the ultimate criterion, why bother about efficiency? The efficiency criterion is used because one can measure the cost of equity in term of efficiency; i.e. it is important to know what efficiency loss is needed to achieve an equitable income distribution. Clearly if output is located on an efficiency frontier then inefficiency is the degree to which an economy is below the frontier. Similarly if one compares two situations, neither of which is on the frontier, an improvement in efficiency may be a deterioration of equity though the trade-off is difficult to measure as long as distributional preferences are not explicitly known. Efficiency is only one element in evaluation, and indeed, not necessarily the overriding one. It is interesting here to point to a solution that is often proposed in the field of law and economics. There it is argued that liabilities and responsibilities should be allocated to the party that can easiest, at least cost, find a solution for it (e.g. see Cooter and Ulen (1988)).

Transition problems

Applying the P criterion to the transition from one situation to another, is problematic. P is a criterion for evaluating the rules of the game, it is a method for evaluating institutions, evaluating decision making procedures rather than specific welfare effects calculations. The evaluation of rules of the game may consist merely of comparing one set of rules with another set, without bothering about the actual transition. One then applies P as a sort of pre-constitutional analysis: comparing different situations as if nobody had already taken up a specific position. The result of such analyses may be that one world is P and another world is not, or that one world P dominates another: "competition is P superior to monopoly", "minimum wage laws are inefficient". But such analysis does not consider the actual transition from one situation to another. And in practice, one hardly ever encounters changes that would benefit all without hurting anyone. Even if an initial situation is not P and the new situation does satisfy P, then the transition will usually involve loosers. If actual compensations to these loosers are not paid, one might apply the rule of hypothetical or potential compensation. However, the contributions of Scitovsky and Kaldor have indicated that this rule is not fruitful, because of its ambiguous results: under hypothetical compensation, both the transition from situation A to B and the return from B to A may be a P improvement. This means that the problem of transition is not adequately solved.

The problem of transition is not only a problem of compensation. Comparing different sets of rules and institutions suggests that one may move freely from one set to another. Clearly, this is not so. Existing situations or historical developments may have an independent influence. They may condition economic behaviour, of individuals and organizations. Or they may influence preferences, as for example, the case of long-lasting fear for hyperinflation in Germany. A change of institutions may be a costly affair. Such effects seem more important for modelling the world than for the nature of the P criterion itself. But since the criterion cannot be applied in a vacuum, shortcomings of modelling easily spill over to shortcomings of applications. The same applies to the criticism that P would be a static criterion. It is the economic model that should allow for the dynamic effects of technological developments, of lifecycles etc. and the P criterion can then be applied just as easily as in static cases. It would only imply that individuals' intertemporal preferences become more relevant, since intertemporal substitution would become the ultimate basis for judging dynamic changes.

Sometimes, critics of the P criterion indeed insufficiently distinguish the criterion itself from the assumptions shaping the analytical environment. For example, the theorems on the optimality of perfect competition also invoke the strong assumptions shaping this environment, but these assumptions do not affect the P criterion by itself. Similarly, the fact that in perfect competition future (unborn) generations do not share in the efficient outcome does not point at the criterion as the culprit. On the other hand, there is an important issue what restrictions one accepts in formulating the optimum problem. The distinction between first-best, second-best, etc. precisely refers to this point. Second-best applications acknowledge unavoidable constraints in some sectors of an economy. Ng (1979) coined the term third-best for the case where both unavoidable distortions and cost of information exist, and Arnott, Hosios and Stiglitz (1988) mention the concept of constrained efficiency for the case where a planner would face the same constraints as agents in the market. Although the restrictions are vitally important for the conclusions that will be obtained, they do not affect the value (or validity) of the criterion itself. Criticism on the criterion referring to the strong assumptions that are often used in its application, is therefore not very relevant.

Similarly, the criticism that many analyses are very partial indeed holds good, but neither goes at the heart of the P criterion itself. Many arrangements or policy measures are studied in isolation, considering just one measure at the time and ignoring other policy interventions or distortions. Yet we know from the theory of second-best that this is not allowed. The practice obviously derives from our limited analytical abilities.

In our view, P is a valuable criterion for pre-constitutional analysis, to assess rules of the game, allowing one to get a long way without interpersonal comparison of utility. It is regrettable that economists make no stronger attempts to define utility as an observable rather than a latent variable. With individual welfare as a directly measurable variable rather than an interpretation *ex post*, stronger statements would come within reach. Practical applications of the P criterion are severely restricted by the ambiguity in the case of actual transitions, the partiality of many analyses, transition problems and the difficulty of working with relative individual welfare functions. Further as indicated the P criterion is difficult to implement as the number of economic activities grows. Surely in larger economies it is difficult to increase welfare without making at least someone worse off. As such the economy is always P, and any policy change is always Pareto inferior. For this reason alternatives to the P criterion are considered.

D. Are There Alternatives for the P Criterion?

As mentioned, labour market watchers and policy makers usually do not discuss labour market performance explicitly in terms of P efficiency. They are more inclined to apply a number of directly measurable indicators of results. The list includes variables such as levels and growth rates of wages, income, labour productivity, total factor productivity, employment, unemployment, frictional unemployment, participation. Also, there are indicators like job quality, sex and ethnic wage differentials, and complex indicators such as the labour market's ability to absorb shocks. In addition, there are computed measures indicating the underutilization of productive capacity such as the extent production is below an economy's production frontier (i.e. X-inefficiency).

The use of such variables in day-to-day discussions does not preclude the relevance or implicit use of efficiency concepts. Flanagan observes, in his contribution to this volume, that at the beginning of this century perfect competition was the theoretical notion behind labour market policies, in particular behind the regulations laid down in the law. In other words, the regulations were motivated by the expected efficiency of a particular institutional environment. This indeed seems to be the field where we should apply the concept of P efficiency: the rules, regulations and laws. P is a criterion for rules of the game, for evaluating a structure, and not for measuring actual outcomes. The connection between P and such performance indicators is very remote.

For most of the performance indicators, theory does not define an optimum level that can be used as a practical standard of evaluation. What is the optimal growth rate of wages, or what is the optimal rate of unemployment or participation? Actual evaluation usually takes place by comparison over time or across countries, and there is said to be reason for concern if for example productivity growth is falling or lagging behind other countries. Such discussions may lead to interesting observations, but obviously lack a rigorous basis.

Another problem in applying performance indicators would seem to be the hidden role of preferences. Maybe the only exception are measures like the "production gap". Producing less than possible given resources utilized would seem to be unambiguously bad, serving no useful purpose at all. On the other hand, evaluating labour unemployment rates immediately runs into the problem of voluntary versus involuntary unemployment and how to evaluate leisure. Even indicators like growth rates, job quality, job security or income security bring almost any result as overall welfare depends on a population's preferences in trading off one for another of these welfare measures.

The decisive role of preferences is of course well known from economic theory. For example, allocations in two countries would be P if they were realized according to perfect competition. But comparisons by income or productivity levels would not be meaningful: each country has reached efficiency relative to its own preferences (hence, equilibrium prices) and resources. Each country would be superior to the other at its own preferences and inferior at the other country's preferences. Performance indicators are meaningful if one agrees on preferences and if they are conditioned on available resources. Agreement on preferences is certainly conceivable, but seldom the subject of systematic economic analysis. The application of performance indicators indeed usually proceeds on the implicit assumption of agreement on preferences, e.g. on the desirability of high growth rates of national income and of low unemployment rates.

So, the conclusion should be that P and performance indicators indeed serve different purposes. P is a criterion that can be used to evaluate structural features, such as rules, regulations and institutions. Actual performance of an economy can be measured with the performance indicators, assuming of course, one accepts the underlying preferences, such as "more growth is always better". One may also relate the performance indicators scores to an economy's regulatory and institutional features. But again, using such results for normative purposes is conditional on the implicit preferences.

The case of evaluating labour markets may be similar to the problem of commodity markets. Industrial organization theory argues that not only may policy intervention fail to realize perfect competition, but it may even be undesirable. "Workable competition" may be all that is feasible. Moreover because monopoly profits both may be the source and reward for innovation, dynamic considerations may favour restricted competition. "Structure-conduct-performance" models have become popular, yielding many empirical studies relating market structure and market performance.

Empirical work on the performance of different labour market institutions has been started by considering the optimal degree of centralization/decentralization of labour contract negotiations. According to Calmfors and Driffill (1988) both the strongly centralized, corporatist bargaining structure (e.g. Sweden, Austria) and the strongly decentralized negotiations (e.g. U.S., Japan) generate more favourable inflation and unemployment levels than countries which are neither centralized nor decentralized (e.g. the Netherlands). At strongly centralized bargaining parties can internalize the macro-economic effects of their negotiations. Decentralized bargaining has the advantages that comes with a competitive structure.

Another approach might be to apply the micro based frontier production function method (Aigner, Lovell, and Schmidt, 1977). Essentially this technique originated to identify "inefficient" firms whose outputs lagged behind the outputs of other firms, holding inputs constant. By applying this technique to a national economy, one can determine whether this economy produces more abundant output (but in reality a utility bundle) than any other economy, *holding resources constant.*

The approach is to fit an economy-wide production function using each country as a data point (optimally time-series cross-section analysis should be performed):

$$Q_{it} = Q(X_{it}) + v_{it} + u_{it}$$

where Q is output, X is a vector of economic inputs, i indexes the country, t indexes time, v is a normally distributed error term, and u is a non-positive half-normally or exponentially distributed error. The one-sided error u which can be identified for specific countries (see Jondrow *et al.* (1982)) represents inefficiency in the production process, since as indicated it measures the extent a particular country's output lags others, holding inputs constant. Fixed effect estimation techniques can be used when there are pooled cross-section times-series data (Polachek and Yoon, 1990).

One can question whether using aggregate output data adequately addresses questions concerning overall economy-wide efficient allocation. Conceivably, an economy can be efficient in one sector, but inefficient in another. Using aggregate output can camouflage each sector's performance. One could argue that were there internal sector-specific inefficiencies then the country would not achieve "efficient" production levels overall. Consequently to measure "efficient" production one might want to disaggregate. As such even the most efficient country can be inefficient in *some* sectors. Sector-specific assessments of inefficiency are contained in Good, Johnson and Sickles (1986), Gaynor and Polachek (1987), Grabowski and Pasurka (1988) and Kumbhakar (1988).

Obviously a shortcoming of the frontier production function approach is essentially to assume that a country's objective is to maximize GNP. Equity is not considered. However, in a sense equity may be more important than efficiency. To get around this shortcoming, it is possible to use the same frontier estimation approach but to apply a uniform welfare function across all countries. Instead of Q representing output, it would represent welfare. The problem here though is to determine an appropriate welfare measure. But even if an appropriate measure can be found one must be careful to consider post-tax welfare levels. What appears as inefficiency may be efficient once one appropriately controls for income transfers.

With this method too, one should be careful to account for how different economic policies affect outcomes. For example certain policies such as unemployment insurance, health insurance, welfare arrangements, and others vary widely across countries, yet economic outcomes such as the male-female wage gap, secular changes in labour force participation, wage structure and others are very similar. Other economic outcomes such as union power differ. Examining inter-country differences in policies and outcomes should lead to understanding the causes that underlie outcome differences.

The simplest example is a country's production process itself. Scarce energy resources could lead to a more labour intensive technology. However observing a labour intensive technology does not necessarily imply inefficiency. A country merely appears inefficient because it uses more labour than other countries. On the other hand from a global perspective there may very well be inefficiency. Why should the country be producing that product at all? Why not merely import the product and stick to producing only those outputs for which there is a comparative advantage? If this is the case then again one can detect the inefficiency via the frontier production technique. But if for example tariffs or high transportation costs preclude trade, then what appears to be inefficient need not be inefficient at all. Instead an institutional variable, namely tariffs, is generating inefficiency.

Perhaps the easiest way to identify such factors is to correlate the data on one-sided inefficiency residuals (u_{it}) generated from the frontier estimation with country institutional attributes. Correlating will enable one to isolate the institutional variables that identify why some countries excel in certain areas and others do not. Here the trick is to utilize the most appropriate institutional country attributes so the analysis can make economic sense.

E. Conclusion

Clearly the inter-country variation in economic well-being is large. For example, in 1987-1988 real GDP varied from about 700 US dollar per capita in less developed countries like Bangladesh, to about 5500 US dollar in Eastern Block countries like Hungary, to about 11500 US dollar in European countries like the Netherlands, and finally to about 18000 US dollar in highly advanced economies like the US. Worker wages and well-being clearly vary as well. Even among developed countries in 1991 hourly manufacturing worker compensation indices vary from 131 in Norway to 109 in the Netherlands, 100 in the US, 88 in Japan, 55 in New Zealand, and down to 19 in Portugal and 12 in Brazil. The motive for this chapter is to seek methodologies to evaluate not just worker well-being across countries, but also to devise ways to determine what country and labour market institutions as well as government policies increase labour market efficiency making workers better off.

The usual neoclassical criterion is Pareto optimality. An economy is Pareto optimal if any status quo deviation results in at least some economic units becoming worse off. If so, one cannot make anyone better off without hurting at least someone.

Clearly if a country is not Pareto optimal welfare for all can be increased. Thus one approach to evaluating well-being is to determine which countries are Pareto-efficient.

As indicated in this chapter, such a task is formidable. For one welfare is difficult to measure. Common economic indicators such as earnings, wealth, or job security are not completely appropriate. They measure only one aspect of welfare but do not encompass overall well-being. For example earnings represents a money metric but it does not value leisure, nor does it account for compensation over the lifetime. Secondly, even if this indicator or others were adequate, equity issues concerning how an individual values the welfare of another are not included. These "externalities" are important because often they motivate governmental welfare type transfer payments. Third, there are many measures of well-being but there are no clear notions which of the myriad of welfare measures is the best. Thus when using any one as a welfare measure does not mean that finding an inefficient country implies that all can be made better off in terms of other welfare measures. A fourth problem confounding evaluation is that even if P-efficiency were easily discernible one has no way of ranking efficiency across countries. Fifth and perhaps most important is that improvements in large diverse economies unlikely occur without hurting at least some. Thus while P-efficiency is valuable to economic theorists studying narrow policies with theoretical population welfare functions the P-efficiency criterion is less than ideal for policy makers.

We thus propose an alternative technique based on frontier estimation. Frontier estimation entails measuring inefficiency as the extent to which data lie below a boundary function. The technique is mostly applied to firms by fitting production function models. Inefficiency is the degree to which a particular factory's output lags maximal levels. For our case, a country's inefficiency can be defined by using countries as units of observation instead of factories. Here inefficiency is measured as the extent to which a particular country's output lags others holding inputs constant. One is not confined to technical production inefficiencies since by holding output constant, one can use income level and distribution indices as the dependent variable. Here shortfalls define welfare losses. Correlating these welfare deficiencies with country institutional characteristics as well as government policies gives an indication what institutional processes promote efficiency and equity.

Even with this approach there are problems. For example, it is not obvious what constitutes the appropriate dependent variable, whether it should be output, whether it should be worker wage, or whether some other welfare measure is preferable. Again externalities are difficult to measure, as even earnings distribution measures do not determine how one evaluates the welfare of another. Nevertheless, despite these difficulties, at least the prime benefit over the P-efficiency approach is that frontier estimation simplifies inter-country comparisons.

Clearly none of these techniques can be applied if one has no information about what data are available in each country. For this reason we commissioned studies on twelve diverse countries on four continents. Included are countries with rather capitalistic economies as well as countries with more socialist economies. By using the information gathered in these following chapters it is hoped that the techniques described in this chapter can be applied not only to evaluate relative labour market performance but in addition to assess how institutional characteristics affect worker well-being.

REFERENCES

Aigner, D.J., C.A.K. Lovell, and P. Schmidt (1977), Frontier Estimation of Stochastic Frontier Production Models, *Journal of Econometrics*, 6(1), 21-37.

Arnott, R., A. Hosios and J. Stiglitz (1988), Implicit contracts, labour mobility and unemployment, *American Economic Review*, 78 (5), 1046-1066.

Arrow, K.J. and G. Debreu (1954), Existence of an Equilibrium for a Competitive Economy, *Econometrica*, 22, 265-290.

Arrow, K.J. and F.H. Hahn (1971), *General competitive analysis*, San Francisco: Holden-Day.

Calmfors, L. and J. Driffill (1988), Centralisation of wage Bargaining and Macro-economic Performance, *Economic Policy*, 6, 12-61.

Cooter, R. and T. Ulen (1988), *Law and Economics*, Glenview: Scott, Foresman and Company.

Blaug, M. (1980), *The Methodology of Economics*, Cambridge: Cambridge University Press.

Freeman, R.A. and J.L. Medoff (1984), *What do unions do?*, New York, Basic Books.

Gaynor, M. and S. Polachek (1987), Measuring Ignorance in the Market: A New Method with an Application to Physician Services, Paper presented at the American Economic Association Meetings, Chicago.

Good, D., R. Johnson and R. Sickles (1986), Allocation Distortions and the Regulatory Transition of the US Airline Industry, *Journal of Econometrics*, 33, 143-163.

Grabowski, R. and C. Pasurka (1988), The Technical Efficiency of Northern and Southern US Farms in 1860, *Southern Economic Journal*, 54, 598-614.

Gravelle, H. and R. Rees (1981), *Microeconomics*, London: Longman.

Hartog, J. (1988), Poverty and the measurement of individual welfare, *Journal of Human Resources*, 23(2), 243-266.

Hartog, J. (1990), Labour market policies from a neoclassical perspective: implementing the trinity, in: K. Groenveld, J.A.H. Maks (eds.), *Economic Policy in the Market Process, Success or Failure?*, Amsterdam: North Holland.

Hartog, J. (1992), *Capabilities, allocation and earnings*, Boston: Kluwer Academic Publishers.

Hartog, J. and J.J.M. Theeuwes (1990), Low productivity and social inequality, Working paper, Amsterdam/Leiden.

Hennipman, P. (1981), De verdeling in de Paretiaanse welvaartstheorie, in: *Inkomensverdeling en Openbare Financiën*, P.J. Eijgelshoven and L.J. van Gemerden (eds.), Utrecht: Spectrum.

Hochman, H.M. and J.D. Rodgers, Pareto-optimal Redistribution, *American Economic Review*, 59, 542-557.

Jondrow, J. and C.A. Knox Lovell, I.S. Materov and P. Schmidt (1982), On the estimation of technical inefficiency in the stochastic frontier production function, *Journal of Econometrics*, 19, 233-238.

Kumbhakar, S. (1988), On the Estimation of Technical and Allocative Efficiency Using Stochastic Frontier Functions: The Case of US Class 1 Railroads, *International Economic Review*, 29, 727-743.

Mortensen, D.T. (1986), Job search and labour market analysis, in: O. Ashenfelter and R. Layard (eds.), *Handbook of Labour Economics*, Amsterdam: North-Holland.

Ng, Y. (1979), *Welfare Economics*, London: MacMillan.

Polachek, S. and B. Yoon (1990), Panel Estimates of A Two-Tiered Earnings Frontier, Paper presented at the Third Conference on Panel Data, ENSEA, Paris (June).

Rosen, S. (1985), Implicit contracts, *Journal of Economic Literature*, XXIII (3), 1144-1175.

Spence, A.M. (1974), *Market Signalling*, Cambridge: Harvard University Press.

Tobin, J. (1970), On Limiting the Domain of Inequality, *Journal of Law and Economics* XIII (2), 263-277.

Ulph, A. and D. Ulph (1989), Labour Markets and Innovation, *Journal of the Japanese and International Economies*, 3, 403-423.

Labour Market Contracts and Institutions
J. Hartog and J. Theeuwes (Editors)

CHAPTER 2

THE UNITED STATES:
Decentralized Heterogeneity

Robert J. Flanagan*

A rich variety of employment arrangements frustrates any search for the "typical" employment contract in the United States. While the data on U.S. employment relationships can be organized by categories that are believed to facilitate analysis – e.g., union vs. nonunion, public vs. private – the variance of outcomes within these categories can be as instructive as any "on average" generalizations. Nevertheless, the distinction between individually-determined and collectively-determined employment arrangements provides a useful point of departure. The former are established in nonunion, hierarchical settings by what appears to be unilateral employer action but what may be individually-determined "implicit contracts" or "invisible handshakes." The latter emerge in the union sector, where the employee's objectives for the collective bargain, established by a voting process within unions, confronts the employer's objectives in a bargaining process. On average, strikingly different outcomes emerge from these two settings, but each setting also yields a striking diversity of outcomes.

This chapter begins with a brief review of the evolution of the employment relationship in the United States, and current labour market structure. Section II then describes the current institutional and legal environment of the U.S. employment relationship. The "tilt" toward arrangements in the union sector risks overemphasizing arrangements that now directly cover only about 16 percent of employment, but facilitates comparisons with collective bargaining arrangements and outcomes in more unionized economies. The third and longest section reviews the evidence on all major elements of the employment contract – wage payment methods, fringe benefits, hours of work, duration of the employment relationship (labour turnover), and the allocation of risk. An overall evaluation concludes the chapter.

---

* Graduate School of Business, Stanford University, Stanford, California. The author is grateful to the Graduate School of Business, Stanford University for research support.

A. The Evolution of Employment Institutions

From a comparative perspective, the distinguishing feature of the employment relationships that arise in labour markets in the United States is the limited extent to which they are influenced by collective bargaining and statutory regulation. Lacking this perspective, most participants in U.S. employment relationships would no doubt dispute the word "limited". Nevertheless, employment is dominantly nonunion, and many aspects of employment contracts determined by collective bargaining or statute in other countries are a matter for market determination in the large nonunion sector in the United States.

On the other hand, the form of employment relationships has changed substantially during the 20th century and has not been immune from institutional changes any more than those changes have been immune from the nature of employment relationships. At the beginning of the century, the Common Law provided the legal framework for the employment relationship, and unions barely existed outside of the skilled crafts, leaving foremen and plant production managers free to define the employment relationship in factories. These individuals, who made the hiring, termination, and wage decisions in plants, were guided mainly by short-run production considerations. Hiring, lay-offs and wages were more or less discretionary, and favouritism and prejudice often influenced these decisions (Jacoby, Chapter 1). Job attachment was transient, and turnover and economic insecurity were high. Foremen used this insecurity to try to motivate greater effort.[1]

During the first half of the 20th century this system gave way in medium and large firms to "internal labour markets," characterized by extensive promotion-from-within, explicit company-wide policies governing hiring, promotions, transfers, and lay-offs, and greater economic security. As an organization-wide employment policy became an end in itself, authority over employment relationship shifted from foremen to personnel departments to ensure uniformity of application. The underlying motivational assumptions also changed radically. Contrary to the foremen's "drive" system, internal labour markets sought to motivate workers by rewarding their contributions to the firm with greater economic security. As modern economic theories stress, internal labour markets were also mechanisms for building specific human investments, screening performance, and reducing turnover costs.

---

1. One observer described the foremen's "drive system," the prevailing production-employment system of the day, as "the policy of obtaining efficiency not by rewarding merit, not by seeking to interest men in their work ... but by putting pressure on them to turn to a large output. The dominating note of the drive policy is to inspire the worker with awe and fear of the management, and having developed fear among them, to take advantage of it." (Slichter, 1919, p. 202)

Although long advocated by personnel professionals, these changes occurred mainly in two periods of significant external stimulus. During World War I, tight labour markets, threats from expanding (although still limited) union influence, and the government's interest in stabilizing the war production effort all stimulated the regularization of employment relationships in larger firms. During the Great Depression, a rapid growth of unionization following legislation ensuring that the interests of workers rather than employers were paramount in determining union representation, stabilized the employment relationship directly (via union contract) and indirectly (by stimulating nonunion firms to abandon old employment practices in an effort to forestall unionization). (Section II of the chapter discusses the development of collective bargaining institutions.) Subsequent legal developments, while often later and more modest than in other countries, reinforced these tendencies in the broad shape of employment arrangements.

A.1 Labour Market Structure

The pattern of employment emerging from these developments is easily described. Most of the key changes in the industrial distribution of employment (Table 1) parallel developments in other advanced countries – a declining (but very small) share in agriculture, declining share in the goodsproducing sector and an increasing share for services. Employment in the government sector is notable for three reasons, however. First, direct public employment accounts for a small fraction of employment in comparison to other countries. Second, changes in state and local government (SLG) dominate changes in the aggregate government share of employment. Third, the federal government's share of employment peaked 30 years ago and is now at its lowest point in the postwar period. After significant growth following World War II, the SLG share of employment peaked in 1975 and since then has slowly declined. These figures may surprise those who have followed political commentary about the size of the public sector in the United States.

Changes in the occupational distribution of employment (Table 2) largely parallel those in the industrial distribution. For the first time in this century, however, the shares of two white-collar categories, professional/technical workers and clerical workers, fell during the 1980s. For the manufacturing sector only, there are data on the mix of production and nonproduction workers. These show a steady increase in the share of nonproduction workers, most notably in durable goods manufacturing where they comprised a third of employment by the late 1980s, (U.S. Bureau of Labor Statistics, 1989, Table 72).

The employment data in the preceding tables represent a mixture of full-time and part-time employment. Table 3 provides data on the distribution of full-time and part-time employment and labour force.

Table 1. Employment Distribution by Major Industrial Sector, 1950-89 (percent)

	1950	1955	1960	1965	1970	1975	1980	1985	1989[d]
Agriculture[a]	13.7	11.3	9.2	6.7	4.7	4.2	3.6	3.2	2.9
Goods-producing industries[b]	35.3	35.9	34.3	33.7	31.7	28.1	27.4	24.7	22.9
Nongovernment Services[c]	39.5	40.7	42.6	44.2	46.7	49.4	51.7	55.9	58.3
Government	11.5	12.1	14.0	15.5	16.9	18.3	17.3	16.3	15.9
Federal	3.7	3.8	3.8	3.7	3.4	3.4	3.1	2.9	2.7
State & Local	7.8	8.3	10.2	11.8	13.2	14.9	14.3	13.4	13.2
Total	100	100	100	100	100	100	100	100	100

[a] Agriculture includes forestry and fishing.

[b] Manufacturing, mining and construction.

[c] Transportation and public utilities, trade, finance insurance, real estate, and personal, professional and business services.

[d] Preliminary data.

Source: U.S. President, *Economic Report of the President*, February 1990, Tables C-32 and C-43

Table 2. Occupational Distribution of Experienced Civilian Labor Force, 1900-1987 (percent)

	1900	1910	1920	1930	1940	1950	1960	1970	1980	1987
White-collar workers	17.6	21.0	25.0	29.4	31.1	36.6	42.2	47.5	52.2	55.9
Professional and technical	4.3	4.6	5.4	6.8	7.5	8.6	11.3	14.6	16.1	15.8
Managers	5.9	6.5	6.6	7.4	7.3	8.7	8.5	8.1	11.2	14.6
Clerical	3.0	5.2	8.0	8.9	9.6	12.3	14.9	17.8	18.6	15.6
Sales	4.5	4.6	4.9	6.3	6.7	7.0	7.5	7.0	6.3	9.0
Manual workers	35.8	37.5	40.2	39.6	39.8	41.1	39.7	36.6	31.7	27.6
Craft workers	10.6	11.4	13.0	12.8	12.0	14.2	14.3	13.9	12.9	12.1
Operatives	12.8	14.4	15.6	15.8	18.4	20.4	19.9	17.9	14.2	11.3
Labourers (nonfarm)	12.5	11.8	11.6	11.0	9.4	6.6	5.5	4.7	4.6	4.3
Personal-service workers	9.1	9.4	7.9	9.8	11.8	10.5	11.7	12.9	13.3	13.4
Domestic	5.4	4.9	3.3	4.1	4.7	2.6	2.8	1.5	1.1	0.8
Other*	3.6	4.5	4.5	5.7	7.1	7.9	8.9	11.3	12.3	12.6
Farm workers	37.5	30.4	27.0	21.2	17.4	11.8	6.3	3.1	2.8	3.1
Farmer and Farm managers	19.9	16.3	15.3	12.4	10.4	7.4	3.9	1.8	1.5	1.2
Farm labourers	17.7	14.2	11.7	8.8	7.0	4.4	2.4	1.3	1.3	1.9

Note: From 1900 to 1930, employment data relate to "gainful workers." from 1940 on, data related to civilian labour force. 1980 and 1987 data are not strictly comparable because they relate only to the *employed* labour force 16 and over. Data for 1987 are not strictly comparable because of definition changes.

* Included are attendants, barbers, cooks, guards, janitors, police, practical nurses, ushers, waiters, and so forth.

Source: 1900-1950: U.S. Bureau of the Census, *Historical Statistics of the United States*, Colonial Times to 1957 (1960). Table D72-122

1960: U.S. Bureau of the Census, *Census of Population 1960*. Subject Reports, PC(2)-7A, 1967, Table 1.

1970: U.S. Bureau of the Census, *Census of Population 1970*. Subject Reports, PC(2)-7A, 1972, Table 1.

1980: U.S. President, *Employment and Training Report of the President* (Washington, DC: U.S. Government Printing Office, 1981), p. 149.

1987: U.S. Bureau of Labor Statistics, *Employment and Earnings*, 34, 1 (January 1988), Table 20

Table 3. Full-time and Part-time Jobs and Labour Force, 1970-88 (percent)

Year	Employment			Unemployment			Labour Force
	Total	Full-time[a]	Part time	Total	Looking for full-time work	Looking for part-time work	Part-time
All workers, 16 years and over							
1970	100	84.8	15.2	100	78.3	21.7	15.4
1975	100	83.4	16.6	100	82.2	17.8	16.7
1980	100	83.1	16.9	100	82.1	17.9	16.9
1985	100	82.6	17.4	100	81.7	18.3	17.4
1988	100	82.8	17.2	100	80.0	20.0	17.3
Men, 20 years and over							
1970	100	94.6	5.4	100	91.6	8.4	5.5
1975	100	93.8	6.2	100	93.6	6.4	6.2
1980	100	93.6	6.4	100	94.5	5.5	6.4
1985	100	92.7	7.3	100	93.6	6.4	7.3
1988	100	92.6	7.4	100	93.0	7.0	7.4
Women, 20 years and over							
1970	100	76.6	23.4	100	79.9	20.1	23.2
1975	100	75.6	24.4	100	82.3	17.7	23.8
1980	100	76.4	23.6	100	81.6	18.4	23.3
1985	100	76.1	23.9	100	81.0	19.0	23.6
1988	100	77.1	22.9	100	79.9	20.1	22.8

[a] Includes workers who usually work full time but are on part time for economic reasons (less than 2 percent of employment).

Source: U.S. Bureau of Labor Statistics, 1989, Table 12

The data for individuals 20 years and over is particularly useful, since it covers workers who for the most part are beyond schooling and can consider permanent job attachments. Part-time jobs are a much more important source of work for women than for men, but for at least the past 20 years, increasing female labour force participation has not been accompanied by changes in the shares of full- and part-time work among women. Overall, there has been only a small increase in the part-time share of employment since 1970, and this has been entirely among men. For workers over 20 years of age, the preferences of the unemployed for full-time and part-time work seem closely matched to the distribution of employment opportunities. For teenagers, however, the market appears to offer a lower proportion of part-time jobs than job seekers prefer.

B. Institutional Environment

The discussion of U.S. employment arrangements cannot be taken much further at this point without specific information on the institutional environment.

B.1 Legal Framework

The Common Law, which rested on the theory of competitive labour markets in which extensive choice on both sides of the market provides workers and employers with symmetrical power in determining the terms and conditions of employment, provided the earliest legal framework for employment relationships in the United States. This Common Law framework placed no significant restrictions on the terms of employment that an employer could offer. At the same time, the U.S. Constitution accorded considerable latitude to the states in determining conditions of employment, largely because of the division among the states over the issue of slavery at the time the constitution was written. Southern states, where slavery was widespread, were unwilling to grant the federal government full authority over the employment relationship for fear that a coalition of northern states would vote to end slavery. Although the slavery issue was resolved in the 19th century, the Constitution restricted federal policy to *interstate commerce*, and debates over the respective responsibilities of the federal and state levels of government influenced the structure of employment regulation well into the 20th century.

Workers' compensation legislation provides a key example of how a constitutional framework resulting from an accident of history decentralized public policies pertaining to the employment relationship. While the Common Law held employers liable for injuries resulting from their negligence, several permissible defenses precluded or limited the amount of compensation that injured workers could collect in practice. In the face of soaring industrial accidents in the first decade of the 20th century (e.g., in the railroad and mining industries), several states passed workers' compensation laws, but the only federal law covered the railroad industry, which was clearly *involved* in interstate commerce. (In contrast, it was claimed that manufacturing activities did *not* constitute trade between states.) These statutes simultaneously established a no-fault insurance system[2] that assured compensation to injured workers, limited employers' liability to the compensation payment, and introduced experience rating, which provided some incentive for employers to reduce accidents by investing in safety. By 1920, 42 of the 48 states passed such laws, and now laws exist in all states. But the laws vary considerably in average wage replacement, and administration. Some of the variation reflects the unwillingness of some states to impose costs that they believe will place companies at a competitive disadvantage. A uniform federal statute could break through this prisoners' dilemma and might have been passed, but the U.S. Constitution was believed to preclude such federal activity. Although the constitutional issue was resolved in 1937 by Supreme Court decisions permitting federal regulation of activities, such as manufacturing, that *affect* interstate commerce, no federal statute has yet supplanted the state-based policies in this area.

The legal framework for the employment relationship established by Common Law and the U.S. Constitution was eventually supplemented by two important waves of federal statutory employment law – the first in the 1930s and the second since the 1960s. Fundamental to statutory developments in the 1930s was a rejection of the competitive labour market model in favour of the proposition that employers inherently had superior bargaining power – although only over some workers. One effect of federal legislation in this period was to establish minimum employment standards. The Fair Labour Standards Act (discussed in section III below) established minimum wages, maximum hours, and premium pay for overtime work, but exempted executive, administrative, professional and sales employees. A second effect was to provide employees with a mechanism for supplementing minimum standards. The National Labour Relations Act (discussed in section II below) provided statutory rights to concerted activity and collective bargaining, but initially these rights were restricted to employment where a majority of the workers favoured unionization.

A third effect was to extend statutory insurance against employment related risks beyond workers' compensation. The structure of some of the resulting social insurance programs again reflects the influence of conflicts within the federalist system. The key federal statute, the Social Security Act of 1935, established a retirement income program for older workers that was later amended in 1939 (notably to provide income to a surviving spouse), in 1954 (to provide income for disabled workers

---

2. No-fault insurance systems provide benefits even when an employer is not negligent or otherwise at fault. Thus, under the no-fault workers' compensation systems in the various states, employers are held liable without fault.

and their families), and in 1965 (to provide hospital and medical insurance to people 65 and over). Individuals become eligible for payments by working a certain amount of time in jobs covered by the law (now over 90 percent of employment). Payroll taxes assessed on current employees and their employers (up to a maximum taxable annual income) finance the system.

The Social Security Act also provides the basis for an unusual Federal State unemployment insurance system, under which the federal government establishes minimum guidelines and oversees the operation and performance of the system, while the states are free to enact their own laws as long as they comply with federal standards. Government action in this area followed decades of private efforts by unions, union-management groups, and some industrial groups to establish unemployment insurance plans. Most of these encountered actuarial and administrative difficulties, and none could cope with the scale of joblessness in the 1930s. By 1935, only one state had passed a law.[3] Concerns that a purely federal plan would be unconstitutional because of the states' responsibility for the regulation of industry led to the peculiar federal-state formulation. Although the constitutional issues were resolved by the late 1930s, there is still no uniform federal policy, since states determine eligibility and the amount and duration of benefits. All states now have programs financed by federal and state payroll taxes (up to an annual maximum). Interest in preventing unemployment as well as cushioning its effects led to the experience rating of state payroll taxes. Experience rating is incomplete, however, so that firms with the most stable employment patterns effectively subsidize firms with very high lay-off rates.

A second wave of employment law began in the 1960s with the passage of statutes forbidding employment discrimination (on the basis of age, race, sex, religion, or national origin), and regulating occupational health and safety (extending the objective of accident prevention at the workplace inherent in the experience-rating of workers' compensation further by providing for the establishment and enforcement of mandatory federal job safety standards and health standards), pensions (setting minimum standards for private pension programs), and plant closures (requiring advance notice to employees of plant closures or mass lay-offs).[4]

---

3. Munts (1976, pp. 74-75) described the perceived prisoner's dilemma confronting each state: "Even in a political climate of crisis, states could not overcome a natural reluctance to disadvantage their own industrial development by imposing taxes on business." As in the case of workers' compensation, arguments that lowering risks would lower equilibrium wage rates (costs) apparently received little weight.

4. The key statutes are the Title VII of the Civil Rights Act of 1964, the Occupational Health and Safety Act of 1970 (OSHA), the Employment Retirement Income Security Act of 1974 (ERISA), and the Worker Adjustment, Retraining and Notification Act of 1989 (WARN).

Table 4. Union Membership in the United States, 1897-1984 (in thousands)

Total		Private Sector		Public Sector					
				Total		Federal Government		State/Local	Govt. (SLG)
Year	US Members	Members	% of Private Emp.	Members	% of Public Emp.	Members	% of Federal Emp.	Members	% of SLG
1897	455	444	3.5	11	–	11	–	–	–
1900	932	917	6.4	16	–	16	–	–	–
1910	2,169	2,109	10.1	61	–	51	–	–	–
1920	4,823	4,664	17.1	165	–	135	–	21	–
1930	3,750	3,482	13.3	268	8.5	244	–	–	–
1935	3,650	3,337	14.2	312	9.0	272	–	–	–
1940	7,297	6,848	24.3	449	10.7	336	–	–	–
1945	12,254	11,674	33.9	580	9.8	390	13.9	159	5.1
1950	14,294	13,550	34.6	744	12.3	510	–	–	–
1955	16,127	15,341	35.1	786	11.4	509	–	–	–
1960	15,516	14,613	31.9	903	10.8	541	23.8	307	5.0
1965	18,269	15,638	30.8	2,631	26.1	755	–	1,913	–
1970	20,990	16,978	29.1	4,012	32.0	1,082	39.6	2,958	30.1
1975	22,207	16,397	26.3	5,810	39.6	1,147	41.7	4,586	38.4
1980	20,958	15,273	20.6	5,695	35.1	1,049	36.6	4,567	34.1
1984	18,306	13,013	16.6	5,295	33.1	1,020*	37.1*	4,251*	32.7*

Note: Membership figures are the average annual, dues-paying, full-time equivalent membership of private and public sector bargaining organizations. Bargaining organizations include unions and professional associations that engage in collective bargaining. State and local government data for 1945 and 1960 professional associations and are not directly comparable with later years.

* 1983 data

Sources: Troy and Sheflin, 1985, Table 3.92 and Appendix A

These laws provide broader coverage than the employment protection legislation of the 1930s by dropping the distinctions between exempt and nonexempt and between union and nonunion employees (again without underlying economic analysis or explanation).

B.2 Union Membership

One of the most distinctive features of the American labour movement is its slow growth and relatively modest representation of American workers. In both absolute terms and as a percentage of nonagricultural employment, union membership grew slowly and somewhat erratically prior to the mid-1930s in the face of determined employer opposition and nonsupportive judicial interpretations of the Common Law (Table 4). In the private sector, brief periods of membership growth associated with tight labour markets and, notably, a moratorium on employer opposition during World War I were quickly reversed by higher unemployment and renewed business hostility (as during the 1920s). Unions barely existed in the public sector.

Structurally, the labour movement consisted mainly of craft unions, which represented workers in a single occupational group (usually a skilled trade), and which were organized into the American Federation of Labour (AFL), whose main function was to coordinate organized labour's political activities. These activities have never been tied to any particular political party, however, and U.S. labour unions have in general accepted the capitalist system and focused on the division of the economic pie.

High unemployment continued to contribute to falling union membership in the early 1930s, but following dramatic changes in the legal environment and the structure of the labour movement, membership doubled during the late 1930s and continued to grow rapidly through World War II. The legal changes (see below) provided workers with the rights to bargain collectively and effectively removed the major judicial and employer methods of opposing union development. In addition, a new labour federation, the Congress of Industrial Organizations (CIO), began to organize workers by industry rather than by occupation. The new industrial unions organized many of the large massproduction unions that craft unions had been ill-equipped to organize. None of these developments influenced unions in the public sector, however, where employees were not accorded similar rights and where strikes were prohibited. The two federations merged into the present AFL-CIO in 1955 just before the share of union members in nonagricultural employment and the labour force began a slow decline.[5] The decline accelerated notably after 1978, when the absolute number of union members also began to fall.

---

5. Not all unions affiliate with the merged AFL-CIO, but independent unions no longer represent a significant proportion of union workers.

The federation, while nominally the pinnacle of the labour movement, in fact has very little authority over the national unions. The original labour federation, the AFL, was established by the national unions largely to arbitrate disputes over organizing jurisdictions and to provide political representation on issues of general interest to the labour movement. These unions insisted that the federation follow two principles – national union autonomy and exclusive jurisdiction – which remain relevant in varying degrees to this day in the AFL-CIO. Under national union autonomy the federation has no authority over the internal affairs of its constituent national unions or their membership. (Indeed, the national unions, not union members, belong to the federation.) Thus, no labour federation in the United States has conducted collective bargaining, or set up strike funds, which might be used to influence the policies of particular national unions. The federation is also constitutionally forbidden from interfering in national union practices regarding admissions to unions, apprenticeship programs, discipline of union members, and internal union government. In short, decision-making over all aspects of union economic policies is effectively decentralized to the national union level. Exclusive jurisdiction meant that one and only one national union would be accorded the right to organize workers of a particular skill or performing a particular type of work. (Awarding jurisdiction was originally the AFL's sole authority over the national unions, but even this power was eroded by the National Labour Relations Act representation election procedure.)

Union density, the proportion of employees belonging to unions, varies significantly by demographic group, occupation, industry, and region in the United States. As of the 1980s, union density was higher for men than for women, higher for blacks than for other races, and higher for full-time than for part-time workers. Membership declined for each of these groups during the 1980s, however. Union density remains higher among blue-collar workers than white-collar workers, but even in the unskilled and craft positions that were traditional bastions of union strength, coverage has fallen to about one-quarter of employment. Union density in industries of traditional union strength reveals a similar story, while unionization in sectors of rapid employment growth, such as trade and services, has always been low. Indeed, the most startling revelation in the data by industry is that union members now comprise little more than 12 percent of nonagricultural employment in the private sector. Unionization in the public sector, particularly at the state and local levels, has grown substantially since the mid-1960s, and the effect of the relatively high density for government workers on the frequently-reported average density masks the slim grip that American unions have on workers in the private sector (U.S. Bureau of Labor Statistics, 1981b, Table 5; U.S. Department of Labour, 1991, Tables 1,2; Gifford, 1988).

These variations in union representation by sector are important in interpreting at least two sets of claims regarding influences on union membership in the United States. The first concerns the general decline in union representation visible in Table 4. This is sometimes attributed to the changing industrial and regional structure of employment – shifts from manufacturing to services, from blue-collar to white-collar jobs, and from the industrial northeast (the "rustbelt") to the south and west (the "sunbelt"). Clearly, these are shifts from sectors with historically high union representation rates to sectors with lower rates, so there is some sense to the claim. Equally clear from the tables, union representation rates for nongovernment workers have been declining in all sectors since the 1970s, so that changes in the employment distribution are only part of the story. The best estimates suggest that perhaps 30 to 40 percent of the decline can be attributed to this factor (Farber, 1985). Factors common to all sectors must explain the rest of the decline.

The second claim is that state "right-to-work" laws inhibit union representation. These are laws that prohibit the negotiation of union security clauses – contractual provisions that require workers hired into a unionized establishment to become a union member within a certain period of time (usually 30 to 90 days).[6] Right-to-work laws exist mainly in southern states, where community resistance to unionization was high historically and union membership is low, leading some to conclude that the law has stifled union representation. Empirically, the difficulty with the argument is that representation was low in the South before the laws were passed. Conceptually, the error, common to the measurement of many institutional impacts, is the assumption that institutions (in this case right-to-work laws) are exogenous. The missing question is: Why do some states pass such laws while others do not? When studies account for the fact that the passage of such laws tends to reflect preexisting attitudes towards unions, the laws themselves appear to have no independent influence on the degree of unionization (Farber, 1984).

B.3 Employer Organizations

American employers have not formed nationwide associations for the purpose of collective bargaining and policy negotiations with the government, although such associations are common in most European countries. The failure to unite to pursue common employment objectives may to some degree signal the diversity of employment objectives in American industry. Bargaining structures are comparatively decentralized, for reasons noted below, and the nationwide labour federation, the AFL-CIO has no authority to bargain for the diminishing minority of U.S. workers who belong to unions. Moreover, the federalist constitutional system also contributed to the underlying diversity of employment arrangements by leaving important public policies influencing employment to state determination. Political lobbying by the two major employer associations, the Chamber of Commerce and the National Associ-

6. These laws constitute a rare Congressionally-sanctioned exception to the principle that federal legislation takes precedence over state legislation in areas where the U.S. Congress chooses to legislate.

ation of Manufacturers, includes employment issues, but coordination for collective bargaining is left for more decentralized arrangements. These consist mainly of multi-employer bargaining groups formed as a joint union-management convenience in certain industries discussed further below.)

B.4 Legal Regulation of Labour Relations

The third major actor in U.S. labour relations is the government, but whereas most aspects of the legal environment of the labour market address substantive aspects of the employment relationship, such as wages, hours, fringe benefits, health and safety, and the like, the legal regulation of union-management relations embodied in the National Labour Relations Act (NLRA) is almost entirely directed at procedural aspects of the relationship. The NLRA was the last piece of pro-union legislation pertaining to the collective bargaining relationship. Passed in the midst of the Depression (1935), the objectives of the Act were to reduce labour disputes and the associated disruptions of production and to encourage collective bargaining, in the belief that if unions were successful in raising the wages and purchasing power of workers, consumption demand would increase.[7]

The NLRA provides a statutory guarantee of the right of workers to engage in concerted activities, including but not limited to organizing unions, bargaining collectively, and striking in support of contract demands. The law established two broad mechanisms to secure and enforce these rights. First, the NLRA established a government-supervised election procedure to determine which union, if any, should represent employees in collective bargaining. The purpose of the representation-election procedure was to reduce strikes over union recognition (a common source of strikes and violence prior to the Act). A union receiving the support of a majority of the employees in an election becomes the exclusive bargaining representative of all employees in the bargaining unit. (A subsequent amendment to the Act allows bargaining-unit employees to request decertification elections to determine whether a majority of employees continues to support the union as bargaining representative. Only about 0.25 % of the unionized work force has participated in decertification elections in recent years.) Exclusive representation imposes on the union the duty to represent and bargain for all employees in the unit, including those who voted against union representation and those who do not belong to the union. At the same time, employers are required to deal with employees through the union rather than individually. Exclusive representation effectively protects the monopoly position of a union within the bargaining unit by excluding rival unions. It also means that employers

7. Although widely and correctly interpreted as pro-union legislation, the Act did not have the unanimous support of organized labour. The AFL unions in particular worried that it would improve the fortunes of the new industrial unions (Gross, 1974).

negotiate with only one union per bargaining unit. On the other hand, the legal obligation to bargain for and represent all employees in the bargaining unit raises a free-rider problem for the union – employees who do not support the union nevertheless can receive the benefits of union activities. This has encouraged unions to develop union security arrangements, which in turn have provoked the right-to-work legislation discussed earlier.[8]

Table 5. Unfair Labour Practices Under the National Labour Relations Act

Employers may not:		**Unions may not:**	
(1)	Interfere with, restrain or coerce employees in the exercise of their rights to join labour organizations and to bargain collectively.	(1)	Restrain or coerce employees in the exercise of their rights to join or to refrain from joining a labour organization (but union security arrangements are permitted).
(2)	Dominate or interfere with the formation or administration of any labour organization or contribute financial or other support to it.	(2)	Force an employer to terminate or otherwise discriminate against an employee (unless the employee refuses to pay union dues).
(3)	Discriminate against individuals supporting a labour organization with respect to any term or condition of employment.	(3)	Refuse to bargain collectively with an employer.
(4)	Discharge or otherwise discriminate against an employee because he has filed charges or given testimony under the NLRA.	(4)	Engage in a secondary boycott (e.g., strike a party not involved in a labour dispute to bring economic pressure against one who is).
(5)	Refuse to bargain collectively with the union representing the employees.	(5)	Charge exorbitant initiation fees.
		(6)	Force an employer to pay for services that are not performed.
		(7)	Engage in "organizational" picketing to pressure an employer to recognize a union without are presentation election.

8. Union security arrangements require that employees in a bargaining unit either belong to the union or (in some arrangements) pay a service fee to the union. In 1980, 83 percent of major private sector collective bargaining agreements contained a union security provision (U.S. BLS, May 1981, pp. 23-24). In 1974, the latest date for which data are available, 34 percent of public sector agreements had such clauses (U.S. BLS, 1975, p. 10).

Second, the NLRA proscribes certain "unfair labour practices" – employer and union activities that might interfere with or restrain employees seeking to exercise their rights under the Act. (Table 5 provides examples of the more important categories of unfair labour practices.) To implement these provisions, an administrative agency of the federal government, the National Labour Relations Board (NLRB) was established to conduct elections for union representation and to investigate, prosecute, and adjudicate unfair labour practice charges.

The passage of the NLRA had major consequences for American unions. Under the NLRA, the bargaining unit, or group of employees eligible to vote in the representation election, is either determined by agreement of the union and employer, or, failing this, a determination by the National Labour Relations Board. The choice of union depends on a vote of employees in the unit rather than an award of jurisdiction by the labour federation. Also, once majority rule, rather than economic power became the criterion for establishing a bargaining relationship, unorganized employees rather than employers became the targets of union organizing efforts and employer defenses.

B.5 Bargaining Structure

Decentralized determination of employment contracts is characteristic of the union as well as the nonunion sector in the United States. Few realize that over 150,000 collective bargaining agreements specify employment arrangements for unionized employees. Some of the comparative decentralization of collective bargaining in the United States can be traced to the somewhat "federalist" relationship between the AFL-CIO and the national unions, which precludes bargaining by the federation. The representation election procedure established in the NLRA also encourages smaller bargaining units. As noted, when labour and management cannot agree on the appropriate bargaining unit for a representation election, the NLRB determines the unit. During the early years of the NLRA, the NLRB tended to give more weight to union preferences for relatively small units to encourage the spread of collective bargaining. When the statute was amended in 1947, Congress prohibited the Board from using the extent of employee support for unions as the sole criterion for determining an election unit. Subsequently, the Board has held that extent of organization is nevertheless one of the factors that may be considered in determining which employees are eligible to vote in a representation election. After leaning toward the establishment of multiplant election units during the 1950s, the NLRB has increasingly permitted single-plant election units. Because so many election units are proposed and accepted at the plant and company level, collective bargaining tends to occur close to the workplace in the United States. This is another instance where the specific legal environment has contributed to the decentralization of employment institutions.

Negotiating units are not necessarily coextensive with election units, however, and notwithstanding the general tendency toward decentralization, collective bargaining occurs in a wide array of bargaining structures. One purpose of Table 6 is to contrast bargaining structures determining major collective bargaining agreements (covering 1000 or more workers) in 1980, with those observed in 1988 after the collective bargaining system experienced significant economic shocks. (The tens of thousands of agreements covering less than one thousand workers are largely the outcome of negotiations at the plant or company level.) In 1980, singleplant negotiations (between a union and an employer or plant manager) determined employment arrangements in 30 percent of major agreements. Multiplant negotiations within a single company accounted for another 30 percent of the contracts. Multi-employer negotiations determined over 40 percent of major collective bargaining agreements (covering about half of the workers included in these agreements).

Bargaining structures are not distributed randomly across industries, and the patterns visible in the 1980 data reflect economic influences on the level of bargaining. Multi-employer bargaining structures are most prevalent in nonmanufacturing industries with substantial competition between small- to medium- sized firms in local or regional product markets (for example, construction, hotels and restaurants, supermarket chains, etc.) and least prevalent in the oligopolistic market structures common in durable goods manufacturing industries. Since U.S. labour law will only sanction multiemployer bargaining established by consent of both negotiating parties, the arrangement must offer joint benefits in sectors where it appears. What are these joint benefits?

Multi-employer bargaining reduces the potential scope for consumer substitution. Employers can offer a united front and be assured that the ultimate agreement will impose the same compensation rate on all participants in the negotiations. Moreover, unions will find it difficult to sustain long strikes when strike support resources must be spread over the entire membership. Reducing the elasticity of product demand is also favourable to the union, however, since fewer jobs will be lost for a given wage increase. Since this bargaining structure creates a bilateral monopoly, its effect on bargaining outcomes cannot be predicted. (This would seem to be a prerequisite for an arrangement formed by mutual consent.) However, empirical evidence indicates that after controlling for characteristics of industries and workers, wages tend to be higher under multiemployer bargaining units in local product markets than in single employer units (Hendricks, 1975; Hendricks and Kahn, 1984; Feuille, Hendricks, and Kahn, 1981). Multi-employer agreements rarely extend beyond local or regional product markets in the United States, for the stability of such associations is threatened by the greater potential for the emergence of nonunion firms and because it becomes more difficult to formulate a bargaining position that is agreeable to all when members of the association differ in their internal efficiency, susceptibility to nonunion competition, and the like.

Table 6. Structure of Major Bargaining Units, by Industry, 1980[a] and 1988[b] (percent distribution)

All Agreement		Single Employer						Multi Employer	
		Total		Single Plant		Multi Plant			
	%	1980	1988	1980	1988	1980	1988	1980	1988
All Industries	100	60	79	30	51	30	28	40	21
Manufacturing	100	86	98	53	66	33	32	14	2
Food	100	63	100	37	68	27	32	37	0
Apparel	100	19	60	6	40	13	20	81	40
Chemical	100	100	100	89	72	11	28	0	0
Primary metals	100	99	100	55	58	44	42	1	0
Machinery (nonelectr)	100	98	100	68	50	30	50	2	0
Electrical machinery	100	97	100	66	90	31	10	3	0
Transportation Equip	100	96	100	40	53	56	47	4	0
Nonmanufacturing	100	35	63	8	38	27	25	65	37
Communications	100	100	100	5	51	95	49	0	0
Construction	100	1	36	c	22	1	14	99	64
Hotels & restaurants	100	10	65	3	65	6	0	90	35
Retail trade	100	53	77	11	32	41	45	47	33
Service	100	29	70	14	55	15	15	71	30
Utilities	100	96	100	26	52	70	48	4	0

[a] Labour Agreements covering 1000 workers or more, as of January 1, 1980.
[b] Labour Agreements covering 500 workers or more, as of January 1, 1988.
[c] Less than 0.5%

Sources: U.S. Bureau of Labor Statistics, 1981a, p. 19; Cleveland State University, Industrial Relations Center, May 1989, Table 1.8

Single employer (companywide) bargaining is more typical in markets with a few large producers (such as automobiles, rubber, meatpacking). Until the 1980s, the union would begin bargaining with the "target" company selected for the bargaining round, and the terms established at the target became the "pattern" that was extended to other companies in the same industry in subsequent negotiations. These structures are generally advantageous to unions, for if a strike occurs only a fraction of the union's membership (those employed at the target company) will draw strike benefits, and the union's financial resources will therefore support a longer strike than if the union faced a multiemployer bargaining unit. At the same time the target company risks losing customers to unstruck competitors. The limited empirical evidence available indicates that unions achieve more generous contracts in company-wide bargaining units than industrywide bargaining units, in national product markets, contrary to the findings for local product markets. (Hendricks, 1975; Hendricks and Kahn, 1984; Feuille, Hendricks, and Kahn, 1981).

During the 1980s, collective bargaining responses to increased competitive pressures and a deep recession disrupted many traditional bargaining structures in the United States. A comparison of the data for 1988 with the data for 1980 in Table 6 indicates the major developments.[9] The most dramatic change in official bargaining structures is the shift from multiemployer to single plant bargaining. In non-manufacturing, multiemployer bargaining determined employment conditions in about two-thirds of the bargaining units in 1980 but in a little over a third of the units in 1988. Only in construction were a majority of the bargaining units multi-employer near the end of the decade. Official multiemployer bargaining virtually disappeared from the manufacturing sector. Single-plant bargaining increased substantially in virtually all industries. Although not reflected in these data, effective multiemployer bargaining also declined as many pattern bargaining arrangements broke up in favour of single-employer bargaining. In short,the response to more competitive product market pressures during the 1980s further decentralized the determination of employment arrangements in the union sector.

The relatively decentralized bargaining structure found in U.S. collective bargaining has an important influence on the scope of labour agreements. As a rough rule of thumb, the more centralized the bargaining structure, the more limited the scope of employment arrangements covered by the agreement. It is very difficult for a relatively centralized agreement to address effectively the wide variety of labour relations problems faced by the many plants, firms, or industries subject to the agree-

9. In the 1988 data, major agreements cover 500 or more workers. Even with this change in definition, which seems sensible given the general decline in union membership during the 1980s, the total number of contracts covered by the data is much lower. Nevertheless, comparing the data for 1980 and 1988 at the industry level should provide a reliable picture of changes in bargaining structures.

ment. Negotiators tend to focus on issues, such as wages and hours of work, that have a common meaning and method of application across companies, while issues of variable importance across firms may be ignored, despite their importance to some workers. Decentralized agreements tend to have greater scope because they confront less heterogeneity, and U.S. contracts tend to be quite detailed.

B.6 Conflict and Conflict Resolution

Decentralized bargaining produces more negotiations than centralized bargaining and more opportunities for negotiations to break down. During most of the postwar period both strike frequency (strikes per thousand workers) and strike duration (number of working lost per thousand workers) has been comparatively high in the United States. During the 1970s, between 1 and 3 million workers were involved in the 4000 to 6000 work stoppages occurring each year. (Work stoppage statistics include a small number of lockouts.) Collection of these statistics was curtailed in the 1980s, but a more limited series indicates a significant decline in work stoppages.

The U.S. Constitution provides no right to strike, but federal labour relations statutes guarantee the right to strike in the private sector. Oddly, the right to strike in the private sector does not carry with it an absolute right to reinstatement after a strike ends. The U.S. Supreme Court has held that in a normal economic strike, the employer has a right to hire permanent replacement for striking employees. Once the strike is over, strikers receive preference for reemployment only as vacancies become available. The employer is not obliged to dismiss replacements. Most federal and state government legislation prohibits strikes by public employees; strikers have no rights to reinstatement. Private-sector employers have a right to lock-out workers when a labour agreement has expired and collective bargaining has reached impasses.

The threat or event of a strike is the main mechanism of conflict resolution in the private sector. While federal law provides a set of emergency disputes procedures that may be invoked by the president, these are rarely used and in any event delay rather than substitute for a strike. Since strikes are forbidden in the public sector, most states have provided third-party procedures – notably arbitration – to resolve disputes over the contents of a collective bargaining agreement. Such "interest arbitration" is virtually unheard of in the private sector. On the other hand, "grievance arbitration," in which an arbitrator adjudicates disputes over the interpretation and application of a previously negotiated agreement, is incorporated in virtually all private-sector agreements to minimize the likelihood of "wildcat" strikes during the term of the agreement.

C. Outcomes

Implicit and explicit contracts can include understandings on hours of work, employment levels, compensation, the allocation of economic opportunities and risks, and methods of resolving disputes over the interpretation or application of the contract. Here again there is no "typical" contract in the United States. Union and nonunion outcomes differ on average, practices vary significantly within each sector, and legal requirements play a small role in comparison to European countries.

C.1 Legal Influences on Wages and Hours

Most regulation of work time is found in the federal Fair Labour Standards Act (FLSA) passed in 1938. This statute establishes minimum wages, maximum weekly hours of work (40), and overtime pay of 150 percent of the base ("straight-time") rate for hours exceeding the weekly maximum. Adjustment of the federal standards requires statutory action, which occurs infrequently, and to date Congress has rejected proposals for automatic adjustments of FLSA standards – notably indexing minimum wages to general wage or price movements. However, employers do not have to pay minimum wages and overtime rates to employees who are exempt from the statute – executive, administrative, professional and sales employees who are not paid on an hourly basis and whose monthly or annual salaries exceed statutory thresholds. Moreover, the FLSA does not forbid the use of either individual or group incentive payment systems to either exempt or nonexempt employees. States may establish standards for sectors not covered by the FLSA (e.g., agriculture and the public sector) and may also establish stronger standards (higher minimum wages or lower weekly hours) for sectors subject to the FLSA.

Most states also have worker protective legislation that prohibits or limits work by women and/or children in certain jobs. For example, child labour laws commonly restrict the hours that children can work and prohibit the employment of children in dangerous jobs. State laws prohibiting women from working on jobs that required lifting a certain amount of weight, etc. have given way to more recent federal anti-discrimination statutes that require judging suitability for employment on the basis of individual rather than group attributes.

C.2 Employment and Working Time

Hours of work, employment levels, and employment duration determine the quantity of work provided through employment contracts. The first two aspects are discussed now, while a discussion of employment duration, which depends on such factors as labour turnover and retirement appears in the section on employment risks.

(a) Hours of work

There has been very little trend in average weekly hours in the goods producing sector of the economy since the passage of the FLSA. While average hours have declined in the service sector, notably in retail trade, this development reflects the growth of part-time employment in this sector rather than systematic changes in normal full-time weekly hours schedules (U.S. Bureau of Labor Statistics, 1989, Tables 75 and 77). Unfortunately, the rather modest interindustry variation in average weekly hours reinforces the misconception that maximum hours legislation greatly limits the choice of hours schedules in U.S. labour markets. ("Everybody works 40 hours.") Data on the distribution of hours worked by individuals in full-employment years offer a rather different message (Table 7). Just over 40 percent of employees work the "normal" schedule of 40 hours per week (about half work 35-40 hours), and the rest are distributed more or less symmetrically above and below this amount. Industrial averages clearly obscure the amount of choice in labour markets.

Table 7. Percent Distribution of Hours of Work per Week, Nonagricultural Industries

Hours of Work	May 1969		May 1979		May 1989	
1-14	5.5		5.4		4.6	
15-29	10.1	} 20.7	11.6	} 23.5	11.7	} 22.7
30-34	5.1		6.5		6.4	
35-39	6.8	} 49.3	7.3	} 49.8	6.8	} 47.4
40	42.5		42.5		40.6	
41-48	13.1		10.9		10.8	
49-59	9.3	} 30.0	9.0	} 26.6	11.2	} 29.9
60 and over	7.6		6.7		7.9	
Total at work	100.0		100.0		100.0	
Average hours	39.7		38.8		39.5	

Source: U.S. Bureau of Labor Statistics, June 1969, Table A-22; June 1979, Table A-26; June 1989, Table A-27. The figures are obtained from household interviews in the Current Population Survey. Detail may not add to total because of rounding

There has been very little research into differences in hours worked by union and nonunion employees. Time series estimates indicate that the presence of unions has a negative effect on annual full-time hours worked. Cross-section estimates produce a more complicated picture, however. An analysis of time worked in 1978 found unions associated with lower weekly hours for white men but higher weeks worked and annual and weekly hours worked for white women. Union impact on hours also differed substantially by occupation (Earle and Pencavel, 1990).

(b) Employment levels

The choice of employment level rests almost exclusively with employers in both the nonunion and union sectors. As noted, legal regulations place few restrictions on the employment decisions of employers in either sector. Union contracts in the United States accord great detail to the wage and fringe benefit aspects of the collective bargain, but generally recognize the choice of employment level as a management right. Historically, some unions developed work rules producing inefficiently high employment levels, but with the exception of limitations on subcontracting work previously done in the bargaining unit (found in 58 percent of collective bargaining agreements covering at least 1000 workers in 1980), these practices do not appear to be widespread. In 1980, provisions fixing employment as well as wages and provisions limiting crew sizes existed in 11 percent and 12 percent of such contracts respectively (U.S. Bureau of Labour Statistics, 1981).

Negotiations in the 1980s produced significant work rule concessions by some unions, and by 1988 all categories of employment restrictions had diminished in major agreements. Some unions, noting that wage concessions in the early 1980s had failed to halt declining employment of union members, began to negotiate a new generation of job security agreements in the late 1980s. These agreements purported to insulate specified employment levels in the face of a variety of economic shocks.[10]

C.3 Compensation

Since the writings of Adam Smith, economists have recognized the relevance of a rather broad definition of compensation, including both monetary and nonmonetary elements, for the allocation of labour resources. Labour contracts, both implicit and

10. Three-year contracts negotiated by the United Automobile Workers (UAW) with the Ford Motor Company and General Motors in 1987 established a guaranteed employment number (GEN) – the 1987 employment level – at each plant and limits the situations in which actual employment can fall below the GEN. The companies agreed not to close any additional plants during the term of the agreement and not to lay-off workers except for a downturn in sales. In the latter case, laid-off workers must be rehired when sales rebound (rather than working longer hours, for example). The companies also agreed to replace a fraction of the workers lost through normal attrition. Under these agreements, the GEN at each plant must be maintained if jobs decline for reasons other than slow sales. Workers in these jobs enter a special pool from which they may be assigned to training, another job or some other activity. Their normal wages are paid from a special job security fund (Schlesinger, 1987).

explicit, and statistical agencies continue to recognize only the monetary component of economic compensation, and so the issues associated with wages and fringe benefits dominate the ensuing discussion. This is not meant to imply an unimportant role for nonpecuniary aspects. Indeed, public policies seeking to produce greater equality can produce significant inequality in labour markets when directed only at monetary outcomes.

(a) Wage payment methods

Three general wage payment methods, alone or in combination, cover most work – time-based payments, individual incentive payments, and group incentive payments. Time payments are by far the most frequent in the United States, followed at a distance by individual incentives (piece rates or sales commissions), and group incentive systems, in which remuneration is linked to some measure of the performance of the organization rather than the performance of the individual (Table 8). Data on payment systems in effect in major union agreements appear in Table 9. While the data in the two tables are not strictly comparable, they do not indicate major differences in wage payment methods between the two sectors.

Table 8. Percentage of Employers With Alternative Time and Incentive Pay Systems, 1980 (percent)

	Plant and Service	Office and Clerical	Professional and Technical	Sales	First-Level Supervisors	Middle Managers
Time Systems						
Hourly rate	86	43	16	9	11	6
Weekly rate	5	21	19	17	18	13
Month rate	8	30	40	43	36	40
Annual rate	5	11	28	26	34	39
Incentive Systems						
Individual	11	–	*	7	*	*
Group	5	–	*	3	*	2

* Less than 1 %.

Note: Percentages may sum to more than 100 % due to multiple plans used by an employer for a particular occupational group.

Source: Bureau of National Affairs, Inc., 1981, p. 6

Table 9. Percentage of Major Collective Bargaining Agreements With Alternative Time and Incentive Pay Systems, 1988 (percent)

	All Agreements	Production Workers	Professional	Production and Professional	Clerical
Time Systems	98	98	90	100	100
Hourly or daily	80	83	62	94	25
Weekly or monthly	5	1	10	0	50
Hourly and weekly	12	14	19	10	25
Incentive Systems	28	n.a.	n.a.	n.a.	n.a.
Individual	21	24	10	13	0
Group	7	n.a.	n.a.	n.a.	n.a.

n.a. not available
Source: Cleveland State University, 1989, Table 3.3

Time payments. The applicable time unit for time-based payments broadens as one moves toward higher-paying occupations, with hourly time payments most frequent for blue collar and clerical workers. This reflects in part the distinction between exempt and nonexempt employees in the Fair Labour Standards Act. In a career sense, time payment systems do not literally reward individuals solely for putting in time, for advancement and retention may be tied to performance appraisals and merit plans.

Table 10 profiles the frequency of various types of pay increases received by different employee groups. Salaried workers' compensation increases were tied more closely to individual performance than those of hourly workers, and among hourly workers, merit pay increases are rare among union workers. (In contrast, the weight given to longevity or seniority is greatest among union workers.) Upper level salaried employees, especially corporate officers, are much less likely to receive across-the-board increases (general, cost-of-living adjustment (COLA), or longevity) than are other employees.

Wage commitments in implicit contracts with white-collar workers are for about one year – shorter than in most union contracts. About 80 percent of employees are covered by formal salary plans specifying pay rates and/or pay ranges for each job. Rate ranges are typical of formal plans, and merit reviews are the main procedure for determining a worker's position in the salary range. Merit reviews may also play a role for the 20 percent of white-collar workers subject to individual salary determination (Personick, 1984). To the extent that merit reviews take length of service into account, the influence of seniority on nonunion white-collar salaries may be greater than Table 10 indicates.

Table 10. Types of Private-Sector Pay Increases Given in the United States, 1974-75

Employee Class	Type of Increase (Percentage of Firms Employing a Given Type of Worker Providing a Given Type of Increase)			
	General	Merit	COLA[a]	Longevity
Union hourly	87	10	39	27
Nonunion hourly	69	49	10	17
Nonexempt salaried	49	88	11	7
Exempt salaried[b]	41	87	9	3
Officers	25	91	4	1

a "COLA" increases are cost-of-living based raises that may be automatic or discretionary but are given across the board.

b "EXEMPT" employees are those not covered by the overtime provisions of the Fair Labor Standards Act. They are generally in professional, managerial, or administrative positions.

Source: The Conference Board. Inc., 1976

Merit pay systems are not uniformly successful, however, and about 16 percent of companies with merit systems express dissatisfaction with their plans. Difficulties with merit pay systems illustrate the conflict between companies' desires to motivate their employees and workers' aversion to risk. If merit pay is a large component of compensation and is viewed as unpredictable or out of a worker's control because it is applied inconsistently or with favouritism, then it increases uncertainty among workers. On the other hand, a merit system in which workers know how their work will be rated can reduce some of their uncertainty about future pay increases.

Individual incentives. Estimates of the prevalence of individual incentives systems, such as piece rates and sales commissions, vary widely in the United States, but it does appear that the use of piece rates has been declining. The estimates reported in Table 8 are at the low end of the spectrum. Another study suggested that 36 percent of manufacturing firms had incentive and bonus plans covering production or operations workers (Conference Board, 1976). A 1970 study by the BLS found that about 14 percent of plant workers (20 percent in manufacturing) in medium to large firms received individual incentive payments and that the use of incentives had declined during the 1960s. A later study of manufacturing found further diminution in incentive payment systems during the 1970s (Cox, 1971; Carlson, 1982). These averages mask the highly varied incidence of individual incentive payments by industry and occupation (Seiler, 1984). Incentive systems are most suitable in work settings where both the amount produced by an individual and the quality of output can be easily monitored. Several studies indicate that incentive workers in the United States earn a wage premium of 10 to 15 percent over time workers, but the premium has not been decomposed into motivational and sorting effects (Mitchell et al., 1990, pp. 52-5).

Group incentives. Three general types of group incentive plans can be found in U.S. industry. So-called "gain sharing" plans link the pay of a group of employees to improvements in some measure of internal productivity. Gains attributable to productivity improvements are shared with management. "Profit sharing" plans provide a share of profits in a designated pay period to employees. There is apparently considerable but untallied variation in the exact profit sharing formulae used in various companies. Finally, various "employee-stock-ownership" plans (ESOPS) provide some ownership rights to certain classes of employees.

Table 11. Profit sharing, Savings, and Stock-Purchase Plans in Major Collective Bargaining Agreements (percent)

Agreements	All Agreements	Profit sharing Plans		Saving Plans		Stock Purchasing Plans	
		1980	1988	1980	1988	1980	1988
Private Industry*	100	2	7	5	12	2	8
Manufacturing	100	3	11	8	12	4	11
Nonmanufacturing	100	1	4	2	11	1	6

Workers	All Workers	Profit sharing Plans		Saving Plans		Stock Purchasing Plans	
		1980	1988	1980	1988	1980	1988
Private Industry*	100	2	22	5	28	2	23
Manufacturing	100	3	47	7	47	3	48
Nonmanufacturing	100	1	3	3	14	1	4

* Agreements covering 1000 workers or more, January 1, 1980 or 500 workers or more on January 1, 1988.

Sources: U.S. Bureau of Labor Statistics, 1981a, p. 49; Cleveland State University, Industrial Relations Center, May 1989, Table 3.9

About 19 percent of full-time employees participated in profit sharing and ESOP plans in 1986 in medium and large firms, a sample that probably overstates the general use of these payment methods (U.S. BLS, 1987, Table 75). Profit sharing was distinctly less common in the union sector (Table 11). In 1980, for example, only 2 percent of major collective bargaining agreements in the private sector included profit sharing plans as part of worker compensation. Another 2 percent of the agreements provided for employee stock ownership plans. Fewer than 200,000 workers were covered by agreements with such plans. During the early 1980s, profit sharing became a more important element of the compensation package of many union workers, particularly in the manufacturing and transportation sectors, where increased foreign competition and deregulation augmented the effects of a deep recession on employment. By 1988, profit sharing plans appeared in about 7 percent of the agreements and covered over 20 percent of the workers (and almost half in manufacturing) of the workers covered by major agreements.

This pattern reflects the nature of union decision-making. The median union member (voter), whose preferences determine the nature of contracts that can be ratified, is protected by seniority arrangements from lay-offs during moderate cyclical fluctuations. Since a fixed-wage policy is equivalent to a fixed-income policy for high-seniority workers, they are unlikely to support profit sharing in normal times. Employment risks are borne by the least senior employees. When unusually severe economic developments threaten the employment and earnings of the median union member, as occurred during the 1980s, however, profit sharing arrangements that spread the risks of income variation more evenly may be accepted in an effort to enhance job security.

(b) Fringe benefits

Fringe benefits, including legally-required social-insurance contributions (for unemployment insurance, workers' compensation, and Social Security or retirement) and privately provided benefits (such as holiday pay, vacation and sick leave, private pensions, and private health and life insurance) have grown to be a significant element of worker compensation and employer costs since the Great Depression. National income data show that compensation other than wages and salaries barely existed in 1929. The share of supplements to wage and salary income grew during the Depression with the passage of federal and state legislation mandating social insurance programs for retirement and unemployment. The surge of union growth during this same period and into the 1950s provided impetus for the growth of private fringe benefits, directly through collective bargaining, and indirectly as nonunion employers sought to reduce their employees' interest in unions by providing more generous fringe benefits. These data indicate an approximate doubling in the share of "supplements" in compensation over the past 25 to 30 years, and only in the 1980s does the share level off at about 16.5 percent of employee compensation (U.S. President, 1990, Table C-24).

While national income statistics provide a useful description of longterm trends, they understate the importance of private fringe benefits in total compensation, because they include holiday, vacation, and sick pay as wages. Data published from a Bureau of Labour Statistics survey of employer costs provide a more comprehensive guide to the relative importance of specific fringe benefits (Table 12).[11] By the late 1980s, nonwage benefits comprised almost 30 percent of employee compensation costs in U.S. private industry. (The figure drops to 24 percent if one prefers to consider supplemental pay as part of wages and salaries.) Legally required benefits constitute about a third of all benefit costs. Paid leave and insurance are among the larger private benefit expenditures.

Table 12. Hourly Employer Costs for Employee Compensation, Private Industry, 1989

	Percent of Total Compensation			Percent of Total Benefits		
Total compensation	100.0					
Wages and salaries	72.7					
Total Benefits	27.3			100.0		
Legally required	8.9			32.6		
Social Security		5.9			21.5	
Federal unemployment		.2			.8	
State Unemployment		.8			2.8	
Workers' compensation		1.9			6.9	
Private benefits						
Paid leave	18.4			67.4		
Vacation		7.0			25.6	
Holidays						12.8
Sickness						8.8
Other						3.3
Insurance		6.0			30.0	4.4
Pensions and savings		2.9			10.6	
Supplemental Pay		2.4			8.8	
Premium pay						2.9
Nonproduction bonuses						1.1
Shift pay						
Other		.1			.4	

Source: U.S. BLS, 1989, Table 1

11. For a more limited sample, time series data on the cost of various fringe benefits as a percent of payroll comes from the biennial U.S. Chamber of Commerce survey of large manufacturing establishments. Using payroll as the base inflates the importance of fringe benefits in total compensation. Nevertheless, the series is presumably reliable for trends, and shows an increasing importance in all categories of fringe benefits until the 1980s (U.S. Chamber of Commerce).

Both the level and the share of fringe benefits in compensation are higher in union than in nonunion firms (Table 13). Only private fringe benefits are subject to negotiation in collective bargaining, and most of the union-nonunion benefit differential emerges in the areas of insurance, pensions and premium pay. The difference in the composition of union and nonunion pay packages again appears to reflect the fact that the former are ratified by vote of the membership while the latter are determined by managers concerned about retaining their most mobile employees. Unions must therefore negotiate contracts that satisfy the median worker, who in general will be older than the "marginal" or most mobile workers. Since most fringe benefits have more appeal to older than younger workers, unions are likely to bargain for generous fringe benefit provisions. One result of the larger share of fringe benefits in unionized employment is that estimates of the effect of unions on wages will in general understate the true union-nonunion compensation differential.

Table 13. Hourly Employer Costs for Employee Compensation, by Union Status, Private Industry, 1989 (percent of total compensation)

	Union			Nonunion		
Total compensation	100.0			100.0		
Wages and salaries	66.4			74.4		
Total Benefits	33.6			25.6		
Legally required	9.7			8.7		
Social security		5.7			5.9	
Federal unemployment		.2			.2	
State unemployment		.8			.7	
Workers' compensation		2.6			1.7	
Private benefits	23.9			16.9		
Paid leave		7.3			7.0	
Vacation			3.9			3.4
Holidays			2.4			2.4
Sickness			.7			.9
Other			.3			.3
Insurance		8.3			5.3	
Pensions and savings		4.2			2.6	
Supplemental Pay		3.8			2.0	
Premium pay			2.6			.9
Nonproduction bonuses			.5			.9
Shift pay			.7			.2
Other		.3			.0	

Source: U.S. BLS, 1989, Table 3

The cost data do not indicate the fraction of workers covered by various fringe benefits. Table 14 provides this information for workers in the private sector and in state and local governments. Virtually all workers in the private sector receive paid vacations and holidays, life insurance, and medical care. These benefits are less prevalent in state and local government employment. (Some of the difference reflects peculiarities of the occupational mix; public school teachers do not generally receive contractual vacations, for example.) As noted elsewhere, the level of these benefits provided often varies with length of service. Fewer workers receive paid leave, paid lunch breaks or long-term disability or accident insurance. Over the past decade coverage has increased most rapidly for paid sick leave and dental care.

Table 14. Percent of Full-Time Employees by Participation in Employee Benefit Programs, Medium and Large Firms, 1978, 1986 and State and Local Governments, 1987

Employee benefit program	Private Sector		State & Local Government
	1979	1986	1987
Paid holidays	99	99	81
Paid vacations	100	100	72
Paid personal leave	19	25	38
Paid lunch period	13	10	17
Paid rest time	75	72	58
Paid funeral leave	n.a.	88	56
Paid jury-duty leave	n.a.	93	98
Paid military leave	n.a.	66	80
Paid sick leave	56	70	97
Sickness and accident insurance	65	49	14
Long-term disability insurance	49	48	31
Medical care	97	95	93
Dental care	49	67	59
Life insurance	96	96	85
Defined benefit pension	87	76	93
Defined contribution	n.a.	60	9

Notes: Participants are workers covered by a paid time off, insurance, retirement, or capital accumulation plan. Employees subject to a minimum service requirement before they are eligible for benefit coverage are counted as participants even if they have not met the requirement at the time of the survey. If employees are required to pay part of the cost of a benefit, only those who elect the coverage and pay their share are counted as participants. Benefits for which the employee must pay the full premium are outside the scope of the survey. Only current employees are counted as participants; retirees are excluded.

n.a. Data not collected

Source: U.S. Bureau of Labor Statistics, August 1989, p. 583

(c) Union wage effects

The decentralization of collective negotiations in the United States produces hard bargaining because decentralized bargaining provides no assurance that competitors will face the same labour costs. Wage payments rarely deviate from contractually-specified rates; wage drift in the private sector is virtually unknown. Moreover, with no legal extension of negotiated terms and conditions to other firms, distinctive union-nonunion compensation differences emerge.

There have been many estimates of wage differences between union and nonunion workers that first adjust statistically for other differences between the two groups that might influence wages. After a careful review of over 200 econometric studies, H.G. Lewis concluded that the union relative wage advantage probably averaged 15 percent between the mid-1950s and the late 1970s (Lewis, 1986). (Unadjusted wage differentials are generally higher, and even most "adjusted" estimates may overstate the true union wage differential, which appears to reflect in part compensation for unfavourable and difficult-to-measure nonpecuniary aspects of union employment (Duncan and Stafford, 1980).)

The average union wage effect conceals considerable variation across bargaining situations and over time. Union relative wage effects are higher in nonmanufacturing than in manufacturing industries, and higher in construction (particularly craftsmen) than in other nonmanufacturing industries. There is substantial variation by industry, and in a few highly competitive industries, such as textiles and apparel, unions appear to have no effect on wages. In manufacturing, where industrial unions usually negotiate equal absolute wage increases for all occupations, union wage impact is generally largest for labourers, next highest for operatives, and lowest for craft workers. The union wage impact is also much higher for blue-collar workers than for white-collar workers. As a consequence, unions achieve large relative-wage increases for blacks and other workers who are disproportionately employed in the low-wage jobs where the union wage impact is greatest. As noted earlier, union workers receive more fringe benefits than nonunion workers, so the union impact on total compensation exceeds the impact on wages. Within the public sector, unions in state and local governments have had more moderate effects on the relative wages of their members than unions in the private sector. Public sector unions also appear to have had larger effects on fringe benefits than wages, although the evidence is less complete than for the private sector.

In periods of inflation, the effects of the automatic cost-of-living-adjustments (COLAs) found in many multi-year collective bargaining agreements often raise union wages more rapidly than nonunion wages. Between 1969 and 1982, for example, the average union wage premium rose by about 13 percentage points, peaking at over 25 percent of nonunion wage in the early 1980s. The growth in the union relative wage produced a massive quantity adjustment with substitutions in both consumption (e.g., greater import penetration) and production (e.g., relocation of production facilities and greater capital intensity) as well as reduced compliance with the National Labour Relations Act. For several years unions accepted the large membership losses described earlier in Table 4 before agreeing to pay concessions, including wage cuts or freezes and alterations in COLA formulae. As a result, the union wage premium has declined in every year since 1982 (but has not yet returned to its 1969 level).

C.4 The Allocation of Risk in Employment Contracts

Employment contracts seek to provide both employers and employees with greater certainty about the terms and conditions of employment, yet all employment contracts confront an uncertain future. One approach to uncertainty is to establish short-duration contracts, so that contract terms can be frequently adjusted to unexpected events. On its face, this appears to be the dominant approach in nonunion employment relationships in the United States, where compensation tends to be adjusted at least annually. Note, however, that the modern literature on implicit contracts suggests that even frequent adjustments to changes in the "weather" may be circumscribed by implicit understandings regarding the long-term treatment of employees in a career relationship with a firm.

Where negotiations between employer and employee representatives establish an employment contract, both parties have an incentive to reduce negotiating costs by lengthening the duration of the contract, and during most of the postwar period the average duration of collective bargaining agreements in the United States increased to about three years in the private sector. (Contract durations shortened in some sectors during the 1980s as union and management negotiated various wage concessions.) State-and-local government contracts tend to be for shorter periods.

(a) Adjusting to contingencies

Multi-year union contracts typically preset most terms of employment based on a forecast of future economic conditions but make certain benefits contingent on future events. Collective bargaining agreements in both the private and public sectors provide for wage adjustments during the term of the agreement (Table 15). The data in Table 15 illustrate two typical features of U.S. collective bargaining agreements. First, noncontingent, deferred wage increases are more common than increases that are contingent on economic events. Deferred wage increases are often granted in response to union requests for an "annual improvement factor" (reflecting an implicit forecast of general productivity increases over the life of a contract) and in response to the negotiators' general forecasts of future economic events, such as inflation and unemployment. Such deferred increases involve risk to both parties, depending on the sign of the realized forecast error. Moreover, because deferred wage increases do not respond to actual economic events during the contract period, employment fluctuations are likely to be larger than they would be if wage increases were linked more closely to economic performance.

Table 15. Wage Adjustments During the Term of a Collective-Bargaining Agreement

	Percent of All Agreements in Sector[a] with Provisions for:			
	All Agreements	Escalator (cost-of-living) Adjustments	Deferred Wage Increases	Contract Reopening
Private industry[b]	100	49	89	21
Manufacturing	100	64	90	16
Nonmanufacturing	100	34	88	25
State and local Government	100	15	52	24
State	100	8	35	32
County	100	10	44	31
Municipal	100	20	66	15
Special District	100	50	50	21

a Percentages may add to more than 100 because some agreements have more than one type of wage adjustment provision.
b Agreements covering 1000 workers or more, January 1, 1980.
c Agreements in effect on January 1, 1974.
Source: U.S. Bureau of Labor Statistics, 1981a, p. 55; U.S. Bureau of Labor Statistics, 1975, p. 25

Second, the most common form of contingent wage provision in U.S. collective bargaining agreements is a "cost-of-living" adjustment (COLA) – a formula that automatically adjusts wages to changes in a general index of consumer prices. During inflationary periods up to 60 percent of major collective bargaining agreements (mainly multi-year contracts) have included COLA clauses. (Few contracts permit an alternative approach to contingencies – reopening a contract before its scheduled expiration date.) Explicit COLAs are rare in nonunion employment arrangements, although econometric evidence indicates that general price increases are a determinant of nonunion as well as union wages. Price changes receive more econometric weight in determining union wages, however, in the mid-1980s, COLAs provided an average of 65-75 percent compensation for increases in consumer prices and COLAs providing complete compensation for consumer price increases are rare. The most common COLA formula in the U.S. provides for a uniform cents-per-hour wage increase for a specified absolute change in the price index, thereby narrowing the wage structure. The formulae are renegotiated periodically to prevent indefinite erosion in the degree of compensation.

Recent studies suggest that the extent of COLA protection is related to the nature of the risks that firms face – for example, the extent to which changes in the price of a firm's output is correlated with the general price index – and to the risk preferences of employers and employees. The fact that COLA coverage is incomplete shows that employers as well as workers must be risk averse, and evidence increasingly indicates that the variety of COLAs observed in the U.S. reflects patterns of risk sharing in which both employers and employees are only partially insured for the risks incurred during a long-term labour agreement (Ehrenberg, Danziger and San, 1983; Card, Hendricks and Kahn 1985).

An alternative form of contingent contracting would index changes in compensation for union members to the general performance of the firm via profit sharing, employee stock ownership, or worker ownership of the firm. We have already seen that these arrangements are rare in collective bargaining agreements in the United States (Table 11), and the absence of such plans reveals much about the allocation of risk among unionized workers in the United States. As noted earlier, the inflexibility of standard wages increases the reliance on lay-offs in adjusting to recessions. Since lay-offs dominantly occur according to the reverse seniority principle, discussed in the following section, less-senior workers bear the burden of adjustments to economic shocks. Protected by seniority from lay-offs during moderate cyclical fluctuations, the most senior workers are likely to oppose profit sharing, which would mitigate lay-offs but would also threaten their income security by spreading the burden of adjustment to economic shocks more evenly across union members.

By the mid-1980s, a few unions in economically distressed firms or industries in the U.S. began to accept limited profit- sharing or stock-purchase plans instead of normal noncontingent wage increases (Flanagan, 1984). In another departure from past practice, some of these same unions demanded and were given representation on the company's board of directors to facilitate monitoring decisions influencing the company's performance. The most extreme form of profit sharing is worker ownership of a company, and in the face of the economic challenges of the 1980s, there have been a few dramatic examples of unionized workers assuming ownership of firms. It is too soon to form any generalizations about the outcome of these ventures, but this ultimate assumption of risk by workers raises many questions including: Why should a worker-owned firm be inherently more profitable? Are traditional forms of collective bargaining appropriate in a setting of worker ownership?

(b) Seniority

The traditional industrial relations literature distinguishes two links between seniority (length of service) and employment status. *Benefits seniority* entitles workers with more seniority to more fringe benefits. As seniority increases, workers generally become eligible for longer vacations, additional sick leave and paid holidays, supplemental unemployment benefits, and more generous pension, insurance and health benefits, for example. *Competitive status seniority* governs the allocation of economic opportunities within an organization. As seniority increases, workers are less likely to be laid off and more likely to qualify for promotions, transfers, and overtime work, for example. In combination, benefits seniority and competitive status seniority therefore raise income and reduce the uncertainty of the income stream. Length of service rules provide an important mechanism for allocating risk over time.

The industrial relations literature often describes competitive status seniority as a mechanism for choosing who will benefit from certain economic opportunities and who will not, while benefits seniority involves no such choice between employees. To the extent that risk reduction is a fringe benefit, however, this is a dubious conceptual distinction, since competitive status seniority simply increases employee's entitlement to this benefit with time in service.

Nonunion employers have reasons to accord at least some weight to seniority as long as employee productivity is positively correlated with length of service. There are many reasons why a positive correlation would be expected. One is provided by standard human capital theory, which argues that a worker's productivity in the market and in the firm increased over time from the respective effects of general and specific training. Moreover, some argue that experienced workers are more likely to train junior workers if they know that trained junior workers will not become competitors for their jobs. Competitive status seniority arrangements remove that threat (Marshall and Briggs, 1989, p. 194). Principal-agent considerations (motivating worker-agents whose effort cannot be continually monitored at low cost by owner-principals) also can produce a positive correlation between seniority and wages (Lazear, 1981).

In fact, benefit and competitive status seniority appear in both union and nonunion employment relationships in the United States, but competitive status seniority receives greater weight in the union sector. Table 10 provides evidence from one survey. In addition, a survey of 400 companies revealed that seniority was the most important factor affecting promotions in 41 percent of the union firms but in only 3 percent of the nonunion firms and that seniority afforded much greater protection against lay-off in unionized firms (Abraham and Medoff, 1984, 1985). The use of seniority in promotion and lay-off decisions was also more prevalent among the unionized firms in a 1987 survey by the Columbia Business School (Delaney, Lewin, and

Ichniowski, 1989). One large survey of collective bargaining agreements found seniority provisions in 90 percent of the contracts (Bureau of National Affairs (BNA), 1986). Clearly, union members use their collective organization to elevate the seniority criterion over the norms established in nonunion employment arrangements.[12]

Why do the collective choices of workers place so much emphasis on the seniority criterion? The dominant labour relations explanation rests on fairness considerations. Very early applications of seniority in employment seem to have been in civil service systems to counter political favouritism in employment decisions. Unions favour the seniority criterion because it is an objective measure, easy to observe, monitor and enforce, that reduces managerial discretion and favouritism in personnel decisions.

Why did this particular method of countering discretion become the norm when other rules could serve the same purpose? For example, random selection for promotion and transfer decisions, and worksharing – equal reductions in hours of work – could be used instead of lay-offs by seniority. The ascendancy of seniority is probably a direct consequence of determining employment arrangements by voting (e.g., contract ratification votes) rather than hierarchical decision-making. Since the median union voter will generally be older than the most mobile worker in a nonunion firm, the tendency to emphasize seniority over mechanisms involving a more equal sacrifice is understandable in the union sector. The development of unemployment insurance systems in individual states beginning in the 1930s became another reason for preferring lay-offs by seniority over worksharing. Union leaders argued that the total wage income of workers would now be larger under a lay-off system, for those losing their job could now collect unemployment benefits.

Seniority would seem to have the potential to be divisive among workers, since the least-senior employees bear most of the risk of business fluctuations. Why doesn't seniority tear an organization apart? Earlier in the century before the development of unemployment insurance systems, this concern led unions in particularly volatile industries to adopt some degree of worksharing over a general reverse seniority system. More generally, the divisiveness of seniority ultimately seems to rest on whether or not employees view themselves as being in a career relationship with a

---

12. Even in collective bargaining agreements, however, seniority is rarely established as the sole criterion for allocating opportunity. In the BNA sample, seniority has some role in determining promotions in 73 percent of the contracts but was the sole factor in only 5 percent. Over half the contracts provided for some consideration of seniority in determining transfers, but it was the sole factor in only 8 percent. The more common arrangement is to use seniority to choose among employees of equal ability. Even for lay-off decisions, where seniority plays some role in 89 percent of the contracts, it is the sole consideration in just under half of the agreements.

firm. If so, the instability of income earlier in their career is merely an investment in lower risk in their more senior years.[13]

Seniority does not provide direct control over the bargaining agenda in unions. Contract ratification and other important union decisions proceed by one-member, one-vote. Nonetheless, the uses of seniority in many unions certainly influences how votes will be cast on specific issues, with the result that collective bargaining agreements look different than they would without seniority – for example, the greater preference for fixed-wage over flexible wages or profit sharing.

C.5 Termination of Employment Contracts

Implicit and explicit employment contracts are terminated by voluntary or involuntary job separations, retirement, and death. The general patterns are reasonably well-documented. Employer-initiated and worker-initiated job separations peak early in the employment relationship, and the probability of either a lay-off or a quit declines with job tenure. Over one-half of the men and about one-quarter of the women over 30 years of age hold jobs that will last at least 20 years (Hall, 1982), but job tenures are somewhat shorter than typically observed in Europe and Japan (OECD, 1984). On average, quit rates are lower and lay-off rates higher in union than in nonunion employment (Freeman and Medoff, 1984). The major public policies influencing the duration of employment pertain to dismissal regulation, pensions, and mandatory retirement.

(a) Dismissals

In the nonunion sector, the common law and its underlying economic assumptions has had a pervasive impact on the legal framework for dismissals. The basic common law principle is that employers and employees have symmetrical rights to terminate an employment arrangement for any reason. It is therefore said that under common law, the duration of employment is "at the will of the employer," although the importance of quits in the U.S. economy indicates that the will of the employee is also important in terminating employment relationships. Explicit dismissal statutes have not supplanted the common law at either the federal or state level of govern-

---

13. More senior workers in some unions have at times countered demands of less-senior workers for work sharing with this argument. In discussing lay-off policies in railroad unions during the Great Depression, for example, Slichter reports: "The long-service men, who were sure of their jobs, opposed spreading the work and favoured strict adherence to the seniority rule. They argued that they had borne the burden of unemployment in earlier depressions when they were junior men and that they were now entitled to steady work." (Slichter, 1941, p. 125)

ment in the United States. From these facts, outside observers often conclude erroneously that the country has no dismissal policy.

Since the 1930s, a sequence of statutes made piecemeal incursions on the ability of employers to dismiss for any reason. The National Labour Relations Act (discussed earlier) prohibits employers from dismissing or otherwise discriminating against workers for their union activities. State fair employment practice legislation as well as Title VII of the federal Civil Rights Act of 1964 prohibit employment discrimination (including dismissals) on grounds of race, sex, religion, colour, or national origin. Public employees are protected against arbitrary dismissals and public school teachers can even acquire tenure under civil service acts. All of these laws alter the symmetry of the common law stance in the sense that they circumscribe the employer's freedom to terminate the employment relationship in some situations while leaving the employee's freedom to quit unchanged. But while many employees are protected against dismissal on the basis of the characteristics noted above, there is no general legislative protection against unjust dismissal.

In the presence of this statutory vacuum, other institutions have acted to limit an employer's right to dismiss. American collective bargaining agreements generally require that dismissals be "for just cause" and establish grievance arbitration procedures to adjudicate disputes over individual dismissals. During the 1980s, moreover, the judiciary in most large states increasingly found exceptions to the "employment-at-will" doctrine. The courts in some states effectively recognize the existence of implicit employment contracts based upon oral promises, statements in personnel manuals, length of employment, and the like. In other states, employees cannot be fired legally for activities in support of public policies (like preventing health and safety violations, or bringing antitrust violations to light). In a few states a "covenant of good faith and fair dealing" is recognized, which invalidates dismissals that do not follow a company's procedures.

The odds of an employer being challenged by litigation over a dismissal are still probably lower in the United States than in most European countries. This is particularly true for dismissals of blue-collar workers. The monetary consequences of a successful suit are much greater in the United States, however. In Europe successful challenges to dismissals produce compensatory monetary awards and/or reinstatement. Successful litigants in the United States also obtain compensatory damages, but courts permit compensation for longer periods of time. In reviewing damages permitted under European laws during the first half of the 1980s, I found ceilings on compensatory awards ranging from $2,200 (in Sweden) to normal earnings for a twelve-month period (in Germany). During the same period in the state of California, compensatory awards averaged $344,000 (Flanagan, 1987, pp 195-197). The major difference between the potential monetary costs of dismissals in Europe and the United States, however, is the availability of punitive damages for certain categories of unjust dismissals in the United States. These can be quite large, since they are meant to punish. (The standard instruction to juries is to "consider an amount that will make the defendant (firm) take notice.") Punitive damage awards in California averaged $557,300 during the first half of the 1980s. On balance, it seems that differences in dismissal incentives between the United States and Europe have been overstated.

While no federal statute governing standards for dismissals has emerged, Congress passed the Worker Adjustment Retraining and Notification Act (WARN) in 1989. This statute requires businesses employing 100 or more employees to give 60 days advance written notice of plant closures or mass lay-offs to employees "who may reasonably be expected to experience an employment loss as a consequence of a proposed plant closing or mass lay-off" and to state and local government agencies.[14] Companies may give less than 60 days advance notice if they encounter unforeseeable business circumstances or natural disasters. Although some collective bargaining agreements have had advance notice provisions, surveys indicate that over the period 1983-87 only 20 percent of all displaced workers received written advance notice and only 7 percent received such notice two or more months in advance of lay-off. While the law may bring about a distinct change in practice by covered firms, there are distinct limitations on the scope of its coverage.

(b) Pension and retirement

Public and private pensions influence the duration of labour contracts through their effects on retirement incentives. Private pensions can have a further influence through their effect on labour turnover.[15] Social security now covers over 90 percent of the labour force, and we have seen in Table 14 that over two thirds of private-sector employees and virtually all state-and-local-government employees are covered by pensions. Among the private schemes, pensions comprise a larger fraction of compensation when unions are present.

Employers may provide either defined benefit or defined contribution pensions. Under *defined benefit plans*, which cover more workers, employers promise to provide benefit of a certain size upon retirement and are responsible for funding the pension

---

14. Workers must file suit in federal courts to enforce the provisions of this law. Remedies include lost wages and fringe benefits to affected employees, fines of $500 per day up to 60 days to the local government, and attorneys fees.

15. Although the effects on contract duration are emphasized here, these are by no means the only efficiency issues raised in the now vast literature on the economics of pensions. Another central question, which could be addressed in an analysis of fringe benefits, is why private pension schemes exist.

benefit obligation. Pension benefits may be a specified sum or a fraction of earnings (usually in the last few years of work life). Under *defined contribution* plans, employers promise only to contribute certain amounts into a pension fund each year. The size of the ultimate benefit therefore depends on the size of contributions (often supplemented by employee contributions) and investment returns. Defined-contribution plans offer greater uncertainty about retirement income, and those who stress the insurance function of pensions argue that this accounts for the fact that defined benefit plans are more common.

Public and private pensions influence the duration of employment attachments most obviously by specifying the age and condition of retirement. While 65 may be the most common "official" (although no longer mandatory[16]) retirement age for maximum benefits, most pension plans offer early retirement alternatives. Some recent studies indicate that under many common alternatives, workers should rationally accept early retirement, and in fact a large proportion of the work force retires before age 65.

Private pension plans also influence employment attachments through their *vesting* provisions, which establish how long an employee must work for an organization before becoming eligible to receive pension benefits (upon retirement). Workers who leave an organization lose rights to unvested pensions, so that plans with long vesting periods discourage labour mobility. Federal legislation passed in 1974 and 1986 provided for more liberalized vesting rules for private pensions. The most recent legislation cut the period for full vesting from 10 years of service to 5.

D. Concluding Remarks

It is hard to ignore the multiplicity of contractual arrangements that emerge in the union and nonunion segments of U.S. labour markets. The central role of the concept of "equilibrium" in economics implies more similarity in labour market outcomes than is justified by the facts. That so many employment arrangements can coexist for long periods signals the potential importance of analyses and interpretations supporting multiple equilibria in labour markets.

Legal influences have contributed to both a decentralization (greater variation) of employment arrangements and a decentralization (and variation) of employment

---

16. The most direct legal restriction in this area used to be federal legislation mandating retirement at age 65. (There is at least one economic argument that mandatory retirement is an important element of implicit career employment contracts (Lazear, 1979).) The 1978 amendments to the Age Discrimination in Employment Act raised the mandatory retirement age to 70 years, and further amendments in 1986 outlawed mandatory retirement entirely for most firms.

policies. While social scientists are well-advised to consider the endogeniety of legal institutions, one cannot rule out the importance of certain accidents of history, particularly given the difficulty of changing institutional structures inherited from such accidents.

The statutory legal framework for employment relationships in the United States proceeds from a rarely-examined assumption that there is an inherent inequality of bargaining power in labour markets. Yet, statutory limitations on coverage imply that only some groups suffer a disadvantage in bargaining. The basis for the presumption that some workers (mainly blue-collar and lower level clerical employees) face a world of monopsony and hence need statutory intervention on their behalf, while others faced an entirely different set of labour market opportunities requiring no parallel statutory intervention has never been clearly articulated, but has had an important impact on both the design of legislation and its subsequent interpretation by the judiciary. The tension between the prevailing economic assumption underlying many statutory interventions in the labour market and modern economic theories of the employment relationship is clearest in the case of labour turnover, where economic theories stress forces that bind employers and employees and make turnover costly for employers as well as employees. A reevaluation of the economic foundations of much statutory intervention would appear to be overdue.

REFERENCES

Abraham, Katharine G. and Medoff, James L., Length of Service and Layoffs in Union and Nonunion Work Groups, *Industrial and Labour Relations Review*, October 1984, 38. 87-97.

Abraham, Katherine G. and Medoff, James L., Length of Service and Promotions in Union and Nonunion Work Groups, *Industrial and Labour Relations Review*, April 1985, 38, 408-20.

Blinder, Alan S. (ed.), *Paying for Productivity: A Look at the Evidence*, Washington: Brookings, 1990.

Bureau of National Affairs, *Basic Patterns in Union Contracts*, 11th ed. Washington: Bureau of National Affairs, 1986.

Bureau of National Affairs, *Wage and Salary Administration*, PPF Survey No. 131 Washington: Bureau of National Affairs, 1981.

Card, David, An Empirical Model of Wage Indexation Provisions in Union Contracts, *Journal of Political Economy*, June 1986, Part 2, 94, S144-75.

Carlson, Norma W., Time Rates Tighten Their Grip on Manufacturing Industries, *Monthly Labour Review*, (May 1982, 105 15-22.

Cleveland State University, Industrial Relations Center, *Characteristics of Major Private Sector Collective Bargaining Agreements*, January 1, 1988, Report 8801-1, May 1989.

The Conference Board, *Compensating Employees: Lessons of the 1970s*, Report No. 707 New York: Conference Board, 1976.

Conte, Michael A. and Svejnar, Jan, The Performance Effects of Employee Ownership Plans, in: Blinder, (ed.), pp. 143-171.

Cox, John Howell, Time and Incentive Pay Practices in Urban Areas, *Monthly Labour Review*, December 1971, 94, 53-56.

Delaney, John Thomas, Lewin, David and Ichniowski, Casey, *Human Resource Management Policies and Practices in American Firms*, BLMR 137, Washington: U.S. Department of Labour, 1989.

Duncan, Greg and Stafford, Frank, Do Union Members Receive Compensating Wage Differentials?, *American Economic Review*, June 1980, 70, 355-71.

Earle, John S. and Pencavel, John, "Hours of Work and Trade Unionism", *Journal of Labour Economics*, January 1990, 8, S150-S174.

Ehrenberg, Ronald G., Danziger, Leif and San, Gee, Cost-of-Living Adjustment Clauses in Union Contracts, *Journal of Labour Economics*, July 1983, 1, 215-45.

Ehrenberg, Ronald G. and Milkovich, George T., Compensation and Firm Performance, in: Morris M. Kleiner *et al.* (eds.), *Human Resources and the Performance of the Firm*, Madison, Wis.: Industrial Relations Research Association, 1987, pp. 87-122.

Farber, Henry S., The Extent of Unionization in the United States, in: Thomas A. Kochan (ed.), *Challenges and Choices Facing American Labour*, Cambridge: MIT Press, 1985, pp. 15-43.

Farber, Henry S., Right-to-Work Laws and the Extent of Unionization, *Journal of Labour Economics*, July 1984, 2, 319-52.

Feuille, Peter, Hendricks, Wallace E. and Kahn, Lawrence M., Wage and Nonwage Outcomes in Collective Bargaining: Determinants and Tradeoffs, *Journal of Labour Research*, Spring 1981, 2, 39-53.

Flanagan, Robert J., Wage Concessions and Long-Term Union Wage Flexibility, *Brookings Papers on Economic Activity*, 1:1984, 183-216.

Flanagan, Robert J., Labour Market Behavior and European Economic Growth, in: R.Z. Lawrence and C.L. Schultze (eds.), *Barriers to European Growth: A Transatlantic View*, Washington: Brookings Institution, 1987, 175-211.

Freeman, Richard B. and Medoff, James L., *What Do Unions Do?*, New York: Basic Books, 1984.

Gifford, Courtney D., *Directory of U.S. Labour Organizations*, 1988-89 ed., Washington: Bureau of National Affairs, 1988.

Gross, James A., *The Making of the National Labour Relations Board: A Study in Economics, Politics, and the Law*, 1: 1933-37 Albany: SUNY Press, 1974.

Hall, Robert E., The Importance of Lifetime Jobs in the U.S. Economy, *American Economic Review*, September 1982, 72, 716-24.

Hendricks, Wallace E., Labour Market Structure and Union Wage Levels, *Economic Inquiry*, September 1975, 13, 401-16.

Hendricks, Wallace E. and Kahn, Lawrence M., The Demand for Labour Market Structure: An Economic Approach, *Journal of Labour Economics*, July 1984, 2, 412-38.

Hendricks, Wallace E. and Kahn, Lawrence M., *Wage Indexation in the United States: Cola or Uncola?*", Cambridge, MA: Ballinger 1985.

Hutchens, Robert, Seniority, Wages, and Productivity: A Turbulent Decade, *Journal of Economic Perspectives*, Fall 1989, 3, 49-64.

Jacoby, Sanford M., *Employing Bureaucracy: Managers, Unions, and the Transformation of Work in American Industry*, 1900-1945 Columbia University Press, 1985.

Lazear, Edward, Why is There Mandatory Retirement?, *Journal of Political Economy*, December 1979, 87, 1261-84.

Lazear, Edward, Agency, Earnings Profiles, Productivity and Hours Restrictions, *American Economic Review*, September 1981, 71, 606-20.

Lewis, H. Gregg, *Union Relative Wage Effects: A Survey*, Chicago: University of Chicago Press, 1986.

Marshall, F. Ray and Briggs, Jr., Vernon M., *Labour Economics: Theory, Institutions, Policy*, 6th ed., Boston: Irwin, 1989.

Medoff, James L. and Abraham, Katharine G., Experience, Performance, and Earnings, *Quarterly Journal of Economics*, December 1980, 95, 703-36.

Mitchell, Daniel J.B., Lewin, David and Lawler III, Edward E., Alternative Pay Systems, Firm Performance, and Productivity, in: Blinder, 1990, pp. 15-88.

Munts, Raymond, Policy Development in Unemployment Insurance, in: Joseph P. Goldberg, Eileen Ahern, William Haber, and Rudolph A. Oswald (eds.), *Federal Policies and Worker Status Since the Thirties*, Madison, Wisc.: Industrial Relations Research Association, 1976, Chapter 4.

Organization for Economic Cooperation and Development, *Employment Outlook*, Paris: OECD, September 1984.

Personick, Martin E., White-Collar Pay Determination Under Range-of-Rate Systems, *Monthly Labour Review* 107, December 1984.

Schlesinger, Jacob M., Ford-UAW Job Security Clause Contains $ 500 Million Cap on Payouts to Workers, *Wall Street Journal*, September 21, 1987.

Seiler, Eric, Piece Rate vs. Time Rate: The Effect of Incentives on Earnings, *Review of Economics and Statistics*, August 1984, 66, 363-76.

Slichter, Sumner H., *The Turnover of Factory Labour*, New York, 1919.

Slichter, Sumner H., *Union Policies and Industrial Management*, Washington: Brookings, 1941.

Slichter, Sumner H., Livernash, Robert and Healy, James, *The Impact of Collective Bargaining on Management*, Washington: Brookings, 1959.

Troy, Leo and Sheflin, Neil, *Union Sourcebook*, West Orange, N.J.: Industrial Relations Data and Information Services, 1985.

U.S. Bureau of Labour Statistics, *Characteristics of Agreements in State and Local Governments*, January 1, 1974, Bulletin 1861, Washington: U.S. Department of Labour, 1975.

U.S. Bureau of Labour Statistics, *Characteristics of Major Collective Bargaining Agreements*, January 1, 1980, Bulletin 2095, Washington: U.S. Department of Labour, 1981(a).

U.S. Bureau of Labour Statistics, *Earnings and Other Characteristics of Organized Workers*, May 1980, Bulletin 2105, Washington: U.S. Department of Labour, September 1981(b).

U.S. Bureau of Labour Statistics, *Employee Benefits in Medium and Large Firms*, > 1986, Bulletin 2281, Washington: U.S. Department of Labour, 1987.

U.S. Bureau of Labour Statistics, *Employment and Earnings*, Washington: U.S. Department of Labour, June 1969, June 1979, June 1989, and January 1990.

U.S. Bureau of Labour Statistics, *Handbook of Labour Statistics*, Bulletin 2340, Washington: U.S. Government Printing Office, August 1989.

U.S. Chamber of Commerce, *Fringe Benefits and Employee Benefits* (biannual).

U.S. Department of Labour, *News*, "Union Members in 1990", Press Release 91-34, February 6, 1991.

U.S. President, *Economic Report of the President*, Washington: U.S. Government Printing Office, 1990.

Labour Market Contracts and Institutions
J. Hartog and J. Theeuwes (Editors)
1993 Elsevier Science Publishers B.V.

CHAPTER 3

AUSTRALIA:
The Search for Fair Employment Contracts through Tribunals*

Richard Mitchell** and Peter Scherer***

A. Background

A.1 Labour Market Structure and Social Security System

The Australian labour market derives from a pattern of settlement by Europeans established in the nineteenth century. Its development over the last 100 years has been characterized by a steady diminution in the employment share in agriculture and mining, and a gradual increase in manufacturing share (Table 1), accelerating during World War Two and reaching a peak in the late 1950s of 29 percent, but thereafter diminishing in favour of service sector growth (Withers, 1987: 257). However, even 100 years ago, Australia was a highly urbanized and service-oriented society, with a lower percentage of the workforce engaged in agriculture than other settler countries such as the USA, Canada and Argentina (Table 2).

This urban and service-oriented nature of the workforce, however, went with an atypically high share of output attributable to primary production (i.e. agriculture plus mining), a pattern which continued at least until 1950 (Table 2). Thus Australian labour market institutions developed in an unusual context: urbanized, but with economic development often dominated by primary industries with high value of output per person employed. The issue of how to distribute the gains (or losses) made on world markets by primary industries which directly employed only a small minority of the workforce was a frequent cause of social tensions. This could well be one reason why the system of labour contracts which developed in Australia put such an emphasis on economy-wide distributional fairness. It has only started to move away from this emphasis over the last decade.

---

* The opinions expressed in this chapter are authors' own and do not engage the institutions to which they belong.

** Department of Business Law, Melbourne University, Australia.

*** OECD, Paris, France.

Table 1. Industry Distribution of Employment, 1901-1990 (percentage)

Year	Rural	Mining	Manufacturing	Building	Trade and Transport	Finance and Property	Other	Total Employment	Employment Females as percent of total
1901	25.4	7.6	14.6	9.5	20.0	1.2	21.7	1461	–
1911	24.2	4.9	18.5	12.8	21.1	1.3	17.2	1914	18.8
1921	23.8	2.5	19.5	10.7	21.3	1.8	20.4	2113	20.1
1931	25.8	2.5	18.4	6.4	22.7	2.4	21.8	2056	22.9
1941	16.4	1.8	25.6	4.7	19.1	1.7	30.7	3042	23.1
1951	13.9	1.7	28.2	9.6	23.9	2.7	20.0	3589	23.1
1961	10.9	1.3	27.0	8.8	22.7	3.4	25.9	4216	25.5
1971	7.9	1.4	26.3	8.6	22.9	4.5	28.4	5420	32.4
1981	6.0	1.3	20.1	7.9	25.6	8.7	30.4	6321	36.6
1990	5.4	1.2	15.3	7.5	25.7	11.67	40.8	7825	41.4

Sources: Glenn A. Whithers, Labour 1900 to 1984, Working Paper No. 28, Department of Economic History, Australian National University, Australian Bureau of Statistics, *Labour Force August 1990* (Cat. No. 6203.0), ABS, *The Labour Force, Australian Historical Summary 1966 to 1984* (Cat No. 6204.0); Michael Keating, *The Australian Workforce 1910-11 to 1960-61*, Canberra: Department of Economic History, ANU, 1973, p. 392.

Much of the growth in employment in the service sector which has occurred in Australia over the last fifty years has been on the part of women, whose share of total employment has increased from 23 percent in 1951 to 41 percent in 1990 (Table 1). This growth has in turn come about through the entry of married women into the labour market: from a participation rate of 34 percent as at the 1947 Census, their participation rate had reached 53 percent in 1990. (Withers, 1987; ABS, 1990).

Table 2. Sectoral Shares in Selected Countries (percentage)

Employment				Output			
Years	Primary	Industry	Service	Years	Primary	Industry	Service
Argentina							
1900/4	39	25	36	1900/4	38	13	49
1925/9	36	27	37	1925/9	32	17	51
1947	27	30	43	1950	17	32	52
				1980	11	62	53
Australia							
1901	32	26	40	1900	30	19	51
1933	27	30	43	1930	23	23	55
1947	18	38	45	1950	33	31	36
1981	8	28	64	1980	12	30	57
Canada							
1911	39	27	34	1926	23	26	51
1921	37	27	37	1935	18	26	56
1950	22	35	44	1950	17	36	47
1980	7	27	66	1980	11	31	59
United Kingdom							
1901	15	42	44	1907	13	33	55
1931	13	43	44	1935	7	37	56
1950	9	46	46	1950	9	42	49
1980	4	37	59	1980	7	33	60
United States							
1899	39	25	36	1899/1903	21	23	56
1929/37	23	25	52	1927/37	11	26	62
1950	14	35	51	1950	10	36	54
1980	5	30	66	1980	6	30	64

Source: Michael Carter, "The Service Sector", pp. 195-228, in: Rodney Maddock and Ian W. McLean (eds.), *The Australian Economy in the Long Run*, Cambridge UP 1987, p. 199.

Australia's social security system is relatively unique. Apart from pensions for government employees, social security provisions are based on the provision of a general social safety net, and not on social insurance principles. As a result, there is a close similarity between the basic entitlements of those unable to work due to illness, of the unemployed, and of the recipients of government old age pensions. The entitlements are not a function of previous income, and therefore provide a rate of income replacement for those who were previously in employment which is quite generous for those on low incomes, but is much lower than is common in Europe for those with median incomes. Furthermore, they are subject to means tests which reduce the rate of support in the light of the income and assets of the family. Such means tested provisions have been extended in recent years, and now cover payments (such as family allowance) which were free of such provisions in the past.

A.2 Labour Laws and Institutions

(a) Origins

The Australian labour market is extensively legally regulated by statutory tribunals invested with compulsory powers of conciliation and arbitration. Generally speaking, the activities of most employers, in most sectors of the economy, are subject to the legal determination of employment conditions which are set down in the awards of these tribunals. In legal terms, the award system introduces into the employment contract a "floor" of rights under the terms and conditions of employment. Such norms are characteristic of civil law systems such as those on the European continent (see Hepple and Fredman, 1986:94), but are not a feature of the British common law system. Nevertheless, they have come to dominate the regulation of labour contracts in Australia in a legal system which is otherwise based upon common law jurisprudence.

The system of compulsory arbitration was introduced in New Zealand and Australia in the wake of a series of major strikes, and severe economic depression, in the 1890s. Voluntary arbitration was attempted in this earlier period (in some colonies), but failed owing to the almost total collapse of trade union power. In response to this imbalance of power between employers and unions, and the general economic and social instability of the 1890s, middle class "liberal" politicians, supported by labour politicians, introduced measures for the resolution of industrial disputes by quasi-legislative regulation. Their aim in introducing such measures was to attempt to eliminate, or at least reduce, the level of strikes, and also to provide a form of joint regulation by employers and unions. The system of compulsory arbitration was first introduced in New Zealand (1894), and was then adopted in two Australian States (Western Australia 1900, and New South Wales, 1901). Most importantly, however, when the Australian Federation was constituted in 1901, it was given power for the settlement of interstate industrial disputes by means of conciliation and arbitration.

The Federal government introduced its compulsory arbitration scheme in 1904, and it subsequently became the mechanism whereby the guiding principles used for setting employment conditions were established.[1] The federal tribunal has jurisdiction over federal employment, employment in federal territories, and over disputes "extending beyond the bounds of any one state". As a result, employment in most industries and occupations is split between jurisdictions, although most workplaces will be covered predominantly or wholly by one jurisdiction. Over the years, a pattern has grown up under which National Wage Cases (which now occur at least once a year) lay down general principles which are then applied throughout the award system, with supplementary hearings to settle matters or detail as necessary in each particular industry. This means that, in spite of the complexity of the award system, general decisions are made and passed throughout the wage structure relatively simply.

The nature of these tribunals has varied greatly over time and between jurisdictions. Originally, the tribunals began with a mixture of conciliation "boards" and arbitration "courts". However, the early experience was that the "boards" were ignored or by-passed, and therefore by the early 1900s, most arbitration systems had abandoned the "dual" model and opted for a single court exercising powers of conciliation and arbitration. This single body was highly "judicial" in structure and appearance, though in fact it exercised both the judicial powers of conciliation and arbitration *creating* rights. This practice was brought to an end in the *Federal* jurisdiction in 1956 when the Australian High Court ruled that it was unconstitutional for one body to exercise both judicial and non-judicial power. As a result the Federal tribunal was split into two bodies: one a body (now called the Australian Industrial Relations Commission) responsible for conciliating and arbitrating industrial disputes (and issuing awards to settle them) and the second a body (now the industrial division of the Federal Court) responsible for interpreting awards and applying judicial sanctions for breaches. This split of responsibilities has also been instituted in most of the tribunals of the federal states, although in these cases there was no constitutional requirement to do so.

The legacy of judicial status has meant that most tribunals – federal and state – have two grades of members. For example, the federal Industrial Relations Commission has a President and (at the moment) 14 Deputy Presidents, all of whom hold

1. The Federal government of Australia may enact legislation only where there is an enumerated power in the Constitution. The separate State governments have plenary legislative authority within their own domain, and are not, therefore, constrained by the specification of certain powers. Federal and State legislation is, therefore, possible in the same areas of subject matter, and conflicts may arise. However, in the event of such conflict, s.109 of the Federal constitution states that the Federal law will prevail, and the State law will be invalid to the extent of the inconsistency. The principal power for the Federal government to regulate industrial relations is found in s.51 (xxxv) of the Constitution which empowers the government to make laws for the settlement of interstate industrial disputes by conciliation and arbitration.

office until they reach the statutory retirement age (65), and 32 Commissioners (often former union and employer association officials), who hold office for (renewable) terms of seven years. Most (but now not all) of the 15 Presidential members are qualified lawyers, and all have the same rank, status and precedence as a Judge of the Federal Court[2], but in recent years members of other professions (notably economists) have also been appointed.

Cases are generally heard initially by one member of the Commission, but important cases and appeals are heard by so-called "full benches" composed of at least three members, including at least one Deputy President. The Commission is one body, but its members are divided into "panels" with responsibilities for particular industries. The members of the Commission thus develop an expertise in particular industries, although they are periodically re-assigned (by the President) as circumstances require.

(b) The award system

Whilst there are differences between the various Federal and State systems, the underlying principles of their institutional operation are common to all. The tribunals have the power to take control of most industrial disputes, with or without the approval of the parties. Where the matters in dispute cannot be settled by conciliation (or bargaining), arbitration is employed. Arbitration takes a quasi-legal, adversarial form – parties serve claims upon each other, witnesses are called, evidence examined. The decision of the arbitrator (the award) is legally enforceable upon the parties to it.

Several further points should be noted about these institutional arrangements. First, each of the systems has an administrative apparatus through which claims are processed, unions registered, agreements filed and so on. Second, each has an associated body which is responsible for the inspection of workplaces and the enforcement of awards. Thirdly, legal matters are dealt with by a court system within, or associated with, the arbitral system. Finally, industrial action by parties to a dispute is genrally legally prohibited – though these prohibitions are not effective in practice.

Industrial awards are, in effect, a form of legislation. They are made by statutory process and they are legally enforceable by statute. The reach of awards is very extensive. In many instances Federal awards determine the terms and conditions of employment of State government employees.

---

2. However, this "judicial" status has never been absolute: arbitrators with supposed judicial status have been excluded from hearing important cases, or have not been re-appointed when legislation has replaced one tribunal by another: for background and details of a recent case, see Kitay and McCarthy (1989) and Kirby (1989).

The content of major industrial awards is extremely wide ranging. It covers, primarily, the basic elements of the wage/effort exchange – wages, allowances and penalty rates, various forms of leave, holiday, hours of work, overtime and so on. Beyond that, however, awards also deal with matters such as union rights and security, the rights to hire and dispose of labour, discipline and various forms of grievance and disputes procedure.

The term "award" derives from the quasi-judicial origins of the Australian tribunals: an "award" is a general term for a tribunal decision. Nonetheless, today a substantial proportion of "awards" result from the certification by tribunals of agreements between the parties, with relatively few or no matters being actually decided by the tribunal. Since the parties will almost always be governed by an existing award most negotiations are about award variations. The tribunals predominantly operate as mediators, and can become involved in the negotiations when either party requests – or, on occasion, at their own initiative.

Such bargains can have a narrow or a wide effect. Many awards apply to particular workplaces or enterprises.[3] Others will be the result of agreements between unions and employers' associations. In these cases, certification as an award makes the agreement enforceable: in particular, the terms and conditions of employment prescribed become binding on all members of the employers' association which signed it. It can also lead to the "extension" of a collective agreement to cover all firms engaged in the industry: in state jurisdictions, this will be achieved by declaring a "common rule", in the federal jurisdiction, other employers will be "roped in" by being served demands by the union. In most cases, certification is semi-automatic, but the tribunals do have the right to refuse to certify agreements "not in the public interest". Certification offers advantages to both sides: it makes terms and conditions enforceable by unions, and it allows employers to take advantage of terms in commercial contracts which specify contract prices can be varied if labour costs, as specified in awards, are charged. However, the regulation of terms and conditions by unregistered collective agreement is quite widespread. Some industries and enterprises currently supplement their award conditions with private agreement on such matters as health and safety, union security and dismissals. The legal status of these private agreements is unclear, though the weight of authority supports the view that such agreements have approximately the same legal status as the voluntary collective agreements characteristic of the United Kingdom. The terms of such agreements may, however, be enforceable as terms of the individual contract of employment.

---

3. The Australian Workplace Industrial Relations Survey (AWIRS), conducted between November 1989 and May 1990, found that eight percent of workplaces with at least 20 employees reported awards or appendices to awards which were specific to their enterprises, and a further 12 percent reported agreements certified or registered with the tribunals which were localized in their application. (Callus *et al.*, 1991: p. 196).

It is of course important not to exaggerate the voluntary nature of this process. Negotiations with employers take place in the context of a union's right to seek a hearing before the tribunals if the employer refuses to negotiate. Many employers who negotiate agreements in these circumstances might decline to do so if unions did not enjoy access to the tribunals.

Australian award structure is extremely complex. Australian unions originally had a craft basis rather similar to that in the UK. Over the years, this form of unionism has become attenuated, so that now most unions are of a broad occupational or industrial character. However, the award structure still reflects some of these origins, with some awards applying to particular occupations, and with most employers finding the awards and conditions of their workforce being covered by a number of awards (although only one award or set of awards would apply to any particular individual employee). This situation is generally recognized as undesirable, both by employers and by the union movement. Nonetheless, progress in rationalising the award system and union structure has been very slow.

Industrial action to force changes over matters of rights contained within awards, or conflicts of interest, is usually prohibited or greatly restricted at law. However, such legal restrictions are usually ignored by unions in practice, particularly those which apply under the industrial legislation. On the other hand, employers have been able to take effective steps against industrial action where they have proceeded under the civil law. In general, compliance with the award system under the Accord between the Labour Party government and the trade union movement has been brought about by pressure exerted within the union movement itself. Unions which have sought to go outside the award system for improvements in pay and conditions have been isolated and industrially defeated (e.g. airline pilots, food processors).

The function of the tribunals in determining wage rates by award process has been an important device in maintaining a relatively controlled and centralized wage policy. Although the wage fixation powers are shared between Federal and State tribunals, since the 1920s the pattern has been for State tribunals to follow the decisions of the Federal authority. There have, however, been two recent major episodes in which the centralized control of wages under arbitration has broken down. The first of these was in the early 1970s, when the failure of the enforcement of awards mechanism induced widespread direct action in pursuit of above award wage claims. The second, in 1981/82, came about as a result of the failure of the (then) centralized system of wage indexation and the temporary withdrawal of the tribunals from the practice of hearing applications for the *general* increase of wages. In both instances, there was an upsurge in wages and industrial disputes, fuelling inflation. This in turn led to recession, rising unemployment and declining real wages.

(c) Recent developments

In 1983, shortly before the election of the first Labour government since 1975, the Australian Labour Party entered into a "Prices and Incomes Accord" with the peak trade union body, the Australian Council of Trade Unions (ACTU). Under the Accord, trade union commitment for a centralized system of wage fixation – largely wage *restraint* since the mid 1980s – was exchanged for greater participation in government decision making. The Accord has produced substantial changes in relation to many aspects of micro-economic reform, including industrial relations, industry policy and industry training. It has also brought about a new emphasis in industrial relations upon matters of deregulation, efficiency and productivity.

This bargained approach to wages and industrial relations at government level has led to a somewhat different role on the part of the industrial tribunals. The substance of the arrangements in National Wage Cases (before the Federal tribunal) since 1983 has usually been the subject of agreement between the ACTU and the government prior to the tribunal hearing. Thus, the tribunal's decisions, which have tended to follow the Accord arrangements, have been less independent and autonomous than in previous periods.[4]

Changes to the *external* structure of awards (i.e. the way awards fit into various industries, occupational groupings, etc.) is undergoing change but very slowly. The shape of these awards will depend in future upon the union restructuring programme which is taking place through amalgamations and other legal processes.

The main recent change in the *internal* structure of awards has been a series of moves to eliminate very fine occupational distinctions and to arrange their structure to facilitate career paths and skill upgrading. These moves were pioneered in the metal industry, with the "initiative" coming from both the employers' federations and unions. Thus, in the proposed 1990 Metal Industry Award, the internal structure of the award was to undergo change, whereby in excess of 340 horizontal job classifications were to be replaced with three skill areas, each comprising a 14-point career path.

Beyond the metal industry, award restructuring generally has been fostered in two key National Wage Case decisions. The first of these (March 1988) introduced the "Restructuring and Efficiency Principle" under which wage increases were allowed in relation to the offsets obtained through direct bargaining over the elimination of

4. Australian industrial tribunals have had to maintain a fine balance between their role as the independent arbitrators of industrial disputes, and the requirements of government economic policy. In general it would be fair to say that the activities of the tribunals have been consistent with government's approach to wage outcomes for most of this century.

restrictive work practices, over the re-organization of work and over the training and reskilling of workers.[5]

The key changes introduced under this principle included changes to payment methods, the introduction of award restructuring (including the broadbanding of job classifications, and the development of career paths), greater freedom in the use of part-time and casual labour, the reduction of demarcation barriers, the greater spread of hours for the working of ordinary time, greater flexibility in the selective use of overtime, and in the operating time of the plant. There were few changes implementing performance-based pay, and other merit systems.

The second case (August 1988) introduced the "Structural Efficiency Principle", under which wage increases were guaranteed for a major award restructuring exercise under which job classifications would be reduced and rationalized and provision for multi-skilling, training and career paths provided.[6] It remains too early to assess the effectiveness of the award restructuring exercise. The early evidence suggests, however, that whilst considerable progress has been made on paper in the rationalization of job classifications, the creation of career paths and in job training, management has failed to adapt to these changes, and has failed to give its attention to task design and training in practice.

A fundamental change in the system, at least in principle, was introduced in October 1991, when the Federal Commission, for the first time, devolved the determination of employment conditions to enterprise or establishment level negotiation. It remains to be seen how many enterprises actually engage in such negotiations – thus far, most have occurred in the metal industry, where preparatory negotiations at the industry level have been taking place over a period of years.

(d) Private arrangements vs legal rules and collective agreements

Awards which prescribe minimum terms and conditions of employment cover the vast majority of Australian employees (80 per cent in 1990 – see Table 6 below). The mechanism by which this comes about is discussed in greater detail below, when the legal structure of the award system is discussed. However, there are three important areas of employment which the award system does not affect. Firstly, outside the public sector, managerial employees are not generally covered by the system. While their occupations may have minima applicable to them (for example,

---

5. The Restructuring and Efficiency Principle was introduced in the *National Wage Case 1987*, (1987) 17 *Industrial Reports* 65.

6. The Structural Efficiency Principle was introduced in the *National Wage Case August 1988*, (1988) 25 *Industrial Reports* 170.

in some general award covering clerical employees) , their actual terms and conditions are so far above those minima that the awards are to all intents and purposes irrelevant. Secondly, most persons who do not have the status of an employee, and who work either as a self-employed person, or as an independent contractor, are not covered by industrial awards.[7] The third exception is the freedom of any of the parties to an employment relationship to agree to terms and conditions of employment which brings excess of the minima laid down in the award. Such "over award" conditions, which are usually negotiated at the establishment level, have historically been one of the main issues in industrial conflicts.

One of the features of the system which has been practised under the Accord between the government and the union movement since 1983 has been that the union movement has, in general, desisted from making collective claims for betterments in over award conditions. However, employers and employees remain at liberty to reach uncoerced agreements which are outside the award framework.[8]

B. Unions and Employers' Associations

B.1 Union Membership Rates

The introduction of the compulsory arbitration system gave rise to a great increase in the numbers of trade unions, in the levels of union membership and also in the density of union membership as a proportion of the overall workforce.[9] These developments were in large part due to the fact that unions were required to register as organizations "representing" the workforce in the arbitration process. Unions were

7. The definition of an "employee" in Australia is the subject of complex common law principles, which distinguish between an employee properly so called, and various other forms of work relationships including contracting, sub-contracting, agency relationships and partnerships. With only slight exceptions, the awards of arbitration apply only to the "employee" category. See briefly B. Creighton and A. Stewart (1990), pp. 95-104.

8. 11 percent of workplaces with more than 20 employees report they use agreements which are not registered with the tribunals (Callus *et al.*, 1990: p. 196).

9. The role given to trade unions by these provisions led to their early rapid growth. Bain and Elsheikh estimate that union density in Australia grew from 15 per cent in 1907 to 42 per cent in 1920. There was a brief decline in the mid-1920's, but by 1927 membership had reached about 46 per cent. The density level declined during the depression years of the 1930's, but recovered slowly during the Second World War years, and in the after-war years. Membership peaked at about 59 per cent in 1954. A period of stagnation followed, during which unions failed to organize service sector industries and saw a slow decline in union density. This decline was reversed in the period from 1971 to the early 1980's, but since then density has declined and in 1988 officially measured to be in the range 53 per cent and 41 per cent, although there is some disagreement over which of these two extremes is the more accurate (see note 11).

thus crucial to the success of the systems – and they were provided with legally protected conditions as a result of their registration. Whilst they were essentially self-governing, they were provided with corporate status, preference in employment[10] for their members, and monopoly organization over particular industries and occupations. Such monopolies come about because the rules of each union prescribe the occupations or industries in which it is entitled to recruit. The Registrars who must approve union rules have, in general, been required by legislation to restrict jurisdictional disputes by avoiding overlaps in potential membership. However, such overlaps frequently occur – and hence, jurisdictional disputes have, at times, been common.

Table 3 documents trends in union membership rates since 1976 in Australia. It can be seen that union density has declined steadily over this period.[11] The decline is general, and has in fact been more dramatic amongst full-time than part-time employees, and also more rapid in the private than in the public sector, although union density has fallen there also. This process has continued in the very favourable political climate in which unions have operated during the 1980s, when Labour governments were in office, both federally and in the majority of Australian states. Union membership remains highest in those industries such as communications, which are overwhelmingly in the public sector, and also remains high in mining. It should be added that there is no sector of the economy from which unions are excluded in the way that they are from most of the service sector of the US economy; for example, in Australia the union density rate is respectable in finance, property and business services.

Union density is lower among part-time than full-time employees, and lower among women than men. However, Table 4 suggests that these differences are in large part at a function of the type of employment contract. "Casual" employees who do not receive annual leave or sick leave entitlements (although the minimum rates payable are adjusted upwards to compensate) are much less likely to be union members than "permanent" employees. Over one quarter of female employees but only just over one tenth of male employees have this type of contract, and this is an important influence on aggregate density.

---

10. That is, an award could (but often did not) require that, other things being equal, a member of a union should be given preference in hiring: a relatively un-rigorous "closed shop".

11. There are two different sets of statistics issued by the Australian Bureau of Statistics on trade union membership. The first of these is the annual collection *Trade Union Statistics* (Cat. No. 6323.0). It is based on returns from union officials. These are inflated by several factors such as the inclusion of unemployed, retired or non-financial members. The second set, generally regarded as the most accurate, is *Trade Union Members* (Cat. No. 6325.0), which is derived from household surveys. Table 3.2 is based on this series.

Table 3. Union Membership as a Proportion of Employees (per cent)

	1976	1982	1986	1988
Total	51	49	46	42
Full-time employees	–	52	47	43
Part-time employees	–	33	40	39
Males	51	49	46	42
Females	43	43	39	35
Age group				
15-19	43	31	28	27
20-24		44	42	36
25-34	52	51	48	43
35-44	52	52	48	45
45-54	58	57	53	47
55-59	62	61	55	51
60-64	60	59	53	45
65+	24	25	12	9
Sector				
Public	–	73	71	68
Private	–	39	34	32
Industry				
Agriculture, forestry, fishing and hunting	20	20	15	13
Mining	63	64	72	63
Manufacturing	57	54	51	48
Electricity, gas and water	83	78	82	80
Construction	57	50	48	47
Wholesale and retail trade	27	28	25	23
Transport and storage	73	72	67	62
Communication	88	85	80	76
Finance, property and business services	42	42	34	28
Public administration and defence	72	63	60	61
Community services	56	54	52	49
Recreation, personal and other services	41	36	29	26

Sources: Australian Bureau of Statistics, *Trade Union Members August 1988*, Cat. No. 6325.0), Canberra: ABS, 1989.

Table 4. Union Density by Occupation and Permanent Casual Status, 1988

Occupation	Males			Females			Persons		
	Permanent employee	Casual employee	Total	Permanent employee	Casual employee	Total	Permanent employee	Casual employee	Total
Managers and administrators	20	8	19	19	3	17	20	7	19
Professionals	41	13	39	57	23	50	47	20	44
Para-professionals	57	18	54	52	29	48	55	25	52
Tradespersons	54	26	52	30	12	25	53	23	50
Clerks	54	7	52	30	9	26	36	8	32
Sales persons and personal service workers	25	22	24	42	24	33	34	24	30
Plant and machine operators and drivers	70	31	66	62	22	54	69	28	64
Labourers and related workers	59	22	51	57	19	42	59	21	48
Total	50	21	46	42	19	35	47	20	42
Total employees	3,127.8	415.7	3,543.5	1,821.2	737.3	2,588.4	4,949.0	1,1152.9	6,101.9

Sources: Australian Bureau of Statistics, *Trade Union Members August 1988*, Cat. No. 6325.10), Canberra: ABS, 1989.

B.2 Union Structure

Australia's union structure is still characterized by a large number of very small unions which, however, account for a very small proportion of the total union members (see Table 5). Large Australian unions are generally interstate Federations, with semi-autonomous branches in each State (these are necessary because most unions need to represent members in State tribunals as well as Federal ones). The small unions are generally those representing small occupational groups, often in the public sector, and often confined to a particular State. Another important aspect of Australian trade union structure concerns its pattern of organization, which sees unions organized along a number of different lines, including craft unions, general conglomerate unions and unions which are industrial in nature. Several problems are said to flow from this multi-union structure, including resource problems, demarcation and jurisdictional disputes, lack of strategic cohesion and so on.

Table 5. Number of Unions and Number of Members according to Size of Union, 30th June 1989

Size of Union	Number of Unions		Number of Members	
	Number	Per cent of total unions	Average number per union	Per cent of total number
Under 10	38	12.7	45	0.1
100 and under 250	31	10.4	170	0.2
250 and under 500	26	8.7	341	0.3
500 and under 1,000	41	13.7	703	0.8
1,000 and under 2,000	42	14.0	1,417	1.7
2,000 and under 3,000	12	4.0	2,466	0.9
3,000 and under 5,000	25	8.4	3,950	2.9
5,000 and under 10,000	19	6.4	7,309	4.1
10,000 and under 20,000	19	6.4	13,755	7.7
20,000 and under 30,000	12	4.0	26,620	8.7
30,000 and under 40,000	10	3.3	35,017	10.3
40,000 and under 50,000	6	2.0	45,177	7.9
50,000 and under 80,000	7	2.3	64,723	13.3
80,000 and over	11	3.7	127,983	41.3
Total	299	100.0	11,406	100.0

Source: Australian Bureau of Statistics, *Trade Union Statistics, Australia, 30 June 1989* (Cat. No. 6323.0), Canberra: ABS, 1990.

A number of initiatives were made in the Federal Industrial Relations Act 1988 and by further amendment to that Act in 1990, to encourage some rectification of these size and structural inadequacies. Union amalgamation laws were liberalized, and the minimum size of registered unions was increased from 100 to 1,000 members, and then to 10,000 members. Provisions were also created whereby union membership rights in particular industries and occupations could be compulsorily varied by order of the Federal tribunal. Finally, no *new* registrations of unions were to be accepted unless the applicant unions are organized along industry lines.

There is now only one national trade union centre – the Australian Council of Trade Unions (ACTU) – which incorporates blue collar and white collar private sector and public sector unions. The ACTU has been remarkably successful in co-ordinating union policies over the last few years, and in ensuring adherence on the union side to the agreements arising out of the Accord between the union movement and the Federal Labour Government. The ACTU has also been instrumental in promoting the reform of trade union structure. In 1987, it proposed a strategy for the reduction of the number of unions to no more than 23 unions based upon industry lines.

B.3 Union Recognition Arrangements

Union recognition is readily attained in Australia owing to the character of the arbitration system. Once a union is registered under either Federal or State system they are guaranteed rights to represent workers in their area of coverage, and to obtain an award covering the employment conditions of those workers. They do not require the direct recognition by the employers of their members, nor are they required to demonstrate a level of support amongst the workforce other than the level of membership required for registration. There is, therefore, nothing to be gained by employers in refusing recognition. In order to obtain registration, however, unions are required at least to demonstrate that they are bona fide organizations representing their members, and there is strict scrutiny of union rules to ensure that democratic and orderly decision making processes take place. Although in strict legal terms unions may not register when an existing registered union may cover their members, this has not prevented the proliferation of unions with overlapping coverage of the workforce. One of the recently developed functions of the tribunals has been the resolution of jurisdictional disputes which result from these overlaps.

It is common for awards to extend rights of entry to union officials for the purpose of carrying out an inspection of the work and interviewing employees. Many awards also provide workplace union delegates with the right to carry out the union's business during worktime.

B.4 Employer Organizations

In contrast to Australian unions, Australian employers are disunited, and in fact have become increasingly so in recent years. The Confederation of Australian Industry (CAI) is the "peak" employer body, taking a lead role in National Wage Cases and in tripartite bodies set by the government, such as the Economic Planning Advisory Council and the National Labour Consultative Council. However, in recent years the Business Council of Australia – an organization comprised of the Chief Executives of the fifty largest private sector companies – has increasingly taken a stance on industrial relations matters which is separate to that of the CAI, and has made independent submissions to National Wage Cases. Furthermore, several employer organizations which were affiliated to the CAI have left, including for example the National Farmers Federation and the Metal Trades Industry Association, and now appear separately before the tribunals. The arbitration system itself is partly responsible for this paradox. Employer organizations are service organizations which compete for membership among small businesses. The small employers generally want the organizations to which they belong to resist union claims, and not to negotiate. This makes it very difficult for the employer organizations to bargain with unions in the way which would be familiar in, for example, Europe, where such organizations are led by large employers. There are a number of notable exceptions to this – in the metal industry, for example, negotiations do take place between employers associations and the relevant unions in a manner reminiscent of European negotiations. But in most other industries, the process is not yet well developed.

B.5 The Scope and Sources of Australian Regulation of Employment Conditions

(a) The extent of award coverage

It is a critical feature of Australian industrial relations that awards have an extremely wide coverage regardless of the participation in bargaining or arbitration by employers or employees. From the employee's perspective, union membership is immaterial to award coverage. In the Federal system all employees of employers bound by awards are covered by the award. Employers are widely covered because of the practice of serving demands upon all employers in the industry, thereby making them parties to the dispute to be arbitrated. Employers who were not initially parties to the dispute which resulted in an award may be "roped-in" by the unions serving on them a set of demands. The "paper" dispute which results is then "settled" by a tribunal decision which extends the initial award to the "roped-in" employers. (This procedure is similar in purpose to the "extension" laws found in various European jurisdictions).

Table 6. Percentage of Employees affected by Awards, etc. Australia, April 1954, May 1963, May 1968, May 1974, May 1985 and May 1990[a]

	April 1954	May 1963	May 1968	May 1974	May 1985			May 1990		
					Total	Sector		Total	Sector	
						Public	Private		Public	Private
Males										
Affected by										
Federal awards, etc.	44.3	42.3	43.8	43.7	40.0	44.3	37.7	38.0	48.0	33.8
State awards, etc.	44.3	44.4	41.8	40.6	40.5	50.8	35.0	37.3	49.9	32.0
Unregistered collective agreements	(11.4	13.3)	1.6	1.1	2.9	2.7	2.9	2.0	0.3	2.6
Not affect by awards, etc.	(	)	2.8	14.6	16.6	2.2	24.4	22.7	1.8	31.6
Total employees	100.0	100.0	100.0	100.0	100.0	100.0	100.0	100.0	100.0	100.0
(thousands)					(2974.3)	(1037.4)	(1936.9)	(3174.1)	(944.9)	(2229.2)
Females										
Affected by										
Federal awards, etc.	37.2	31.0	31.0	30.2	21.6	28.7	18.5	23.2	33.0	19.0
State awards, etc.	54.9	59.7	60.6	62.0	63.4	65.2	62.6	58.4	63.9	56.0
Unregistered collective agreements	(7.9	9.3)	0.8	0.5	2.4	4.1	1.7	1.9	0.4	2.6
Not affect by awards, etc.	(	)	7.6	7.3	12.6	2.0	17.2	16.5	2.7	22.4
Total employees	100.0	100.0	100.0	100.0	100.0	100.0	100.0	100.0	100.0	100.0
(thousands)					(2028.6)	(616.0)	(1412.6)	(2478.2)	(749.9)	(1728.3)
Persons										
Affected by										
Federal awards, etc.	42.4	39.3	40.1	39.2	32.6	38.5	29.6	31.5	41.3	27.3
State awards, etc.	47.0	48.5	47.3	47.8	49.8	56.2	46.6	46.5	56.1	42.4
Unregistered collective agreements	(10.5	12.2)	1.4	0.9	2.6	3.2	2.5	2.0	0.4	2.7
Not affect by awards, etc.	(	)	11.3	12.2	15.0	2.1	21.3	20.0	2.2	27.6
Total employees	100.0	100.0	100.0	100.0	100.0	100.0	100.0	100.0	100.0	100.0
(thousands)					(5002.9)	(1653.4)	(3349.5)	(5652.2)	(1694.8)	(3957.4)

a Figures for 1954, 1963 and 1968 exclude the Northern Territory and the Australian Capital Territory

Source: Australian Bureau of Statistics, *Incidence of Awards, Determination and Collective Agreements, May 1974*; *Incidence of Awards, Australia, May 1985*; *Award Coverage, Australia, May 1990* (Cat. No. 6315.0)

In the State jurisdictions, awards operate as common rules applicable to all employers and employees within the scope of the award, which may be industrial or occupational by definition.

Table 6 shows trends in coverage by awards over the last 35 years: the data include negotiated collective agreements which are registered with federal and with state tribunals respectively. It will be seen that the proportion of employees not covered by awards etc. has grown gradually but steadily, and by 1990 accounted for 20 percent of all employees and 28 percent of private sector employees. The declining coverage is confined to the private sector, but affects both males and females, and seems to be occurring with respect to both federal and state awards. Table 7 explores this question further by identifying the groups with the lowest award coverage. These prove to be two particular groups: managerial, executive, etc. employees (of whom only one third are now covered by awards) and employees in small firms. It is noteworthy that, as far as small firms are concerned, the variation in coverage by size is observed for federal awards only; state awards seem to cover large and small enterprises fairly uniformly. This suggests that the process of serving "roping in" demands does tend to miss small employers, leaving them less likely to be covered by federal awards than are large employers. However, the decline in award coverage in the private sector during the 1980's is not due to this differential pattern: it affected both federal and state award coverage, with the decline in state award coverage being if anything greater.[12]

Various proposals have recently been implemented or suggested for diminishing the reach of compulsory arbitration through awards, by allowing the parties to enter into voluntary agreements which exclude the application of awards.[13] The relevant provision of the Federal Industrial Relations Act 1988 provided for the certification of agreements even where they did not conform to the guidelines laid down in Federal awards, although the Federal Commission still retained the power to refuse certification on public interest grounds. However, these provisions were not sufficiently flexible to allow many employers and unions to enter into the kinds of arrangements considered appropriate to the needs of their enterprises and industries. It is apparent from Tables 6 and 7 that an increasing number of private sector employers in particular have been ignoring award conditions in entering into employment contracts, and doing so independently of the certified agreements provision (since such "certified agreements" would still be included as coverage by a registered federal or state agreement in the statistics).

---

12. On the other hand, few employers seem to operate completely freely of the award system: amongst workplaces with five or more employees, only one percent, employing one percent of employees, report that they are not covered by any awards at all. (Callus *et al.*, 1991, p. 40).

13. For example see ss. 115-117 of the Federal Industrial Relations Act 1988; the Niland *Green paper* (pp. 39-40).

Table 7. Incidence of Awards by Type of Employee and by Employer Unit Size, 1985 and 1990

	Covered by Awards, Determinations and Collective Agreements						Not covered		Total ('000)	
	Federal		State		Unregistered					
	1985	1990	1985	1990	1985	1990	1985	1990	1985	1990
All Employees	32.6	32.0	49.8	46.5	2.6	2.0	15.0	20.0	(5002.9)	(5652.2)
Managerial,										
executive etc.	15.5	15.2	21.7	15.9	5.5	2.6	57.3	66.3	(603.9)	(618.2)
Non-managerial	34.9	33.5	53.6	50.3	2.3	1.9	9.2	14.3	(4399.0)	(5034.0)
Full-time	39.8	38.5	50.5	46.1	2.3	1.8	7.4	13.6	(3503.7)	(3829.2)
Part-time	15.9	17.6	65.8	63.8	2.3	2.0	16.0	16.6	(895.3)	(1204.9)
Private Sector										
Employees: total	29.2	27.3	46.6	42.4	2.9	2.7	21.3	27.6	(3349.5)	(3957.4)
Employer Unit Size:										
under 30	17.2	15.1	45.3	40.0	3.1	4.1	34.3	40.8		
20-49	30.3	26.0	49.2	39.6	2.5	2.2	18.0	32.2		
50-99	32.0	30.8	50.2	45.2	1.1	2.6	16.7	21.4		
100-499	37.3	31.2	44.8	46.5	2.2	2.0	15.5	20.3		
500-999	41.1	36.0	44.4	44.4	1.5	1.6	13.0	18.0		
1000 and over	38.2	44.4	48.4	39.9	2.4	1.3	11.0	14.2		

Source: Australian Bureau of Statistics, *Incidence of Awards, Australia, May 1985*; *Award Coverage, Australia, May 1990.*

Changes are to be made to the Federal Industrial Relations Act in 1992 designed to rectify these difficulties. Their thrust is to allow for greater flexibility in the certification of appropriate enterprise agreements. The most important change is that the Federal Tribunal will no longer have the power to refuse to certify an agreement on general "public interest" grounds. As long as an agreement applies only to a single bargaining unit (i.e. a single business or place of work), the Commission *must* certify it, provided it does not disadvantage employees, taking into account their employment conditions as a "total" package. Various other safeguards apply, but the thrust of the new provision is to considerably enhance the power of the parties to arrive at agreements which do not comply with award conditions.

(b) Restrictions on employers

One of the main constraints of awards is the extent to which they restrict the employer's ability to alter the size of his/her labour force freely according to market conditions. Awards frequently regulate aspects of manning levels, and further restrictions may apply to the shedding of labour where rules of seniority and strict standards of redundancy compensation usually apply (see Section 6(b) below for details of restrictions on collective lay-offs). Although these restrictions have largely remained unaltered by the award restructuring process of post 1987, the internal flexibility of the employer has been improved by changes to work scheduling, overtime, and ordinary time span of hours.

(c) Direct legislation

A number of conditions of employment are determined outside the award system by direct legislation. In particular, safety standards are laid down by inspectorates which are set up by State and Territory governments. Similarly, workers compensation legislation is a matter for State legislation.

One important area in which responsibility is shared in a very complex manner between the arbitration tribunals and State administration and legislation is the apprenticeship system. Federal awards have traditionally supported the apprenticeship system by prescribing that young people cannot be employed in apprenticeable trades other than as apprentices. However, the actual regulation of apprentice education, and the provision of off-the-job classroom training, has been the responsibility of State administrations. The current restructuring process is expected to involve a complete overhaul of this (by now) archaic training system, and the age requirements with which apprenticeship had been associated will be replaced by a general entitlement to continual training, combined with a revision of the awards structures to eliminate narrow craft boundaries. The implementation of these changes will require that the

State government administered educational institutions, which provide classroom training, also reorient their course offerings, and it is quite possible that this will be one of the slowest parts of the system to change.

(d) Federal government

The Federal government's powers to make laws regulating labour are relatively restricted[14], and for that reason, if for no other, it does not directly prescribe the terms and conditions of employment of Australian workers. Even in instances where such direct regulation would be constitutionally permissible (i.e. in respect of the Federal government's own employees, or of employees employed in Federal territories) the approach has been to allow arbitration tribunals to regulate employment conditions. On the other hand the Federal government has established a national Occupational Health and Safety Commission which is now suggesting national health and safety standards; it lays down fiduciary requirements for pension schemes (enforced by making conformity with these requirements a condition for tax concessions); and it has now passed legislation requiring enterprises to expend a certain minimal proportion (one per cent) of their wage bill on training, with tax sanctions for non-compliance. The Federal government also influences employment policies through financial support, such as subsidization of child care facilities, income support for those who have exhausted their employer-based sick leave entitlements, tax concessions for pension and child care provisions by employers, and the general provision of means tested flat-rate old age pensions, to which occupational superannuation is an adjunct.

(e) Private Arrangements

As mentioned earlier, private arrangements between employers and employees, or employers and unions, are commonly made in the form of "over award" conditions, or in respect of matters which cannot, or are not, dealt with in the award. Where the arrangements are made between individual employees and the employer, these conditions will usually form part of the individual's contract of employment, and be enforceable by the employee under a civil law process.

Where the arrangements are made between the union and the employer, the position is less clear. It is doubtful, in such cases, that the arrangement will be enforceable between union and employer. On the other hand, it is likely in the normal course of events, that such terms arrived at in the collective agreement will become implied

14. See note 1, above.

into the contracts of the individual employees, and thereby become civilly enforceable.[15]

It is also now clearly established that awards themselves are capable of forming part of the contract of employment, and that they may therefore provide an employee with a contractual avenue of enforcement in addition to the statutory powers available under the various Acts.[16]

C. Outcomes

C.1 Working Time Regulation

Working time regulation in Australia has been determined by collective bargaining, interacting with tribunal decisions. Standard weekly hours (after which overtime rates are payable) were initially 48 hours, were reduced to 44 hours over the period 1925–1934, to 40 hours in the late 1940s, and finally fell to 38 hours as the result of a bargaining round originally instituted in the metal trades in 1981. The standard vacation period has also been raised through tribunal decisions, and reached a standard of 4 weeks per annum in 1975, where it has remained to date. It can be seen from Table 8 that 90 per cent of full-time workers benefit from annual leave provisions, but a little under a third of part-time workers do. In Australia, those who do not benefit from the provisions of annual leave and sick leave entitlements are generally categorized as "casual employees" and the award system usually prescribes a premium on their hourly wage to compensate for this. Such prescriptions are so universal that the Bureau of Statistics actually defines casual employees as those who are not entitled to receive either annual leave or sick leave benefits, a definition which of course begs the question somewhat, as it is quite possible, under this definition, for "casual" employees to remain with one employer for an extended period of time.

Legal holidays are legislatively prescribed, and are determined by the administrations of the various States, though most of them are celebrated nationwide. In general, the award system simply validates such holidays, requiring employers either to release employees or to pay a penalty rate for work on prescribed public holidays. Some awards provide for special holidays in the particular industry with which that award is concerned.

---

15. This consequence flows from the decision in *Gregory* v *Philip Morris*, (1988) 80 *Australian Law Reports* 455 (Federal Court of Australia).

16. *Gregory* v *Philip Morris*, above.

Table 8. Proportion of Employees receiving Particular Benefits, 1984 to 1989

Benefit	Full-time employee			Part-time employee			Total		
	1984	1988	1989	1984	1988	1989	1984	1988	1989
Sick leave	92.8	90.7	90.6	32.5	30.8	30.5	82.5	79.1	78.3
Annual leave	93.2	91.4	91.2	32.3	30.8	30.3	82.8	79.7	79.8
Long service leave	75.5	73.2	74.6	23.9	22.6	25.1	66.7	63.4	64.4
Superannuation	46.1	49.0	54.7	7.5	9.9	16.5	39.5	41.4	46.8
Goods and services	21.8	15.1	15.6	19.6	17.1	18.9	21.4	15.5	16.2
Transport	19.2	17.9	19.7	6.7	5.2	5.3	17.1	15.4	16.7
Shares	1.8	3.2	2.9	0.7	1.0	0.5	1.6	2.8	2.4

Source: Australian Bureau of Statistics, *Employment Benefits Australia August 1989* (Cat. No. 6334.0), Canberra: ABS, 1990.

C.2 Restrictions on Working Hours or Participation

The award system does, as mentioned earlier, prohibit the employment of minors in "apprenticeable trades" except as apprentices, in order to protect the apprenticeship system. It also restricts women's employment in "unsuitable" hours and attempts to regulate "outwork" – that is contracting out at piece rates of work, in particular in the clothing trade. However, the latter regulations are difficult to enforce, since it is in the interests of neither the outworkers or their contractors to report that they are working in violation of the regulations.

Retirement ages are not, on the whole, prescribed in awards. However, businesses and employers usually adopt the age at which employees become eligible for government pensions (65 for men, 60 for women) as the age around which supplementary retirement benefits are built. The continuation of this policy must be placed in some doubt, however, as a result of legal change prohibiting discrimination in employment on the basis of age. In recent years, early retirement schemes have become more common, particularly in the public sector. However, except in a few cases of mass redundancy in the recession of 1982, little of this trend to early retirement seems to be the product of collective pressures.

C.3 Wages

In order to understand the Australian wage structure, it is necessary to distinguish between "award wages" and actual earnings. Award rates consist of a series of very complicated tables or schedules which define the minimum rates to be paid for particular occupations, or for persons employed in particular industries, according to their classification or grade. In general, these minima are not necessarily intended by the tribunals to be the actual rates to be paid, though in industries or occupations with an excess supply of labour, they frequently are. However, in many industries particularly mining, printing and the metal trades, a significant proportion of average earnings is constituted by "over award payments", which are the result of direct negotiation between unions and management at the enterprise level, or (less frequently) as the result of individual agreements between workers and their employers. In 1990, 68 percent of workplaces, employing 57 percent of all employees, made over-award payments to some employees: in 23 percent of these workplaces, all employees received such payments.[17]

To add to the confusion, over the last ten years the tribunals have started to respond to union demands for the protection of low paid workers by prescribing "supplementary payments" which are payable *only* if over award payments are not made or if

17. Callus *et al.*, 1991, pp. 241-242.

their current level is less than the prescribed supplementary payment. The purpose of this is to eliminate perceived inequities due to the large variation in over award payments that has grown up in the marketplace and to implement a more "solidaristic" wage policy for particular skill categories. Such measures clearly will tend to reduce the ability of the over award payment system to produce inter-enterprise differentials which reflect market circumstance. However, at the same time, the union movement has over the last year accepted that there should be a shift in emphasis to enterprise-level negotiation. It is not clear how well enterprise bargaining will fit with the levelling tendency of the supplementary payments system.

Table 9. Composition of Average Weekly Earnings; Full-time Adult Non-Managerial Employees, May 1988 (percentage)

	Average weekly ordinary time earnings				Overtime	Total (= 100%)
	Award or agreed base rate of pay	Payment by measured result	Over-award and other pay	Total ordinary time		
Private Sector						Aus. $
Males	82.4	2.1	2.7	87.3	12.7	493.30
Females	94.0	0.5	1.9	96.5	3.5	383.70
Public Sector						
Males	92.2	0.2	0.7	93.7	6.3	511.20
Females	97.9	0.0	0.1	98.0	2.0	454.90

Source: Australian Bureau of Statistics, *Distribution and Composition of Employee Earnings and Hours Australia May 1988*, (Cat. No. 6306.0), Canberra: ABS, 1989.

For many parts of the labour force, however, these complexities do not apply. For most employees in the public sector, and some in the private sector, awards have been recognized as being "paid" rates; that is, the rate prescribed in the award is the rate actually paid to the employee. For this reason, over award payments in the public sector are quite small, but on the other hand this can cause problems of co-ordination in wage setting between these two systems. In particular, in the past the tribunals were plagued with a feedback from increases in paid rates awards on the grounds that they had become uncompetitive in the labour market compared with over award payments paid elsewhere and the tendency for over award payments not to be reduced when the award rate was increased. It is really only since the introduction of the negotiated Accord between the union movement and the government that these issues have been reconciled in a series of principles for wage determination laid down in National Wage Cases. which then guide all members of industrial tribunals, and which are generally also applied by the State tribunals.

The total wage bill is therefore the weighted sum of a number of components:

Managerial earnings (largely determined outside the award system);
Average weekly earnings of full-time non-managerial employees, which can be disaggregated into:

* overtime earnings,
* ordinary time earnings of full-time employees which can in turn be disaggregated into:
  - award or "agreed" rates of pay,
  - over award payments,
  - payments by measured result.
* earnings of part-time non-managerial employees.

Table 9 shows average weekly earnings disaggregated in this way.[18]

C.4 Piece Rates and Performance Related Pay

Table 10 summarizes some available evidence on the importance of piece rates in Australia. Amongst full-time non-managerial adult employees, 7.8 per cent of males and 1.1 per cent of females received part of their earnings as payment by results in 1975, and that these percentages had fallen to 4.8 per cent and 0.4 per cent respectively in 1983, although the latter figure was undoubtedly affected by the recession which then affected Australia. Most of those receiving such payments worked in manufacturing – 14.2 per cent of males and 3.6 per cent of females working in manufacturing received such payments in 1975. Only in two industries – basic metal fabrication and mining – did a substantial proportion of employees receive such payments. Also, even for those receiving, payment by results represented only 30 per cent of average earnings for all employees, and even less for women. Interestingly, though, this ratio remained stable even though the proportion of employees to which it applied halved.

---

18. Table 3.6 shows "over award" and other pay in the private sector to be quite a low proportion of overall earnings, in fact to be only about one-fifth of the importance of overtime earnings. This is almost certainly an underestimate. The reason is that the survey instrument used to gather these data asks employers to nominate either the award or the "agreed base rate of pay" for a sample of their employees. In many cases, the "agreed base rate of pay" will be considerably above the award and for this reason the employer in fact disregards the award and quotes that aggregate figure in the survey. Thus the true margin between the minimum described in the awards system and actual rates is probably much greater than that shown in Table 3.6.

Table 10. Importance of Payment by Results in Australian Wage System for Full-time Adult Non-managerial Employees, by Industry, 1975 and 1983

		Basic Metals	Textiles, Clothing and Footwear	All Manufacturing	Mining	All Industries
Proportion of employees receiving such payments (per cent)						
Males	1975	50.0	–	14.2	36.0	7.8
	1983	42.7	–	–	37.4	4.8
Females	1975	–	8.1	3.6	–	1.1
	1983	–	–	–	–	0.4
Payment by results: Average payments to those receiving such payments as a proportion of average earnings for all employees (per cent)						
Males	1975	19.4	–	22.5	33.6	29.5
	1983	19.7	–	–	33.9	29.0
Females	1975	–	26.1	19.3	–	17.0
	1983	–	–	–	–	16.0

Source: Derived from Peltz *et al.* (1985), who used published and unpublished data from Australian Bureau of Statistics, *Distribution and Composition of Employees Earnings and Hours Australia May 1975 and May 1983* (Cat. No. 6306.0).

As a result of strong union opposition to its introduction in the 1920s, payment by measured result has never attained the same importance in Australian wage setting as it has in a number of European countries. The relative unimportance of piece rates in the Australian wage structure is significant. It helps to account for the recent success of the system in holding the rate of growth of wages to a little less than price rises, thus encouraging strong employment growth from 1983 to early 1990. The absence of the continuous plant level bargaining which is an inevitable result of the need to fix rates for new tasks in a payments-by results system, has been a key feature of the system's recent success in keeping wages growth under control. There has been only a very slight increase in the incidence of performance-based pay as a result of the recent development in Australian award restructuring.[19]

19. In 1990, 34 percent of employees worked in workplaces at which some non-managerial employees received performance-related payments (Callus *et al.*, 1991, p. 243)

Employee compensation in Australia only rarely reflects the performance of the enterprise, except perhaps for managerial salaries. The level of profit sharing and other equity sharing schemes is poorly developed at this point of time: in 1990, workplaces with profit sharing schemes employed five percent of all employees, while those with share ownership schemes employed 14 percent.[20] Such schemes are not encouraged by tax concessions. Perhaps as a result, unemployment can climb sharply if economic conditions worsen (as happened in 1982 and has also occurred in 1990). The union movement is now supporting moves to make earnings more responsive to enterprise performance and in one or two instances this has been reflected in the terms of agreements registered under the Federal Industrial Relations Act 1988. The development of performance based pay concepts might conceivably result in more "gain" sharing at a micro level and a consequent reduction in employment fluctuation.

C.5 Gender Discrimination

Wage discrimination – particularly on the grounds of sex – has been attacked with some success by the award system itself. Prior to 1969, the basic wage paid to women was less than that paid to men, while margins for skill were less, by design, for "women's occupations" such as clothing machinists and nurses. When, in 1969 and 1973, the tribunals decided to eliminate such segregation, they had as a guide the explicit discrimination previously practised. As a result, the differential between female and male earnings approximately halved, having initially been comparable with the ratio which existed then (and has persisted until now) in the United States.[21] Recently, the issue has again been revived: some women's groups have argued that poor advocacy robbed some groups, such as nurses, of full compensation for past discrimination in 1973-75. Drawing on recent US debates, they have called for "comparable worth" to be used as a guideline for another revision of earnings. However, except for the extension of parental leave mentioned earlier, further extra provisions for women have not been attained.

C.6 Other Terms and Conditions of Employment

Most terms and conditions of employment in Australia are determined by the award system with the Federal and State systems working quite closely together. This is true of general rules for defining the standard work week, and rules prescribing

20. Callus *et al.*, 1991, p. 242.

21. For a further discussion of trends in female.male earnings differentials see J. Stackpool-Moore, "From Equal Pay to Equal Value in Australia: Myth or Reality", *Comparative Labour Law Journal*, Vol. 11 No. 3 (1990), pp. 273-294.

compensation for dismissal (such compensation is a relatively recent innovation in Australia, and is generally much less generous than job security provisions found in European practices).

Table 11. Proportion receiving sick leave and superannuation, 1989

		Proportion Receiving	
		Sick leave	Superannuation
Age	15-19	56.6	15.8
	20-24	79.7	35.7
	25-34	82.0	49.2
	35-44	80.4	54.1
	45-54	81.7	59.0
	55-59	81.4	59.4
	60-64	78.1	52.9
	65+	51.7	22.0
Sector	Public	98.4	73.2
	Private	89.6	48.3
Status	Permanent	97.8	56.2
	Casual	– (*)	9.5
Sex	Male	85.2	55.0
	Female	68.9	35.8
All employees		78.3	46.8

(*) The ABS *defines* casual employees as those entitled to neither annual leave or sick leave in their main job. In 1989, these comprised 20.0 per cent of all employees.

Source: Australian Bureau of Statistics, *Employment Benefits Australia August 1989* (Cat. No. 6334.0), Canberra: ABS, 1990.

Other benefits prescribed by the Award system are:

* Annual leave entitlements (generally 4 weeks per annum for "permanent" employees);
* "Sick leave" income support by the employer at full rates of pay (for the initial days) or half rates of pay (for a further period) for a defined total number of days per year;
* Minimum rates of contribution to employment-related superannuation funds (that is funds providing retirement benefits, though in Australia these are often awarded as a lump sum on retirement rather than as a pension). The custom of paying lump sum benefits – which, unlike annuities, are viewed as capital

endowments and have been taxed at a low rate – is related to the means tested pension system, in which some capital assets (such as the family home) are exempt from the means test. These provisions were extended during the 1980s as a result of union action which eventually resulted in a number of awards requiring employers to make contributions (initially 3 per cent of the wage bill). Tables 8 and 11 summarize the portion of employees benefiting from major employment benefits, most of which are prescribed in awards of the tribunals.

It will be seen that there has been a slight fall in the proportion receiving "standard" benefits such as sick leave and annual leave – due, apparently, to a growth in "casual" employment. Receipt of other benefits not generally prescribed in awards – such as goods and services paid "in kind", and the provision of transport equipment (usually a company car) have stagnated. Shares – which are generally available to upper management groups only – have however been made available to a larger minority, though still a small one. The main change has been the spread of superannuation provisions, largely as a result of the spread of requirements for employer contributions throughout the award structure.

There have been a number of other provisions which have largely come out of tribunal decisions. One of these is a general entitlement to maternity leave, which has recently been generalized to a parental leave entitlement. Under these provisions, an expectant mother is entitled to take a year off without pay and to be reinstated at the end of that period, and is also entitled to share that entitlement with her partner. She and he are now also entitled to take this leave by working part-time, so that the total period can extend to up to 2 years.

Table 8 also summarizes the current extent of some fringe benefits. Until recently, taxation savings were an important reason for the growth of such benefits. However, since 1986 employers have had to pay a special tax on the value of benefits they supply to employees. This "fringe benefits tax" has reduced the incentive for such provisions to be extended in place of open salary increases.

C.7 Termination of Labour Contracts

(a) Individual employees

In the usual type of indefinite hiring arrangement, employees may quit the job by giving the appropriate notice. Notice may be specified in the contract, but for most employees the proper period of notice to terminate the contract will be specified in the award: in the typical case, one week on either side. Technically if the employee quits the job without giving due notice, the employee may be sued for breach of contract and/or prosecuted for breach of the award. In practice it is almost unknown for either of these consequences to occur.

Employers may terminate the employee's contract without notice in cases where, by reason of some misconduct, incompetence or disobedience, the right to summarily dismiss arises. However, in most instances employers are required to give due notice, as specified in the contract or award, and where no such notice is specified, to provide the employee with "reasonable" notice. Where an employer wrongfully dismisses an employee, or fails to give the appropriate notice, the employee may pursue an action for breach of contract or breach of award. Such cases are quite common, and have become more significant both in number and substance with the advent of an "unfair dismissal" right in Australia awards and statutes.

(b) Collective lay-offs

Until relatively recently, in cases of an employer wishing to lay-off the whole or part of his or her labour force in response to economic downturn the only requirement was that the correct period of notice be given to terminate the contract of employment. There was no uniform set of guarantees for job security of the sort which have been common in European countries since the 1960s although some provisions began to emerge in Federal and State awards in the late 1970s. However, in a major test case brought by the ACTU in the early 1980s[22], the Federal tribunal determined certain levels of job protection in the Metal Industry Award, and these have become the established minima across industry generally.

In awards where these termination, change and redundancy (TCR) clauses apply, employees now have the following protections:

- *termination by notice*: ranges from 1 week's notice for an employee with 1 years service or less to a maximum of 4 week's notice for an employee who has served more than 5 years with that employer. An additional 1 week's notice is given to employees of 45 years of age in certain circumstances;
- *redundancy termination*: severance payments are calculated according to length of continuous service, ranging from nil for a person employed for less than 1 year to a maximum of 8 weeks pay for an employee with more than 4 years standing with that employer. Severance pay is additional to the notice due on termination;
- *unfair dismissal*: federal awards may now also contain a provision prohibiting dismissal on grounds which are "harsh, unjust or unreasonable".

---

22. *Termination, Change and Redundancy Case*, (1984) 8 *Industrial Reports* 34; 9 *Industrial Reports* 115.

(c) Termination at will and unfair dismissal

There is no general concept of termination at will in the Australian system of regulation. An employer retains a fairly broad freedom to dismiss employees, or to declare them redundant, with the appropriate notice.

However, since the mid 1980s, unfair dismissal provisions in federal awards, coupled with the operation of State legislation has extended the protection for employees and correspondingly diminished the employer's power to dismiss with notice. Even where the appropriate notice is given by the employer, unless there is a "fair" reason for dismissal, compensation or reinstatement may be sought by the former employee.

(d) Restrictions on employees after termination

Apart from certain implications under a contract that an employee will not attempt to undermine the employers business, or seduce away his or her clients, there are no restrictions upon the behaviour of the ordinary worker. Virtually no awards, and only certain classes of contracts contain express restrictions upon an employee's working or trading activities beyond the termination of the relationship. In this select class of cases – usually in the case of senior employees who are privy to important information concerning the organization – restraints may be placed upon the employee's right to compete with the former employer, or to set-up a similar business, or to work with a competitor. However, such restraints cannot be open ended, and must be reasonable in terms of their period of operation and their area of coverage.

D. Conclusion

The Australian method of regulating labour contracts through arbitration of interest disputes has long been the object of fierce criticism. This has centred on the system's failure to achieve the industrial peace which is its supposed objective. Although the number of working days lost by strikes in Australia is not very high, the number of strikes and the number of workers involved is as high or higher than in most Western countries (Table 12). The system itself can be held partly responsible for this: since it is designed to settle disputes, short strikes to attract attention to grievances and to demonstrate the seriousness of a dispute are, perversely, encouraged. At least in the past, unions tended to approach the tribunals as supplicants, not bargainers, and did not consider the rights they were "awarded" through this process to require any commitment to industrial harmony.

Table 12. Measures of Stoppage Activity: Annual Average 1962-1981

	Number of stoppages per 100,000 employees	Number of workers involved per 1,000 employees	Number of days lost per 1,000 employees	Average number of workers involved per stoppage	Average number of working days lost per stoppage	Average number of working days lost per worker involved
Australia	45	229	497	495	1048	2.1
Austria	n/a	15	27	n/a	n/a	2.1
Belgium	5	19	188	452	4664	9.5
Canada	10	49	765	500	7813	17.1
Denmark	6	30	162	563	2389	4.0
Finland	51	141	448	415	2365	3.9
France	18	117	195	734	1141	2.0
Germany (FR)	n/a	8	47	n/a	n/a	3.8
Iceland	83	206	1407	435	2722	10.5
Irish Republic	17	46	695	274	4180	14.9
Italy	26	518	1347	2401	5512	3.4
Japan	6	42	113	702	1878	2.6
Netherlands	1	5	25	1053	6399	3.7
New Zealand	27	78	205	285	780	2.7
Norway	1	4	43	349	4805	14.2
Spain	13	126	474	785	2775	3.2
Sweden	2	14	91	488	3454	7.1
Switzerland	–	–	3	134	1672	10.3
United Kingdom	11	67	386	660	3814	6.2
United States	6	28	474	429	7361	17.3

Source: Stephen W. Creigh, "Australia's Strike Record: the International Perspective", pp. 29-51, in: Richard Blandy and John Niland (eds.), *Alternatives to Arbitration*, North Sydney: Allen & Unwin, 1981.

In virtue of the statutory award system, Australian industrial regulation is inevitably highly legalistic. The senior members of Australian industrial tribunals are mostly lawyers who enjoy judicial (or quasi-judicial) status and benefits. The regulation of labour contracts has established an industrial jurisprudence which is foreign to basic common law principles. The reason for the adoption and development of this method of contract determination lies outside the legal system itself. Australian compulsory arbitration was based upon the notion of "fairness" – that the labour contract should be based upon a "just" set of principles rather than upon pure market forces. This supposition was derived in turn from the problems which were caused by the industrial and social dislocation in the big strikes of the 1890s. Australian industry, and the Australian economy, it was thought, could only develop if the forces of capital and labour could be made to work together in reasonable harmony. "Fair employment conditions", tariff protection and a racially exclusionary labour force policy were the principles which sustained this development from Federation in 1901 until the 1960s.

In so far as the "employment contract" element of this arrangement was concerned, the process which developed brought the workers (represented by their unions) before industrial tribunals seeking minimum employment conditions in respect of most aspects of their employment. One apparent advantage of the system is that it gave the tribunals a power to influence the wage outcome at a macro level. This has, however, often been criticized. In the past, the system was held responsible for maintaining a floor under real wages in Australia which reduced Australian competitiveness and which was used to justify protective tariffs which distorted the economy. Wage inflation was encouraged by unions' efforts to achieve wage increases additional to award standards where market conditions allowed, and then to use the tribunal system to spread the benefits more widely in a search for "comparative wage justice". Over time, employers who could not afford to pay the award wage went out of business[23], and those who remained in business came to rely upon the centralized award wage structure as their defence against further union claims.

Since 1983 (the year of the Accord), the unions have made "no extra claims" commitments, and the tendency for wage drift due to union pressures has been removed. At the same time, the tribunals themselves have tightened their own wage setting criteria in order to avoid the "wage-wage" spirals which had occurred at times as a result (for example) of differences in policies between state and federal tribunals. As a result, earnings growth appears to have been held to a rate below that which would have been expected on the basis of past experience.

---

23. The main exception is in agriculture. Farmers could and did substitute family labour and capital equipment for hired labour, but have remained strong opponents of the award wage system.

Critics of the system have advanced two reasons for scepticism on the supposed benefits of the Accord. One is that, in the labour market circumstances of the 1980s, wage costs would have risen even more slowly if the "floor" provided by the tribunals had been removed. This argument, however, is implausible in the light of the strong employment growth which occurred from 1983 to 1990 (see Chapman and Gruen, 1989).[24] The other is that the micro economic costs of the rigidities of the system have been too high: lower inflation has been bought at the cost of inflexibility and inefficiency. Recently, the Australian union movement has itself become convinced of the need for structural adjustment in the economy, and of the importance of labour market flexibility in that process. This has led to the centralized tribunals prescribing by award the flexibility in individual employment contracts which is natural to an unregulated wage system. Also current proposals under the accord envisage a greater scope for enterprise level bargaining. It is still not clear whether this process will in fact lead to the workplace adjustment which its proponents regard as necessary.

However, on this issue an old problem in interpreting Australian debates presents itself. Many business spokesmen criticize the system for imposing rigidities. However, very few employers have proved willing to operate outside that tribunal's jurisdiction: each appears to fear union power would make any such an attempt too costly. Non-Labour governments, responding to the fears of business lobbies, have baulked at making strike action in pursuit of interest claims lawful.[25] In Australia, at least, escaping from historical inheritances has proved very difficult.

During 1992, the debate has continued, with the parties opposed to the federal Labour government proposing to reform the system, possibly using as a model the radical changes introduced in New Zealand in 1990. Changes of this magnitude would need to be introduced in a co-ordinated manner at federal and state level to be effective. However, even when federal and state governments have been of the same political persuasion, concerted action of this sort has always proved difficult to achieve in Australia.

---

24. In an earlier study, Beggs and Chapman (1987) concluded that the decline in strike activity observed in the first three years of the Accord's operation was greater than would be expected from economic conditions, and that no such change was observable for Canada, the UK or the USA for the same period.

25. For example, in 1989, the New South Wales government decided not to implement the crucial recommendation 34 in the "Niland" Report (1989), to the effect that, in certain circumstances, strikes in pursuit of interest disputes should be lawful.

REFERENCES

A.B.S. (Australian Bureau of Statistics), *The Labour Force* (Cat. No. 6203.0), August 1990.

A.C.T.U. (Australian Council of Trade Unions), *Future Strategies for the Trade Union Movement* (Melbourne, May 1987).

A.C.T.U./T.D.C., *Australia Reconstructed.* Report by the A.C.T.U./T.D.C. Mission to Western Europe. (A.G.P.S., Canberra, 1987).

B.C.A. (Business Council of Australia), *Enterprise Based Bargaining: A Better Way of Working*, Vol.1. (Melbourne, July 1989).

G.S. Bain and F. Elsheikh, *Union Growth and the Business Cycle* (Blackwell, Oxford, 1976).

J.J. Beggs and B.J. Chapman, Declining Strike Activity in Australia, 1983-85: An International Phenomenon?, *Economic Record*, Vol. 63, No. 183, December 1987, pp. 330-339.

J. Borland, B. Chapman and M. Rimmer, *Microeconomic Reform in the Australian Labour Market.* Paper presented to Conference on Micro Economic Reform, Centre for Economic Policy Research, Research School of Social Sciences, A.N.U., 1990.

R. Callus, A. Morehead, M. Cully and J. Buchanan, *Industrial Relations at Work* (Australian Government Publishing Service, Canberra, 1991)

B.J. Chapman and F. Gruen, *An Analysis of the Australian Consensual incomes policy: the Prices and Incomes Accord.* (Paper presented to the Conference "The Art of Full Employment", University of Limburg, Netherlands, 1989.) Discussion Paper 122, Centre for Economic Policy Research, Australian National University, Canberra, 1990.

B. Creighton and A. Stewart, *Labour Law: An Introduction* (Federation Press, Sydney, 1990).

S. Crean and M. Rimmer, *ILO Study on the Adjustment Problems of Trade Unions in Industrialised Market Economies: Australia* (National Key Centre in Industrial Relations, Monash University, 1990).

R. Curtain, *Emergence of Workplace Bargaining Within a Centralised Wages System: The New Industrial Relations in Australia* (Working Paper No. 2, National Key Centre in Industrial Relations, Monash University, 1990).

[K. Hancock], *Report of the Committee of Review on Australian Industrial Relations Law and Systems* (4 Vols.) (A.G.P.S., Canberra, 1985).

B. Hepple and S. Fredman, *Labour Law and Industrial Relations Regulation in Great Britain* (Deventer: Kluwer, 1986).

M. Kirby, The Removal of Justice Staples and the Politics of Australian Industrial Arbitration, *Journal of Industrial Relations*, Vol. 31, No. 3, September 1989, 334-371.

J. Kitay and P. McCarthy, Justice Staples and the Politics of Australian Industrial Arbitration, *Journal of Industrial Relations*, Vol. 31, No. 3, September 1989, 310-333.

S. MacIntyre and R. Mitchell (eds.), *Foundations of Arbitration: The Origins and Effects of State Compulsory Arbitration, 1890 - 1914* (Oxford University Press, Melbourne, 1989).

R. Mitchell, Labour Law Under Labor: The Industrial Relations Bill 1988 and Labour Market Reform, *Labour and Industry*, Vol. 1, No. 3 (October 1988), pp. 486-504.

R. Mitchell and M. Rimmer, Labour Law, Deregulation and Flexibility in Australian Industrial Relations, *Comparative Labour Law Journal*, Vol. 11, No. 4 1990.

[J. Niland], *Transforming Industrial Relations in New South Wales*, Vol. 1 (Green Paper) N.S.W. Government Printer, February 1989.

D. Peetz *et al.*, *Pay Incentives: Payment by Results and Employee Financial Participation in the Australian Wage System* (Canberra: Internal Policy Discussion Paper, Wages and Income Policy Division, Department of Employment and Industrial Relations, 1985).

M. Rimmer, *Enterprise Awards: Are They More Flexible?*, (Working Paper No. 6, National Key Centre in Industrial Relations, Monash University, 1990).

M. Rimmer and J. Zappala, Labour Market Flexibility and the Second Tier, *Australian Bulletin of Labour*, Vol. 14, No. 4 (September 1988), pp. 564-591.

P. Scherer, The Nature of the Australian Industrial Relations System: A Form of State Syndicalism?, in: G.W. Ford, J. M. Hearn and R. D. Lansbury (eds.), *Australian Labour Relations: Readings* (Macmillan, Melbourne, 4th ed. 1987), pp. 81-101.

G.A. Withers, *Labour 1900 to 1984*, Working Paper No. 28, Department of Economic History, Australian National University, 1987.

Labour Market Contracts and Institutions
J. Hartog and J. Theeuwes (Editors)

CHAPTER 4

NEW ZEALAND:
From Legal Regulation to Legal Deregulation: 1968-1992*

Alan Williams**

A. Introduction

On 15 May 1991, the New Zealand government passed into law an entirely new piece of legislation entitled the Employment Contracts Act. The new statute which came into force on 19 August 1991, replaced all other enactments relating to industrial relations. Needless to say, given its scope and contents, the relatively short period following its introduction in December 1990, saw the proposal become the focus of enormous controversy. For what was being formally suggested had the effect of rendering nearly one hundred years of industrial legislation, virtually obsolete. In sum, a tradition of centralist intervention by the state into the regulation of the labour market, usually as prime mover, that began with the passing of the Industrial Conciliation and Arbitration Act of 1894 (the IC and A Act) came to both a symbolic and administrative end. For the changes incorporated in the new legislation, totally altered the nature of the formal rules and institutional processes that had shaped the centralist tradition of labour market regulation in New Zealand, since 1894.

Critics who perceive of the changes contained in the new legislation as having quite literally the qualities of total discontinuity between systems as found in Piore and Sabel (1984), have tended to overstate the reformist case. For it must be borne in mind that the history of industrial relations law was born of a reformist impulse, and that this has made itself manifest quite frequently in the past, most often, when some new statutory intervention failed in practice. Indeed it is safe to argue that what is at issue when the 1991 ECA is analyzed is not so much the notion of reform per se, but its purposes and directions.

The latest legislation actually replaces two other statutes, the 1987 Labour Relations Act, and the 1988 Public Sector Act, both of which introduced large and substantive

* Thanks are due to Massey University Research Fund for grant support during the project.

** Department of Human Resource Management, Faculty of Business Studies, Massey University, Palmerston North, New Zealand.

changes which were still in the process of "bedding in" when the current government introduced the new law. It must also be remembered that only fourteen years earlier, the Labour administration of the day had introduced an entirely new statute, the 1973 Industrial Relations Act, which had totally superseded, the original IC and A legislation, the foundation of the entire system. The new legislation despite the sweeping changes it has introduced may thus be seen in a very real sense, to be the culmination of reformist intentions which date back to the early 1970s.

The 1991 ECA also has provided an important demonstration effect, in light of the fact that it incorporates in legal and operational form the processes of labour market de-regulation that constitute one of the major theoretical constructs of labour market flexibility (Layard and Calmfors, 1986; Atkinson, 1987; Boyer, 1988; Blyton and Morris, 1991; Pollert, 1991). As discussion below will reveal the process of labour market de-regulation in New Zealand has advanced much further and faster than that of any other OECD economy. This chapter will examine and attempt to analyze the reformist process as it has evolved since the late 1960s. In doing so it will analyze both the major legislative enactments that have shaped reform, and some of the pressures both political institutional and economic that have shaped the process. The balance of the study will consider in some detail the structural and operational aspects of the new law and will conclude, with a speculative discussion as to the possible and consequential outcomes of de-regulation.

A.1 Reflections on the Origins of Labour Market Regulation in New Zealand

The question immediately arises, where can the origins of this reformist impulse which has taken its most recent shape in the legislation of 1991 be found? There is some degree of consensus, that it has been shaping steadily since the late 1960s, when serious questions began to be asked about the increasing bureaucratic rigidities that encased both employers and trade unions in a centralized, highly legalistic and complex set of both substantive and procedural rules. What had been entered on the statute book in 1894, as a highly innovative means of controlling industrial conflict (Howe, 1991) had become by the end of the 1960s in need of further reform. It took a highly symbolic incident in 1968 to activate the processes whereby change was to be achieved.

The evolution of the New Zealand industrial relations system in the period since 1894 has been characterized by its high degree of state regulation and administration through the medium of statute and prescribed formal practices (Stone, 1962; Woods, 1963; Williams, 1984; Holt, 1986). Over time the agencies set up under the original legislation, most notably, the Arbitration Court (comprising of two lay representatives and a presiding judge) began to take on functions additional to their original prescribed tasks. This was partially due to government intention and also to the fact that the Court as a legal institution was not subject to the normative rules that governed other aspect of the judiciary.

It was in fact allowed wide freedom in the application of its statutory rules, and needed after legal test, to be guided only by the doctrine of equity and good conscience. Its primary task became identified with the setting of occupational wage rates as operational minima, together with such additional non-wage payments as may be prescribed by conditions of employment. The balance of the award's clauses became standardized over time and frequently remained quite unchanged from one term to another.

The actual levels of wages then became subject to local labour market conditions, and the award rate for a given occupation in a specific industrial location, would be advanced usually in percentage terms to become a prevailing rate. This in turn, would be strongly influenced by such relative factors as labour market tightness. Until the middle 1970s, when unemployment began to perceptibly rise, albeit slowly, actual payments exceeded the award rate quite significantly in some industrial districts, as employers "paid the going rate" for specific industrial skills.

(a) In search of wage equity: The role of General Wage Orders (GWO)

During the 1920s, the industrial bench had been vested with the power to make general wage orders, through changes to the existing law. This arose from the fact that over periods of time the industrial awards of the Court, which were the main vehicle through which the terms and conditions, as well as the minimum wage rates of all occupations covered by trade unions and registered under the IC and A Act, were set, would find larger unions making net gains, while smaller unions lagged behind. The GWO process was designed to bring some degree of equity into the wage market by an order that all prevailing award rates be raised by a given percentage. In reality the process simply lifted the tail, and left the pattern of occupational differentials in place.

By 1968, the processes whereby a GWO was obtained had become a stylised ritual. The President of the Federation of Labour, representing all private sector unions would lodge a case for a GWO in the name of a key union, usually the carpenters. Because occupational awards crossed sectoral boundaries in industry, and carpenters were found to be employed in all of them, this had the required general effect. The claim would be heard by the court, and the Executive Director of the New Zealand Employers Federation would file a formal opposition to the claim. Expert witnesses would then be called, with the Government Statistician appearing in a somewhat Gilbertian role, first arguing for an increase and then when called by the employers, against it.

The Court would then adjourn and its judgement would follow conventionally two weeks later. It was always for an award, and usually delivered either the percentage figure asked for, or some lower figure on the "split the difference" principle. The economy would then face a strong wage shock, as the increase was added on to all industrial awards that were currently in force.

(b) The catalyst for change: the Nil Order of 1968

With all solemnity, the ritual began in 1968 with an unforeseen series of events in the background. There had been a major international downturn in wool prices which had inevitably had an adverse effect in Australasia. The Court, not for the first time in its long history, but certainly in the matter of a GWO case, took the question of current economic circumstances into the decision making processes. It ruled that with uncertainty in one of New Zealand's most important export markets that was being reflected in falling farmers' incomes, always a barometer for GWO decisions, it would be unwise to burden the economy with the wage shock that a GWO would entail. As a consequence the Court decided it would make a nil award.

The decision was to raise serious doubts about the whole system. The parties in collusion, sought through a loophole in the language of the GWO procedures to bring another case. Despite the fact that Sir Robert Muldoon then Minister of Finance characterized the second procedure as an "unholy alliance", the Court was prevailed upon to make a new order. In the event it was to prove a hollow victory, since it clearly exposed to view the inadequacy of the GWO procedures. But it did more than that.

In effect, it gave to T.P. Shand, the Minister of Labour, for whom, long tenure in the post and international exposure to labour market practices elsewhere had raised notions for major reform, a very important opportunity to criticize the system. His wondering aloud and in public forums about the efficacy of an industrial relations system, whose principles could be found in New Zealand's colonial and purely rural past, and its applicability in an increasingly industrial present, began the debate that was to lead to the first major changes to be made to the New Zealand industrial relations system since its inception in 1894.

B. The System on the Eve of Major Legal and Institutional Change

It is difficult to explain to those whose experience of labour market systems locate their primary dynamic within the collective bargaining process, that in the New Zealand case the bargaining process became largely uncoupled over time, from the means whereby settlement would be achieved. The IC and A tradition certainly permitted collective bargaining in the first instance, but required as a quid pro quo for formal recognition as bargaining agents, that all matters that remained outstanding between the parties, should be subject first to the process of mediation, and where that failed to arbitration.

As the preamble to the 1894 statute states, the act was intended to encourage the growth of trade unions of both workers and employers as well as for the settlement of industrial disputes, but after due and formal registration as what came to be called an arbitration union, the right to strike or lockout was forbidden under penalty of deregistration. It was therefore compulsory conciliation and arbitration that was the price of compliance with the law, and due recognition as a trade union.

It is a matter of historical consensus that the perceived need to regulate for the control of industrial conflict, emanated from the major industrial unrest that was the great maritime strike of 1890. This had begun in the major ports of Australia, and had spread to New Zealand through common membership in seafaring unions. As a consequence the progenitor of the IC and A legislation who was essentially the sole ideologue in a Liberal cabinet of very pragmatic reformers determined to regulate the labour market and after some four years of effort succeeded in doing so. For Reeves (1902), his industrial relations law was conceived as an experiment, the direction of which, he later frankly admits was to take on a life of its own. Thus by 1901, his original presumption that mediation would be the key process of dispute settlement, had been shattered by an amendment (Williams, 1976) to the legislation that permitted the parties to by-pass mediation and go straight to arbitration.

It was a decision that was to shape the whole direction of the industrial relations system and contribute in no small part to the problems of functional rigidity that were created as the process became highly formalized. The arbitrated award virtually dominated the entire industrial relations system and by the 1960s, had become a highly ritualized process. It was this that the reformers set out to change in the period down to the passing of the 1973 Industrial Relations Act.

B.1 The Award Structure and the Representational Process

(a) The problems of inflexibility in customary practice

On the eve of the major changes that took place in 1973, the New Zealand system was characterized by the centrality of the industrial award as not only a regulative instrument, but also as the primary reason for its existence. For under the 1954 IC and A Consolidation Act the activities of the parties were constrained to the procedures laid down for the promulgation of a new award to cover an industry or occupation that was not already within the system's ambit.

Most of the activities of the Court however were concerned with the renewal of existing awards which were coming to the end of their specified terms. While many of the Presidents of the Arbitration Court insisted that the parties exhaust the mediation process before going to arbitration, this legal requirement was often honoured in the breach. There was always a history of tension between the system and the perceived needs of the parties, and in the modern period this led to the growth of bargaining practices increasingly outside the ambit of the arbitral function. By the 1970s, actual arbitration in cases accounted for about 5 % of settlements. The balance, was settled through the conciliation process.

(b) The arbitral process

The procedure in either case required the creation of an industrial dispute, and under the traditional process, matters would inevitably end up before the Arbitration Court. At this point the parties were relieved of any further control over events. The Court would require them to present their views on the issues that were outstanding. It would then withdraw and make a judgement that would uni-laterally define the terms of the award. This would then be binding on the parties without right of appeal. Failure to comply was then presumed to be punishable by the Court. This emphasis on arbitration which was the hall mark of the 1950s and 1960s, meant that the Court's fixture list would often mean a smaller union in particular, would have to wait sometimes many months for a decision which was incumbent upon its formal appearance before the industrial bench. It was problems like these that informed the need to make change an imperative and shaped the deliberations that led to the passing of the 1973 legislation.

(c) The regulative controls over trade union membership

Trade union membership had become compulsory in New Zealand under an amendment to the IC and A Act, passed by the first Labour government in 1936. A National government which came to power in 1961 proceeded to abolish the compulsory clause in the act, but was persuaded, with employers supporting the claim, to introduce the concept of unqualified preference (for union members; see below). Trade unions were empowered to police the process and the task of ensuring that all employers would comply, was made extremely difficult, due to the relative small size of firms. At the time of writing for example, the average size of a company labour force in membership of the country's largest regional employers' association (Auckland), is ten persons. But the problem was further compounded by the fact that the number of trade unions duly registered under the law, was out of all proportion to the size of the active labour force.

(d) The pattern of union membership under the IC and A

According to official returns by the Department of Labour for 1971, there were 350 trade unions formally registered under the IC and A Consolidation Act of 1954. Of these 127 had under 100 members (the legal minimum was 7), a further 236 had less than 500 members, and 268 had less than 1000 on their books. Of the 350 listed in the department's annual report to parliament, only 44 could muster a membership in excess of 2000. This pattern of membership distribution gives weight to the contention of Howells (1970), that many of the smallest unions, and there were 73 listed who had less than 50 members, were little more than groups of workers in similar occupations who had combined simply to obtain the benefits of a registered award.

The result has been an industrial labour movement dominated by sectional interests and very often fragmented on key issues. What is interesting is the fact that the deliberate localization of union membership which was incorporated in the original statute, became the focus of a multi-partisan view that fewer and larger unions were needed.

(e) Employee representation in the public sector

By contrast with the private sector, public sector employees were covered by an entirely separate legislative history. Their terms and conditions of employment were governed by the central principle of the state as a single employer, represented in turn, by a surrogate body the State Services Commission. The process of negotiation between the designated service organizations representing public employees, which were constitutionally defined as voluntary bodies, and the SSC, incorporated the doctrine of equity and fair relativity. The operational presumption was traditionally invoked, that the setting of terms and conditions for public sector employment should incorporate relativities based on designated occupational awards in the private sector, and also included the notion that the rewards of professional workers, for example lawyers, in the state sector, should take into account factors based on comparison with peer groups in private practice. The central statute covering state sector employment prior to the primary reforms of the mid 1980s, was the 1977 State Sector Conditions of Employment Act.

(f) Institutional rights and the law in the private sector

In a sense the law itself was a surrogate in New Zealand, for those institutional rights, that in Europe for example, have been the subject of political as well as industrial conflict, between trade unions and employers. On the other hand the operational means by which such rights were assured often proved to be contentious when attempts were made to apply them. The problem of obtaining compliance with award rules specifying compulsory membership, for example, was partially resolved by the process of unqualified preference which gave unions the power to regulate employment. This could be achieved by invoking the unqualified preference clause in an award, where after the normative period of fourteen days from the start of employment, a worker not already a member refused to join.

It became conventional practice among employers to agree to such a clause during the process of conciliation (which was first introduced in 1908), and superseded mediation. An employer who had agreed to the admission of such a clause, then incurred a statutory duty, if the worker refused to join the union on any grounds other than conscience which then required formal testing before a tribunal, to dismiss the recalcitrant worker. In effect this meant that the law permitted the operation of what was a post-entry closed shop.

Terms and conditions such as these could also be extended across industries through what became national awards. The Arbitration Court on application could insert a blanket clause, which extended the terms of an award, not only to employers who were the original parties in the dispute, but also to employers who were not so listed in the terms of coverage. The principle even became extended toward the end of it's active life, to new firms entering the industry after the award came into force. For many small employers setting up in business for the first time, the realization that they were bound by an existing industrial award was often only made apparent, when a union official called with the news, in the process of checking membership numbers, in the firm's labour force.

In sum, the industrial labour movement found the source of its formal powers not through the medium of its own collective will, but rather through statutory rights, such as the granting to a registered trade union with coverage over more than 50 % of the potential membership the exclusive coverage and representation of a given occupational class which could not be challenged by any other group claiming the same representational duty. The reciprocal requirement as previous discussion has already indicated involved the voluntary abrogation of rights ranging from the autonomous control over strike action, often honoured in the breach, to make provision of social and related services for the sole benefit of the membership.

(g) The problems of a national identity for trade unions

The representation of collective interests through forms of national organization has always presented the industrial labour movement in New Zealand, with a range of organizational as well as ideological problems. The Federation of Labour (FOL) which came into existence in 1936, was led sequentially, and until relatively recently, by leaders who espoused a highly idiosyncratic approach to such questions as labour market reform, being more concerned with maintaining the status of the FOL, and the viability of its formal and informal relationships with government and the state agencies.

The FOL was not really faced with the choice of an alternative strategy, since it could only act on behalf of an affiliate if it was invited to do so. The rigidities of the system also mitigated against the development of a reformist view, and the absence of a viable and national system of shop steward training for example made it difficult to raise the administrative consciousness of trade union officials. The organization also suffered from two other quite important limitations.

The widely scattered, and diverse nature of trade union organizations as well as their inherent weaknesses in time of real conflict often found the FOL leadership actively engaged in industrial disputes that were really the province of the unions concerned, rather than finding time to plan overall strategies for the longer term. The result would often lead to direct confrontation with government, since there was also an active tradition of involving the Minister of Labour directly in major disputes. It also faced the problem that it could only be guaranteed a sympathetic ear by government, when there was a Labour administration in power. The 1950s and 1960s were thus barren years even if the FOL had had the collective will, the organizational strength and the leadership ability to carve for itself an independent role in labour market reform.

More recently an amalgamation has been achieved between the private sector FOL and the Combined State Unions, the CSU, to form the New Zealand Council of Trade Unions NZCTU. But as the events of 1991 have demonstrated, industrial history tends to repeat itself, and as in the great strikes of 1912-13 and 1951, industrial labour however determined, has proven no match for a government determined to use its full powers to either suppress direct action or unilaterally change the law.

(h) The pattern of employer representation

The IC and A rules pertaining to membership in industrial unions of workers applied in the same way to employers. The original law permitted any 7 workers to form a trade union and allowed any 4 owners to register as industrial unions of employers. Initially, this deliberately localized form of organization saw the development on the workers side of regional trades and labour councils, which would attempt to organize multiple occupational interests around such common causes as the need to bring all employers under the control of the legislation, through the extension of the terms of awards.

By contrast, the formal and national organization of employer interests through an appropriate institutional arrangement, actively pre-dates the emergence of a confederation of trade unions. For while it was not until 1916 that the first and ultimately abortive attempts were made to organize a truly national grouping of worker organizations, a federation of autonomous employer associations has been in existence in New Zealand since 1902. The conventional advancement of employer interests has been carried on essentially under a two tiered structure. At the regional level, and there are four associations each with its own dedicated staff centred in the four largest cities in New Zealand, an employer not wishing to maintain a specialist staff for the purpose, could contract out, through membership of the local branch of a given regional association, for a wide range of industrial relations services, including most importantly, advocacy requirements at times of award renewal.

By contrast the national federation, which had its own dedicated staff, acted as the main agency for the progressive forwarding of employer interests at the appropriate levels of interaction with government, state agencies, amongst large private sector firms and in the international context within bodies such as the ILO, the OECD and the EC. A primary focus of federation activities for example, has always been the shaping and direction of industrial legislation with employer interests in mind. This role has intensified considerably over the last several years, and there is clear evidence that federation inputs into the process of shaping the 1991 ECA were formative in the fundamental sense of the term.

(i) Limitations on the role of the national federation

On the other hand, the federation has never been able to develop a single employer position in issues, and has often (Boston, 1984) found itself contradicted in the public arena by the action of some of its larger and sectoral members. The regional associations are in fact very protective of their autonomy as independent agencies, and see the federation as a vehicle for the advancement of common interest. It has also had serious difficulties not only in sustaining, but actually developing a leading role in such important areas as the control of wage settlements in the collective name of all employer interests. As New Zealand moves into the 1990s with a virtually deregulated labour market the question the Employers' Federation faces with the New Zealand Council of Trade Unions, the national successor to the old FOL and the Combined State Unions, is uncertainty as to any future role that central organizations may play in such an industrial relations environment.

C. The Era of Legal, Institutional and Operational Change

The impetus for reform put in train by the nil award of 1968, survived both long debates and arguments, and a change in government before it took final legal form in the 1973 Industrial Relations Act. The changes were hailed in public comment as being the most far reaching since the passing of the IC and A Act in 1894. Yet there is an element of paradox involved at the same time. For while the purpose of the legislation was to free up the system, modernize it and make it more amenable to changes imposed by such major factors as the growth of collective agreements outside the framework of the award process, the engine of reform was still driven by the state, and the industrial law was still seen as the means to achieve successful outcomes.

C.1 The 1973 Industrial Relations Act

The passing of the 1973 Industrial Relations Act, signalled both the symbolic and the administrative end of the IC and A era. The primary changes introduced by the legislation betray strong American influences since the concept of a dispute was totally changed. Under the old regime, a dispute was the means whereby the processes leading to the making of an industrial award could be initiated. The new law abandoned what had often become a purely administrative procedure, and in its place created a dual status, for industrial disputes. Disputes of interest were defined as those arising as a function of the actual negotiation process. By contrast the disputes of rights procedure (s. 117) widened the concept of personal grievance (Williams, 1984) by introducing the notion of unjustified dismissal (Hughes , 1989, p. 1813) in place of the common law principle of wrongful dismissal. There was also a statutory requirement to write into awards and industrial agreements, either a customized procedure for handling personal grievances or the standard clauses laid down in the legislation.

(a) The key legislative changes

The new act also made some important administrative changes. Under Part III (s. 26), the power to settle disputes of interest was taken away from the now defunct Arbitration Court and vested in an Industrial Commission, which acted as a tribunal. Meanwhile under Part IV, the old Court reconstituted as a Labour Court, with powers of record, was deputed under (s. 47) to deal with disputes of rights and any matters of law referred to it by the Industrial Commission.

Two further bodies were created, an Industrial Relations Council charged with the task of advising government in matters relating to manpower policies and general industrial matters. It was also somewhat belatedly required to advise government on codes of labour market practice. In the event, it was destined to fall into disuse, since its role had been virtually pre-empted by the new law. By contrast, two quite powerful administrative policies were introduced. A new Industrial Conciliation Service was created under (s. 63) which was empowered to settle disputes of interest upon the application of one or other of the parties. It also recognized the need for early and sometimes informal intervention in industrial conflict by the creation under (s. 64) of a dedicated Industrial Mediation Service, staffed by specialists.

The political decision to recognize the need for more flexible arrangements was also a recognition of the fact that informal bargaining practices were growing in the interstices of the award system, often in the form of in-house agreements which were then not subject to formal registration required of industrial awards. The new law introduced (s. 65) the formal recognition of bi-lateral agreements of this kind that were in fact the voluntary settlement of disputes of interest. This had the very important consequence of introducing for the first time (Smith, 1984, p. 350), the notion of the collective agreement as a recognisably legal instrument.

The Industrial Commission proved to be short lived institution in what with hindsight, was its first term as an operational tribunal. With the return of a National government in 1975, the incoming Prime Minister (Sir Robert Muldoon) re-imposed his personal preference for arbitration. This resulted in the introduction of a modified form of the Arbitration Court, divided this time into three separate units, each intended to cover sectoral activities with the full bench combining for major decisions. Under the 1977 IRA, these revitalized institutions were empowered to hear under (s. 48) both disputes of interest and disputes of rights. The alternative form of reference of disputes to Conciliation Councils, with the results to be duly registered as awards under Part V of the 1973 legislation was also retained, since it was clearly working well.

(b) Interventionism and incomes policies: some vexed issues

Again with hindsight what had been intended as a major change in both rules, conventions and practices, proved to be a prologue of things to come. The late 1970s was to see considerable pressure being exerted on the wage fixing system. The period from 1968 onward was to be one of wage controls exerted through both legal and administrative regulations. Within the period down to 1984, the New Zealand labour market came under the purview of: the Stabilisation of Remuneration Act (March 1971-March 1972), the Stabilisation of Remuneration Regulations (March 1972-December 1972), the Economic Stabilisation Regulations (August 1973-June 1974), two periods of Wage Adjustment Regulations (July 1974-August 1977), the General Wage Orders Act (August 1977-August 1979), the Remuneration Act (August 1979-June 1982) and a Wage Freeze (June 1982-July 1984).

Government intervention on this scale came in direct response to deteriorating terms of trade and rising inflation, which steadily worsened during the 1970s. It was also strongly influenced by the strategic use made by trade unions of the essentially interlocked nature of wage fixing as they evolved a response to government efforts to control wages, in the face of manifest uncertainties with regard to New Zealand's economic future.

A natural propensity to develop a wage round approach to award settlements which had developed in the old IC and A system, was given further impetus by the 1977 application of wage controls. Considerable restrictions imposed on collective bargaining during the period, as a consequence the wage round gained in strategic importance during the latter part of the 1970s. As a general rule, the main trend setting awards such as the metal trades, drivers and electrical workers, settled in the opening period between September and October. Other groups would then follow in the subsequent period between October and March of the following year.

What was significant at the turn of the 1980s (Boston, 1984, p. 37) was the excessive rigidity found in both award and prevailing (actual) wage rates. During the 1979-1980 wage round, the core rate for fitters in the metal trades award became the benchmark and some 92 % of all settlements ended up within 1 % of that figure. It fell to 80 % in the 1980-1981 round and was back to 92 % in the 1981-1982 period. While the actual percentage distribution of settlements in terms of their degree of concentration has been contested (Deeks, 1990), the fact that rigidities of a considerable order did occur, was a clearly major influence upon both the Prime Minister's decision to impose a freeze in July 1992, and upon strategy adopted later by the post 1984 Labour government, is not in doubt.

A number of factors may be attributed as causal inputs. The occupational basis of the award system, made it easy for wage movements to cross sectoral boundaries. In addition the Arbitration Court as well as other pay fixing bodies had insisted in turn that historical pay relativities between various groups be maintained. This traditionally allowed the question of relativities to over ride any other consideration, such as the employer's ability to pay, or the application of productivity as a yard stick for wage increases.

Stability and continuity in turn played their part (Boston, 1984, p. 37) and together with pre-1980s government practice of accommodative monetary policies, now called by the current Prime Minister, the age of "borrow and hope", which was often reflected in the response of those employers who were able to pass on increased wage costs in their final market prices, and who saw nothing to be gained by trying to prevent flow on effects.

C.2 The 1987 Labour Relations Act: Introducing Further Change

The year 1984, was to see yet another change of government, with the return to power of Labour with a considerable majority. The history of the next six years (the parliamentary term is three years) was a period of quite fundamental political, economic and social change. The New Zealand voter was suddenly faced with an ostensibly centre-left government, which had adopted a free market approach to reform and was determined to release the economy from its protectionist carapace. In the event the price was exceedingly high. Loss of favour with the electorate, despite the fact that the government was returned with an increased majority in 1987. Internal dissension and bitter ideological wrangling also saw three successive Prime Ministers take office during the second half of the government's final term.

(a) Labour's contribution to labour market reform

The Labour government's contribution to labour market reform is important for three distinct reasons. In the first instance they were clearly concerned to improve employer-employee relationships as signalled in the title of the principal legislation. The purpose of the 1987 Labour Relations Act was to create a system where the parties could be made simultaneously more effective and accountable to their various constituencies for their actions. The primary direction of policy was thus to create a framework where order, efficiency and viability could co-exist.

The second important development aimed to eradicate the dual system, whereby state servants and private sector employees were located in quite separate industrial relations environments. The direction taken by government policy was strongly influenced by its larger economic strategy. As part of its economic de-regulation package, government proposed initially, to uncouple some twelve government departments whose functions included trading in products and services and make them state owned enterprises, under the 1987 State Owned Enterprises Act.

This was designed to have the effect of changing both the occupational status and the terms of employment, for senior managers (Walsh, 1988) who would then enter in competition with candidates from the private sector, the upper echelons of the new corporations. In the process the prevailing doctrine of equity and fair relativity would give way to what had been the subsidiary purpose of recruitment and retention. The outcome would leave a much smaller group of senior officials in charge of what would become the core public service.

The third key change saw the balance of the clerical and non administrative persons in the public service, moved under Part IV of the 1987 LRA. This meant that their terms and conditions would no longer be set under an independent statute and the enabling legislation that effected these changes, the 1988 Public Sector Act also replaced the prevailing State Servants Conditions of Employment Act, 1977. Designated service organizations who had represented the various occupations in public employment were also required to change their status in order to retain rights of representation. They were required to formally register as trade unions and they also faced another problem. Under the LRA, the minimum number of members required to form a trade union was raised from 30 to 1000.

Both private sector unions and service organizations whose current rolls often fell well below this figure, were given three choices and a moratorium in order to make them. They could amalgamate, recruit, or simply disband. Some 60 private sector unions and 15 state organizations were as a consequence given a two year period to accommodate these major changes. Official data for 1989 (NZ Official Year Book, 1991, p. 384) which excluded the groups just cited, estimates that there were 136 trade unions registered in 1989, covering an aggregate membership of 460,000 and with an average membership per union of 3382.

The process of amalgamations has continued to develop, and the NZCTU plan for a series of German style industrial confederations is proceeding. Unfortunately, since under current labour law, trade unions are no longer required to register membership numbers with the Department of Labour. It is therefore extremely difficult to obtain hard data on the current state of trade union membership. Estimates in the popular press currently put the combined membership of the NZCTU at between 450,000 and 500,000.

(b) Significant labour initiatives and their effects

The fact is often lost sight of in the controversies that have surrounded the 1991 ECA, that Labour had put into the 1987 legislation several quite important new provisions that were reflective of its own perceptions of labour market reform. It was clearly constrained in the task, by the fact that a balance had to be struck between what it saw as the need for regulative changes, and the maintenance of its traditional basis of support in the industrial labour wing. The problem was further compounded by the fact that a considerable balance of voting power was held by middle class voters whose support for labour was conditional upon the appeal of its larger policies of economic de-regulation.

One major change of significance involved the status of trade unions. Under the IC and A system, they had been constrained in terms of their roles and functions to the carrying out of those tasks defined by law that related to the formalization and maintenance of industrial awards. This meant that they were expressly forbidden to engage in any social, educational or welfare functions on behalf of their memberships. Under the 1987 LRA, they were granted full status as organizations able to carry out any functions on behalf of their members, that did not conflict with the normal restraints imposed on the private citizen by the common law. In addition their officers were required to be more accountable to the membership, and such accountability was required to be written into union rules.

But there were a number of stings in the reformist tail. Under (s. 98-107) of the act, they were required to modify their exclusive rights to occupational representation through the introduction of the principle of contestability. This meant that where a group of workers wished to change their representational arrangements, the right to represent could be contested by another union, with the final decision going to a secret ballot of the members.

This change was clearly introduced to actively encourage unions to raise the quality of their services to members, and to throw away their unfortunate image in some quarters as institutional debt-collectors, empowered to claim fees without reciprocal obligations to offer services. It was also intended to facilitate the more rapid growth of larger sectoral unions, since smaller unions already facing the problem of finding large numbers of new members would be encouraged either to amalgamate or leave coverage to their larger colleagues. On the other hand, critics claim (Harbridge and McCaw, 1989), that the real impact of the 1987 LRA was to change the relative power relationship in the labour market in the employers' favour.

The most contentious change introduced by the government from a trade union point of view was the loss of the unilateral right to go to arbitration. Labour had come to power with an important problem confronting them. How to ease the labour market out of a two year wage freeze without a wage explosion caused by deferred wage demand? This possibility was further complicated by the fact (Treasury, 1984) that the practice had grown up in the wage rounds prior to the freeze, for unions to activate second tier bargaining. This was done by taking the benchmark award rate using it as a wage floor and then targeting specific industries to make employers' mark up the prevailing rate for that occupation.

The claim was also made that cases existed of third tier agreements where the prevailing rate would then be used in specific company situations to lever the wage level up even further. The existence of unilateral arbitration could then be used as an implicit threat on the presumption that what the employer refused a tribunal would later grant, on the application of the trade union concerned.

It is clear that government had heeded the warning of Treasury that the return to normal labour market conditions would be placed at risk unless the problem was addressed. As a result trade unions faced a new choice. They could seek an industrial award from the newly re-constituted Arbitration Commission, which would give them the right to arbitration. Alternatively, they could seek to place themselves under four other defined forms of collective agreements, ranging from a composite multi-union single site agreement under (s. 166), a conjoint (single) award (s. 137) covering a number of unions in the same plant who agreed to the same terms and conditions or a bi-lateral agreement between a trade union and a single employer (s. 164). All of these had relative degrees of coverage under the central system. Finally, provision under (s. 152) of the legislation allowed the parties to simply move their arrangements outside the ambit of the system altogether. Unions who choose this then lost their rights of enforcement under the law and were required to take issues like enforcement to the civil courts.

The introduction of these alternatives that duly recognized the importance of the pressure for collective agreements more closely fitted the operational needs of specific industrial situations, gives a clear indication of the important growth of collective bargaining and burgeoning flexibility (Deeks, 1990) within the labour market system. The new law also permitted strikes to be treated as lawful under (s. 233) provided they were caused by matters arising under disputes of interest.

In turn, the Labour Court had its jurisdiction extended in matters relating to industrial torts and was also empowered to rule in situations where the introduction of new technologies were deemed to have created "new matters", not covered by the terms of an existing award or collective agreement. The government also tried to regulate for post-wage freeze consensus, by laying down formal ground rules for a tri-partite wage conference to precede each annual wage round.

(c) The integrative role of the 1988 Public Sector Act

While the LRA tended to overshadow the other changes taking place in the industrial law, it is important to recall that the 1988 Public Sector Act also played an important role in integrating private and public sector industrial relations. Within the retained core public service, contractual arrangements, often of the fixed term type, began to replace incremental arrangements based upon external comparisons. A number of the state owned enterprises having passed into private hands, and with government now intent upon reducing public expenditure, there has been a resultant and increasing emphasis on fixed term contracts, and a stronger movement towards performance based terms and conditions of employment.

Effectiveness, accountability and order those responsible for the LRA would claim, were the primary motivational forces driving labour market reform between 1984 and 1990. It must be noted that in parallel with these changes the government also introduced a major law, the 1990 Wage Equity Act, which attempted to push forward equity in employment and took as its central concept the argument of comparable worth. The act was destined to barely survive its formal introduction. Its repeal was signalled by the opposition during the election campaign of 1990, and it became the first statutory casualty claimed by the new government.

It is clear that the processes of labour market reform had come a long way by the time that a change of government occurred in 1990. The new administration had made much of the fact that the Labour government had not proceeded to de-regulate the labour market with the same enthusiasm that it had attacked other sectors of the economy. It had also made it very clear that once it attained office, it would proceed to make major changes to industrial relations law. The most important of these would be the introduction of the principle of the labour contract which would shape in totality, the future relationship between the employer and the employee. The legal formalization of these intentions and their institutional shape will provide the balance of discussion in this chapter.

D. The Emergence of Labour Contracts: the Legislation of 1991

Upon entering office in October 1990, the new National government proceeded to activate its promise to increase the momentum of labour market reform. An immediate casualty as has been already noted was the Wage Equity Act, which had in fact come into force on 1 October 1990. The new administration acted with confidence since its return to office had been preceded by the greatest political landslide in New Zealand's history. By October 1990, a bill introducing the new legislation was before parliament. It called for the formal reintroduction of voluntary trade union membership, and the removal of their exclusive rights to represent occupational groups. In addition, the blanket principle in award coverage was to be removed and the notion of freedom of association was introduced. But the central focus of the legislation was to be the employment contract in either single or collective form.

D.1 The Scope and Form of Labour Contracts

Employees with the repeal of the 1987 LRA were to be permitted to choose whether they wished to be represented by a third party or simply look after their own interests in direct negotiations with the employer, which would lead to the establishment of an individual contract in what was essentially the English common law form. Alternatively the same individual could choose to be bound by a collective contract to which his or her employer was a party. In turn, a collective contract under the meaning of the new law would be one which would bind an employer and two or more employees. Employment contracts were to be the only means whereby the rights and responsibilities of the parties were to be formally laid down. In addition, the question of whether or not an employee was covered by an individual or a collective document became a matter for the parties to decide. The whole thrust of the legislation said (Bradford, 1991) was to create a new flexible bargaining environment.

The intentions of the government as made clear in the 1991 Employment Contracts Act, became the focus of intense trade union hostility. Mass stoppages were called and widespread opposition was voiced. A sample of 400 submissions to the Select Committee (Department of Labour, 1991) found 71 in support, 188 opposed and a further 141 that were technical in nature and expressed no opinion on the veracity of the proposals. No less than 62 petitions, 830 written submissions and 530 sets of oral evidence were admitted during parliamentary hearings. There can be no doubt that these did have an influence on the final drafting of the law, but when the document was reported back to parliament its main components and legal direction remained unchanged.

D.2 The Major Areas of Structural and Institutional Change

In moving the final reading of the proposed legislation the government proposer advised the House of Representatives, that ten major areas of change were to be found in the new law. They were in sequence:

(a) A single jurisdiction for all employment contracts

The previous legislation had collective agreements in the class of bi-lateral arrangements under (s. 152) were not subject to enforcement in the Labour Court, but required that the parties take the matter forward as a civil action. The new law intended to bring all contracts under the same jurisdiction.

(b) The introduction of new institutions

After the Department of Labour test polled interested parties, the decision was taken to replace the Labour Court and the Conciliation Service with a new Employment Court while at the same time it was proposed to introduce an Employment Tribunal. Under new arrangements that were aimed at both cost reduction and the prevention of long delays for hearings, this latter body would take on both an adjudicative and a mediation role. The Court was charged with the duties of appellate function, dealing with disputes of rights and matters of contractual interpretation. Tribunal decisions could be the subject of appeal to the Court on points of law which would be in turn, based upon a review of the evidence presented by the parties before the Tribunal.

(c) The extension of personal grievance and rights machinery

Historically both the Arbitration and Labour Courts had taken the view that access to grievance procedures and services for the resolution of rights disputes were conditional upon trade union membership. In other words they applied the rule that free riding was not permitted. The new legislation removed this disability on the non-union member, and made access free from any form of conditional requirement. The second schedule to the ECA laid down a standard procedure to cover due process, on the grounds that this substantially improved the individual employee's protection in the work place.

(d) The extension of the principle of procedural fairness

The original draft of the legislation made access to disputes of rights and personal grievance procedures subject to the filing of the intent to grieve, within 28 days of the issue being raised. Clearly under pressure from external opinion, this period was raised to 90 days in the final draft.

(e) The question of harsh and oppressive contracts

The possibility that macho managers would use the new legislation in order to create total control over their work forces, was strongly canvassed by opponents of the new law. As a result, government placed a clause in the legislation (s. 57) which granted access for an appeal to the Employment Court by any party who could justifiably claim that the defined terms and conditions of their contracts constituted a harsh and oppressive work regime under the meaning of the ECA.

(f) Toward a code of minimum employment conditions

The absence of mechanisms in the new legislation that would protect employees in the period when they moved from under the LRA to the new system, was strongly noted by the Select Committee of parliament that dealt with the legislation. It was suggested that matters such as: statutory holidays, sick pay, bereavement and domestic services leave which had been written into awards and collective agreements under mandatory rules, form a minimum code of contractual requirements. The compromise was to be arranged through the development of a minimum code of employment conditions, as well as changes to legislative provisions outside the ECA.

The most significant of these involved the Social Security Act. Critics had pointed out that the conditional requirement that employees refusing a job offer incur a benefit stand down period of 26 weeks, was seen as the means whereby a macho or unscrupulous employer might be tempted to make unreasonable offers especially to young, part-time and casual workers, mindful of the monetary costs of refusal. Accordingly (Shipley, 1991), the terms relating to job refusals under (s. 65) of the Social Security Act was to be altered.

A definition of "good and sufficient reason" was introduced for workers under 20 years of age, newly established as the watershed between youth and adult employment. They would be permitted to refuse an offer, where the payment was less than either the unemployment benefit entitlement, or the training benefit entitlement plus $15 per week. The figures set for the new arrangements were: For unemployed persons in the age range 18-20, $123.17 net. For persons aged 16-17 currently on a training benefit, $101.14 net. Those over the age of 20 were presumed to come under the protection of the Minimum Wage Act, and could also claim assistance where it was required under the Guaranteed Minimum Family Income Scheme.

(g) The concept of the bargaining agent

At the fulcrum of the new bargaining process, the government introduced the concept of the bargaining agent. It had the affect of virtually creating a free market for services in employee representation. It was presumed that such a provision in which trade unions could compete with a variety of other individuals and agencies for the right to represent, would bring a natural stability over time into the new system. It was also made possible for a bargaining agent to be joined under the terms of the appropriate final contract.

(h) Variations of contractual arrangements during term

This had the effect of voiding the notion of new matters that had been formalized in the 1987 LRA. The contents of a contract were now to be allowed to be modified during the duration of their term. Such variations were to be arrived at by mutual agreement.

(i) Changes to strike and lockout provisions

Under the ECA, the absence of a labour contract will provide grounds whereby one or other of the parties can strike or lockout. The only limitation imposed by the new law directly relates to issues that arise over the scope of the bargaining unit, if it involves other employees. It is clear that to permit such an action, would transgress the principle of freedom of association. Employers also have the right to suspend both striking and non-striking workers where direct industrial action is currently taking place.

(j) Rights of access granted to bargaining agents

This category of change is really an extension of the principle of right of access that was contained in the earlier statutes.

These changes in sum signal the main thrust of the new legislation. The law has now been in place for eight months, and continues to arouse controversy and no little confusion. It is now time to consider some of its operational functions in somewhat more detail.

E. Some Functional Aspects of the New Industrial Relations

E.1 The Structure of Employment Contracts

The new legislation has really introduced two quite distinct provisions for the negotiation of employment contracts. For the individual employee two choices are now available. Either to proceed on a personal basis or to nominate a bargaining agent, who may be another person, the existing work group or a dedicated organization. All matters involving content, scope and administration during term then become subject to negotiations between the parties. The new rules governing the bargaining process are specified in the 1991 ECA, Part II.

(a) Individual employment contracts without a bargaining agent

It is important to note that provisions are now established for the formal negotiation of an individual contract, which may co-exist with a collective contract at the same time, providing its terms and conditions are not inconsistent with the collective document. On the other hand if no such contract exists, the single employee and the employer may proceed providing what is negotiated is not ultra vires. Protection is also extended by the rule that individual contracts must contain procedures for the resolution of rights disputes, as well as the various minima specified in related legislation, such as: the Holidays Act, the Wages Protection Act and the Minimum Wage Act, if these are not expressly written into the contract.

The procedure is allowed to lapse if there is no agreement. It is then presumed that the only contractual agreement that exists is implied by common law. Alternatively, the previous terms of employment can become the basis of an individual contract, clearly as a transitional measure, or if an existing collective contract is already in place, it will cover the individual worker, in the absence of a customized arrangement. The contract may be in writing, and the employee has the right to insist that it be so and that a copy be made available on application to the employer. Finally, terms may be varied at any time to accommodate local conditions and the contract may be voided for any duly specified reason.

(b) Collective employment contracts with a bargaining agent

A collective employment contract may cover all or any of an employer's work force. In addition 2 or more employers may enter into a collective employment contract with any or all of the workers in their conjoint employment. After nomination of a recognized bargaining agent, the parties then proceed to negotiations. In the absence of a settlement the principles already specified in the case of individual contracts come into force. In addition parties may be added in the form of new entrants into employment, either under common terms or as co-existent individual arrangements. Unlike the individual arrangement, collective contracts must be in writing and contain a specified expiry date. Voiding for a reason is permitted and the contract may be varied during its term by mutual agreement. Where 20 or more employees are engaged and covered by its terms, the document must under law be duly registered with the Department of Labour.

(c) Procedures for personal grievances

The provisions for the handling of personal grievances are found in Part III of the ECA and simply follow the arrangements that were laid down by the 1987 LRA. There is however an additional clause (s. 26(b)) that makes the need to place an effective grievance procedure in every contract a mandatory requirement. Because of their change of status, trade unions are now excluded from the grievance process, unless they have been duly nominated as bargaining agents. Unfortunately, suggests (Geare, 1991, p. 9) this has the effect of making informal settlements of grievances, extremely difficult.

In the matter of remedies similarities with the LRA are again present. The model procedure found in the current legislation does not contain a right of appeal against decisions. But under (s. 95) an appeal to the Employment Court against a decision handed down by the Employment Tribunal is allowed. In addition where an employment contract contains its own specially designed procedure, the same right of appeal may be written into the document.

F. Procedures for the Enforcement of Contracts

There is a statutory requirement under Part IV of the legislation that all employment contracts are to contain procedures for the settlement of disputes. These are defined as matters arising in relation to the interpretation, application or operation of an employment contract. By simply substituting the terms "award" or "agreement" in the text, we find the law has retained the disputes of rights procedures laid down in the 1987 LRA.

(a) Terms for the enforcement of employment contracts

The terms of (s. 43(d)) now specify that the process of enforcement of employment contracts is a matter to be decided by the parties. This raises the vexed question of the power of an employee working under an individual contract to both specify its terms and to ensure that the employer will operate it fairly. The answer suggests (Wedderburn, 1986) is highly problematic, since the common law principles which now underpin the ECA, utilize the "polite fiction" that the parties share an equality of power. The situation is slightly less fraught in the matter of collective contracts, since as Geare (1991, p. 10) has noted, trade unions where designated can be parties.

(b) Penalties incurred for breach of contract

The imposition of penalties for breach has always been a major problem in New Zealand. Attempts for example, to impose fines on trade unions have always proved difficult, often because of inability to pay. The authorities in turn have been reluctant to impose the latter of the law, by penalising trade union officers for default, despite the fact that under the previous law they could be made accountable for breach as individual persons.

Where breach of contract is now proven, the Employment Court is empowered to impose a fine of $2000 where the transgressor is an individual employer or employee, and up to $5000 where the defendant is company or a corporation. Where notice of enforcement has been served, failure to comply can lead in the case of an individual to a term of up to 3 months in prison and a fine. Where inability to pay is claimed, the Court may then rule that an order for the sequestration of property be made.

The balance of the legislation contains various enabling procedures and administrative details. In addition it tidies up some of the ambiguities that were contained in the statutes that is now supersedes.

G. Some Speculative Views on the New Law

This chapter has attempted to establish that the processes of labour market reform found in the 1991 Employment Contracts Act, can find lineal descent in a long tradition of the experimental use of the law to regulate the New Zealand labour market. As a consequence what the new legislation reflects is a change in tempo and the direction of reform, rather than the working out of some revolutionary agenda. On the other hand the ECA does mark quite an important shift in both ideology and value systems. These underlie what are perceived to be the imperatives of survival faced by a small open economy, in an economic world where competition is globalizing and where new forms of relationship have to be developed along the Pacific rim.

At the same time it would be dangerous to overstate the strength of continuity as a major construct of reform. While there were serious ideological ambiguities in the Labour government's commitment to economic reform, the new administration is clearly an offspring of that re-emergent centre-right tradition that has committed itself to free market policies in other parts of the world since the early 1980s. This has been reflected in the fact that the current government has if anything, strengthened the policy emphasis on monetary issues that began with the initial Labour administration in 1984. Since 1990, there has been if anything an even greater stress on reducing inflation. The social price has been an inevitable and rapid rise in unemployment.

It is also clear that government policy was influenced by two other important considerations. The fact that it could act with impunity in the matter of commitment to various special interests. The historical identification of the industrial labour movement with the Labour party, and its functional integration into the party structure required that any policy of labour market reform take cognisance of trade union interests. By contrast National government in power is able to act without any form of residual or functional obligation of that kind.

The second important variable involved the role of two major pressure groups. The evidence is in the public domain, that the New Zealand Employers' Federation played a formative role in both the design of the legislation and in its public presentation. In addition, the Business Round Table, a powerful group representing all of the large business interests in the country, and dedicated to free market principles, ran a parallel public campaign calling for the structural reform of the labour market. It is also a fact that both bodies were calling for reforms of the kind that were later introduced, for some considerable time before the election campaign. While the time frame in which the legislation was introduced covered barely seven months, government can claim, perhaps with some justification, that information about much of what it intended to do was already in the public domain, and that their landslide victory at the polls could be seen as a mandate to act.

There can be no doubt that these factors exerted a major influence on the direction that labour market reform has taken. The direction of government policy in regard to the labour market is now linked to the twin ideas that the effective protection of New Zealand's economic future can only be achieved by the development of free markets in all aspects of economic life. It is now calling for the development of an "enterprise culture" and proposes to place alongside the 1991 ECA a comprehensive industrial training act, which will introduce the right to skill development into employment contracts. If there is an element of discontinuity in the tradition of labour market reform it lies in the fact that its motivation in 1991, was not based upon the intrinsic needs of the labour market, but upon a larger determination to extend the power of market forces across the entire economy. In that sense, the labour market constituted a "last frontier" for de-regulation.

The pressure on government to continue the reform process in the labour market has recently taken on a new direction. Both the Director General of the Employers Federation and a very senior member of the Business Round Table, have publically suggested that the next step in the de-regulative process should entail the abandonment of the notion of employment contracts altogether. What they propose is that terms and conditions of employment should simply be treated as normative contractual arrangements, presumedly in the common law sense.

The idea of a labour market consisting solely and presumedly of independent contractors, may well prove too advanced a concept for event the most dedicated free market advocates, especially with an election pending in October 1993. If it is introduced one thing will be certain. It will be on the traditional basis of the state legislating through statute law.

APPENDIX ONE

The following tables are presented as a statistical summary of the activities of the New Zealand industrial relations system, prior to the passing of the Employment Contracts Act,1991. They are both a summary of the work of the various agencies, and an indication of the effects of existing legislative changes upon the activities of the parties.

Table 1. The Work of the Labour Court
(for the period 1/7/90 to 31/12/90)

Applications Outstanding at 1/7/90	360
Applications Received in period	622
Decisions Finalised	186
Applications Withdrawn	347
Applications Outstanding at 31/12/90	469

Note: The balance outstanding does not tally with the other totals due to the fact that some decisions are multiple rather than single cases.
Source: Department of Labour Report, for the Period 1/7/90 to 31/12/ 90 Appendices to the Journals of the House of Representatives, G. IHY, 1991, p. 43.

Table 2. The Work of the Arbitration Commission
(for the period 1/7/90 to 31/12/90)

(1) Conciliated Settlements	
(a) Outstanding at 1/7/90	62
(b) Completed Settlements Received	108
(c) Partial Settlements Received	0
(d) Settlements Registered	137

(2) Collective Agreements	
(a) Outstanding at 1/7/90	42
(b) Submitted	237
(c) Withdrawn	8
(d) Registered	250
(e) Outstanding at 31/12/90	21

(3) **Composite Agreements**	
(a) Outstanding at 1/7/90	1
(b) Submitted	35
(c) Registered	0
(d) Outstanding at 31/12/90	2

(4) **Redundancy Cases**	
(a) Outstanding at 1/7/90	0
(b) Submitted	165
(c) Withdrawn	5
(d) Registered	143
(e) Outstanding at 31/12/90	17

(5) **Work of the Mediation Service**	
(a) Personal Grievances Submitted	577
(b) Disputes of Rights	79
(c) Interest Disputes filed with the Chief Mediator	208
(d) Informal Hearings	7
(e) Other	24

Source: Department of Labour Report, op. cit. p. 44.

Table 3. The Number of Industrial Unions in the Private Sector 1986 and 1989

Year Ending	Number of Unions	Aggregate Membership	Average Size
1986	227	489,763	2157
1989	136	460,000	3382

Notes: (1) These figures do include the 31 state sector voluntary unions who were required to become registered under Part VII of the LRA, 1987.

(2) The figures do not include the 60 private sector unions who had been granted a moratorium of two years in order to bring membership leve to the 1000 minimum prescribed by the Act, or the 15 state organisation who were doing the same.

(3) Total trade union membership for New Zealand in 1989 was 611,000

Sources: OECD Employment Outlook, July 1991, p. 101.
New Zealand Official Year Book, 94, 190, p. 384.

Table 4. Trade Union Density Rates in New Zealand in 1988

Industrial Sector	Percentage Rate
Manufacturing	58.0
Financial/Business/Services	42.0
Community/Social/Personal Services	50.7
Construction	39.0
Skilled Trades	53.0
Transport/Communication	67.0
National Average (1988)	50.5

Decennial Percentage Change in Density of Unionisation	
Between 1970-1980	+19.0
Between 1980-1988	−23.5

Source: OECD Employment Outlook July 1991, p. 103.

Table 5. The Distribution of Trade Unions by Size and Proportion of Membership Coverage After the LRA, 1987: 1988-1989

Union/Size by Category	1988	1989	Increase/ Decrease
0-99	54	26	−28
100-500	40	26	−14
500-1000	80	18	−62
1000+	80	97	+17

Note: (1) The trend toward less but bigger unions has been endorsed by all the parties as a positive bi-partisan policy.

Source: New Zealand Official Year Book, 94, 1990, p. 384.

Table 6. Industrial Stoppages in New Zealand: 1985 - 1989

Year	Number of Stoppages	Number of Workers Involved	Working Days Lost
1985	383	182,154	756,432
1986	215	100,633	1,329,054
1987	193	80,092	366,307
1988	172	103,981	381,710
1989	163	85,844	168,743

Note: The "blowout" for working days lost in 1986, is attributed to 12 strikes in the meat exporting industry. Some 43,184 workers were involved, 986,780 working days were lost and $93,743,927 in wages were forfeited.

Source: Ministerial Briefing by the Hon. Helen Clark, 12 September 1990.

Table 7. Hourly Rates ($NZ) in Paid Employment in Non-Agricultural and Manufacturing by Gender, Plus Movements in Consumer Prices: 1987 - 1990

Year	Males	Females	Total
(1) Non-Agricultural Activities			
1987	12.49	9.92	11.46
1988	13.70	11.01	12.61
1989	14.47	11.70	13.83
1990	15.45	12.45	14.19
(2) Manufacturing			
1987	11.87	8.61	10.95
1988	12.89	9.61	11.99
1989	13.51	10.17	12.62
1990	14.37	10.77	13.43
(3) Changes in Consumer Prices (1980=100)			
1987	230.9		
1988	245.6		
1989	259.6		
1990	275.6		

Note: The figures constitute the mean of all estimates supplied.

Source: ILO Bulletin of Labour Statistics, 1991 (2), p. 100 and p. 110.

Table 8. Estimates of Real Unit Labour Costs in Business, Manufacturing and Services in New Zealand: 1985-1988
(average for period = 100)

Category	1985	1986	1987	1988
(a) Business	94.1	98.2	99.5	95.2
(b) Manufacturing	97.3	96.4	100.5	97.2
(c) Services	98.7	96.7	98.3	94.6

Source: OECD Employment Outlook, July 1991, p. 57

APPENDIX TWO

THE EMERGING PATTERN OF CONTRACTUAL OUTCOMES

It is still difficult to establish a clear grasp of the impact of the ECA,1991 on labour market behaviours in New Zealand. Difficulties have been complicated by the fact that there are a significant number of collective arrangements which came into force prior to 19 May 1991, which are now coming to full term.

What follows is the reporting of trend indications of the basis of returns on contracts involving 20 or more employees as at July 1992. The New Zealand Department of Labour has processed some 456 contracts to July 1992, which covers 111.684 employees, or 8 % of the labour force. They advise the following trends appear to be emerging.

Most contracts to date appear to be enterprise based (multi-firm) and the incidence of self representation appears to be on the increase. Basic wage movements appear to fall for the most part into two broad bands, either zero or 2 %. Some 46.2 % of employees obtained a pay increase of 1 % or more, equal to or better than the rate of inflation.

Almost 50 % of employees received a zero wage increase. It is also noticeable that contracts are not locking in wage increases above the rate of inflation. Some 228 of the 456 contracts noted have introduced the concept of remuneration packages. The principal recipients appear to be smaller groups of employees. Such arrangements reveal that 43 % of these contracts have obtained more than the average wage increase of 2 %. In addition they retain overtime penal rate clauses of the standard ratio form of 1.5 on the hourly rate for Saturdays and 2.0 for Sundays.

Overtime is conditional in many contracts, with just over 50 % containing appropriate clauses. But it is also reported that serious modifications are being made to the penal rate ratios, with 21.7 % of contracts revealing the removal of the additional differential for Sunday work. Remuneration packages also indicate a distinct trend toward performance related remuneration together with the incorporation of individual allowances into either a compounded wage rate or a single allowance.

While the forty hour week remains the standard measure for contracts, there is evidence that employers are treating the working week as a span of time in which target hours are to be worked. This appears to be leading to the extension of hours of work within the forty hour norm, but more attuned to the exigencies of short run surges in work requirements.

Some 73 % of contracts have terms of between 9 to 15 months duration. a further 11 % have a term of more than 18 month.

In the matter of trade union coverage, estimates of the number of employees who have been effectively "de-collectivised" run as high as 300.000. Despite this unions appear to be holding the line on collective bargaining despite a reported 20 % fall in membership. Real evidence is sketchy at this time, but there would appear to be a serious need for a code of minimum employment that both complies with the requirements of various international standards and conventions, and protects the rights particularly of employees in small firms located in regional locations, that are increasingly beginning to feel the effects of an emergent dual labour market.

The overall effect of the law on the collective bargaining process reveals that there has been a significant decline in activity in sectors such as: agriculture; food and beverage production; textiles and clothing; paper and printing; retailing, building and construction and transport. By contrast it remains strongly preferred in: utilities production; wholesaling; communications; finance and the public sector.

REFERENCES

Atkinson, John, Flexibility and Fragmentation? The United Kingdom Labour Market in the Eighties, *Labour and Society*, Vol. 12, No. 1, 1987: 87-105.

Boston, Jonathan, *Incomes Policy in New Zealand*, Wellington, Institute for Policy Studies and Victoria University Press, 1984, p. 337.

Blyton, Paul, and Jonathan Morris (eds.), *A Flexible Future; Perspectives for Employment and Organisation*, Berlin, de Gruyter, 1991.

Boyer, Robert, *In Search of Labour Market Flexibility*, Oxford, Clarendon Press, 1988.

Bradford, Max, Reporting Back Speech to the New Zealand House of Representatives, on the Employment Contracts Bill, Wellington, *Hansard*, 23 April 1991.

Deeks, John, New Tracks, Old Maps: Continuity and Change in New Zealand Industrial Relations: 1984-1990, *New Zealand Journal of Industrial Relations*, Vol. 15, No. 1, August 1990: 99-116.

Department of Labour, Statement by the Hon. William Birch, *The Dominion*, 24 April 1992.

Geare, Alan, The Employment Contracts Act, 1991, Research Centre for Industrial Relations and Labour Studies, Department of Economics, University of Otago, Discussion Paper, 91/01, June 1991.

Harbridge, Raymond, Collective Bargaining in New Zealand: the early Effects of New Legislative Arrangements, Communication to the 3rd European Congress of the International Industrial Relations Association, Bari, Italy, 23-26 September 1991.

Harbridge, Raymond, and Stuart McCaw, The First Wage Round Under the Labour Relations Act, 1987: Changing Relative Power, *The New Zealand Journal of Industrial Relations*, Vol. 14, No. 2, 1989: 149-168.

Harbridge, Raymond and James Moulder, Freedom to Bargain: a Review of the First Year of Bargaining under New Zealand's Employment Contract Legislation, Communication to the 9th World Congress of the International Industrial Relations Association, Sydney, 30 August-3 September 1992.

Hughes, John, *Labour Law in New Zealand*, Sydney, The Law Book Company, 1989: 1893.

Holt, Michael, *Compulsory Arbitration and Conciliation in New Zealand: the First Forty Years*, Auckland, Auckland University Press, 1986.

Howe, Kerry, P., *Singer in a Songless Land: A Life of Edward Tregear*, Auckland, Auckland University Press, 1991.

Howells, John M., Concentration and Growth in New Zealand Trade Unions: 1900-1966, *Journal of Industrial Relations*, Vol. 12, January 1970: 39-51.

Layard, Richard, and Lars Calmfors (eds.), *The Fight Against Unemployment*, Cambridge, Mass, MIT Press, 1986.

New Zealand Department of Labour, Contracts, No. 3, July 1992.

New Zealand Official Year Book, 94, 1990: 384.

Piore, Michael J. and Charles, Sabel, *The Second Industrial Divide: Possibilities for Prosperity*, New York, Basic Books, 1984.

Pollert, Anna, *Farewell to Flexibility?*, Oxford, Basil Blackwell, 1991.

Reeves, William. P., *State Experiments in Australia and New Zealand*, 2 Vols, Melbourne, 1902.

Stone, Russell, The Origins and Development of the Industrial Conciliation and Arbitration Act: 1894-1937, in: Sinclair, Keith, and Robert Chapman (eds.), *Studies of A Small Democracy*, Auckland, Blackwood and Janet Paul, 1963.

Shipley, The Hon. Jennifer, Statement in the House of Representatives, *Hansard*, 23 April 1992.

Smith, Ian S., Is Employment Properly Analysed in Terms of Contract?, *New Zealand Universities Law Review*, Vol. 6, 1974-75: 341-66.

The Treasury, *Economic Management*, Wellington, Government Printer, Vol. 2, ch. 13.

Walsh, Patrick, The Struggle for Power and Control in the New Corporations: the First Year of Industrial Relations in State Owned Enterprises, *New Zealand Journal of Industrial Relations*, Vol. 13, No. 2, 1988: 190-199.

Wedderburn of Charlton, Lord, *The Worker and the Law*, 3rd. ed., Middlesex, Penguin Books, 1986.

Williams, Alan, Industrial Relations, in: Lane, Peter, and Paul Hamer (eds.), *Decade of Change: Economic Growth and Prospects in New Zealand: 1960-1970*, Wellington, Reed Research Studies, 1973.

Williams, Alan, *Industrial Militancy in New Zealand: The Contributing Influence of the Industrial Conciliation and Arbitration Act, and Its Administration, 1894-1908*. Unpublished Ph.D. thesis, Massey University, 1976.

Williams, Alan, *Power, Conflict, Control, Recurring Themes in Industrial Relations Theory*, Palmerston North, Dunmore Press, 1984.

Woods, Noel S., *Industrial Conciliation and Arbitration in New Zealand*, Wellington, Government Printer, 1963.

Labour Market Contracts and Institutions
J. Hartog and J. Theeuwes (Editors)

CHAPTER 5

THE JAPANESE LABOUR MARKET:
Its Institutions and Performance

Yoshio Sasajima*

A. Introduction

A.1 The Structure of the Labour Market

(a) Changes on the labour supply side

The Japanese labour market has been changing rapidly. With regard to the labour supply side, it can be first pointed out that the aging of the labour force has been rapid, reflecting the aging of the population. The share of those aged 55 years and over in the total labour force was 16 per cent in 1980, and 20 per cent in 1990. It is expected to reach 24 per cent by the year 2000. This trend toward the aging of the labour force will continue until around 2025. Though the young population in the labour force has gradually been increasing until now, it is forecasted that it will start declining rapidly after 1995, reflecting the long-run trend of the declining birth rate.

Second, more and more women have been participating in the labour market. The participation rate of women increased from 46 per cent in 1975 to 50 per cent in 1989. It increased especially for middle-aged married women. The trend is expected to continue in the near future. Third, the educational attainment of the newly-hired has been improving year after year. The enrolment ratio of secondary and higher education is in an upward trend, registering about 94 per cent for secondary education and 37 per cent for higher education in 1989. Among women who enter higher education, about half enrol in two-year colleges and the remaining half in four-year colleges, while almost all men taking higher education enrol in four-year colleges. Since many of those who do not enter higher education spend two or three years in vocational school, about half of the same birth cohort spend somehow a few years in school after their graduation from senior high school. As a result, new college graduates accounted for about 47 per cent of those newly-hired among the new school leavers in 1989.

* Professor, Faculty of Economics, Meijigakuin University, Shirogane-dai, Minato-ku, Tokyo.

(b) Changes on the labour demand side

With regard to the labour demand side, it can be first pointed out that a shift toward the service sector has been taking place in the economy. The proportion of employment in tertiary industry increased from 47 per cent to 58 per cent between 1970 and 1989, and is expected to reach 62 per cent in 2000. The increase is especially striking in the wholesale and retail trade and in restaurants, and personal and business services. Second, the proportion of white-collar workers among the employed has been increasing. The proportion increased from 37 per cent to 48 per cent between 1970 and 1989, and is expected to reach 55 per cent in 2000. The increase is especially pronounced in professional and technical occupations. Third, part-time employment is rapidly expanding. In Japan, the definition of part-time workers is not yet clear, which makes it difficult to estimate the size of the part-time employment. If they are defined as employees in non-agricultural industries who actually worked less than 35 hours in the survey week, part-time employment in 1989 was 6020 thousand out of 45920 thousand, a 54 per cent increase over the 1980 level. On the other hand, full-time employment increased by 14 per cent in the same period. The definition just employed is not proper, however. This is because they include many full-time workers who worked short during the week. Another reason is that there are many workers who are said to be part-time workers in the firm, but who work more than 35 hours a week.[1] Thus, if they are defined as those whose contract status in an enterprise is part-time workers, then part-time employment in 1989 was 5060 thousand. Adding to this "arubaito workers",[2] who are in fact part-time workers, total part-time employment becomes 7100 thousand. It should be mentioned that the size of employment at a temporary employment agency, 380 thousand in 1989, is relatively small although it is increasing. The reason why it is rather small is that the jobs open for those from temporary employment agencies are restricted to certain fields by the Worker Dispatching Law. There are two types of the agency, the one dispatching its own employees and the other dispatching workers in the register.

---

1. The distribution of part-time workers according to weekly hours worked is as follows; those working less than 35 hours account for 63 per cent, those 35 to less than 49 hours for 32 per cent, those 49 hours and over for 4 per cent.(Management and Coordination Agency, *Special Survey of the Labour Force Survey*, February 1989).

2. The term "arubaito" (from the German Arbeit) is generally used to refer to part-time and/or short-term employment. The most common form of arubaito is casual, part-time work done by students at nights and weekends in and around the large cities. One survey indicated that 64 per cent of Japanese college students were regularly engaged in this sort of work.

(c) Other changes

The Japanese economy has been expanding quite rapidly since the end of 1986, which has led to a severe labour shortage situation in the labour market. The current unemployment rate has been around 2.1 per cent since the beginning of 1990. The labour shortage is especially acute in low-paid and low-skilled jobs such as dirty, dangerous and demanding jobs. In response, many illegal foreign workers have been penetrating into these job markets. Another important development is the wide spread phenomena of a reduction in working hours in the form of additional paid leave, five-day work week, a week long vacation and so on. The labour shortage problem has led many companies to reduce working hours, which in turn may enable them to more easily recruit workers. Although shorter hours seem to worsen the labour shortage situation, historically working hours has been reduced substantially during the labour shortage period. It is being repeated. Another important development is the changing attitude of workers toward their job. The major work force of many companies is slowly changing from one with workers born before and during the Second World War to one with workers born after the war. The latter grew up in affluent times and were more educated than the former generation, so their values are different from the former generation. According to a government survey, the proportion of those who regard work as making their everyday life worthwhile is declining. The sense of identity with their company is also weakening.

A.2 Social Security System

There are four social insurance schemes, which are intended to protect workers from various expected and unexpected causes. The unemployment insurance scheme started in 1947 with the enactment of the Unemployment Insurance Law. In 1974, the Law was revised so as not only to cover unemployment benefits, but also to cover various employment programmes such as training, employment stability, improvement of job environment and so forth. Unemployment benefits, 60 to 80 per cent of previous daily wages of an unemployed person, are paid for a certain period, which is set according to the age of the unemployed and the length of his contribution to the fund. Those aged under 30 years receive a benefit for 90 to 180 days, those aged 30 to 40 years for 90 to 210 days, those aged 45 to 54 years for 90 to 240 days, those aged 55 to 64 years for 90 to 300 days. The previous daily wages are calculated by dividing gross earnings of the last six months by 180 days. In addition, those unemployed from designated areas and industries are entitled to an additional 90 days benefit. The areas and industries are designated according to their employment situation by the Ministry of Labour on the basis of the related laws. The premium rate for unemployment benefit, one per cent of gross salary, is borne equally by employers and workers. The premium for the various employment programmes is paid solely by employers.

The National Employees Pension Scheme (NEPS) started in 1943 with the enactment of the National Employees Pension Scheme Law. The present pensionable age is 60 years for men, and 56 years for women. The pensionable age for women will be progressively raised to 60 years by 2000. The pension amount is composed of two parts, a fixed part and an earnings-related part. The premium, currently 12.4 per cent of wages, is shared equally between employers and workers. It is expected that because of the aging of the population the NEPS will face severe financial problems under the present scheme, and that one option to get around this problem is to raise the pensionable age to 65 years. Even so, it is estimated that the premium rate will increase to about 30 per cent of salary around the year 2020.

The Health Insurance Scheme started in 1922 with the enactment of the Health Insurance Law. The premium rate is also rising, reflecting the aging of the population. The current rate is 8.5 per cent shared equally by employers and workers.

The Workmen's Compensation Scheme is based on the Workmen's Compensation Law of 1947. It is financed by employers' contributions. The premium rate differs from industry to industry in order to reflect the injury rate of each industry. The premium rate also differs among companies in the same industry to encourage them to reduce injuries.

Additional programmes of the social security system include social assistance for poor families and a children's fund designed to aid low-income families with children.

A.3 Brief History of the Labour Law

Japan's major labour laws were mostly enacted after the Second World War. As a way to democratize Japan, the Allied Occupation Army promoted fostering labour unions and the enactment of the Labour Union Law of 1945. Frequent labour disputes prompted the government to enact the Labour Relations Adjustment Law of 1946. The Labour Standards Law of 1947 and the Employment Security Law of 1947 were designed to protect workers, to improve their status in the society, and to improve their employment situation. Also enacted during the immediate post-war period were the Unemployment Insurance Law of 1947, which was later revised and renamed the Employment Insurance Law of 1974, and the Workmen's Compensation Law of 1947. Both the Minimum Wage Law of 1959 and the Safety and Health Law of 1972 were enacted and became independent of the Labour Standards Law. The Employment Measures Basic Law of 1966, which is designed to prepare basic employment policies, and the Vocational Training Law of 1969 (revised in 1985 and renamed the Human Resources Development Law) were enacted under the gradual expansion of the national economy and employment. The Employment Promotion Laws targeted to the physically handicapped and the middle-aged and older people were enacted in 1960 and 1971, respectively. Under the unstable economic growth period after the first oil shock, the Local Employment Measures Law was enacted in 1977 to cope with employment problems arising from the structural changes in the economy. The Equal Employment Opportunity Law was enacted in 1985 under the influence of the worldwide movement for equality between men and women. The Worker Dispatching Law was enacted in the same year. Two social security-related laws, the Health Insurance Law of 1921 and the National Pension Scheme Law of 1943, were enacted before the war.

The laws mentioned above have been revised from time to time so as to reflect changes in the national economy and the labour market.

A.4 Collective Agreement, Labour Contracts and Labour Laws

As will be discussed below, the Japanese rate of unionization is currently around 25 per cent. Almost all collective agreements are concluded between a company and a company-based union. As a result, there is limited scope for collective agreements to influence labour conditions in the unorganized sector. Thus, the contents of the collective agreement are important for the organized sector while the labour legislation plays a significant role in the conditions of unorganized workers. Naturally, labour conditions in Japan differ significantly between the organized sector and the unorganized sector, namely between large companies and small and medium-sized companies. Some kinds of labour conditions do not differ much from the standards required by the labour laws even in the organized sector.

B. The Institutional and Legal Environment

B.1 The Industrial Relations Structure

(a) Labour union structure

The basic structure of the Japanese labour union is mostly enterprise-based organization. Classifying labour unions according to their base, it can be observed that enterprise-based unions account for 94 per cent of all the independent unions (83 per cent of total union membership), occupation-based for 1 per cent (1 per cent), industry-based for 3 per cent (13 per cent) and others for 2 per cent (3 per cent) (Ministry of Labour, *Labour Union Basic Survey*, 1975).

An enterprise-based organization implies one that is organized by the workers within the same enterprise. Generally speaking, workers of each enterprise are organized solely by one union. However, in some large corporations, an independent union is organized at each establishment of the corporation. These independent unions of the same enterprise generally form a federation. As a result, it turns out to be one large enterprise-based union. Thus, almost all unions in Japan are enterprise-based or establishment-based.

The major characteristics of enterprise-based unions are as follows. First, union members are in general restricted to full-time regular workers of the enterprise concerned. Full-time regular workers are here defined as full-time workers with indefinite-term employment contract (see Diagram 1). Both blue- and white-collar workers are organized in the same union as long as they are full-time regular workers. Second, union officials are also restricted to full-time regular workers of the enterprise concerned. Thus, both full-time and part-time union officials assume their position in the union while freezing their positions in the company. Therefore, a full-time union official usually returns to his previous position he used to work for as one of the employees after his service to the union. The typical length of union service is either two or four years.

Diagram 1. Concept of Full-Time and Part-Time Workers

Full-time workers		
(a) regular workers	→	indefinite-term contract
(b) temporary workers	→	fixed-term contract
Part-time workers		
(a) part-time status	→	indefinite-term contract
(b) part-time status	→	fixed-term contract

Notes: (1) Part-time workers are here defined as those whose contract status is part-time status, but it does not necessarily mean that they work substantially shorter than full-time workers. As mentioned in footnote 1 of the text, many part-time workers work almost as long as full-time workers. Part-time workers who work almost as long as full-time workers can be said full-time temporary workers.

(2) The so-called lifetime employment is generally applied to regular workers above. In addition, most enterprise-based unions are organized solely by regular workers as well.

Third, an enterprise-based union has a free hand in the union management and union budget. Although many enterprise-based unions join one of the industrial federations and/or local federations, and may take uniform actions along the lines of the federation, whether or not they take part in such uniform action is decided by each enterprise-based union. These federations are not able to control the decision-making and activities of the enterprise-based unions. The extent to which an enterprise-based union follows the advice and guidelines of the federation are left to the will of each enterprise-based union. The point just made is also true of the relationship between national confederations and industrial federations. Similarly important is the independence of the union finances. How much, and in what way, union dues should be collected are decided by each enterprise-based union. The enterprise-based union contributes a portion of the union dues collected to the budget of the industrial federation, and to the national confederation according to the size of its membership.

It is quite natural to say that labour unions tend to be organized on the basis of each enterprise under the so-called lifetime employment practice, and the seniority wage rule, and strong attachment to the company. The number of independent unions was 72,222 in 1990, much more than in other countries, reflecting the background mentioned above.

In contrast to enterprise-based unions, industrial unions such as the Seamen's Union and occupational unions such as Zenken-souren organize workers in a specific industry or occupation irrespective of their company. In addition, there exist general unions such as Zenkokuippan and Un-yuippan which organize workers irrespective of industry or occupation.

(b) Federations of labour unions

Many enterprise-based unions join the industrial federation organized for each industry. There are more than 200 industrial federations at present. Major industrial federations with more than 400 thousand members are Jitirou (prefectural and municipal workers, 1061 thousand in 1990), Jidousha-souren (automobile workers, 728 thousand), Denki-rouren (electrical machine workers 720 thousand), Zensen-doumei (textile, garment, chemical and distributive workers, 529 thousand), Zenken-souren (construction workers, 481 thousand), and Seiho-rouren (life insurance workers, 457 thousand), Nikkyouso (teachers, 440 thousand)(Ministry of Labour, *Labour Union Basic Survey*, 1990). As mentioned earlier, independent establishment-based unions and their federations are formed in some of the giant corporations. In these cases, the federation is treated in the national scene of the labour movement as one of the industrial federations.

Industrial federations form a national confederation. After a long history, today, there are two major national confederations: Rengou (Japanese Trade Union Confederation) and Zenrouren (National Confederation of Trade Unions). Their membership was about 7614 and 835 thousand workers in 1990, respectively. The difference between the two is found in their political position. Industrial federations in the machinery and metal industries, all being members of Rengou, form the IMF-JC (Japan Council of Metalworkers' Unions, 2306 thousand), irrespective of the difference in their political position, which acts as if it were a national confederation. Similar organizations are Kou-un roukyou (866 thousand), formed mainly by industrial federations in the transportation industries, and Kagaku-roukyou (628 thousand), formed mainly by industrial federations in the chemical and petro-chemical industries.

(c) Employers' organizations

In each region, employer groups form their associations under their name of the region. Also formed are employers' associations for each industry. The central body representing these associations is Nikkeiren (Japan Federation of Employers' Associations). These employers' groups promote solidarity on labour issues in addition to offering such services as collecting relevant information, undertaking public relations work and research work, and proposing labour policies on behalf of member employers. As of 1990, the members of Nikkeiren were 47 regional associations and 55 industrial associations, grouping in total about 30 thousand companies.

Also, other active employers' organizations are Chuuoukai, the members of which are medium-sized and small enterprises, and Shoukoukai for small enterprises.

Although neither Nikkeiren nor other employers' groups participate in collective bargaining on behalf of member employers, they do influence labour-management relations by issuing statements prior to the annual spring labour offensive outlining the employers' basic stand and presenting wage increase levels that are acceptable from the employers' points of view. Every year, Nikkeiren makes public a report on wages and related issues to represent their position. In 1970, it proposed a productivity-based wage determination principle as a rational wage increase standard in order to stop the vicious cycle of the wage-price spiral.

(d) Union membership rates

The unionization rate has been declining in recent years as shown in Table 1. It is noteworthy that the unionization rate differs significantly between groups of workers in the larger and smaller enterprises. In 1990, the rate was 61 per cent for workers in enterprises with 1000 employees and more, 24 per cent for workers in enterprises with 100 to 999 employees, and 2 per cent for workers in enterprises with less than 100 employees (Table 2). The major reason for the difference is that it is easier to form an enterprise-based union in a larger enterprise due to the availability of the necessary staff and funds.

Table 1. Union, Union Membership, and Unionization Rates

Year	Number of Unions	Union Membership (in thousands)	Unionization Rates (in percent)
1945	509	381	3.2
1950	29114	5774	46.2
1955	32012	6286	35.6
1960	41561	7662	32.2
1965	52879	10147	34.8
1970	60954	11605	35.4
1975	69333	12590	34.4
1980	72693	12369	30.8
1985	74499	12418	28.9
1986	74183	12343	28.2
1987	73138	12272	27.6
1988	72792	12277	26.8
1989	72605	12277	25.9
1990	72222	12265	25.2

Source: Ministry of Labour, *Labour Union Basic Survey*

Table 2. Unionization Ratio by Size of Firm and Industry (%)

	1960	1970	1980	1985	1990
Private sector	–	28.5	24.5	24.3	21.9
Public sector	–	82.2	74.5	61.7	–
500 and more	67.1	63.9	61.1	59.9	61.0[(a)]
100 to 499	36.4	30.7	27.8	24.3	24.0[(b)]
30 to 99	8.0	8.9	7.4	6.7	2.0[(c)]
Construction	30.0	25.0	16.2	19.3	17.1
Manufacturing	32.6	38.0	34.7	32.9	30.1
Wholesale and retail trade	–	9.7	10.4	10.6	9.0
Bank, insurance and real estate	–	68.5	56.8	49.9	49.7
Transportation and communication	–	63.9	51.5	56.9	48.3
Utility	–	76.9	79.7	67.9	70.7
Services	27.6	26.2	23.0	20.1	14.8
Government	59.7	65.6	69.1	71.0	74.9
Total	32.2	35.4	30.8	28.9	25.2

Notes: (a) 1000 employees and more; (b) 100 to 999 employees; (c) under 100 employees
Source: Ministry of Labour, *Labour Unions Basic Survey*

The rate is higher in manufacturing, and transportation and communication and lower in the wholesale and retail trade, and services. The unionization of both men and women is declining. Between 1980 and 1990, it declined from 34 per cent to 29 per cent for men, and from 25 per cent to 18 per cent for women.

Total union membership has been around 12 million despite the increase in the number of people employed. About one third of union membership is concentrated in manufacturing while about ten per cent is in transportation and communication, the public sector, and services.

Although there is no data on the union participation rate for age groups, it is estimated that the union participation rate seems to be lower for older workers. This is because older people tend to assume the managerial position under the seniority-based promotion system, managers being treated as non-union members. As a result, the participation rate should be higher for younger people.

B.2 The Bargaining Structure

(a) Type of bargaining

From the foregoing discussion, we know that the bulk of Japanese labour unions is company-based. Thus, almost all wage negotiations take place at the level of each company. As an exceptional case, wage negotiation is held between an employers association and an industrial federation in the case of Zen-nikkai (All Japan Seamen's Union) and Shitetu-souren (General Federation of Private Railway Workers' Unions of Japan). In addition, in companies where some employees are members of a general union, negotiation is held between representatives from the company and those from the general union. In such a case, the companies concerned are generally small or medium-sized.

Similarly, negotiation is held at the company-level as long as negotiated matters are somehow related to the working conditions of all workers in the company. However, in the case of matters related to the working conditions of a specific branch of a company, the negotiation takes place at the company-level or the branch-level depending on the nature of the matters.

Both industrial federations and national confederations play a significant role in formulating wage demands and strike schedules, setting the minimum levels of wage hikes, collecting relevant information, and so forth. In this way, they lead member unions toward a better position in the negotiation. As mentioned earlier, generally they do not participate in negotiations, with some exceptions.

Taking a look at the negotiating members of unions in the collective bargaining held in 1987, those who "negotiated only with the union officials concerned" account for 84 per cent of unions, "negotiated together with officials from the upper organization within the same enterprise" for 18 per cent, and "negotiated together with officials from the upper organization outside the enterprise" for 9 per cent. Though the proportion of the unions involved in collective bargaining in 1987 was 77 per cent, 40 per cent among the remaining "23 per cent" of unions reported that their upper organization was engaged in the collective bargaining in place of them. From the foregoing statistics, the proportion of unions whose upper organizations outside their enterprises were involved in the collective bargaining was 16 per cent. The proportion was larger for smaller enterprises.[3]

(b) Frequency of bargaining

Wage bargaining takes place once a year. Since 1955, many unions have been concentrating their wage bargaining in the spring time. This is called the spring labour offensive. At present, about 80 per cent of union members participate in the spring labour offensive. In the case of enterprises where no union is organized, wage hikes are implemented taking account of the outcome of the spring offensive.

Bonuses, which are a part of wages and are discussed below, are paid twice a year (summer time and year-end) in most companies. The amount of bonus is determined through negotiations between labour and management. In some cases, the amount of both summer and year-end bonuses are decided at the same time, while in others the amount of each bonus is decided at separate times.

The labour conditions and other matters other than wages are taken up and negotiated at the same time as wage negotiations in most bargaining. Since the bulk of negotiation time is spent on wage negotiation, other matters are negotiated at a different time in some cases.

B.3 Legal Structure of Collective Agreements

(a) Union's right to represent

On the basis of the National Constitution, any worker can organize a union, demand collective bargaining from the company, and engage in an industrial action. How-

3. Figures here are based on the following survey, Ministry of Labour, *Fact-finding Survey on Collective Bargaining and Labour Dispute*, 1987.

ever, a labour union is required to satisfy certain conditions set by the Trade Union Law if it wishes to be protected under the Law. The conditions are as follows. First, those who represent the interest of management, such as senior managers, must not be members of the union. Second, no financial aid for the union operation is given to the union by the management.

With regard to the number of the unions operating in the same enterprise, one-company-one-union is generally observed in most companies. The proportion of establishments with more than one union was 14 per cent in 1988 according to a Ministry of Labour survey (*Fact-finding Survey of Labour Unions*). The remaining 86 per cent of establishments had one union. Also mentioned is the wide-spread practice of a union-shop agreement between the union and management. The same survey shows that union shop is arranged in 61 per cent of unions surveyed, the proportion being especially higher for larger unions (97 per cent for unions with 5000 members and more, 92 per cent for unions with 1000 to 4999 members). It requires compulsory membership for full-time regular workers.

According to the Trade Union Law, an employer can not refuse a demand for collective bargaining from the union or the upper organization commissioned by the union without good reason. Such refusal is regarded as an unfair labour practice.

Labour unions are guaranteed rights to represent members of the union. Various labour laws prescribe that a union organising more than half of workers in an establishment can conclude with management important agreements on overtime work and holiday work arrangement, flexi-time, safety committee members and so forth.

(b) Influence of negotiated results

The outcome of collective bargaining is applied to all union members in the case of one-union companies. In addition, if a union organizes more than three-fourths of the workers in the company, the Trade Union Law prescribes that the outcome also be applied to non-union members as the general binding power. If more than one union is organized, then the outcome of the negotiation for each union is applied to the members of each union. Whether negotiated results are applied to non-union members is left to the discretion of the employer concerned. In most cases, however, similar terms and conditions of employment are also set to non-union members.

In addition, in the case where the most workers of some kind in a region are under the same collective agreement, then the agreement is applied to workers of the same kind and from the same region at the request of either one or both of parties concerned, on the condition of the approval of the Labour Commission. However, this has so far rarely been implemented, since most collective agreements are concluded on a company basis.

(c) Extent of negotiation over employment

The matters to be taken up in the collective bargaining are not specified in the Trade Union Law. The Ministry of Labour survey of 1987 shows that the collective agreements were concluded for 92 per cent of unions within the last three years. 48 per cent of the collective agreements included regulations concerning dismissal, 45 per cent transfer within the company, 42 per cent temporary and/or permanent transfer to subsidiaries and other companies. Where individual or collective dismissal is regulated by collective agreement, 19 per cent of agreements require union approval for dismissal, while 46 per cent require consultation prior to the dismissal. Where dismissal is not regulated, however, approval or consultation is still needed as an established practice or through joint consultation system (see Table 3).

Table 3. Collective Agreement on Personnel Management

	Extent of union involvement (%)							
	(1)	(2)	(3)	(4)	(5)	(6)	(7)	(8)
Prescribed in agreement								
Dismissal	18.9	46.1	9.1	10.9	3.7	4.5	3.8	2.9
Transfer[(a)]	12.1	31.6	6.5	26.8	10.7	8.4	1.4	2.5
Secondment[(b)]	17.8	33.6	5.8	23.5	7.6	6.3	2.2	3.2
No provision in agreement								
Dismissal	9.4	31.3	9.0	13.6	7.0	12.6	10.3	6.7
Transfer[(a)]	6.4	17.3	6.0	19.6	12.1	24.1	6.7	7.8
Secondment[(b)]	5.8	17.7	4.5	15.8	7.3	23.0	13.5	12.8
Total								
Dismissal	16.6	38.9	8.4	11.5	3.4	7.9	7.9	5.4
Transfer[(a)]	9.0	23.7	6.2	22.8	11.5	17.0	4.0	5.4
Secondment[(b)]	10.9	24.4	5.0	19.0	7.5	15.9	8.7	8.5

Legenda: (1) approval needed from union; (2) consultation with union; (3) opinion solicited from union; (4) notice to union needed prior to the decision; (5) notice to union needed after the decision; (6) nothing; (7) others; (8) no answer.

Notes: (a) transfer within the company; (b) temporary and permanent transfers to subsidiaries and/or related companies.

Source: Ministry of Labour, "*Fact-finding Survey on Collective Agreement*", 1987

Table 4. Matters Discussed at the Joint Consultation

Matters discussed	(1)	Extent of union involvement			
		(2)	(3)	(4)	(5)
On management issues					
Management policy	56.5	77.6	8.5	11.7	2.2
Production/sales plan	59.5	66.3	12.5	18.6	2.5
Management organization	59.6	61.3	13.0	19.4	6.3
New technology/rationalization	55.8	39.3	18.5	37.5	4.6
On personnel management					
Recruitment/job assignment	50.9	42.2	21.1	29.3	7.4
Transfer/secondment to subsidiaries	58.3	29.0	17.6	37.0	16.4
Laid-off, dismissal	61.9	10.6	8.4	55.7	25.2
On labour conditions					
Working system	79.2	11.1	11.7	57.9	19.4
Working hours/holidays	85.8	9.1	9.6	56.3	25.1
Safety/health	85.6	11.5	17.8	61.9	8.8
Compulsory retirement age	69.9	13.1	6.9	48.4	31.6
Wages/bonuses	69.9	16.2	4.4	52.7	26.6
Retirement benefits	65.7	16.6	5.5	49.7	28.3
On other issues					
Education/training	63.3	40.9	18.8	32.8	7.5
Fringe benefits	81.5	14.8	20.4	56.5	8.3
Recreation activities	72.8	16.5	22.0	53.1	8.4

Legenda: (1) proportion of establishments where the matter concerned is discussed; (2) explanation to union; (3) opinion solicited from union; (4) consultation with union; (5) approval needed from union

Source: Ministry of Labour, *Survey on Communication between Labour and Management*, 1989

With regard to the introduction of new technology, 34 per cent of agreements require prior consultation, 32 per cent prescribe some regulation concerning deployment due to such introduction, and 31 per cent include an employment security clause.

In Japan, the labour-management joint consultation system is not legally required, but widely spread.[4] Since most Japanese unions are company-based, both union and management representatives for joint consultation tend to be the same as, or similar to, those for collective bargaining. In other words, it is often difficult to tell joint

4. 58 per cent of establishments within companies with 50 or more employees have some form of labour-management consultation, with the percentage being higher among larger corporations. The percentage is 78 per cent for establishments with a union and 39 per cent where no union is organized (Ministry of Labour, *Survey on Labour-Management Communication*, 1989).

consultation from collective bargaining. It should be noted that in many cases labour-management joint consultation is held to discuss matters in detail before moving to the stage of collective bargaining. Table 4 shows the types of matters to be taken up in the consultation.

(d) Handling of industrial disputes

The labour commissions, set up under the provisions of the Trade Unions Law, are prepared to solve the labour disputes. These commissions, composed of representatives from labour, management and public-interests, operate at both the national and local levels. Representatives from labour, generally officials of a major industrial federation, represent both union and non-union members. The Labour Relations Adjustment Law, coupled with the Trade Union Law, is designed to bring stability to industrial relations by preventing and/or solving speedily labour disputes. The Law prescribes the procedures of the labour dispute adjustment, there being conciliation, mediation and arbitration. Any one of these means can be initiated at the request of either labour or management or at the initiative of the commission. Among these, mediation and arbitration are rarely employed to handle disputes. With regard to labour disputes in industries such as transportation, postal service, communication, electricity, gas, water-supply, medical services and so forth, the Law requires a union to inform of its industrial action 10 days prior to the action, and contains an injunction clause which enables the Prime Minister to request the postponement of the action for 50 days.

Since state corporations (the postal service, forestry, printing, the mint) are prohibited from engaging in any act of dispute by the National Enterprise Labour Relations Law, compulsory adjustment means can be employed as a final resort after all efforts such as conciliation and mediation fail to solve the problem.

According to the Trade Union Law, a strike can not be conducted without a majority decision based on the direct and secret ballot of either union members or union delegates elected by the direct and secret ballot of union members. In this way, easy actions of strikes are prevented. In fact, most unions do not start a strike without the consent of two thirds of their members. Lock-outs are not prescribed in the Law at all.

(e) Developments in labour disputes

The number of labour disputes, the number of participants in such disputes and the days lost thereby declined sharply during the recession in the wake of the first oil shock as the rate of inflation declined (Table 5).

Table 5. Labour Disputes

Year	Total disputes	Strikes for more than half a day/lockouts		
		Disputes	Workers involved (in thousands)	Working days lost (in thousand days)
1973	9459	3326	2235	4604
1974	10462	5211	3621	9663
1975	8435	3391	2732	8016
1976	7974	2720	1356	3254
1977	6060	1712	692	1518
1978	5416	1517	660	1358
1979	4026	1153	450	930
1980	4376	1133	563	1001
1981	7660	950	247	554
1982	7477	944	216	538
1983	5562	893	224	507
1984	4480	596	155	354
1985	4826	627	123	264
1986	2002	620	118	253
1987	1839	474	101	256
1988	1879	498	75	174
1989	1868	362	86	220

Source: Ministry of Labour, *Labour Dispute Survey*

Since then, the days lost per worker have been quite low compared to other industrialized countries. In addition, the duration of disputes is quite low by international standards. The main causes of labour disputes are related to the amount of wage increases and bonuses.

The reasons why the number of labour disputes and days lost are relatively low are as follows. In Japan, with enterprise-based unions, a better business performance leads to better labour conditions and the employment stability of union members. Thus, labour unions tend to be concerned with the business performance of their company. Therefore, labour unions tend to restrain themselves from engaging in labour disputes which might lead to a lessened degree of competitiveness of the company concerned. In addition, after the first oil shock, competition between companies became severe while the prospect of the economy became uncertain. Thus, Japanese labour unions took account of the economic situation.

C. Outcomes

C.1 Working Time

(a) Weekly hours

Work hours are regulated by the Labour Standards Law of 1947. Statutory hours of work were set at 48 hours a week at the time of the enactment. The amended law came into effect in 1988, reducing the standard work week from 48 to 40 hours. In response to the sharp decline, however, a grace period was introduced. Initially, the statutory hours of work were set at 46 hours, which was followed by 44 hours in 1991. However, it is not yet decided when the full implementation of 40 hours a week will be put into effect. The Government wishes to implement it as soon as possible, hopefully in the early 1990s.

With regard to the actual weekly hours in the collective agreement and/or work rules (scheduled weekly hours of work), the distribution of workers according to scheduled weekly hours is as follows; 35 per cent of workers for less than 40 hours, 16 per cent of workers for exactly 40 hours, 21 per cent for more than 40 to 44 hours, 28 per cent for more than 44 to 48 hours (Ministry of Labour, *General Survey on Wages and Working Hours System*, 1989).

(b) Restrictions on overtime and holiday work

The regulations concerning overtime hours and holiday work are based on Article 36 of the Labour Standards Law. This article stipulates that employers can request their employees for overtime and holiday work if and only if management and the workers' representative (or labour union) conclude a general agreement and submit it to a local labour standards inspection office. The agreements are typically renewed every three months. Thus, the maximum working hours vary from company to company, reflecting differences in this agreement between companies. There is no legal regulation concerning maximum working hours. However, the Ministry of Labour set up a guideline for overtime hours in 1989, in which the maximum overtime hours were set at 50 hours a month and 450 hours a year. The Ministry of Labour advises companies of various industries based on the guideline.

The minimum overtime premium prescribed by the Labour Standards Law is 25 per cent, as is the premium for night work which is defined as work between 10 p.m. and 5 a.m. It should be noted that overtime pay is calculated on the basis of scheduled monthly wages. As discussed in C.2(c) below, bonus payment accounts for a fairly large proportion of total annual wages which are composed of scheduled and non-scheduled monthly wages and bonuses. However, bonuses are not taken into account in the calculation of overtime pay. From these facts, the effective premium rate for overtime hours is negative in Japan.[5]

The overtime hours actually worked in 1989 were 188 hours for all industries, and 240 hours for manufacturing industries. Both figures cover both blue- and white-collar workers. The overtime premium for working hours beyond 8 hours is 25 per cent in 90 per cent of companies (with 30 or more employees). 8 per cent of companies offer 25 to 35 per cent of the overtime premium, and only 2 per cent of companies offer more than 35 per cent. With regard to holiday work, 83 per cent of companies offer 25 per cent of the overtime premium, while 12 per cent offer 25 to less than 50 per cent and 5 per cent offer more than 50 per cent.

(c) Annual paid leave

Statutory annual paid leave, which is prescribed by the Labour Standards Law, is 10 to 20 days in accordance with years of service. One year of service with an attendance record of more than 80 per cent entitles a worker to 10 days of annual paid leave. The leave increases by one day with every additional year of service, up to a maximum of 20 days.

Average annual paid leave actually entitled was 15.4 days in 1989. In addition, in many companies workers are entitled to special paid leaves such as year-end and new-year holidays, summer vacation, May day, company anniversary day etc. An average worker was entitled to 7.2 days of special paid leave in 1989, so that the total paid leave was 22.6 days (Ministry of Labour, *General Survey on Wages and Working Hours System*, 1989).

The problem concerning annual paid leave is that it is not fully used up every year. For example, only 7.9 days of the 15.4 days entitled were taken in 1989. In this way, the rate of utilization of annual paid leave has been about 50 to 60 per cent in recent years. If the 22.6 days above is referred to, then 15.1 days (=7.9 days + 7.2 days) were utilized, the rate of utilization being 67 per cent.

The reasons why the leave is not fully utilized are as follows. First, making use of annual leave is not compulsory. Second, a utilization plan is not arranged in most companies. In general, plants are not closed down altogether for annual paid leave. Third, those not making use of annual paid leave tend to be regarded as working hard and earnestly under the open space office system. Those regarded as working

---

5. Suppose premium rate for a specific company being 25 per cent. Suppose also annual amount of bonuses of the company being equivalent to 4 months' salary. Then the effective premium rate of overtime becomes -6.2 per cent (12/16X1.25=0.938, 0.938-1.000=-0.062).

hard are likely to get a better personal evaluation and promotion. Fourth, paid annual leave tends to be reserved for unexpected sickness. A paid sick leave scheme is not common in Japan. The National Health Insurance programme is designed to compensate for lost wages with a three-day waiting period, but many workers tend to be afraid of an unfavourable effect on personal evaluation due to the absence. Fifth, the attitude of the labour unions is not strong enough to change the situation. Since wages paid to workers remain unchanged regardless of taking annual paid leave, unused leave can be said as working days for nothing. It is estimated that working for nothing as a result of the incomplete use of annual paid leave is worth 2.5 trillion yen (20 billion dollars) in 1990.

(d) National holidays

National holidays designated by the National Holidays Law are as follows; 1st January (New Year's Day), 15th January (Coming-of-Age Day), 11th February (National Foundation Day), 21st March (Vernal Equinox Day), 29th April (Green Day), 3rd May (Constitution Day), 5th May (Children's Day), 15th September (Respect-for-the-Aged Day), 23rd September (Autumnal Equinox Day), 10th October (Health-Sports Day), 3rd November (Culture Day), 23rd November (Labour Thanksgiving Day), 23rd December (Emperor's Birthday). When a national holiday comes on a Sunday, then the following Monday becomes a holiday. In addition, when the 4th of May is neither a Sunday nor a Monday, then it becomes a national holiday. Thus, every year, three consecutive days between 3rd and 5th May are national holidays. Thus, there are 14 national holidays in total.

Those working in the public sector as well as in non-profit organizations do not work on national holidays. In the private sector, whether national holidays are working days or paid leave is decided by each company, and is generally stipulated in the work rules. As a matter of fact, on average, 11 out of 14 national holidays were treated as paid leave in companies with 30 employees and more as of 1989.

(e) Regulations for special groups of workers

The Labour Standards Law stipulates restrictions on working hours for both women and young workers. With regard to overtime hours, women are allowed to work up to 6 hours a week and 150 hours a year in the case of blue-collar workers, and up to 24 hours for every four weeks and 150 hours a year in the case of white-collar workers. However, managerial and professional women are not restricted at all. The enactment of the Equal Employment Opportunity Law led to the amendment of the Labour Standards Law so as to enable women to work more overtime hours. Those aged 15 to 17 years are not allowed to work overtime or on holidays. No restriction is made on older people.

(f) Night work

The Labour Standards Law defines night work as work between 10 p.m. and 5 a.m., and it must be paid with a premium of at least 25 per cent. Night work is in principle prohibited for women workers except for specific groups of workers. They include managerial and professional workers, those in designated industries such as hospitals, restaurants, hotels, services etc, those holding jobs not harmful to women's health and welfare, such as stewardesses, policewomen, TV and radio production, etc. Those aged 15 to 17 years are not allowed to take a job of night work. However, male workers aged 16 and over are allowed to be engaged in night work under the condition of a rotating shift.

C.2 Wages and Salary

(a) Structure of wages

Wages are defined in the Labour Standards Law as everything an employer pays to a worker in return for labour service whatever they may be called. They include wages, salaries, allowances, bonuses, and so on.

One of the characteristics of the Japanese wage system is that wages of both blue- and white-collar workers are generally fixed on a monthly basis. Exceptions are part-time workers, whose wages are generally fixed on an hourly basis, some workers in small and medium-sized companies and temporary workers in large companies whose wages are fixed on a daily basis.[6] The payment of wages is generally made once a month. As can be seen from these facts, there is no difference between wages and salary in Japan. Therefore, the term "wages" is used for meanings of both wages and salary in the present Chapter.

In the discussion below, monthly-fixed wages are considered. Wages that a worker is paid monthly include components of basic pay, scheduled allowances and nonscheduled allowances. The basic pay is determined in consideration of various factors such as educational attainment, job content, years of service, age, experience, competence, etc. The way to determine the basic pay varies significantly between companies. The basic pay is the basis for calculating nonscheduled allowances,

6. In 1978, monthly-fixed wages were practised in 68 per cent of companies with 30 employees and more, daily-fixed wages for 28 per cent, and piece rate wages for 4 per cent.

bonuses and retirement allowances. The scheduled allowances are designed to supplement the basic pay and are paid every month. There are various types of scheduled allowances according to the needs of each company. The scheduled allowances are classified into four categories; namely, performance and incentive allowances, job allowances (position allowances, special job allowances, skill allowances, etc.), living cost allowances (spouse allowances, family allowances, area allowances, housing allowances, etc.), and commuting allowances. Each company pays some of the allowances according to their needs. These allowances are all additive and vary across firms.

Non-scheduled allowance is paid according to overtime hours and holiday work, the premium rates for which were already discussed in C.1. above. Bonuses are generally paid twice a year. The amount of the bonus is determined through collective bargaining where there is a labour union or at the will of the employer where no labour union is organized. Accordingly, the amount varies between companies, but is usually equivalent to four to eight months' wages.

Taking annual wages as equal to 100, basic pay accounts for 55 per cent, scheduled allowances for 10 per cent, nonscheduled allowances for 10 per cent,and bonuses for 25 per cent of total wages.

(b) Piece rate wages

It is quite difficult to grasp an overall view of the Japanese wage system, since it differs considerably among companies. However, it can be noted that only a few companies adopt the so-called piece rate wage system. The proportion adopting this system is only 4 per cent.[7]

Another characteristic is that the basic pay, the most important part of wages, is not necessary linked to the job a worker is engaged in. The factors influencing basic wages were already mentioned above. In any case, a job and its wages are loosely linked, so that transfer of a worker from one job to another can easily and flexibly be conducted without causing any change in wages. This also leads to unclear job demarcation. Thus, it can be said that occupational wage structure is an almost irrelevant concept in Japan.

---

7. See footnote 6.

(c) Profit sharing and equity sharing scheme

The bonus system of Japanese companies is often referred to as a type of profit sharing scheme. In real sense, however, most of the bonus is not directly linked to the profit level of the company. The bonus is in fact classified as a wage cost in book-keeping systems. In addition, many unions and companies do not want an excessive variation in the bonus amount, since the amount is now so large a part of annual wages (Table 6). The variation is larger in the manufacturing industry where economic variation is most pronounced while the variation is much smaller in the service industries and financial industries. The long-term trend shows that the relative share of bonuses in the total annual wage bill has been increasing.

Table 6. Amount of Annual Bonuses by Size of Firm (1987)
(Manufacturing, male white-collar workers; as a multiple of monthly scheduled wages)

Age group	Senior high-school graduates			Four-year college graduates		
	1000- empl.	100-999 empl.	10-99 empl.	1000- empl.	100-999 empl.	10-99 empl.
20-24	4.2	3.5	2.3			
25-29	4.5	3.7	2.8	4.6 (100)	4.0 (83)	3.1 (68)
30-34	4.8	3.9	2.8	4.9 (100)	4.2 (78)	3.1 (60)
35-39	5.0	4.1	2.9	5.2 (100)	4.4 (74)	3.1 (54)
40-44	5.2	4.3	3.0	5.7 (100)	4.7 (71)	3.0 (44)
45-49	5.4	4.5	3.1	6.1 (100)	4.9 (69)	3.3 (40)
50-54	5.3	4.7	3.2	6.1 (100)	4.8 (65)	3.2 (37)
55-59	5.6	4.4	2.9	6.2 (100)	4.5 (62)	3.0 (33)

Note: Figures inside parentheses are differentials of amount between company sizes.
Source: Ministry of Labour, *Wage Structure Basic Survey*

It is noted that in some industries, especially in the retail trade, the amount of bonus is a combination of a fixed part irrespective of business performance and a part closely related to profit or value-added.

The average bonus amount, hence total bonus resources, is negotiated through collective bargaining. Then, the bulk of bonus resources is spent to pay individual workers according to basic wages. The remaining part is paid according to job performance of individual workers. In some cases, a part of the resources is distributed among workers in the form of a flat amount.

Many companies offer a stock ownership programme which enables their employees to buy shares of the company with financial aid from the company. The proportion of the companies which offer such a programme is 92 per cent of those listed on the stock exchange. About 45 per cent of employees in these companies participate in the programmes and own 0.8 per cent of the total shares issued by these companies. The amount of shares per participant was 1.66 million yen (13 thousand dollars) in 1989.

(d) Minimum wage system

The minimum wage system is based on the Minimum Wage Law of 1968 which was enacted to become independent of the Labour Standards Law. There are two ways to determine the minimum wage, one decided by the Minimum Wages Council and the other based on an extension of the collective agreement. However, the latter has rarely been employed until today. There are two types of minimum wage, regional and industrial minimum wages. The regional minimum wage is set for each of the 47 prefectures on the basis of the deliberation of the Regional Minimum Wage Council. In order to maintain uniformity among regional minimum wages, the Central Minimum Wage Council presents guidelines for the revision of the regional minimum wages. The industrial minimum wages are set in a similar way at a national and a regional level. Both the Regional and Central Minimum Wage Councils are composed of public-interest, labour and management representatives. The rate of increase in the minimum wage is largely influenced by the outcome of the spring labour offensive and the rate of increase in the cost of living index. The minimum wage has been revised every year.

The regional minimum wages vary between prefectures and as of March 1990, the average being 3928 yen per day and 491 yen per hour, with the lowest being 82 per cent of the highest. The industrial minimum wages at a regional level also vary between prefectures.

(e) Wage discrimination

The Labour Standards Law prohibits any discrimination in working conditions such as wages, hours of work, etc., on the grounds of nationality, creed and social status. The Law also prescribes equal pay for equal work. From the clauses above, any discrimination as to wages is prohibited. However, as a matter of fact, wages of individual workers are determined in consideration of the various factors as mentioned earlier. In addition, the job content for each worker is not strictly defined, so that the actual job content differs from worker to worker. Thus, it is difficult and almost impossible to find out whether wage discrimination exists against a specific worker or a group of workers. Also important is the fact that the wages of part-time workers must be carefully examined, since the amount of bonuses for part-time workers is significantly smaller than for full-time workers, and retirement allowance, which is a part of wages, is also considerably smaller. It is also pointed out that many part-time workers work in the same way as full-time workers, but their wages are substantially lower than full-time workers.[8]

C.3 Fringe Benefits

Table 7 shows the long-term trend of labour costs in Japan. As can be seen from this Table, monthly wage payments and bonuses account for 83.8 per cent while non-wage labour costs make up the remaining 16.2 per cent. The main non-wage elements are statutory welfare costs (7.9 per cent of total labour cost), non-statutory welfare costs (2.8 per cent), and retirement benefits (4.3 per cent). The share of the recruitment cost and that of education and training cost are relatively small.

Table 7. Labour Cost (in per cent)

	1975	1980	1985	1988
Total labour cost	100.0	100.0	100.0	100.0
Monthly wages and bonuses	86.4	85.1	84.6	83.8
Nonwage labour cost	13.6	14.9	15.4	16.2
retirement benefits	3.3	3.4	3.9	4.2
statutory welfare costs	6.1	7.0	7.7	7.9
nonstatutory welfare costs	3.1	2.8	2.8	2.8
housing service	–	–	–	1.1
medical/health service	–	–	–	0.3
meal service	–	–	–	0.4
private insurance plans	–	–	–	0.2
cultural, sporting and recrational facilities	–	–	–	0.3
supplementary workmen's compensation	–	–	–	0.1
costs for congratulations and condolences	–	–	–	0.1
aid for asset formation	–	–	–	0.1
others	–	–	–	0.3
cost of recruitment	0.2	0.2	0.2	0.3
cost of education/training	0.3	0.3	0.3	0.4
others	0.7	1.0	0.6	0.7

Source: Ministry of Labour, *Survey on Wage and Working Hours System*

8. According to the Labour Force Survey, about 37 per cent of part-time workers worked more than 35 hours a week in March 1989. Calculating hourly wages for both female full-time and part-time workers, we see that an average part-time worker earns 71 per cent of the average wages of a full-time worker. If bonuses are included, this will become 61 per cent (Ministry of Labour, *Wage Structure Basic Survey*, 1989).

The statutory welfare cost represents the employer's share of premiums for various types of social insurance programmes. These cover employees' pension insurance, health insurance, employment insurance, workmen's accident compensation insurance, and the children's fund. Employers must in principle enrol their employees in all four of these insurance systems. The cost of the workmen's accident insurance scheme is met entirely by employers, while payments to the other systems normally take the form of equal contributions by employee and employer. The outline of these social insurance programmes was already described in A.2. above. Non-statutory welfare costs consist of expenditures to subsidize housing, meals, and recreational activities for employees. The details of retirement benefits will be discussed in C.4. below.

From the long-term point of view, the share of non-wage labour costs in total labour costs is increasing. This is mainly due to the increasing rate of premiums for employees' pension insurance, health insurance, and the increasing payment of retirement benefits, reflecting the aging of the population. Since the aging of the population is expected to continue up to 2020, so is the share of non-wage labour cost in the foreseeable future.

One of the characteristics of fringe benefits in Japan is that many companies, especially large companies, offer recreational and welfare facilities to their employees. For example, the proportion of companies with various facilities is as follows. Library 13 per cent (proportion of workers 35 per cent), club rooms 15 per cent (47 per cent), resort hotels 32 per cent (67 per cent), seasonal leisure facilities 27 per cent (57 per cent), employees' clubs 17 per cent (42 per cent), gymnasium 8 per cent (35 per cent), athletic fields 18 per cent (48 per cent), tennis courts 18 per cent (53 per cent), swimming pools 7 per cent (33 per cent), hospitals 11 per cent (27 per cent), clinics 13 per cent (36 per cent), infirmaries 24 per cent (54 per cent), stores 9 per cent, barbers and/or hairdressers 3 per cent, child care facilities 1 per cent.

Many Japanese companies have traditionally provided worker housing as part of their employee welfare systems. According to the 1988 statistics, employers now provide a total of 1,539 thousand housing units, 4.1 per cent of total housing stock. It is also common for companies to provide various forms of assistance to enable workers to acquire their own homes.

C.4 Termination of the Labour Contract

It would be better to mention here the so-called life-time employment practice (LTEP) in Japanese companies. It should first be noted that it is not spelled out in labour contracts but exists on the basis of a tacit understanding between labour and management, and that it is only applied to full-time regular workers (see Diagram

1). The emergence of the LTEP can be traced back to around 1900 when major companies started to encourage their employees to stay long on their payroll through seniority-based programmes such as retirement benefits. Despite such efforts, employers implemented collective dismissals in the times of difficult economic situations. In the immediate post-war period between 1945 and 1955, the unstable economy forced many firms to do the same which often led to severe and sometimes bloody conflicts between management and newly-emerged labour unions. Bearing in mind these experiences, both labour and management became increasingly interested in employment stability. This is the origin of the present LTEP.

Table 8. Employers' Attitudes to Lifetime Employment (%)

Size of the firm	(1)	(2)	(3)	(4)	(5)
Present practices					
5000 or more employees					
Managerial	0.0	63.3	36.7	0.0	0.0
Clerical	0.0	88.9	10.1	0.0	1.0
100 to 300 employees					
Managerial	17.3	72.7	6.3	0.0	3.7
Clerical	7.3	85.4	3.6	2.1	2.1
Expected future practices					
5000 or more employees					
Managerial	1.0	42.9	56.1	0.0	0.0
Clerical	0.0	73.8	23.2	2.0	1.0
100 to 300 employees					
Managerial	14.0	73.6	9.3	0.0	3.1
Clerical	3.6	85.6	6.2	3.6	1.0

Legenda: (1) Employ workers as long as they can work; (2) Employ workers until retirement age; (3) Try to transfer (i.e. transfer to subsidiary companies and/or related companies) older workers before retirement age; (4) Expect workers to leave voluntarily; (5) Others.

Source: Ministry of Labour, *Survey on Changes in the Socioeconomic Climate and Japanese Employment Practices*, 1986

It cannot be overlooked that flexible wage and employment systems (see C.2(a), (b) and (c) above, and D.(b) below) and cooperative union attitudes (see B.2(c) and (e) above, and D.(b) below) contributed to its better functioning. Another important factor is steady growth of the Japanese economy. It should also be noted that both part-time and temporary workers had been playing a significant role of the shock-absorber in recession periods. Since their terms and conditions of employment are much less favourable than full-time regular workers, they certainly constitute a part of the dual labour market.

From time to time, people prepare estimates of the share of workers covered by the LTEP, suggesting that the percentage is relatively low. These estimates are based on the prevailing notion that the system applies only to workers at the larger corporations and in the public sector and not to those who work for smaller companies. It is true that employment stability in smaller companies is much less than that in major companies. But, it should also be noted that LTEP has been widely adopted as a philosophy in smaller firms as well (see Table 8).

(a) Firing and quitting rules and regulations for individual employees

The dismissal of workers is regulated by the Labour Standards Law. In the case of dismissal, the Law requires an employer to inform the worker concerned of his dismissal 30 days in advance, or to pay money equivalent to the average wage for 30 days. However, the rules concerning the dismissal are generally specified in either the collective agreement or the work rules. When a union member is dismissed, the union is involved in the matter in a variety of ways. According to the Ministry of Labour's survey, a union approval is required in 17 per cent of companies where unions are organized. Similarly, consultation with the union is needed in 39 per cent of companies, the advice and opinion of the union in 8 per cent, prior notice to the union in 12 per cent, notice to the union after the dismissal in 3 per cent, no involvement of union in 8 per cent, and other arrangements in 8 per cent (see Table 3 above).

According to the court precedents, even when a dismissal is made due to the economic difficulty of the company, the company is required to show that it is in a severely difficult financial situation, that it made all efforts, such as recruitment freeze, internal transfer, short-time working,etc., to avoid the dismissal, that selection of the workers to be dismissed is rational, that it sincerely consulted the dismissal with the union, and so forth.

In 1988, separations due to termination of contract and economic reasons accounted for 6.4 per cent and 7.1 per cent of total separations, respectively. The proportions fluctuate according to the business cycle. They were 5.4 per cent and 10.5 per cent respectively in 1975 when the Japanese economy was hit hard by the first oil shock (Ministry of Labour, *Employment Trend Survey*).

(b) Rules for collective lay-offs

With regard to the legal regulations for collective dismissal, the Employment Measures Law prescribes that the employer must report the collective separation to the local Public Employment Security Office at least one month before the lay-off. A collective separation is defined as one which incurs the separation of more than 30 employees within a month at a specific establishment. In addition, the Law concerning Temporary Measures for Workers Displaced from Specified Depressed Industries prescribes that an employer must submit an employment plan to the local Public Employment Security Office when more than 30 employees are to be displaced. The employment plan should cover employer's programmes to assist them in their reemployment. Furthermore, the Law concerning Promotion of Local Employment and Development requires an employer to make efforts for employment stability of its employees when the company reduces the size of its activity in a specific area. The Labour Minister can request an employer to take necessary measures for the employment stability in order to prevent the local labour market from deteriorating . The measures for employment stability includes making use of various programmes provided by the Employment Insurance Law. Examples are wage and training subsidy programmes.

(c) Employment termination at will by the employer

As discussed already, it is not possible to dismiss any worker, including part-time workers, merely at the will of an employer. However, in actual situations, such dismissals are likely to happen to some extent in very small companies where no union is organized or in the case of part-time workers. About 350 labour standards inspection offices are spread all over Japan in order to implement the regulations of the Labour Standards Law and to protect workers from such unfair conduct.

(d) Arrangements for severance pay

Retirement benefits, one of the important characteristics of the Japanese compensation systems, are very relevant for severance pay. Like bonuses, retirement benefit plans became generally prevalent in Japanese companies only in the post war period. Today, more than 90 per cent of companies pay retirement benefits.

Benefits take the form of either lump-sum payment or pension or both. At some companies the amount of the lump-sum payment is determined as a multiple of basic pay. Other firms use a calculation formula independent of basic pay. Payments are also made to employees terminating their employment before normal retirement age, though the payment scale is lower when the termination is voluntary, and higher when it is involuntary such as the economic difficulty of a company. The system rewards long service, since the payment multiple rises progressively with the number of years worked. Table 9 shows the standard benefits paid to male employees according to educational attainment.

Table 9. Standard Retirement Benefits
(white-collar workers; as a multiple of monthly scheduled wages)

Years of service	College graduates				Senior high-school graduates			
	involuntary reason		voluntary reason		involuntary reason		voluntary reason	
	1989	1969	1989	1969	1989	1969	1989	1969
1	0.9	0.9	0.2	0.1	0.8	0.9	0.2	0.1
3	1.9	2.3	0.9	1.1	1.9	2.4	0.9	1.1
5	3.2	3.9	1.7	2.1	3.4	4.1	1.8	2.2
10	7.3	9.3	4.6	6.0	7.4	9.1	4.7	5.8
15	12.5	16.1	9.0	11.8	12.3	15.9	8.7	11.8
20	18.8	24.9	15.4	20.7	19.0	24.9	15.2	20.3
25	26.5	35.1	22.8	30.4	26.5	34.5	22.7	29.6
30	35.2	44.9	31.5	40.2	34.0	44.2	30.6	38.8
33	39.6	47.3	37.4	42.6				
35					39.1	49.6	36.4	44.8
37					42.3	52.8	40.9	47.8

Source: Central Labour Commission, *Wage Survey*

In the case of employment termination due to either dismissal or voluntary resignation caused by the economic difficulty of the company, the multiple or formula applied is in general the best one, the same as for involuntary retirement shown in Table 9. But many companies add some premium to these benefits to implement employment adjustment smoothly. In the establishments where a voluntary resignation scheme was implemented during the recession in the wake of the first oil shock, 70 per cent of such establishments added some premium as a result of negotiation with the union. The amount added was less than 25 per cent of the involuntary retirement benefits in 28 per cent of such establishments, 25 to less than 50 per cent in 33 per cent, 50 to less than 75 per cent in 13 per cent, and more than 75 per cent in 26 per cent. In the case of designated dismissals, 40 per cent of establishments added some premium. The amount added was less than 25 per cent of the involuntary retirement benefits in 44 per cent of such establishments, 25 to less than 50 per cent in 23 per cent, 50 to less than 75 per cent in 12 per cent, more than 75 per cent in 19 per cent. Thus, severance payments are all based on voluntary agreement, and not on legal prescriptions.

(e) Restrictions on employees after employment termination

The Japanese Constitution stipulates in its Article 22 that every person shall have the freedom to choose his occupation to the extent that it does not interfere with the public welfare. Thus, it is not possible for a former employer to place any restrictions on its former employees with regard to their new jobs. In the case of national government officials, however, it is necessary to obtain an approval from the National Personnel Authority if an official is going to take a job in the private sector and his/her position in the government is at the director-level or above in the headquarters of the national government. Especially, in the case of a job which is closely related to his/her experience in the national government, he or she is required to wait for two years to take the job.

(f) Compulsory retirement ages, pensions and early retirement

Compulsory retirement ages
90 per cent of companies (with 30 employees and more) require employees to retire after reaching a certain age. For many years the usual retirement age was 55. In recent years, however, many firms raised their retirement age to 60. This is partly in response to deliberate efforts by the government to provide steady employment for older workers. In 1986, legislation (the Law Concerning the Stabilization of Employment for Elderly People) was enacted to require employers to make efforts to set compulsory retirement ages at 60 or above. Many older people wish to work even after the compulsory retirement age as suggested by the fact that the participation rate of those aged 60 to 64 is 71.4 per cent in 1989. In response to their needs, many companies offer job opportunities to their retirees at different conditions. In 1990, the Law was revised to require employers to offer employment opportunities to those aged 60 years and older if they wish to be employed after the compulsory retirement age. At the same time, the Government urged companies to fully implement compulsory retirement ages of 60 years and more with the help of all available means by 1993. In 1991, a retirement age at 60 was either already implemented or to be implemented in more than 95 per cent of firms with more than 100 employees and more.

Pensions
The outline of the National Employees Pension Programme was already described in the Section A. Corporate pension programmes are practised as a part of retirement benefits which were already mentioned above (C.4(d)). The proportion of companies (with 30 employees and more) having such a programme was 51 per cent in 1989. The average corporate pension programme provides retirees with 10 to 20 years of services with a pension for ten years after the age of 60. Many companies give retirees an option in which they can choose either a pension or a lump-sum payment.

Since the lump-sum payment is better treated in the income tax system, many retirees prefer the lump-sum payment. Lump-sum retirement benefits are spent for repayment of housing loan, purchase of private pension, education cost of children, and so forth.

Early retirement

An early retirement scheme for those retiring from the labour market before the pensionable age of 60 is not available in the national employees' pension scheme. However, in response to the aging of the workforce, many companies have implemented early retirement schemes for those quitting the company before the compulsory retirement age. The scheme offers a favourable treatment of retirement benefits in such a way that the benefits are calculated in the same way as separation due to the involuntary reason. In addition, an additional amount is paid in many cases. Generally, the age for early retirement is fixed at 45,50 and 55 years old.[9] Those who opt for early retirement generally continue to work in a different job since the scheme itself is designed so as to encourage them to start a different career at a stage early enough.

D. Conclusions and Evaluation

(a) Recent discussion on regulation of the labour market

As in other industrialized countries, Japan has experienced hard times in employment from time to time, especially during the recession after the first oil shock and due to the sharp appreciation of the yen between 1985 and 1986. However, in the long run, Japan could smoothly adapt to the structural changes in the economy. As a result, the unemployment rate has remained quite low by international standards. It can not be overlooked that both employers and labour sought employment stability on the basis of the so-called lifetime employment system.

Since unemployment has not been a serious problem in Japan compared to other industrialized countries, the flexibility and rigidity of the labour market has rarely been discussed until today.

Thus, the deregulation of the labour market has not been an issue, except for the abolition of the protection clause of women workers in the Labour Standards Law. Regulation of the labour market has rather been tightened for a long time. Recent

9. The Ministry of Labour Survey (*Employment Management Survey*) shows that only 4 per cent of companies provided an early retirement scheme in 1987. However, this was 50 per cent for companies with more than 5,000 employees, and 40 per cent for companies with 1,000 to 4,999 employees.

examples are the employment promotion of older people by the Employment Stability Law for Older People, restriction of the jobs handled by temporary employment agencies, employment promotion of the mentally handicapped by the Employment Promotion Law for the Handicapped, employment promotion of women workers by the Equal Employment Opportunity Law. In addition, new legislation concerning part-time workers is under discussion.

(b) Conclusions

What will be the evaluation of the Japanese labour market as a whole?

First, let us examine the so-called external labour market. The labour mobility rate in Japan is quite low compared to other countries. This is mainly due to the so-called life-time employment practice which seems to be changing gradually but is still widely practised. Taking a look at the personnel management system of companies, both wages and promotion systems are constructed so as to be better with long service, leading to less mobility between companies. With regard to regional mobility, more and more people do not want regional movement due to housing and family reasons. As a whole, it is possible to conclude that the external labour market of Japan is not as flexible as in other industrialized countries.

On the other hand, the labour market within firms, the so-called internal labour market, seems to be very flexible in job assignment and wage determination under cooperative labour relations.

First, labour relations in Japan are quite stable and cooperative thanks to the enterprise-based unions. Since the better business performance of a company tends to bring about employment stability and better labour conditions, an enterprise-based union is ready to cooperate with management to improve productivity for better performance. In the case of the introduction of new technology, for example, the union studies the issue from the point of view of how to solve the problems arising from the introduction, as long as it improves the competitiveness of the company in the market. In addition, in the case of economic difficulty, a union makes concession on wages in order to save employment. Furthermore, since both blue- and white-collar workers are organized in the same union and treated in the same way in terms of labour conditions, confrontations between them rarely occur.

One of the points to be remembered in Japanese industrial relations is that almost all board members were union members in the past. Under the life-time employment practice, most board members were recruited immediately after their graduation from school, joined the company-based union and reached the management level through internal promotion. According to a 1977 survey, the background of the board members of the major companies, which belong to the Douyuukai, one of the major employers' associations, were as follows. 91 per cent were from former employees, 2 per cent from major share-holders, 2 per cent from bankers, 3 per cent from public officials, and 2 per cent from other sources. In addition, according to a 1978 Nikkeiren survey, two thirds of major companies said that at least one board member was a union executive committee member in the past. In addition, 1012 of 6457 board members in such companies surveyed experienced union officials while they were employees of the company.

With regard to wages, individual wages are not set according to what a worker is actually doing as described above (see C.2(a) and (b)). From this fact, workers can be transferred from one job to another without causing a change in wages. Thus, workers themselves also tend to accept job transfers. In general, workers are not recruited for a specific job, but for a broader job assignment. Job demarcation is not clearly specified under such a system, so widely practised multiple-skilled jobs are one of the outcomes of the system.

Although the points just mentioned are certainly advantages of the Japanese pay system, it is not known whether the system attains efficient allocation of workers in the economy as a whole. Recent developments suggest that an increasing number of companies tend to introduce a performance-related component into the basic pay structure. In this way, the pay system has been gradually changing. It may be correct to say that the Japanese-type pay system can be efficient in a manufacturing sector where structural changes are rapidly taking place on the one hand and dismissals of workers are often hard to be implemented on the other.

Another point is that wage increase is negotiated every year which makes it easier to reflect the current economic situation in the wage determination. About one quarter of annual wages are paid in terms of bonuses, which also makes wage costs more flexible. The amount of bonuses is influenced by the business performance to some extent.

REFERENCES

Clark, Rodney (1987), *The Japanese Company*, Tokyo: Charles E. Tuttle.

Dore, Ronald, Bounine-Cabale, Jean, and Tapiola, Kari (1989), *Japan at Work, Markets, Management and Flexibility*, O.E.C.D.

Hanami, Tadashi A. (1982), Workforce Reductions in Undertakings-Japan, in: Edward Yemin (ed.), *Workforce Reductions in Undertakings* (ILO).

Japan Institute of Labour (1979), *Labour Unions and Labor-Management Relations*, The Japan Institute of Labour.

Kuwahara, Yasuo (1989), *Industrial Relations System in Japan*, The Japan Institute of Labour.

Ministry of Labour, *Year Book of Labour Statistics*, various issues.

Ministry of Labour (1990), *Labour Laws of Japan 1990*, Tokyo: The Institute of Labour Policy (Roumu Gyousei Kenkyusho).

O.E.C.D. (1972), *Manpower Policy in Japan.*

O.E.C.D. (1977), *The Development of Industrial Relations-Some Implications of Japanese Experiences.*

Sasajima, Yoshio (1988), *Labor in Japan*, Tokyo: Foreign Press Center.

Sasajima, Yoshio (1991), *Contemporary Labour Problems* (in Japanese), Chu-ou-keizaisha.

Shimada, Haruo and Shirai, Taishirou (1980), *The Japanese Employment System*, The Japan Institute of Labour.

Shimada, Haruo (1978), Labor in the Twentieth Century-Japan, in: John T. Dunlop and Walter Galenson (eds.), *Labor in the Twentieth Century* (Academic Press.

Shirai, Taishiro (ed.) (1983),*Contemporary Industrial Relations in Japan*, The Univ. of Wisconsin Press.

Takanasi, Akira *et al.* (1989), *Shunto Wage Offensive*, The Japan Institute of Labour.

Labour Market Contracts and Institutions
J. Hartog and J. Theeuwes (Editors)

CHAPTER 6

THE AUSTRIAN LABOUR MARKET:
Description and Analysis of Structures and Institutions

Ferdinand Karlhofer* and Ulrich Ladurner*

A. General Information on Labour Market and Social Security

A.1 The Structure of the Labour Market

Austria's economic history since 1945 has been characterized by a long process of catching up with advanced industrial nations (Butschek, 1985). The sharp decline of the proportion of those employed in the agricultural sector (32.6 % in 1951; 7.8 % in 1989)[1] illustrates the rapid process of industrialization. Today, according to most economic indicators, the country ranks in the centre-field of the OECD. By and large, the current changes, both on the labour supply side and on the labour demand side, correspond with general international trends (Butschek, 1990).

(a) Changes on the labour supply side

The structure of the workforce is undergoing changes with respect to three aspects: proportion of employed women, educational level, and age structure. We should also mention the increase of foreign workers since the dismantlement of the Iron Curtain in 1989.

Women: In 1989, 41 % of the total labour force were women, compared to 38 % in 1975. The figure is expected to mount up to 43 % in the year 2000. In 1971, the participation rate was considerably higher among singles (62 %) than among married women (43 %). The latter group, however, has undergone a significant increase (50 % in 1981) while the participation rate of singles is stagnating.

Education: The share of unqualified workers (primary school) has decreased sharply in the last decades (51.5 % in 1951; 29 % in 1989; extrapolation 2000: 19 % to 23 %). At the same time, the portion of employed persons who passed secondary or

---

* University of Innsbruck.

1. The figures given here refer to the total labour force (including self-employed persons).

higher education is increasing. The rate of university and academy graduates, however, will remain lower (7 % in 1989; extrapolation 2000: 4 % to 6 %) than in many other OECD countries. Hence, it is the secondary education which is expected to become more important in the labour market (Biffl, 1991).

Age structure: The age structure of the labour market is determined by two dimensions: the change of the age pyramid ("aging"), and education. The age pyramid shows a significant shift from predominantly younger to predominantly older workers. In the year 2000, only 15 % of the total labour force will be younger than 25 (1990: 20.5 %). The respective share of 25-55 aged employed persons will be 77 %. Evidently, this trend is also influenced by education – the age with which young people start with professional activity is increasing.

Foreign workers: The expansion of economic activities which started in the 1960s and increased in the 1970s, resulted in a pressing demand for foreign workers. In 1979, 171.000 foreign workers had been employed (6.8 % of the dependent labour force). During the economic recession of the early 1980s, the share of foreign workers decreased slightly. In the late 1980s, the trend turned around again. The number of foreign workers rose by 30 % from 1989 to 1990, mainly due to the very unexpected phenomenon of migrants from Eastern Europe after 1989. Just in a country which had, geographically seen, up to then played the role of a "buffer state" against Eastern Europe, migration causes a new situation. Many of the new migrants are employed illegally. On the one hand, illicit work is regarded as a menace to established work contracts, on the other hand, the willingness of immigrants to do everything opens the door for new, miserably paid jobs. The influx of economic refugees favours the re-emergence of low-productivity branches. At present, various bills concerning labour migration are discussed in parliament. The problem will and can be solved only in a broader international context. Since there is no consensus in sight, East-West migration will remain one of the most serious problems in the Austrian labour market, let alone that xenophobia and right-wing radicalism have been rising dramatically in recent years.

(b) Changes on the labour demand side

In the early fifties, almost 50 % of the dependent labour force had been employed in the secondary sector, and another 10 % in agriculture and forestry. Today, following the international trend, the labour market is characterized by a dominant (and further growing) tertiary sector accompanied by a decreasing share of employees in the primary and the secondary sector. As can be learned from Table 1, the share of workers employed in the tertiary sector is about 60 %, while the share of workers in the secondary sector has decreased to 37 %. The rapid change can be gathered from the figures showing the percentage change in the period 1986-9.

Table 1. Labour Market by Economic Sectors 1986-9 (annual average)

SECTOR	Wage and salary earners (000s)				Percentage change 1986-89	Share of total 1989
	1986	1987	1988	1989		
Primary	29.8	28.8	28.3	27.9	−6.4%	0.97%
Secondary	1,079.5	1,063.4	1,058.5	1,067.5	−1.1%	37.30%
Tertiary	1,623.8	1,650.0	1,678.1	1,719.2	+5.9%	60.06%
Others*	47.0	46.2	45.6	47.6	+1.3%	1.66%
Total	2,780.2	2,785.4	2,810.5	2,862.3	+3.0%	100.00%

* Basic military service; motherhood leave.
Source: Hauptverband der österreichischen Sozialversicherungsträger.

In correspondence with sectoral changes, we can observe an increase of white-collar workers at the cost of manual workers. In 1979, 50 % of the dependent labour force were salary earners; the respective figure for 1990 is 55 %, and it is steadily increasing. Compared to other postindustrial societies, however, Austria's share of white-collar workers is still below the average.

Table 2. Employment and Unemployment 1980-90

	dependent labour force (000s)	unemployment rate		
		wage earners	salary earners	total
1980	2,788.7	2.8	1.0	1.9
1981	2,789.0	3.7	1.2	2.2
1982	2,756.8	5.7	1.7	3.7
1983	2.734.7	7.0	2.1	4.5
1984	2,744.5	7.1	2.2	4.5
1985	2,759.6	7.4	2.3	4.8
1986	2,780.2	7.9	2.7	5.2
1987	2,785.4	8.4	3.0	5.6
1988	2,810.5	8.0	3.0	5.3
1989	2,862.3	7.3	2.9	5.0
1990	2,928.7	8.0	3.1	5.4

Source: Wirtschafts- und Sozialstatistisches Taschenbuch 1982-1991.

In 1989, Austria reached the highest level of employment since 1945, covering roughly 2.9 million wage and salary earners. At the same time, the unemployment rate is rising. In international comparison, Austria's unemployment rate had been marginal up to the early eighties (1.9 % in 1980), but increased in the course of the last decade to 5.4 % (1990). Table 2 shows that unemployment hits wage earners much more than salary earners. This indicates that recent changes on the labour demand side are favouring white-collar workers and affecting adversely blue-collar workers (and here again unskilled more than skilled workers). Unemployed persons who passed elementary school only are ranking above average (8.5 %). In all, 47 % of all unemployed persons have passed elementary school only (1990).

A.2 Social Security

The Austrian system of social security has its roots in the nineteenth century when basic laws concerning health insurance and old-age assistance were provided by the state. Important provisions were made in the First Republic (1918-34), especially in social-democratic governed Vienna ("Rotes Wien") where a dense network of social security and public welfare was provided (Talos, 1981). After 1945, Austria was devoted to the economic model of Keynesianism which had impacts on social security, too. In 1970, the social-democratic SPÖ came to power, orienting its social policy on the Scandinavian welfare state and on West German standards. Numerous reforms concerning unemployment insurance, pension funds, vacation privilege, equal status of men and women, motherhood leave, etc., were made during the Kreisky era in the seventies and early eighties (Talos, 1988).

In Table 3 the premiums for social insurance are listed. In some cases, the premiums of salary earners and wage earners are slightly different. In addition to the categories listed below, there are various state-regulated provisions for motherhood leave, early retirement, social security, etc.

Unemployment insurance was introduced in 1920. The present system refers to the Unemployment Insurance Law ('Arbeitslosenversicherungsgesetz') of 1977. The law provides arrangements to prevent or to reduce unemployment on the one hand, and to grant individual financial aid on the other hand. In particular in the 1980s, after a shocking increase of unemployment, special programs of retraining and improvement of job environment took place. The premium for unemployment insurance is 4.4 % of the worker's gross income, borne equally by employer and employed.

Unemployment benefits are granted with regard to four requirements: age; former income; duration of contribution to the fund; in some cases, willingness to participate in retraining programs (long-term unemployed persons). Normally granted to a maximum of 30 weeks, unemployment benefits can be extended up to 156 weeks. The amount of unemployment benefit varies between 40 % and 60 % of the previous wage.

The pensionable age is 65 years for men, and 60 years for women. The pension fund is financed both by employers (12.55 % of the gross salary) and workers

(10.25 %). Due to the expected shift in the age pyramid, the premium rates are expected to be raised significantly in times to come. At present, the ratio between end of career income and pension of workers is 74 %.

Table 3. Social Security Premiums (as a percentage of gross salary)

Category	Premium paid by		
	Employer	Worker	Total
Wage Earners			
Health Insurance	3.15	3.15	6.30
Accident Insurance	1.40	–	1.40
Pension Funds	12.55	10.25	22.80
Unemployment Insurance	2.20	2.20	4.40
Housing Program Contribution	0.50	0.50	1.00
Chamber of Labour	0.50	0.50	2.80
Wage Compensation Contribution	2.80	–	0.10
Insolvency Insurance	0.10	–	1.40
Bad Weather Compensation*	0.70	0.70	2.50
Heavy Labour Contribution*	2.50	–	
Total	25.90	17.30	43.20
Salary Earners			
Health Insurance	2.50	2.50	5.00
Accident Insurance	1.40	–	1.40
Pension Funds	12.55	10.25	22.80
Unemployment Insurance	2.20	2.20	4.40
Housing Program Contribution	0.50	0.50	1.00
Chamber of Labour	–	0.50	0.50
Insolvency Insurance	0.10	–	0.10
Total	19.25	15.95	35.20

Source: Wirtschafts- und Sozialstatistisches Taschenbuch 1991.

* Bad weather compensation and heavy labour contribution refer to specific branches such as construction and metal workers.

Health insurance was first introduced in 1888. Actual regulations refer to the General Social Insurance Law ('Allgemeines Sozialversicherungsgesetz') which came into effect in 1955 and has been revised almost annually since then. The health security fund is financed by employers (3.5 % of the gross salary) and workers (2.5 %). Accident insurance is financed by employers only. The premium amounts to 1.4 % of the workers' gross income for both status groups.

B. Institutional and Legal Features

B.1 The Structure of Industrial Relations

(a) Social partnership

In a study on contemporary Austria, recently published in England, one of the authors states: "The Austrian social partnership (*Sozialpartnerschaft*) has been praised by many of Austria's western neighbours in the past 30 years for everything that is desirable in a modern economy – prudent economic management, healthy economic growth, the epitome of social consensus and compromise, a relatively low incidence of societal (industrial) conflict and political stability." (Sweeny, 1988, p. 182) Although the applause is possibly slightly exaggerated, it would be hard to understand Austrian industrial relations without paying attention to this peculiar feature.

First of all, social partnership is a matter of union power. All things considered, the ÖGB ('Österreichischer Gewerkschaftsbund') appears as one of the strongest unions of the West. Its power is not only based on membership rates but also on external arrangements in the industrial relations system. As a result, the ÖGB has played, from the very beginning in 1945, a decisive role in all social and economic affairs. Making use of its power, the ÖGB was the actual protagonist of the specific Austrian form of corporatism – "social partnership" – which was formally established in 1957. In accordance with corporatist rules the ÖGB has always exercised restraint in "money goals" in favour of "participation goals".[2] In return, however, it succeeded to strengthen its institutional position (Karlhofer, 1988).

With respect to the structure of the social partnership, we have to distinguish between two dimensions: an autonomous one, and a non-autonomous one. The non-autonomous social partnership covers the statutory corporations with compulsory membership such as the Chambers of Labor and the Chambers of Commerce. Both have certain legal rights, including extensive co-determination in questions of social security, employment, agrarian policy, money and credit policy, and labour jurisdiction (Pelinka, 1981).

Autonomous social partnership refers to the voluntary cooperation between employers' federations and labour organizations. This peculiar arrangement – which made Austria to a highly regarded case for scholars on neocorporatism in the 1970s and 1980s[3] – was established after World War II. It had been the declared goal of all relevant political actors to achieve economic recovery. The ÖGB in particular played

2. The terms are borrowed from: Crouch, 1982, pp. 174-183.

3. "There are strong reasons to place Austria first on the scale of neocorporatism since it ranks high on all relevant dimensions." (Lehmbruch, 1982, p. 16.)

a leading role in attempts to guide trade in a corporatist fashion. Experiments followed one another. In 1946, a Central Wage Commission was established. In 1947, this was replaced by the Economic Commission. Between 1947 and 1951, annual agreements were arrived at to stop the wage-price spiral, and in 1957 the Joint Commission on Prices and Wages ('Paritätische Kommission für Preis- und Lohnfragen') was established. In 1963, the latter was complemented by the Council of Economic and Social Advisers ('Beirat für Wirtschafts- und Sozialfragen'). To the present the Joint Commission has been the heart of Austrian corporatism. Its monthly plenary meetings follow quasi-parliamentarian rituals, with the one difference that only unanimous vote is the rule. Any majority vote would violate the principle of voluntary cooperation (Marin, 1982).[4]

The secret of Austria's corporatist success lies in the fact that both types of social partnership – autonomous, and non-autonomous – combine to constitute an effective power in industrial relations and in the political arena. Regardless of whether they are entitled by law or not, the trade associations have a decisive say on all government bills before these are put to the vote in Parliament.[5]

(b) Employers' organizations

Austrian employers are organized in the Chambers of Commerce ('Handelskammern'). Covering the total entrepreneurship by compulsory membership the Chambers are the primary employers' association for collective bargaining with the trade unions. Each of the nine provinces (Länder) has its own Provincial Chamber of Trade and Industry ('Landeskammer der gewerblichen Wirtschaft'), while the representation on the national level is the task of the Federal Chamber of Economy ('Bundeskammer der gewerblichen Wirtschaft'). Representative functions are distributed among political groups; the members of the Chamber Council ('Kammerräte') are elected every five years. The Austrian Federation of Employers and Trades People ('Österreichischer Wirtschaftsbund'), a formal subgroup of the Austrian People's Party ('Österreichische Volkspartei' – ÖVP), holds the absolute majority since 1945.

---

4. This is, admittedly, a very academic consideration since both partners – the Chambers of Commerce and the Chambers of Agriculture on the one side, and the ÖGB and the Chambers of Labour on the other – are represented with an equal number of delegates. The representatives of the government, including the Federal Chancellor, are, since 1966, non-voting members of the Joint Commission.

5. One of the most important examples is the Industrial Labour Relations Scheme, part of the new Labour Constitution Act ('Arbeitsverfassungsgesetz') of 1974, which was negotiated and approved by the "social partners" before it was passed by Parliament.

Representing extremely heterogeneous interests of members, beginning with grocers and ending with big enterprises, the Chambers are permanently faced with problems of internal conciliation. Hence, one of the most powerful organizations based on voluntary membership is the Federation of Austrian Industrialists ('Vereinigung Österreichischer Industrieller' – VÖI). Organizing roughly 2.400 members (i.e. companies) which employ about 85 % of the Austrian industrial labour force in the private sector, the VÖI is a well-financed and influential representative of industrialists' interests (Faulhaber, 1980).

(c) Labour union structure

The structure of Austrian trade unionism can be summarized as follows: monopoly of one union federation; high density rate (56 % of the dependent labour force are organized); high degree of concentration (14 affiliates); high degree of centralization both of the umbrella organization and the affiliates; incomplete industrial unionism – white-collar workers in private business are organized in a separate union (Traxler, 1982).

First of all, there is only one federation of unions in Austria: the Austrian Trade Union Federation ('Österreichischer Gewerkschaftsbund' – ÖGB). Its 14 affiliates (until 1991: 15) don't even have a legal status of their own (in the strict sense, they are not affiliates but sub-groups of the ÖGB) – only the ÖGB is officially registered. The ÖGB's monopoly of workers' representation has historical and organizational reasons: On the one hand, the federation was founded in 1945, in a situation when the country was occupied by the Allies (until 1955); only an unbroken unity offered a chance of success. The "secret" of the ÖGB's monopoly, however, can be found in its internal structure: from the very beginning, virtually all political groups, even communist splinter groups, were granted the status of (more or less) formal factions in the federation. Being even privileged in the federation's representative boards (with respect to the support they have among the rank-and-file), minority groups don't really have strong motives to separate and found unions of their own. In fact, it would be easy to found a union. The freedom of association allows the foundation of a union without any formal restrictions. The big hurdle, however, would be to be granted the status of a party in wage regulations (depending on a representative number of members).

(d) Union membership

In 1990, the total union membership was 1.6 million resulting in a unionization rate of 56 %. While the absolute number has been constant since the 1970s, the unionization rate has been slightly declining in recent years. In other words, the ÖGB cannot keep pace with the increase of the total labour force (Table 4).

Table 4. Union Membership, Status Groups, and Unionization Rate

Year	Unionization rate*	Number of affiliates	Membership of federation (in thousands)	Membership by status groups (in per cent)		
				private business		public service
				blue-collar	white-collar	mixed
1950	66.5	16	1291	58.5	12.3	29.3
1955	67.5	16	1398	58.2	14.0	27.8
1960	65.8	16	1501	56.7	16.1	27.2
1965	64.8	16	1543	54.8	17.8	27.3
1970	63.6	16	1520	52.3	18.4	29.4
1975	59.8	16	1588	48.8	19.8	31.4
1980	59.6	15	1661	46.1	21.4	32.5
1985	59.0	15	1671	43.1	21.8	35.1
1986	58.4	15	1671	42.8	21.9	35.3
1987	57.8	15	1653	42.6	21.9	35.5
1988	58.5	15	1644	42.4	21.8	35.9
1989	57.5	15	1644	42.2	21.7	36.1
1990	56.2	15	1645	42.1	21.5	36.4
1991	–	14	–	–	–	–

* Percentage of total dependent labour force.
Source: Union reports.

There are no figures published about the unionization rates by the size of enterprises. It can be estimated, however, that the respective rates are above average in enterprises with more than 1000 employees (80 % to nearly 100 %)[6], and below average in smaller enterprises.

The proportion of female union members has been constant in recent years (31 % of the total membership). A good deal of women are employed in small-sized service sectors enterprises; hence the unionization rate of this group is significantly smaller (42 %) than that of men (67 %).

6. There are no legal provisions for closed shop arrangements in Austria. In large enterprises, however, the works councils put "gentle" pressure on workers to join the union. As a result, in particular in nationalized iron and steel industries, only a marginal number of blue-collar (less than 5%), and a small number of white-collar workers (less than 20%), are not organized.

The structural change of the labour market strongly affects the membership by status groups. The former leading blue-collar unions, steadily decreasing, now altogether make up the minority in the ÖGB. Moreover, white collar workers and public-service employees are organized in large-scale unions, while most of the blue-collar unions are small-sized. The gap between large and small unions is increasing continuously.

(e) Other labour organizations

Workers' interests are not only represented by labour unions. There are two additional institutions to be mentioned: the Chambers of Labour, and Works Councils.

Aside from associations with voluntary membership, the regulation of industrial relations by corporatist institutions is of considerable importance. Virtually all relevant status groups are organized in self-governed chambers: employers, farmers, physicians, lawyers, etc. And there is also a respective institution for employees.

The idea to establish Chambers of Labour ('Kammern für Arbeiter und Angestellte', in practice called 'Arbeiterkammern') has its roots in the nineteenth century. The Austrian labour movement (which has been dominated by social democrats throughout its history) demanded for a counterpart of the Chambers of Commerce which had been erected after the revolution of 1848. Eventually, in 1920, two years after the collapse of the Habsburg monarchy, the Chambers of Labour Act ('Arbeiterkammergesetz') was passed by parliament.

The Chambers of Labour are bodies corporate in public law ('Körperschaften des öffentlichen Rechtes'), organized on a federal basis with the Austrian Conference of the Chambers of Labour ('Österreichischer Arbeiterkammertag') functioning as their national body. Every employee, with the exception of public servants and agricultural workers, is a compulsory member and pays 0.5 % of his gross income. Chamber of Labour elections are held every five years; all members above the age of 18 years are eligible to vote. Altogether, the chambers have traditionally been dominated by the social democrats (69.8 % of the total vote in 1989) followed by the conservatives (29.1 %) who hold the majority in two of the nine Länder (Tyrol, Vorarlberg).

The co-existence of Chambers and trade unions has never caused frictions. On the contrary, observers (and the actors themselves) use to circumscribe the relationship as a "symbiotic" one – many chamber officials are at the same time union leaders. All things considered, Austrian trade unions are a long sight stronger than might be gathered from the figures of union revenues and membership rates.

The representation of workers' interests at plant level is very similar to the German system. As early as 1919 the Works Councils Act ('Betriebsrätegesetz') was passed by parliament. In 1974, the Betriebsrätegesetz was integrated in the Labour Constitution Act ('Arbeitsverfassungsgesetz') regulating both the rights of workers' representation and the handling of industrial conflict. The law provides that from 5 employees upwards a works council ('Betriebsrat') is elected. (In practice, however, only a very small number of enterprises with less than 20 employees really have a Betriebsrat).

Elected by all employees (every 3 years), not only by union members, the Betriebsräte hold a key position for union power. They are protected by law and carry on the day-by-day work of the unions. The relationship between works councils and unions is one of interdependence. The enterprise is the domain of the works council, whereas the union is dominant at the supra-plant level. The works council relies upon information, legal advice, and various support provided by the union. The union depends on the activities of the works council which undertakes the recruitment of, and service to, members. The overwhelming majority of works council members are union members (nearly 100 % of blue-collar, and about 85 % of white-collar representatives).

B.2 The Bargaining Structure

(a) Regional and sectoral structure of bargaining

In principle, wage negotiations take place at the level of aggregated economic branches. Hereby we have to distinguish between federal-, province-, and company-based negotiations. In addition, there are collective agreements made for home-workers, and agreements concerning minimum wages. As a matter of fact, federal-based agreements are binding for lower-level (in particular province-based) negotiations which merely adjust regional differentials.

Table 5 shows the distribution of collective agreements: the bulk of contracts are made at the level of the provinces (62 %); another 27 % are made at the federal level. But this does not quite correctly mirror the real structure of collective bargaining. What appears, at first sight, as a strongly decentralized system, is virtually strongly centralized. There are two ÖGB affiliates functioning as "energizing" unions: the union of metal workers, and the union of public servants. Both use to submit their wage claims first, and they are followed by other branches. Province- and company-based agreements don't differ very much from the results achieved by the afore-mentioned groups. Most collective agreements, in particular wage agreements, are made for the term of one year. Exceptions are occasionally made with skeleton agreements concerning, e.g., reduction of working hours.

Table 5. Collective Agreements (1988)

ÖGB-Affiliate (Unions)	Federal	Province	Company	Home-workers	Minimum	Total
Salaried Employees	47	42	3	–	13	105
Artists, Media and Free-lance Employees	14	18	2	–	–	34
Wood and Construction Workers	31	45	4	–	–	80
Workers in the Chemical Industry	9	10	2	–	–	21
Railways Employees	–	3	–	–	–	3
Workers in the Printing Industry	5	–	–	2	–	7
Transport, Storage and Communication Workers	17	10	5	–	–	32
Catering and Personal Services	3	18	–	–	24	45
Workers in Agriculture, Forestry and Horticulture	3	22	1	–	–	26
Workers in Food Industry	18	106	7	–	–	131
Metal, Mining and Energy Workers	4	–	–	–	–	4
Workers in Textile and Leather Industry	11	100	–	9	–	120
Total	162	374	24	11	37	608

Source: Tätigkeitsbericht des ÖGB 1988, Wien 1989, p. IV/12.

Collective agreements are, in principle, made for the total dependent labour force in private industries (public servants, including post and railways, have separate bargaining structures). In this respect, the Austrian system of collective bargaining differs strongly from other systems. Roughly 56 % of the dependent labour force are organized in the monopolistic ÖGB (cf. below); but virtually all wage and salary earners are subject to collective agreements arranged by the ÖGB. Exceptions are only made for a small number of entrepreneurs who are, by very extraordinary reasons, not members of employers' organizations.

(b) The union's right to represent

The Austrian system of collective bargaining is to a high degree regulated by the Arbeitsverfassungsgesetz. The law specifies the bargaining structure as follows: Collective agreements ('Kollektivverträge') are legally binding on the signatory parties and their members. Employees are even then subject to an agreement when they are not members of a signatory party provided that their employer is under a contract. Analogous rules for outsider employers do not exist unless a signatory party moves for an extension of the scope of an agreement.[7] In this case the conciliation board ('Arbeitsgericht') can declare a collective agreement to a standing rule.

According to the Works Constitution Act, the right to make collective agreements is granted both to corporations under public law (chambers) and to associations with voluntary membership. In practice, the Chambers of Business make use of their right, while the Chambers of Labour relinquish for the benefit of the ÖGB. It is noteworthy that the ÖGB's de facto monopoly in collective bargaining derives from the Chambers of Labour which can determine whether they disclaim for their right or not. Since the Chambers and the ÖGB are strongly linked by personal unions and party interests, there is virtually no scope for additional, competing unions. Collective agreements are without exception made between the Chambers of Business and the affiliates of the ÖGB.

(c) Handling of industrial conflict

The regulation of industrial relations by law is exceptionally far-reaching. The major part of labour law provisions are obligatory, in so far, as contracts must not remain below the specified standards. Thus, it might be amazing that the ultimate means of

---

7. Since virtually all dependent workers are members of either the Chambers of Labour or the unions, it is the task of the latter to take care of those enterprises which are not covered by collective agreements. Usually, their appeals (which are based on the results of other branches) are granted by the conciliation board.

conflict: the strike, is not regulated at all. As early as 1870 the Coalition Act ('Koalitionsrecht') laid down that strikes do not affect employment contracts. This has not been basically changed up to this day, the state emphasizes its neutral role in case of strikes. All litigations emerging from strikes are subject to private-law respectively to public law jurisdiction. As for the latter, it has oriented itself on two questions throughout the Second Republic: Was the strike an official one (did the union call for strike)? and Was the strike the ultimate means after all attempts of conciliation had broken down (principle of ultima ratio)? Scholars in labour legislation agree that the jurisdiction is diffuse and inconsistent. That there have never been any efforts to create a strike law, might be due to only one but most important fact – Austria ranks worldwide with the countries recording the lowest strike figures (Karlhofer, 1983).

Table 6. Strikes 1980-90

Year	Number strikers	Days lost	Most affected economic sector	
			Sector	Days lost (share of total)
1980	26181	16961	Salaried employees	52%
1981	17115	4023	Salaried employees	62%
1982	91	344	Metal industry	81%
1983	208	514	Metal industry	99%
1984	289	544	Construction industry	52%
1985	35531	22752	Public service	96%
1986	3222	3253	Public service	92%
1987	7203	4822	Public service	69%
1988	24252	8542	Public service	88%
1989	3715	2986	Public service	97%
1990	5274	8870	Food industry	53%

Source: Union reports.

The level of industrial conflicts during the 1980s is documented in Table 6. The strike activities are characterized by the following features: (i) The number of workers involved, as well as of days lost, is extremely low. In only one of the years recorded here (1985) slightly more than one percent of the dependent labour force were participants of strikes. (ii) The average duration of strikes was mostly less than one day. (iii) Without exception, more than 50 % (mostly more than 80 %) of the total of lost days falls on only one union's share. (iv) Most economic branches have been strike-free. The bulk of disputes occurred in the public service (mainly teachers).

Contrary to the (not existing) management of strikes, for all conflicts of lower intensity mediation rules are provided by labour law. As mentioned above, Austrian industrial relations are extremely regulated by law. With respect to industrial conflict, this does not primarily mean substantive but procedural regulation. Cardinal point is the works council operating under public law. According to the legal binding of the actors in industrial relations, the Works Constitution Act provides detailed rules in case of conflict.

Lock-outs are almost unknown in Austria. In only a few cases since 1945 individual employers reacted with lock-outs to strikes, but in no case as an offensive means of supra-plant action (Karlhofer, 1983).

(d) Observations on the balance between private and public provisions

The character of labour contracts is largely shaped by three dimensions: 1. legal protection of the individual employee; 2. collective agreements (Kollektivverträge – KV); 3. company-based agreements (Betriebsvereinbarungen – BV). There is a hierarchy between these dimensions: legal protection must not be repealed by KV and BV, and KV must not be repealed by BV.

1. Legal provisions (covering the whole spectrum from protection against unlawful dismissal to social security) fix precisely defined qualitative or quantitative standards which must neither be failed nor be exceeded. What for this, it does not differ too much from the practices in other European countries.
2. KV are, as mentioned above, the results of free negotiations between employers' and workers' associations. The state does not intervene substantially, but specifies merely the procedural regulation. Legally binding on all contract partners and their members, the major part of KV is focused on wage agreements. Usually, KV on wages are concluded twofold: they include the increase of minimum wages as well as of actual wages.
3. Contrary to KV which primarily refer to the supra-plant level, BV are exclusively confined to the plant level relations. BV are subordinated to legal provisions and KV. Their scope is, according to the Works Constitution Act, defined as a supplement to the before-mentioned. The law distinguishes four types of BV: (i) indispensable BV (a great number of controlling measures must not be introduced without the works councils' consent); (ii) replaceable BV[8]; (iii) enforceable BV (e.g., the modes of payment); (iv) voluntary BV (e.g., fringe benefits).

---

8. A great many of management decisions come only in effect after the works council has been consulted. Computer-aided personnel files, for instance, may only be introduced after the works council has agreed. In case of litigation, the works council has the right to appeal to the conciliation board which can "replace" a management decision by decree. Replaceable BVs cannot be terminated within a fixed time-limit.

It must be emphasized that BV are, actually, much more than merely a supplement to KV. Especially in prosperous branches respectively enterprises, works councils are allowed to bargain for higher wages or better working conditions exceeding the KV by far. Thus, it is not amazing that union delegates of prosperous enterprises frequently exercise restraint in supra-plant negotiations in order to improve their in-plant bargaining position. Success with in-plant wage negotiations strengthens the influence of works councils among the rank and file.

Separate treatments for individual labour contracts are only allowed, in so far as they do not deteriorate the conditions for the employee. The law of equal treatment (Gleichbehandlungsgesetz) forbids the discrimination by sex and, in general, to treat an individual worse than the majority of the employees. It does not forbid, however, to grant special favours to a minority of employees.

C. Outcomes

C.1 Working Time

The working time law (Arbeitszeitgesetz) fixes the maximum permissible number of working hours for the bulk of employees. It is a protective law ensuring that the strain on employees does not exceed a certain limit. Since 1969, when the law was passed, the maximum is limited to 8 hours per day respectively 40 hours per week. Extensions of short duration up to 10 respectively 50 hours are allowed. Exemption permit can be granted by law or by the Works Supervisory Board (Arbeitsinspektorat), under certain circumstances an extension can be subject of collective agreements, too. Concerning the actual working time, only data about the manufacturing industry are available. In this sector, the monthly working time was 145 hours in 1984, decreasing to 140 hours in 1989.

The standard working time can be overstepped by working overtime. In that case, an overtime pay of 50 % is obligatory. In principle, the employee is not obliged to do overtime. Under certain circumstances, however, the employer is allowed to demand overtime work (rejection by the worker would violate the duty of loyalty). In-plant regulations can be based on shop-floor agreements between employers and works councils. According to that, the distribution of weekly working time can be fixed (e.g., 8 1/2 hours from Monday to Thursday, 6 hours on Friday), including arrangements on time and duration of breaks.

As can be seen, there is not much scope for individual contracts. With the exceptions mentioned above, individual arrangements can merely remain below the standard working time, but not exceed them essentially. Thus, the precisely defined limits blockade, or at least impede, to a high extent the various attempts of flexibilization of which two are mentioned in the following:

Flexible working hours ('Gleitzeit'): Flexible working hours means that the individual employee can serve his working hours within a specified scope which, to some extent, allows him the self-determination of his individual schedule. The term Gleitzeit is not explicitly mentioned in the working time law. There is a provision, however, allowing a varying distribution of the standard working hours (e.g., an eight-hour day can be self-organized by the employee between 7 a.m. and 6 p.m).

Flexible working hours on call ('Kapazitätsorientierte variable Arbeitszeit'): This form of flexibilization combines flexible working hours with the employee as a subject for recall. The purpose of that model is unequivocally not for the employee's benefit, but for the utilization of the enterprise's capacity: the distribution of working hours is exclusively oriented on the needs of the firm making the employee, in a sense, a stand-by worker ("stop and go").

Principally, for the latter model the same legal provisions are relevant as for "normal" flexible working time. Based on shop-floor agreements, it can be realized respectively for one week. Any efforts of the employers to extend this model are vehemently opposed by the labour organizations, in particular with regard to an extension of the legal framework. As a matter of fact, however, the unions are lossing ground in defending standardized employment contracts – not in the least because of a good number of part-time employees who definitely prefer a flexible working time.

Annual paid leave is prescribed by law. Employees with less than 25 years of service must be granted 30 workdays per year (five weeks), and employees with more years 36 workdays (6 weeks). In addition, there are 13 official holidays for which, provided they fall on a workday (Monday to Saturday)[9], wages must be paid. The average total of paid working time (including sick-leave) in manufacturing industry is 2043 hours per year, and the total of actual observed working hours is 1674 hours (1990).

The protection of women and young workers is extensive: Juvenile workers are defined as workers younger than 18 years old. There are various provisions protecting young workers from night work, overtime work and piece-work. Women are protected from night work and heavy labour (only 6 women affected in 1990!). Some more rigorous provisions apply for pregnant women.

Night work ("night" defined as 11 consecutive hours including the time between 8 p.m. and 6 a.m.), in particular in combination with heavy labour, is subject of

---

9. Although most workers have a five-day week, Saturday is treated as a working day (hence, "30 workdays vacation" means 5 weeks).

special legal provisions such as: additional paid leave (up to 6 workdays per year); extended medical welfare; specific provisions for early retirement. In 1990, only 11 thousand workers (0.2 % of the total dependent labour force) were affected both by night work and heavy labour.

C.2 Wages and Salaries

Wages are, in principle, subject of collective agreements – the state does not intervene. At any rate, there is a small group of employees who are not covered by collective agreements (e.g., housekeepers); in this case, on the application of a trade union, state agencies have to fix minimum wages.

Wages (blue-collar workers) and salaries (white-collar workers) are, in principle, paid on a monthly basis. Both are paid as gross incomes including all revenues paid by the employer. The proportion of social insurance premiums, listed in Table 4 (see above), varies between 16 and 17 % of the workers' gross income (another 19 to 26 % to be paid by the employer). The tax on wages is determined by the workers' marital status, the size of the family, and the income group (tax progression).

Holiday money ('Urlaubszuschuß') and Christmas money ('Weihnachtsremuneration'), also known as a 13th and 14th monthly wage, are part of collective agreements. Calculated as a share of the monthly wage to be paid twice a year, the remuneration varies between 57 % (textile industry) and 115 % (printing industry); public-sector employees are paid 50 % every three months.

As for measures against wage discrimination, the Austrian labour law provides that no employee must be discriminated against by sex (controlled by a commission for equal treatment). In 1990, a Ministry of Women Affairs was established headed by the former Permanent Under-Secretary of Women Affairs. She has a consultative, in some questions intervening, function in industrial relations as far as women are concerned.

With respect to fringe benefits it must be taken into consideration that the Austrian system of industrial relations is strongly determined by legal provisions. The bulk of enterprises are, now as before, strictly acting along prescribed rules. Additional benefits are mainly granted by large-scale enterprises: e.g., lunch tickets at reduced prices, profit sharing, bonus by seniority (mostly after 25 years of service), support of holiday camps, etc. Gratifications of this kind, however, cannot be granted in an arbitrary manner but are subject of collective agreements to be concluded with the Betriebsrat. Another fringe benefit, a common practice in the tourist industry, is to offer free boarding and lodging for seasonal workers.

C.3 Termination of Labour Contracts

(a) Firing and quitting rules

In principle, two different forms of termination of labour contracts are to be distinguished: the summary dismissal and the notice of employment. As for the first, the employment contract is cancelled immediately. Summary dismissal presupposes a severe reason whereby it were unacceptable to one or both contract partners to work together even for the period of notice.

Contrary to a dismissal, the notice of employment does not require a statement of reasons. The length of periods of notice depends on the employee's status: salaried employees are subject to a specific law (Angestelltengesetz) in which the periods are precisely defined by seniority; the notice of manual workers is not regulated by law but by collective agreements in which date and period are fixed. The periods of notice are usually longer for salaried employees (up to five months). As a matter of principle, however, the periods which have to be regarded by the employee must not be longer than those which have to be regarded by employers.

With respect to enterprises in which a works council is established, the Labour Constitution Act prescribes a special handling of dismissals and notices. Every termination of labour contracts planned by the employer, must be announced to the works council. This does not mean that the works council can prevent the termination, but the employer is obliged to justify it. In particular, the works council is entitled to contest the validity of a termination if it is "socially unwarranted" and the person concerned has been employed more than six months. Specific provisions are effective with respect to certain groups, such as women under protection of motherhood[10], and handicapped persons. Members of works councils are protected by the Labour Constitution Act, they cannot be dismissed or noticed without the permission of the Conciliation Board.

(b) Collective lay-offs

Collective lay-offs are regulated by the Labour Market Promotion Act ('Arbeitsmarktförderungsgesetz'). Enterprises employing at least 100 workers have to give notice of the termination of labour contracts to the Labour Exchange Administration ('Arbeitsmarktverwaltung'), if they intend the lay-off of five or more per cent of the staff. In case of bankruptcy or insolvency the employment contract is not dissolved

---

10. Pregnant women must not be noticed of termination. In addition, women are protected at least four months after the delivery, respectively four weeks after a one-year or two-year motherhood release ('Karenzurlaub').

automatically. At least, to the letter of the law, employees have a legal claim to the observance of periods of termination by the employer. Claims for damages can be addressed to the official liquidator.

(c) Severance pay

Severance pay must be granted after a continuous employment of at least three years. The amount is precisely fixed by compensation laws for salaried employees, and for manual workers, which both were assimilated in 1979. Compensation must be paid if the employment contract is dissolved by the employer, in so far as the employee is not responsible for dismissal himself. Compensation must be paid, too, if the contract is terminated by the employee in the following cases: men at the age of 65 (women 60); early retirement; extraordinary retirement of night-shift workers; women during motherhood release. Compensation pay can also be subject to collective agreements, company-based agreements or individual contracts provided that they do not remain below the limits fixed by law. With the exceptions of construction and agricultural workers for which separate provisions exist, the height of severance pay is graduated as spelled out in Table 7.

Table 7. Duration of Employment and Height of Severance Pay [Abfertigung]*

3 years	2 monthly pays	+	2/12 of all separate pays
5 years	3 monthly pays	+	3/12 of all separate pays
10 years	4 monthly pays	+	4/12 of all separate pays
15 years	6 monthly pays	+	6/12 of all separate pays
20 years	9 monthly pays	+	9/12 of all separate pays
25 years	12 monthly pays	+	12/12 of all separate pays

* There are 14 monthly pays: 12 regular pays plus separate pays referring to a 13th (holiday pay) and a 14th (Christmas bonus) wage (each 100% of a regular pay). Severance pays are composed with regard to regular pays as well as to separate pays.

Source: Wirtschafts- und Sozialstatistisches Taschenbuch 1990, Wien 1990, p. 427.

D. Prospects of Labour Market Performance

Austria's industrial relations system has been a special case in recent decades. There is no other country in the industrialized world where social partnership would be as influential as in Austria. In the late 1970s and early 1980s when the debate on neo-corporatism was fashionable, Austria was regarded as a paradigm of cooperative industrial relations. As a matter of fact, the (formal and informal) cooperation between capital, labour, and the state has been extremely far-reaching in Austria. Even in the political system (in a narrow sense) the "social partners" (i.e. employers' and labour organizations) have used to set a precedent for parliamentary decisions in all social, economic, and socio-economic affairs. The parliament played hardly more than the role of an agent of employers' organizations and the union. Though decreasing, the share of members of parliament representing business and labour interests amounts to nearly 50 % in the early nineties.

In recent years, however, observers perceive a decline of the role social partnership plays in the regulation of industrial relations (Traxler, 1988; Pelinka, 1990). First of all, the structural change of the labour market is to be mentioned. Mainly the ÖGB – having maintained its membership rates even in the 1980s (when the unions in other countries suffered from severe losses) – is faced with a continuous decrease of the unionization rate. In particular white collar workers tend increasingly to be unorganized.

Another point to be mentioned is the disastrous development of the nationalized industries. This sector, covering virtually all basic industries, historically a heritage of the Nazi era which had been saved against claims of the Allies through nationalizations, suffered from a serious crisis throughout the 1980s. As a consequence, parts of it were privatized followed by extensive lay-offs and early-retirement programs. The nationalized industries had been the ÖGB's most powerful bastion where unionization rates of 90 % and more had been common. Students of Austrian industrial relations are presumably struck to learn that many high-ranking managers in the nationalized industries worked their way up with union support. This is definitely over, union power in this sector has been grievously weakened since the mid-eighties (Karlhofer, 1989).

In recent years, there has also been a strong drive against the compulsory membership in chambers which are, as mentioned above, basic pillars of Austria's social partnership. Mainly the Chambers of Labour came under fire after a series of political scandals had been revealed in the late 1980s. In 1991, the Chamber of Labour Act was reformed giving more rights to the members. The Chambers of Commerce, on the other side, are facing similar challenges. There is a growing discontent among young entrepreneurs who more and more reject the traditional style of corporatist interest representation. At present, it is hard to say what role the chambers will play in times to come. Throughout the Second Republic the chambers had been power domains of the grand 'Lagerparteien' SPÖ and ÖVP holding the overwhelming majority among the respective social classes. This has changed thoroughly as can be gathered from recent election results: The percentage of voting shrank dramatically in the Chambers of Commerce elections (from 70 % in 1985 to 62 % in 1990), and still more distressing in the Chambers of Labour elections (from 64 % in 1984 to 49 % in 1989) (Sommer, 1990; Kaufmann, 1991).

Despite the problems the actors are faced with, social partnership has, now as before, a high reputation right across the social classes. Recent opinion polls show that a strong majority of Austrians (63 % in 1990) have a positive attitude to corporatist interest representation (SWS-Rundschau, 1990, p. 395). Doubtless, however, the "social partners" on both sides are, at present, under stress and strongly urged to match with a rapidly changing environment (Talos, 1991).

As pointed out in the sections B and C, the labour market regulation in Austria has been determined both by an extensive labour legislation and corporatist agreements leaving little scope for separate treatments in labour contracts. Yet, there are several things in a state of flux indicating that the scope of corporatist determination is becoming narrower. In 1992, the ÖGB, offering resistance for a long time, gave its assent to a reform of the state-provided labour exchange system giving way for the provision of jobs by private employment agencies. There are also negotiations taking place between employers' associations and the unions concerning the reduction of the weekly working time to 35 hours, and, in exchange, a more flexible handling of individual employment contracts. All this certainly does not point in the direction of serious deregulation. Considering the past four decades, however, there are strong reasons to assume that other parts of the labour market relations, up to now nearly completely controlled by the state and the "social partners", will be opened to free-market rules in the nineties – a process that will presumably be accelerated after Austria's entry into the EC.

REFERENCES

Biffl, Gudrun, Beschäftigung und Bildung im Wandel, *WIFO-Monatsberichte*, Nr. 6 (June 1991), pp. 368-76.

Butschek, Felix. *Die österreichische Wirtschaft im 20. Jahrhundert*. Stuttgart: Gustav Fischer, 1985.

Butschek, Felix, Der Arbeitsmarkt in der Zeit der großen Koalition, *Österreichisches Jahrbuch für Politik '89*, München, Oldenbourg, 1990, pp. 137-165.

Cerny, Josef, *Arbeitsverfassungsgesetz*, Wien: Verlag des ÖGB, 1987.

Crouch, Colin, *Trade Unions: The Logic of Collective Action*, Glasgow: Fontana, 1982.

Faulhaber, Theodor, *Die Vereinigung österreichischer Industrieller*, Wien: Signum, 1980.

Karlhofer, Ferdinand, *'Wilde' Streiks in Österreich – Entstehungs- und Verlaufsbedingungen industrieller Konflikte in den siebziger Jahren*, Wien-Köln: Böhlau, 1983.

Karlhofer, Ferdinand, ÖGB und industrielle Beziehungen – Aspekte des Wandels, in: Rudolf Burger *et al.*, *Verarbeitungsmechanismen der Krise*, Wien: Braumüller, 1988, pp. 283-96.

Karlhofer, Ferdinand, Die Krise der österreichischen verstaatlichten Industrie und ihre Folgen – Zum Funktionsverlust einer Konstante im politisch-ökonomischen System, *Jahrbuch zur Staats- und Verwaltungswissenschaft*, vol. 3, Baden-Baden: Nomos, 1989, pp. 315-33.

Kaufmann, Kurt, Analyse der Handelskammerwahlen 1990, *Österreichisches Jahrbuch für Politik '90*, München: Oldenbourg, 1991, pp. 171-83.

Lehmbruch, Gerhard, Neocorporatism in Comparative Perspective, in: Gerhard Lehmbruch and Philipp C. Schmitter (eds.), *Patterns of Corporatist Policy-Making*, London: Sage, 1982, pp. 1-28.

Marin, Bernd, *Die Paritätische Kommission – Aufgeklärter Technokorporatismus in Österreich*, Wien: Internationale Publikationen, 1982.

Pelinka, Anton, *Modellfall Österreich? Möglichkeiten und Grenzen der Sozialpartnerschaft*, Wien: Braumüller, 1981.

Pelinka, Anton, Sozialpartnerschaft ohne Kammern?, *Österreichisches Jahrbuch für Politik '89*, München, Oldenbourg, 1990, pp. 619-31.

Sommer, Franz, Die AK-Wahl 1989 – Die Wahl der Nichtwähler, *Österreichisches Jahrbuch für Politik '89*, München, Oldenbourg, 1990, pp. 97-118.

Sweeny, Jim, The Austrian Social Partnership, in: Jim Sweeny and Josef Weidenholzer, *Austria: A Study in Modern Achievement*, Aldershot: Avebury, 1988, pp. 182-93.

SWS-Rundschau, vol. 30, Nr. 3, 1990.

Talos, Emmerich, *Staatliche Sozialpolitik in Österreich – Rekonstruktion und Analyse*, Wien: Verlag für Gesellschaftskritik, 1981.

Talos, Emmerich, Alles erreicht? Sozialdemokratische Sozialpolitik in der Zweiten Republik, in: Peter Pelinka and Gerhard Steger (eds.), *Auf dem Weg zur Staatspartei? Zur Geschichte der SPÖ seit 1945*, Wien: Verlag für Gesellschaftskritik, 1988, pp. 247-65.

Talos, Emmerich, Sozialpartnerschaft: Kooperation-Konzertierung-politische Regulierung, in: Herbert Dachs *et al.* (eds), *Handbuch des politischen Systems Österreichs*, Wien: Manz, 1991, pp. 390-409.

Traxler, Franz, *Evolution gewerkschaftlicher Interessenvertretung: Entwicklungslogik und Organisationsdynamik gewerkschaftlichen Handelns am Beispiel Österreich*, Wien and Frankfurt am Main: Braumüller and Campus, 1982.

Traxler, Franz, Von der Hegemonie in die Defensive – Österreichs Gewerkschaften im System der Sozialpartnerschaft, in: Walther Müller-Jentsch (ed.), *Zukunft der Gewerkschaften – Ein internationaler Vergleich*, Frankfurt am Main: Campus, 1988, pp. 45-69.

Labour Market Contracts and Institutions
J. Hartog and J. Theeuwes (Editors)

CHAPTER 7

GERMANY:
Living with Tight Corporatism

Karl-Heinz Paqué*

A. History: The Path to Corporatism

West Germany – and since October 1990 Germany as a whole – has a corporatist labour market. There are strong unions and employers' associations entitled to a wide range of autonomy in concluding collective agreements on virtually all matters of labour relations. There is very little direct government meddling with this autonomy, but quite a bit of indirect public interference through an elaborate legislation on labour and welfare matters as well as a detailed regulation of the bargaining process and industrial action. In briefly summarizing the genesis of German-style corporatism, a distinction should be made between (i) collective bargaining as a genuine concern of the labour movement, and (ii) job protection and welfare legislation as a paternalistic reaction of government to find a political solution to the 'social question'.

A.1 Collective Bargaining[1]

The history of collective bargaining in Germany may conveniently be divided into four periods, which are separated by times of war and/or by severe political turning-points: the Empire from 1871 to the outbreak of World War I in 1914, the Weimar Republic from 1919 to 1933, the National Socialist Regime (1933-1945) and the post-war 'Bonn Republic' 1949-1990, leaving out of consideration the altogether different experience of former East Germany in the last four decades.

Until World War I, legislation did not recognize, let alone sanction the existence of collective agreements. Although coalitions of interests like unions were not pro-

---

* The Kiel Institute of World Economics. Thanks are due to Thomas Tack for competent research assistance.

1. For a history of trade unionism in Germany (which entails the main aspects of collective bargaining) see i.a. Moses (1982), Vols. I and II and Kendall (1975), pp. 89-139, both in English, Hentschel (1983) and Limmer (1988) in German. As to the more narrowly legal aspects, see i.a. Gitter (1987), pp. 4-8 and Söllner (1987), pp. 10-16.

hibited, any contract made by coalitions was simply not legally enforceable. Nevertheless – and remarkably enough – collective bargaining gradually became more frequent: in 1873, a first pioneering agreement was concluded in the printing industry, and shortly before World War I, a still low, but significant 6 % share of all employees was covered by collective agreements. Due to the lack of legal backing and the stiff resistance of employers, collective bargaining lagged well behind the impressive upswing of unionism: the foundation of the first few trade unions in the second half of the 1860s (cigar makers, printers, tailors, woodworkers) was followed by a first – still moderate – rise of total membership figures to about 230 000 in 1890, but then a steep upward movement set in to one million in 1904, about 4.5 million in 1913 and more than 8 million members in 1920-1922.[2] In 1890, a so-called general commission of German Trade Unions had been founded as a first umbrella organization for all industry-based unions; this was to remain for almost 30 years under the highly successful leadership of Carl Legien. Except for a group of Christian and liberally-oriented unions, which gradually lost in relative importance, unionism had strong ties to the Social Democratic Party (SPD) whose rise paralleled that of the unions. Under Carl Legien, the unions remained ideologically close to the SPD – in later years to its reformist wing – but in general turned away from political to more narrowly defined 'labour aims', with the strike weapon being reserved for the purpose of supporting economic, not political objectives. Strike activity was becoming significant in the last two decades before World War I, with peaks reached in the boom years 1905 and 1910 when labour markets were particularly tight. Yet, a breakthrough to collective bargaining was still out of reach, not the least because employers in heavy industry – traditionally the most conservative in Germany who dominated the Association of German Employers ('Vereinigung Deutscher Arbeitgeber', VDA)[3] – firmly rejected it.

In this respect, World War I brought a kind of displacement effect: the Patriotic Auxiliary Service Law ('Hilfsdienstgesetz') of December 1916 mentioned unions for the first time as representatives of labour in a legal document. In November 1918, briefly after the war had ended and a full-scale democracy had replaced the still autocratic regime of the Empire, the umbrella organizations of both employers and unions established the so-called central co-operation ('Zentralarbeitsgemeinschaft') which explicitly acknowledged the principle of collective bargaining as the basis for industrial relations; nine months later, the Weimar constitution unconditionally granted the freedom of coalition. Although the central co-operation was a kind of emergency measure, which did not survive for long as an institution, collective bargaining was subsequently sanctioned by the collective agreements decree of December 1918, the conciliation decree of October 1923 and the law on the establishment of a labour

2. See Kendall (1975), p. 94 and Moses (1982), Vol. II., pp. 511-512.

3. The VDA was founded in 1913, but earlier versions of employers' cooperation had existed since the last decade of the 19th century.

jurisdiction of December 1926; in addition, the law on works councils of February 1920 laid the ground for a labour representation on the plant level, with a limited, but significant influence of the works councils on labour concerns within the firm.[4] In practice, collective bargaining became the rule: during the 'golden years' of the Weimar Republic – after the currency reform in 1923 until the beginning of the Great Depression in 1929/1930 – 11-13 million workers and salaried employees (i.e. about 2/3 of all employees) had collectively negotiated contracts.[5]

All in all, the legal framework and the 'culture' of today's industry-based bargaining took shape in the 1920s. There is only one major exception, namely 'compulsory conciliation'.[6] By the conciliation decree of October 1923 – passed as part of the stabilization package of the currency reform – compulsory conciliation was due if the bargaining parties were not able to find a compromise. The minister of labour appointed a number of semi-professional conciliators for all major industries (19 in 1924, 13 in 1929) who were to chair a conciliation board consisting of an equal number of representatives from the conflicting parties and who had a decisive vote if no agreement could be reached. This gave the conciliators the power to introduce their own judgement about the macroeconomic and distributional issues into whatever wage settlement. In turn, the right to appoint conciliators was allotted to the minister of labour, and it assigned to him an important backstage role in the bargaining process.[7]

---

4. The history and present state of codetermination and company statute legislation is not covered in this chapter as it does not have an immediate bearing on collective bargaining and the labour market in general. For a survey of this matter, see Söllner (1987), pp. 155-206.

5. Roughly speaking, something like 60 % of these contracts were concluded on a company, about 30 % on a regional and the remaining 10 % on a national level.

6. For a broad account of the Weimar experience with compulsory conciliation, see James (1986), pp. 209-245. For detailed historical analyses, see Hartwich (1967), and Bähr (1989). Both authors' moderately positive judgement about the Weimar experience is representative for the dominant view among German historians. – Note that we translate the German term 'Schlichtung' by using the English term 'conciliation', not 'arbitration'. We deliberately do so to conserve the spirit of a cooperative (and corporatist!) effort of the bargaining parties, which the German term conveys and which is clearly lost when speaking of 'arbitration'.

7. In our view, the compulsory conciliation of the Weimar Republic had a very unhappy history. In a way, it uprooted the whole bargaining system: instead of being used as an instrument of last resort, it removed the pressure for agreement from the parties and thus induced them to carry on with maximalist positions and to speculate on the conciliator's likely bias. In all major industries, at least half, usually an even higher share of 'agreements' were implemented via compulsory conciliation. (See Hartwich (1967), pp. 418 (Tab. 15*), 419 (Tab. 16*) and 420 (Tab. 17*) for selected industries.) Nevertheless, industrial relations were and remained relatively bad: strikes and lockouts were frequent events, more so than either before World War I or after World War II. It is worth noting that most compulsory conciliation agreements were explicitly disapproved by one party – in the majority of cases the employer's side – sometimes even by both parties. The employers' associations regularly claimed that the conciliators had a bias towards labour

The Great Depression brought serious disruptions of collective bargaining by the quasi-authoritarian governments of Brüning and von Papen, i.a. an administrative wage cut by almost 10 % at the end of 1931.[8] Under the national-socialist regime, industrial relations were terminated altogether: unions were banned and dissolved and the German Working Front ('Deutsche Arbeitsfront') was founded as a unitary organization of both employers and employees. Collective 'agreements' were ordered by decree and ended in a general wage (and also price) stop in 1936.

After four years of Allied occupation and administration following the end of World War II, the Collective Agreements Act ('Tarifvertragsgesetz') of April 1949 marks the return to a bargaining system which very much resembles that of the Weimar Republic with the one major exception, namely the subsequent absence of any element of compulsory arbitration. Unions and employers' associations as well as their respective umbrella organizations were soon rebuilt, with the unions making an attempt to overcome their traditional division into a large socialist and much smaller Christian and liberal parts. Yet, by the mid-1950s, this attempt had partially failed when a part of the membership with a Christian affiliation split off from the main and most powerful umbrella organization of blue-collar workers, the DGB ('Deutscher Gewerkschaftsbund'), to form the more conservative CGB ('Christlicher Gewerkschaftsbund'), an alliance, which has remained fairly unimportant in collective bargaining.[9] Apart from the new legislation on codetermination in the early 1950s and mid-1970s, the institutional framework of collective bargaining and labour representation on the plant level has been kept quite stable over the last four decades. Measured by the extent of strike activity, the system has been extraordinarily successful, both by historical and by international standards.[10] Yet in terms of unemployment, the record is mixed: the system allowed a quick return to full employment in the course of the 1950s – implying an impressively rapid integration of about ten million refugees from the former Eastern German provinces – but it did not prevent chronic unemployment to re-emerge in the 1970s and 1980s.

---

interests. Apart from the observed asymmetry of approvals, there are reasons to believe that this was in fact so: economically, wage inflation hardly abated until 1930, despite an unemployment rate of more than 8 % most of the time; politically, the ministry of labour was regarded as a citadel of labour interests, and the two ministers in charge between 1920 and 1930 – Heinrich Brauns (from 1920 to 1928), a priest from the Catholic Central Party ('Zentrum') and Rudolf Wissel (from 1920 to 1930), a Social Democrat – were known for their affiliation to the labour movement, the Christian one in the case of Brauns, the socialist one in the case of Wissel. Quarrels within the governments on wage policy – notably between the ministry of economics and that of labour – were frequent and sharp.

8. See James (1986), pp. 223-245.

9. Christian unions have retained a non-negligible influence only in some minor branches of trade and commerce.

10. For a concise evaluation of the macroeconomic performance of the German collective bargaining system up to the late 1970s, see Flanagan, Soskice, Ulman (1983), pp. 208-300.

A.2 Job Protection and Welfare Legislation

The early history of social legislation has only loose links to the history of the labour movement. Oddly enough, the main welfare laws were initiated by conservatives, notably the first Chancellor of the Empire, Otto von Bismarck. He recognized the long-term political rise of the labour movement and countered the threat firstly by suppressing the political wing of the movement, the Social Democrats, and secondly by strengthening the workers' ties to the regime by giving them a material reason to support the state. The first part of the strategy failed completely, but the second part was successful at least in the long run. After all, social legislation in Germany never again lost its characteristic tinge of paternalistic statism although an increasingly reformist labour movement later staunchly defended the welfare institutions and called for their extension.

Legal job protection[11] began as early as 1839 with the Prussian regulation of youth employment. In the four decades before World War I, further regulations were introduced to protect juvenile and so-called home workers and to grant maternity leave. After World War I, the protection of handicapped persons, above all war veterans, and general regulations on dismissals and working time were added. All these elements of labour protection remained and were further extended after World War II.

The German social security system[12] goes back to the legislation promoted by Bismarck in the 1880s. At that time, public health and accident insurance as well as pension funds were established, with a compulsory participation for all workers and a large part of salaried employees.[13] Although public in spirit, the funds were to be run by a formally independent administration, jointly controlled by representatives of both employees and employers on a parity basis. Naturally, unions and employers' associations gained a decisive influence on the funds' working and policy. It is a remarkable fact that the social security system has survived a century with two World Wars and much political turmoil. Of course, contributions and benefits have been vastly extended, in particular during the years of the Weimar Republic and again in the 1950s, and taxpayers' money has been tapped occasionally. In 1927, a public unemployment insurance fund was added and organized analogously to the other elements of the system. It immediately crowded out the 'private' insurance

---

11. For the historical background of the legislation and the welfare state in Germany, see Hentschel (1983).

12. For the historical background, see Hentschel (1983), pp. 9-28, 119-215.

13. There were (and to some extent still are) various limits to compulsory participation in particular for salaried employees with higher incomes. As to contributions, the rule was set that 50 % had to be covered by the employer and 50 % by the employee. By and large, contributions and – in the case of pensions – benefits as well are calculated as a share of gross income.

funds run by the unions for their members. The only major change in the working of the system has been the stepwise move from a fully funded old age insurance to a pure pay-as-you-go scheme; this change was due not only to an erosion and destruction of the fund's wealth in the course of two post-war currency reforms (1923 and 1948), but also to the deliberate political decision in the 1950s to drastically raise and 'dynamize' pensions by more or less indexing them to the wage level.

B. The Institutional and Legal Environment

B.1 Structure of Bargaining[14]

Collective agreements are a pervasive feature of German labour markets. The Federal Minister of Labour and Social Affairs estimates that, in 1990, the number of collective agreements in force was about 32 000, encompassing almost all industries and services and about 90 % of all employees.[15] Only a few branches of the service sector – some non-profit organizations such as churches, political parties, chambers of commerce, etc. – are not covered by collective agreements, but most of them routinely adjust wages and working conditions to the terms fixed in the collective agreements of some closely related chunk of the labour market, above all that for public employees.

Due to the traditional organization of German unions and employers' associations by industrial branches, collective bargaining in Germany is carried out on the industry or plant level. This means that usually one single collective agreement on any major matter of remuneration and working conditions is concluded for all employees in one firm or industry, no matter what occupational groups the employees belong to.

In general, collective agreements are concluded between the relevant union and employers' association of an industry on a regional basis, i.e. – very roughly speaking – on the level of the states ('*Länder*').[16] Some industries such as construction and

14. For a detailed account of the relevant legal rules see i.a. Gitter (1987), Part III, pp. 86-117, Söllner (1987), § 9, pp. 53-63; § 15-18, pp. 119-154. A brief summary in English is provided by OECD (1979), pp. 58-59; p. 65.

15. See, e.g., Bundesministerium für Arbeit und Sozialordnung (1990b), pp. 1-2 where more statistics on the number of collective agreements can be found. Note that, in most branches of industry, separate agreements on different issues coexist.

16. The Federal Minister of Labour and Social Affairs estimates the number of (sectoral and regional) bargaining districts to be about 800. See Bundesministerium für Arbeit und Soziales (1990b), p. 2. Note that the so-called works council – a board of elected representatives of labour on the plant level – which is prescribed by the Company Statute Law for all firms with at least five employees, does not have a mandate for collective bargaining. Among its assigned duties is merely to control that the contracts are in fact observed by the employer. For the tasks

printing have nation-wide or almost nation-wide agreements, but they are clearly exceptions. Quite a few larger firms (at present about 2000)[17] conclude collective agreements on a company basis (so-called 'Firmentarifverträge'), the most prominent examples being the car manufacturer 'Volkswagen' and the public monopoly service firms 'Deutsche Bundespost' (German Postal Services) and 'Deutsche Bundesbahn' (German Railways). Currently, about one quarter of all collective agreements are estimated to have been concluded on a company basis.[18]

As a rule, collective agreements on wages and salaries are concluded for twelve months, with the annual payround taking place mostly in the first quarter of the year.[19] General working conditions (e.g. working time, holidays, etc.) are fixed in so-called framework agreements ('Manteltarifverträge')[20], which usually extend over longer periods than one year; they are not subject to any specific rules or negotiation timing.

B.2 Structure of Industrial Relations

Both trade unions and employers' associations play an important role in economic and political life. This role is at least partly reflected in membership (and related) statistics. In all years since 1951, about 37-41 % of all employees have been union members, with peaks reached in the early 1950s and again the late 1970s and a low in the mid-1960s. If retired persons are excluded, the degree of organization (density rate) turns out to be somewhat lower – around 32-36 % – but the intertemporal pattern remains basically the same.[21]

Among the 16 independent unions united under the roof of the DGB, the metal workers' union ('Industriegewerkschaft Metall') has by far the greatest weight as it covers about one third of all DGB members, a share which has hardly changed in the last two decades. It is followed at some distance by the union of public em-

---

and duties of the works council, which are not the subject matter of this chapter, see Söllner (1987), pp. 178-193.

17. See Bundesministerium für Arbeit und Sozialordnung (1990b), p. 1-2.

18. See Bundesministerium für Arbeit und Sozialordnung (1990b), p. 3.

19. More recently, longer-term wage contracts up to three years became common after virtual price stability had been temporarily reached by the mid-1980s. With the revival of inflation towards the end of the 1980s, the standard period for wage contracts has shrunk again to one year.

20. On the different types of contracts, see Söllner (1987), p. 125, Markmann (1977), pp. 543-544.

21. As to the definitional subtleties of union membership, see Price (1989); as to the intertemporal development of union membership in West Germany and some other countries, see Visser (1986; 1989a,b) and Armingeon (1987).

ployees ('Öffentliche Dienste, Transport und Verkehr', ÖTV)[22] with about 15 % and the union of chemical workers ('Industriegewerkschaft Chemie') with 8-9 % of all DGB members. Within the DGB, the share of female members has increased quite substantially from 15 % in the late 1960s to about 23 % in the late 1980s; this trend could be observed all throughout the 16 DGB unions, with a particularly sharp upswing in the union of public employees (ÖTV), where the membership share of women rose from less than 18 % before 1970 to more than 30 % in the late 1980s.[23]

In practice, only the individual industrial unions – and not the DGB – figure as parties at the bargaining tables. Yet, it is safe to say that the unions' umbrella organization has always served as a powerful instrument for coordinating aims and strategies as well as for political lobbying outside the actual bargaining rounds. Looking over the whole of post-war history, the unions' voice in the sphere of economics and politics has remained remarkably homogeneous, with open frictions within the DGB being the exception rather than the rule. Nevertheless, a fairly stable pattern of moderately differentiated union opinions has emerged and survived, with a more radical stance being taken by the metal workers' and the printers' union, and a more pragmatic line taken by, e.g., the union of chemical workers.

Outside the umbrella organization of the DGB, there is the union of white-collar workers DAG ('Deutsche Angestellten Gewerkschaft') which plays a minor part both in public and at the bargaining table. The DAG is not organized on an industrial basis; its membership comprises salaried employees from all branches of industry. In collective bargaining, the DAG more or less follows the lead of the respective DGB industrial union, without taking an all too active part in actual negotiations. The same holds a fortiori for the bunch of small, mostly Christian unions.[24]

As to the size and structure of the employers' associations, it is very hard to receive anything like reliable quantitative information. It is estimated that there are roughly 1000 so-called industrial associations of various branches of industry. The industrial employers are members only of a given local association, not of the central organiz-

---

22. Note that it is somewhat imprecise to call the ÖTV a union of public employees because (i) there are public employees in some other unions as well (notably teachers in the so-called education and science union GEW), and (ii) there are also private employees in the ÖTV (notably workers in the transport industry). Nevertheless, the large majority of organized public employees are members of the ÖTV.

23. For detailed statistical information on these matters, see Löhrlein (1990).

24. The civil servants' organization, the DBB ('Deutscher Beamtenbund'), is an altogether special case because civil servants do not have the right of collective bargaining. Instead the state has a one-sided constitutional obligation to take care of their concerns. Usually, this is done by more or less indexing their wage increases to those collectively agreed upon for other public employees. Hence the DBB must be considered not as a union proper, but rather as a mere political lobbying group.

ations at the federal or state level, whose membership is composed of the local associations. Hence, the individual employer is only an indirect member of any central organization. At the local level, there are also so-called combined industrial associations where employers of different branches of industry are organized, and which are members of some central industrial organization. A good guess is that about 70 % of all associations are members of the Central Organization of German Employers' Associations ('Bundesvereinigung der Deutschen Arbeitgeberverbände', BDA); 90 % of all employers are estimated to be organized in the various associations.[25]

B.3 The Legal Framework of Collective Agreements[26]

(a) Right to represent

Article 9 III of the German constitution (the 'Grundgesetz' or Basic Law) grants a general right to form a coalition for the purpose of preserving and/or improving one's economic and working conditions. To qualify as a coalition in this sense, any association has to fulfil three additional requirements: (i) It has to be a voluntary association based on private law.[27] (ii) It has to be legally and factually independent, both of its opponent party at the bargaining table and of any third party; thus, on the workers' side, an association (e.g. a union) must be organized on an inter-plant basis to become a genuine coalition since a mere workers' club confined to one firm ('Werkverein') is regarded as being too dependent on that one firm's employment decisions. (iii) The aim of the association must be realistically achievable through the use of bargaining and/or economic pressure although the readiness to strike is not considered as a necessary condition.[28] As both unions and employers' associations in general fulfil these requirements, their right to existence is in fact protected on constitutional grounds. Conversely, Article 9 III of the German constitution is widely recognized as granting a right to refrain from joining a coalition; while such a negative right is not explicitly mentioned in the legal text, it can be inferred from the logic and the spirit of the law, notably its emphasis on the voluntary character of the association.

---

25. Private conversation with staff of the BDA.

26. For a detailed account of the relevant legal rules see i.a. Gitter (1987), Part III, pp. 86-117, Söllner (1987), § 9, pp. 53-63; § 15-18, pp. 119-154. A brief summary in English is provided by OECD (1979), pp. 58-59; p. 65.

27. A minor exception are the guilds ('Innungen'), which have been explicitly accepted as coalitions in the sense of Article 9 III, but which are not strictly voluntary organizations. They are allowed to conclude collective agreements. For details, see Söllner (1987), p. 55.

28. This is the orthodox legal opinion shared i.a. by the Federal Constitutional Court. A minority of legal scholars takes a different view. For details, see Söllner (1987), p. 54-55.

The German Collective Agreements Act ('Tarifvertragsgesetz', TVG) of 1949 sets the legal frame for collective bargaining. Paragraph 2 I-III TVG stipulates that only a union, an individual employer and an association of employers may be party to a collective agreement. In the case of a union, the courts have demanded a certain – yet numerically unspecified – minimum size to make sure that there is at least some economic threat potential to support its collective bargaining position (although, again, the readiness to strike is not required). Umbrella organizations ('Spitzenverbände') like the BDA or the DGB may also conclude collective agreements provided they are properly authorized by their members (§ 2 III TVG) or their statutes explicitly require them to do so (§ 2 IV TVG). The legal competence for collective bargaining and for the conclusion of collective agreements as well as the organization of internal decision-making within the associations are all defined by their statutes, which have to obey generally accepted democratic principles. All collective agreements are documented in a publicly accessible register ('Tarifregister') at the Ministry of Labour and Social Affairs (§ 6 TVG).

As to its content, any collective agreement is to consist of two parts, a 'mandatory' and a 'normative' part. The mandatory part describes the rights and duties of the parties with respect to conclusion, implementation and termination of the agreement, including the peace obligation ('Friedenspflicht'), which states that – for the time fixed in the agreement – it is prohibited to resort to any kind of industrial action (strikes, lockouts, boycotts, etc. or threats thereof).[29] The normative part of the agreement defines the wages and working conditions which – according to § 4 TVG – are to apply to both parties of the agreement. Deviations from the rules of the contract are allowed only in two types of cases, namely (i) if they are explicitly mentioned in the contract, so-called opening clauses ('Tariföffnungsklauseln'), which are very rare in the case of remuneration and general working conditions, and (ii) if employers in practice offer 'better' terms than those specified in the agreement. Thus, the collective agreement fixes a contractual minimum: employers may offer better wages and/or working conditions, but not worse ones.[30]

(b) Coverage of negotiated contracts

In theory, the normative part of a collective agreement applies only to the contracting parties, i.e. in the standard case of an agreement between a union and an employers' association, to all members of both organizations. In practice, however, virtually all organized employers offer the same wage and working conditions to

29. For details, see Gitter (1987), pp. 93-94, Söllner (1987), pp. 86-88. Among legal scholars, there is a consensus that the peace obligation should be considered as a direct 'common sense' consequence of any collective agreement, even if it is not explicitly codified in the contract.

30. For details, see Gitter (1987), pp. 99-101, Söllner (1987), pp. 127-129.

union members and non-members alike.[31] On the other hand, the collective agreement itself must not imply any restriction on the granting of contractual conditions to outsiders: any so-called organizational clause ('Organisationsklausel') which either requires the employer to exclude non-organized workers from employment altogether ('closed shop') or from specific benefits of the collective agreement is illegal.[32]

An important feature of German collective bargaining is the possibility of a political declaration by the Minister of Labour that a specific collective agreement will be generally binding, even for employers and employees who are not among the contracting parties (§ 5 TVG).[33] There are four legal requirements for a declaration of this type: (i) There must be a collective agreement currently in force, not just an expired or a forthcoming one. (ii) There must be a so-called overwhelming importance of the agreement, meaning in legal practice that no less than 50 % of all employees in the relevant sector of a region are employed by the agreement-bound employers. (iii) There must be a so-called public interest in a generally binding agreement, which in legal practice means that the equality of remuneration and working conditions is threatened to be seriously undermined by outsider competition wherever it comes from. (iv) At least one party of the agreement must have officially requested the declaration. If these conditions are met, it is up to the minister of labour to deal with the request: if he rejects it, the agreement will remain non-binding for outsiders; if he accepts it, the issue is brought to a so-called bargaining commission ('Tarifausschuß'), consisting of three representatives of both the employer and the union side, which then decides by majority vote. Only if both the minister of labour and the commission favour the declaration, the agreement can and will be declared generally binding.[34]

A generally binding collective agreement runs counter to the spirit of a strictly private contract even if the contract has been concluded between coalitions of em-

---

31. There is a compelling reason for any organized employer to do so: any unorganized worker employed at sub-contractual conditions in an organized (and collective contract-bound) firm might join the relevant union and thus secure himself the right to the conditions of the collective agreement, at least from the time of his membership on. In turn, the employer is not allowed to dismiss the worker on the grounds of his newly acquired union membership or to enforce an individual contract which obliges the worker not to join a union. Hence, the only sensible economic strategy for any organized employer is simply to grant contractual conditions in the first place. If an employer really wants to avoid the constraints of collective agreements for future labour contracts, he/she has to leave or stay out of the relevant employers' association. Note that, even after leaving an employers' association, the individual employer is still bound by all the collective agreements currently in force. Only after these have expired, he/she is free to adjust wages and working conditions. See Gitter (1987), p. 102; Söllner (1987), pp. 141-142.

32. For details, see Gitter (1987), pp. 102-103; Söllner (1987), pp. 62-64.

33. For details, see Gitter (1987), pp. 102-103; Söllner (1987), pp. 62-64.

34. For details, see Gitter (1987), pp. 106-108; Söllner (1987), pp. 150-153.

ployers, employees and not between individuals. Although the legal obstacles to obtain the relevant declaration are not insignificant, they are not insurmountable either: given the generally high degree of organization of German employers, the lower limit of 50 % contract coverage of employees is certainly not much of a constraint in practice; as courts define the public interest precisely as the defence against an undermining of collectively agreed terms by outsider competition, the legal requirement is tailor-made to shield off any substantial threats from market forces; and in the important bargaining commission, only insider interests – employers' and unions' – are represented. The only potential advocate of outsiders' concerns could be the minister of labour who traditionally has a strong affiliation to organized labour and thus can hardly be expected to act in the outsiders' interest.

The actual practice[35] shows that the declaration of generally binding agreements is used most frequently in sectors with a relatively low degree of organization (e.g. construction, retail trade) and/or a high share of – also weakly organized – female employees (textiles, clothing, retail trade). Prima facie, these are precisely the branches of industry where one should expect a particularly pronounced outside market pressure. Although the number of generally binding agreements in force at any point in time is rather low (about 450-600), it would be too simplistic to conclude that the use of this legal weapon is ineffective; the mere existence of the weapon may signal enough threat potential to prevent outsiders from undercutting wages and working conditions of existing collective agreements. After all, it would be awkward to measure the effectiveness of the penal code by the number of convictions.[36]

(c) Conflict handling: arbitration, conciliation, strikes, lockouts[37]

As long as a collective agreement is in force, any conflict between the parties with respect to its implementation or interpretation must be resolved without recourse to industrial action or the threat thereof. If no solution is feasible through supplementary bargaining, the case may be brought to an arbitration board which, however, must have been established through a collective agreement in the first place. If no

35. For details, see Bundesministerium für Arbeit und Sozialordnung (1990c).

36. There is still another legal basis for the Minister of Labour to interfere with collective bargaining: the Act on the Determination of Minimum Working Conditions ('Gesetz über die Festlegung von Mindestarbeitsbedingungen') passed in 1952 allows the Minister of Labour to fix minimum working conditions if an acceptable social minimum is not achieved through collective agreements. Up to the present, no use has been made of this provision simply because the 'social gap' was soon filled by collective agreements. See Söllner (1987), pp. 153-154.

37. For a detailed account of the legal rules of conflict handling, see Söllner (1987), §§ 11-14, pp. 69-118. A shorter summary is provided by Gitter (1987), pp. 111-118.

such provisions have been made, the case has to be dealt with by public labour courts.

Whenever a collective bargaining round has been declared by at least one party as a failure, the parties may resort to some procedure of conciliation ('Schlichtung') which is barely regulated by German law. In most industries, special agreements have been concluded to set a framework for conciliation after the phasing out of a peace obligation. Most of these agreements stipulate that the peace obligation is extended to the time of conciliation and that a conciliation board is established on a parity basis, with the board's chairman being unanimously agreed upon by both parties. His sole task is to bring the parties together with no consideration for any other – say, macroeconomic – repercussions of a prospective agreement. The conciliation board works out a compromise proposal – usually based on a unanimous or qualified majority vote of its members – and submits this proposal to both parties, which may accept it or not. The conciliation board has no legal means of enforcing a proposal; it is merely providing an instrument of bargaining assistance.[38]

The right to strike and to lock-out is generally derived from the freedom of coalition granted by Article 9 III of the German constitution. Only civil servants are denied the right to participate in industrial action.[39] Virtually the whole legal tradition as to strikes and lockouts is the product of case law, not codification. Basically, a strike is considered legal if the following four conditions are met: (i) At the time of the strike, there is no peace obligation. (ii) The aim of the strike can realistically be part of a collective agreement; hence political strikes are illegal, and so are strikes directed at an aim beyond the competence of the prospective parties (e.g. mere sympathy strikes). (iii) The strike must be led by a party – usually a union – which has the right to conclude a collective agreement; hence wild-cat strikes are illegal as long as they are not 'adopted' by the respective union as their own cause. (iv) The strike must be recognizable as an 'ultima ratio', i.e. the scope for compromise at the bargaining table must have been exhausted – preferably up to a procedure of conciliation – and the strike weapon must be handled in an adequate and fair way,

---

38. If no provisions for a conciliation have been made or if a collectively agreed upon conciliation has failed, there may be a public conciliation under the auspices of the state labour administration. Again, a board of conciliation is formed with the members being chosen by the labour administration from proposals of the union and the employer side, and an impartial chairman appointed with the approval of both parties. Yet, again, the worked out conciliation proposal cannot be enforced without the consent of the parties. There is no such thing as a compulsory conciliation of the Weimar type. A minority of legal scholars holds that, under extreme conditions of a social or economic emergency, a compulsory conciliation may be justified (see Söllner (1987), pp. 117-118). Be that as it may, no such occasion has yet arisen in the history of the Federal Republic of Germany; even cases of voluntary public conciliation have been rare.

39. This is due to the particular legal status of civil servants who are not employees, but rather non-dismissable 'servants' of the state, with a more extensive set of obligations to their 'master'.

which means, e.g., that no violence is used. A major exception to the ultima-ratio principle has been allowed in the case of so-called warning strikes ('Warnstreiks'), i.e. short stops of work (up to 2-3 hours) during the time of bargaining, but after the running-out of the peace obligation. Recent experience shows that unions tend to apply warning strikes in a systematic way, combining them to a chain of locally unpredictable 'strike stings' in different places. The courts have accepted warning strikes – even systematic ones – on the grounds that they symbolically support a bargaining position and thus may speed up negotiations.[40]

A legal strike leads to a mere suspension of the main obligations of a wage contract – work on the side of the employee, remuneration on the side of the employer – with the obligations being resumed as soon as the strike is over. Illegal strikes can lead to injunction or damage claims of the employer against the union and/or the individual employee, depending on whether the strike was union-led or wild-cat.

As to the legality of lockouts, one has to distinguish between an offensive lockout with the employer(s) starting the industrial action, and a defensive lockout with the employer(s) reacting to a strike. Offensive lockouts are legal under basically the same rules as 'offensive' strikes though, in practice, they do not occur because an employer seldom has an explicit aim of cutting nominal wages and/or loosening the working conditions agreed upon in prior contracts.[41] A defensive lockout is considered to be legal if and only if the strike of the union side is designed as a deliberate attack on the solidarity of the employers so that, as a consequence, the so-called 'bargaining parity of weapons' is severely disturbed. Typically, this happens whenever the strike is narrowly focused on a fairly small chunk of the relevant sector and/or region of collective bargaining so that many firms may be tempted to act as free-riders to win market shares at the expense of those firms affected by a strike. As a rough guideline, the courts have held that a share of less than 25 % of all employees in the relevant bargaining region definitely disturbs the parity and gives employers the right to extend the range of conflict up to 50 % of all employees by locking out; if the strike involves 25-50 %, again an extension up to 50 % is acceptable; yet if the share exceeds 50 % in the first place, no further lockout is allowed. The legal consequences of the lockout are – *mutatis mutandis* – the same as in the case of the strike, with a legitimate lockout leading to a suspension of the main contract obligations.

---

40. This has been heavily criticized by some legal scholars since it basically allows a simultaneity of bargaining and industrial action which flatly contradicts the ultima-ratio principle. In practice, however, one may doubt whether, after the end of the peace obligation, a clean separation of bargaining and strike makes such sense anyway. For a discussion of this issue, see Söllner (1987), p. 97.

41. The Great Depression 1930-1932 might have been such a situation; yet, to our knowledge, there was no attempt at offensive lockouts even then.

To ensure a neutral bargaining position of the government, workers on strike or affected by a lockout must not receive benefits from the unemployment insurance of the public social security administration. In practice, this means that they can only draw on the unions' strike funds, which support union members only; non-members are left on their own. In recent years, there has been a fierce controversy on whether the neutrality of the government and public institutions requires that no unemployment benefits must be paid out to those workers who have to stop work as an indirect consequence of a strike. Due to the ever more perfect logistics of many firms, unions went over to focus strikes at some neuralgic points of supply that were likely to hit firms in related branches. By an unambiguous legal adjustment of § 116 of the Labour Promotion Act ('Arbeitsförderungsgesetz') in 1986, which has been vindicated by the Supreme Labour Court, it is now clear that no unemployment benefits are to be paid not only to workers on strike or locked out but also to those workers in a related industry outside the relevant area of collective bargaining who have to stop work as an indirect consequence of the industrial conflict provided they can reasonably be expected to share the bargaining aims that are at stake in the conflict.

As to the internal decision procedures about industrial action within unions and employers' associations, there are hardly any legal restrictions except the general requirement that they have to follow democratic principles. Already in its founding congress in 1949, however, the DGB set up quite elaborate guidelines which members were recommended to follow in case of a prospective strike. Most importantly, these guidelines called for a ballot of all union members requiring a 75 % majority in favour of striking. In the early 1970s, the DGB loosened these guidelines and now leaves it to the member unions whether a ballot is cast or not. In practice, all major strikes have been preceded by ballots because, for publicity reasons, unions like to have some symbol of democratic legitimation. Note that, unlike a prospective strike, a routine acceptance of a contract offer need not be (and usually is not) preceded by any prior voting procedure. Only after prolonged industrial disputes is the final agreement usually submitted to the union members for approval. Even then, however, the members' verdict on the agreement comes down to a mere expression of opinion, which may simply be by-passed by the union leadership, if a re-opening of negotiations looks inopportune and cumbersome.

B.4 Legal Rules versus Collective Agreements

As will become clear in Section C of this Chapter, collective agreements are concluded to regulate a large variety of purposes, from wages to working conditions and job protection. Thus, it is not surprising that legal prescriptions and collective agreements do both cover wide ranges of economic and social life with substantial overlappings being quite frequent. In fact, there is only one range of competence where the parties of collective bargaining operate almost unconstrained by law, namely the level and structure of wages. In a second range – working time and holidays – the legal constraints have gradually become irrelevant in practice during the last four decades as the collectively agreed upper limits on daily working hours and lower limits on annual holidays are by now much more favourable to employees than the ones prescribed by law. In the remaining fields of 'social security' in the broadest sense – safety standards on the job, rules of dismissal, compensation for sickness and disability, job protection for elderly workers, severance pay – the elaborate legal standards are still important, but they have been supplemented by a layer of provisions which are regularly adjusted in collective agreements.

C. Outcomes

C.1 Working Time

The legal framework for working hours[42] is provided by the Working Time Decree of 1938 (amended in 1968, 1974 and 1975). It fixes a regular working time of eight hours per day, including Saturdays, and a 48-hour working week. Different rules apply whenever the nature of the work calls for an unusual time pattern (e.g. in sectors such as agriculture, health services, retail trade). Somewhat stricter rules apply to female and juvenile workers with the latter having a legal claim to a 40-hour working week. The daily working time may be extended to 10 hours either through collective agreements or – up to a maximum of 30 days a year – unilaterally by the employer; in any case, however, an extra-compensation for overtime work must be paid. Work on Sundays is generally prohibited although there are many exceptions above all in the service sector. As to the distribution of working time, the law prescribes an uninterrupted break of at least 11 hours between shifts and a break of 30 minutes (or two breaks of 15 minutes) within any shift of six hours or more. As to paid holidays, the law fixes a minimum of 18 days, for juvenile workers 25 to 30 days.[43]

Today, working time regulations of collective agreements are much stricter than those fixed by law.[44] In 1989, the average contractual working time was about 38.5 hours per week, with a pronounced downward trend towards the union medium-term aim of 35 hours to be reached by the mid-1990s. In most sectors of the economy, weekly working time is now well below 40 hours, with most agreements granting some flexibility as to the choice between an across-the-board cut of daily working

42. See Gitter (1987), pp. 165-172, Söllner (1987), pp. 216-224.

43. For the details of the legislation on holidays, see Söllner (1987), pp. 216-224.

44. For a selection of the contractual rules on working time and holidays in selected industries, see Bundesministerium für Arbeit und Sozialordnung (1990a, 1990b).

time and a more unequal intertemporal distribution of the cut over the working week or longer periods. Some agreements even allow work on Saturday to be included in the regular working time schedule. On average, contractual agreements fix about 29 paid holidays per year; 99 % of all employees now have a contractual claim to at least four, 94 % to at least five weeks of paid holidays per year.[45]

C.2 Wages

There are no legal minimum wages in Germany. Contractual wages per hour or month are calculated on basis of job classification schemes, which are themselves the outcome of prior contractual agreements. Usually, a percentage increase of the so-called base rate ('Ecklohn') for some average job is fixed in collective bargaining and subsequently applied to all other job categories, with explicit deviations only if the occupational wage structure is deliberately changed as happened frequently in the first half of the 1970s.[46] For work beyond the legally fixed regular working time of 48 hours per week, the law prescribes an overtime premium of at least 25 %. In all industries, there are additional overtime premia, which in general amount to 25 % on any overtime work, 50 % for work on Saturdays and 100 % for work on Sundays and holidays, with overtime being defined as the working time above the contractual maximum, not the much higher legal maximum. Depending on the specific working conditions of an industry, a set of different premia for particularly demanding work or extraordinary performance is granted; this also includes provisions for piece rates.[47]

Virtually all contractual agreements provide for two additional wage components above the hourly or monthly wage rate, namely (i) holiday money ('Urlaubsgeld') to be paid once a year – usually in summer – as a share of the gross monthly wage or as a fixed amount commonly somewhere between 300 and 1000 DM, and (ii) a 13th monthly wage popularly known as Christmas Money ('Weihnachtsgeld'), to be paid in November or December, calculated as a share (20-100 %) of the monthly wage.

---

45. In some collective agreements, there are also additional rules on so-called educational holidays, i.e. free time for the employees to participate in especially designed training programmes.

46. Soltwedel (1988), pp. 178-180 provides some numerical evidence on the ironing out of wage differentials in the late 1960s and 1970s.

47. Piece rates are calculated on the basis of a 'normal' working performance per hour, which is supposed to yield the contractual wage per hour plus a 'piece rate charge' to compensate for the psychic stress of this particular kind of work; the rate thus calculated is called the standard piece rate ('Akkordrichtsatz') and figures as a marginal supplementary issue in collective bargaining. To our knowledge, there are no reliable statistics on how frequent the use of piece rates is in practice; yet, it seems safe to say that they play no more than a minor part in industry and no role at all in services.

Wages for apprentices, namely the so-called training compensation ('Ausbildungsvergütung'), are also covered by collective agreements. Roughly speaking, an apprentice in his/her first year is paid 30-40 % of the lowest contractual wage in the industry, a share which rises up to 45-55 % in the third and fourth year of his/her training. Note that this entails a quite dramatic wage differentiation between apprentices and regular workers, which may well be held responsible for the persistently low youth unemployment in Germany compared to other countries.

By law, employers are required to cover 50 % of the compulsory contributions to the employees' old age, health and unemployment insurance and 100 % of the contributions to the mandatory accident insurance. Due to the rapidly rising costs of the social security system in the last two decades, the share of employers' contributions in gross wages rose from 12 % in 1970 to 17-18 % in the second half of the 1980s. Thus – quite independent of collective bargaining – a growing wedge emerged between labour costs to the firm and the take-home pay of the employee.

Note that contractual wage agreements in Germany do not contain any price index clauses, which are even prohibited by law.[48] For whatever reason, profit sharing arrangements and negotiations on employment levels are not common either. Hence the bulk of adjustment pressure is placed on the (mostly annual) bargaining rounds, with fairly rigid conditions prevailing in between. Of course, with mutual consent, a recontracting is possible before an agreement runs out, but that rarely happens in practice.[49]

C.3 Fringe Benefits[50]

Various kinds of fringe benefits are common features of collective agreements in Germany. Typically, however, they merely supplement welfare state provisions, without even remotely reaching the dimensions of the public social security system. Three variants stand out in importance: (i) Most collective agreements provide for a monthly employer's payment of 52 DM which is earmarked for the purpose of long-term saving, with the government adding 13 DM (i.e. 25 %) as a subsidy on basis of a law to promote capital formation of low and middle income earners. As a matter of fact, the whole procedure is by now firmly institutionalized and thus not subject any more to controversial collective bargaining. (ii) By law, wage payments

48. The Central Bank Act ('Bundesbankgesetz') prohibits index clauses in any private contracts except in special cases which have to be explicitly approved by the Bundesbank.

49. Only in 1969, after a wave of wild cat-strikes did recontracting take place on a large scale as industry was hard pressed in the public to give labour its fair share of rapidly rising profits.

50. For a selection of the contractual provisions on fringe benefits, see Bundesministerium für Arbeit und Sozialordnung (1990a, 1990b).

have to be fully continued by a firm for six weeks in cases of illness. In many industries, this period has been contractually extended up to 10 or even 26 weeks. (iii) In some industries – notably construction – there are contractual agreements on pension funds at the firm or industry level.

C.4 Termination of Labour Contracts

(a) Legal rules for dismissal[51]

In general, the termination of labour contracts is ruled by law, not by collective agreements. The standard labour contract is unlimited. In principle, it can be terminated by either party at relatively short notice, usually six weeks in the case of salaried employees and two weeks in the case of workers. While employees are free to quit and for whatever reason, the employer side is bound by an elaborate system of dismissal protection, which applies to all employees who have worked for more than six months in one firm and who are neither apprentices nor employees at the managerial level ('Leitende Angestellte'). According to the dismissal protection law ('Kündigungsschutzgesetz'), a dismissal can only be justified if either (i) the employee is factually unable to do his job or persistently violating his/her contract duties, or if (ii) urgent economic requirements – e.g. a cyclical downturn of product demand, a severe structural adjustment to new market conditions, etc. – make lay-offs unavoidable. In any case, the employer must have exhausted all sensible means of reorganization within the firm; if the cause of the dismissal is a general economic (not a personal) one, he/she also has to take into account social criteria such as age, family status, number of children, seniority and the likely opportunities of the dismissed person on the job market. Any dismissal must be notified to the firm's works council – the board of elected representatives of labour – which may object to it. If this happens and if the employee goes to court, the contract remains in force until a court decision is reached; however, if the continuation of the contract is an unbearable burden to the employer, which can be assumed to be the case in a severe economic crisis, the employer can obtain an injunction to dismiss. Note that the works council's opinion counts only for the interim period up to the court decision, not for the final legal verdict on the contract's destiny.

There is an extended dismissal protection for five groups of employees: (i) any woman during pregnancy and up to four months after confinement, (ii) any parent on (unpaid) 'child-raising holiday' ('Erziehungsurlaub') up to 36 months after the

51. For a detailed account of legal dismissal regulation in Germany, see Gitter (1987), pp. 71-85, Söllner (1987), pp. 281-302.

birth of a child,[52] (iii) any employee drafted for military (or the alternative social) service, (iv) any works council member, and (v) any seriously handicapped person.[53] In cases (i)-(iv) a dismissal is prohibited under virtually all conditions.[54] In case (v), a dismissal must be approved by an assigned public welfare agency which has to strike a compromise between economic and social considerations.[55]

As to large-scale lay-offs, there is a general legal requirement that any plan for a major restructuring (including closure and bankruptcy) of a company with more than 20 employees must be submitted to the works council. Both management and the works council have then to find a compromise between the economic needs of the firm and the social needs of the employees ('social plan'). If no agreement can be reached, an elaborate procedure of conciliation begins; it involves the president of the state labour office and a conciliation board with a non-partisan chairman who is appointed either by unanimous vote of both parties, or, if no agreement can be reached, by the labour court. In the last resort, this conciliation board has the decisive vote on the appropriate shape of the social plan.[56] Usually, all social plans entail severance payments up to a few times the monthly wage, depending on the age and seniority of the dismissed employees. From the early 1970s up to the mid-1980s, there has been a quite substantial increase of severance payments per separation, even in real terms (i.e. corrected for wage and price increases).[57]

---

52. That in effect means that any parent can take off three years and then resume his/her job. In the first 24 months of this time, he/she is entitled to obtain 'childraising money' ('Erziehungsgeld') to be paid out by the government (up to 600 DM per month and child). Note that the legal rules on child-raising benefits are very complex and have been adjusted quite frequently in recent years; in effect, benefits and holiday options have become much more generous so as to give economic incentives to have children.

53. Apart from the regulation of dismissals, handicapped persons are also protected by the legal requirement that at least 6 % of all employees of any company must be handicapped persons. If the limit is not reached, a 'tax' of 150 DM per month and 'vacancy' is levied. For details, see Söllner (1987), p. 235.

54. For works council members, there are some very narrowly defined exceptions to this rule. See Söllner (1987), pp. 296-299.

55. For details, see Söllner (1987), pp. 301-302.

56. Note that, in cases of bankruptcy, the interests of the creditors have to be taken into account. There is a special and very complex law on this matter. As a rough rule of thumb, it stipulates that severance pay should not exceed 2.5 monthly wages and salaries of the employees. For details, see Söllner (1987), pp. 191-192.

57. See Soltwedel (1988), p. 193, Table 12.

(b) Collective agreements on dismissal[58]

Many collective agreements supplement the legal framework of dismissal protection. In particular, three types of contractual arrangements are quite common: (i) A special protection of elderly employees, which usually restricts dismissals after a certain age (e.g. 55 years) and/or a certain threshold of seniority (e.g. ten years of work in one firm). In many cases, the payment of adequate compensation is also required if an elderly employee is relocated within a firm to a less qualified job. (ii) So-called 'rationalization protection agreements' ('Rationalisierungsschutzabkommen'), which provide for severance (or related) pay under a variety of circumstances, with the amount to be paid varying with age and seniority of the respective employee. (iii) A temporary payment to short-time or laid-off workers on top of the benefits from the unemployment insurance, which amount to at least 63 % of the previous take-home pay.

(c) Retirement

In Germany, the legal retirement age, i.e. the age at which pensions can be claimed, is 63 years for men and 60 years for women, with special rules applying to handicapped persons. Since 1984, there are additional provisions for early retirement at an age below 60 (down to 58) years, with the firm covering 2/3 and the unemployment insurance 1/3 of the pension if the retired person is replaced by a hitherto unemployed man or woman. In the wake of this reform, more than 400 contractual agreements on early retirement came about in the years 1984-1988, but most of them were not renewed at the end of the 1980s simply because a tighter labour market made them look somewhat out of place.[59]

(d) Fixed-term contracts

Until 1985, fixed-term labour contracts were allowed only if the nature of the work or of the particular project justified such a special treatment (typically, e.g., in academics). Since 1985, they are generally permitted up to a maximum duration of two years, with no option for a renewal beyond that. As a consequence, any employer may now bypass the tight regulation of dismissals by offering fixed-term instead of unlimited contracts. By now, a fairly detailed statistical stocktaking[60]

---

58. For details, see Bundesministerium für Arbeit und Sozialordnung (1990a,b).

59. Part-time work for elderly employees is still very uncommon as a subject of collective bargaining. For the content of a first agreement of this type on the firm level, see Bundesministerium für Arbeit und Sozialordnung (1990b), p. 15.

60. Büchtemann (1989).

has shown that many firms take advantage of this new flexibility, with about 9 % of all new labour contracts in the private sector being concluded on a fixed-term basis, and about 56 % of the resulting contracts being later transformed into unlimited employment. Hence, to a large extent, firms seem to use the introductory fixed term as a prolonged trial period beyond the standard six months probation time ('Probezeit') which German law grants for any new labour contract.[61]

D. The Prospects After Unification

From an economist's standpoint, the labour market regulation in Germany is an elaborate, tightly-knitted straitjacket, which has both a negative and a positive side. The negative side is a pervasive bias in favour of insider interests; after all, the much celebrated bargaining autonomy of unions and employers disregards outsider concerns altogether, as does the complex legislation on dismissal protection. Whoever is lucky enough to have a job can be certain to enjoy the powerful support of organized interests; yet whoever is stuck outside may find it very difficult to get back again onto the job track. Typically, in times of a poor general growth performance as, e.g., in the one and a half decades after 1973, insiders may simply not be ready to keep back wage demands in real terms and/or to allow for a substantial wage differentiation to give outsiders a second chance.

The positive side is the lack of direct government intervention: incomes policy experiments – often ill-designed and ill-fated – have been virtually absent in West Germany all over the post-war period simply because a well balanced parity of weapons in the bilateral bargaining game has provided a stable and fertile framework for compromise, with no public agency keeping open emergency exits. If one were ready to forget about the dualization of the labour market due to the conflict between insiders and outsiders, one could be quite content with the macroeconomic discipline that the system placed on wage demands. In fortunate times when growth – for whatever reason – persistently outpaces prior expectations (as happened in the 1950s and early 1960s), the system may even generate something like an 'employment miracle' with a large stock of jobless people being rapidly absorbed and full- or even over-employment being preserved over a fairly long time.

In the 1980s there was an extensive public discussions on the merits and demerits of labour market regulations and collective bargaining in Germany, more so than at any time earlier this century. All in all, the policy results of this debate have been rather meagre: except for the liberalization of fixed-term contracting, which is a significant step towards more flexibility, the system of dismissal protection and the bargaining

61. Originally, the 1985 law on fixed-term contracts ('Beschäftigungsförderungsgesetz') was due to expire after five years, but it has been extended to apply until 1995.

framework have remained intact. Toward the end of the decade, the debate gradually died down since the medium- and long-run prospects for output and employment growth seemed to improve considerably. Very recently, however, it has been revived again as a consequence of the economic unification of Germany, which opened up a new chapter in German labour market history that will be dominated by just one issue, namely the huge gap of unemployment between the 'old capitalist' Western part and the 'post-socialist' Eastern part of the united country.

Soon after unification, collective agreements in major industries settled for an East/West-equalization of contractual minimum wages by the mid 1990s. The driving forces behind this development are complex: roughly speaking, they lie in the strong egalitarian aspirations of unions, which met a soft budget constraint on the employers' side that was due to the extensive subsidization of formerly state-owned enterprises in the East.[62] At any rate, the rapid wage equalization has accentuated the East/West imbalance in the labour market, a fact that is increasingly recognized by the public at large. As a consequence, the renewed case for labour market deregulation – above all for allowing special clauses for individual firms in the East to opt out of collective agreements with the consent of their workforces – is likely to receive a much more broad-based support than similar proposals for the West in earlier times. In the end, all this may amount to a fundamental challenge for the German-style system of collective bargaining: today already, many forms in the East either leave the employers' association to escape the contractual straitjacket or simply stay out of the associations in the first place. Others remain members, but simply pay wages below the contractual minimum with the implicit consent of their employees. Given this practice, which unions disdain, but actually tolerate so as not to alienate the local workforce, it will be ever harder for organized labour to block any further steps towards more wage flexibility. After all, unions face a rather uneasy choice: either they stick to their traditional crisis of unprecedented proportions, or they explicitly allow for more flexible working conditions – thus paving the way for a German economy and society with much less corporatist features and thus also much less union influence than in the past. In any event, the sheer extent of the crisis is likely to give a fresh impetus to the rethinking of time-honoured institutions of the labour market in Germany.

62. For a summary evaluation of these matters, see Giersch, Paqué, Schmieding (1992), chapter 6.

REFERENCES

Armingeon, Klaus (1987), Gewerkschaften in der Bundesrepublik Deutschland 1950-1985: Mitglieder, Organisation und Außenbeziehungen, in: *Politische Vierteljahresschrift*, Vol. 28, pp. 7-34.

Bähr, Johannes (1989), *Staatliche Schlichtung in der Weimarer Republik*, Berlin.

Büchtemann, Christoph F. (1989), *Befristete Arbeitsverträge nach dem Beschäftigungsförderungsgesetz (BeschFG 1985)*, Forschungsbericht (Sozialforschung) 183, Wissenschaftszentrum Berlin, Berlin.

Bundesministerium für Arbeit und Sozialordnung (1990a), *Tarifvertragliche Regelungen in ausgewählten Wirtschafts- und Dienstleistungsbereichen*, Stand: 31.12.1989, Bonn.

-- (1990b), *Tarifvertragliche Arbeitsbedingungen im Jahre 1989*, Bonn.

-- (1990c), *Verzeichnis der für allgemeinverbindlich erklärten Tarifverträge*, Stand: 01.07.1990, Bonn.

Flanagen, Robert J., David W. Soskice, Lloyd Ulman (1983), *Unionism, Economic Stabilization, and Incomes Policies – European Experience*, Washington, D.C., pp. 208-300.

Giersch, Herbert, Karl-Heinz Pagué, Holger Schmieding (1992), The Fading Miracle. Four Decades of Market Economy in Germany, Cambridge.

Gitter, Wolfgang (1987), *Arbeitsrecht*, Heidelberg.

Hartwich, Hans-Hermann (1967), *Arbeitsmarkt – Verbände und Staat 1918-1933*, Berlin.

Hentschel, Volker (1983), *Geschichte der deutschen Sozialpolitik 1880-1980*, Frankfurt am Main.

James, Harold (1986), *The German Slump – Politics and Economics 1924-1936*, Oxford.

Kendall, Walter (1975), *The Labour Movement in Europe*, London, pp. 89-139. **Limmer, Hans** (1988), *Die deutsche Gewerkschaftsbewegung*, 12th edition, Munich.

Löhrlein, Klaus (1990), Mitgliederzahlen: Entwicklung und Verteilung nach Gewerkschaften und DGB-Landesbezirken, in: Michael Kittner (ed.), *Gewerkschaftsjahrbuch 1990*, Cologne, pp. 67-74.

Markmann, Heinz (1977), Tarifverträge – II: Tarifvertragspolitik, in: W. Albers et al. (ed.), *Handwörterbuch der Wirtschaftswissenschaften*, Vol. 7, Stuttgart, pp. 540-553.

Moses, John A. (1982), *Trade Unionism in Germany from Bismarck to Hitler 1869-1933*, Vol. I and II, London.

OECD (1979), *Collective Bargaining and Government Policies in Ten OECD Countries*, Paris, pp. 58-67.

Price, Robert (1989), Trade Union Membership, in: R. Bean (ed.), *International Labour Statistics*, London, New York, pp. 146-181.

Söllner, Alfred (1987), *Grundriß des Arbeitsrechts*, 9th edition, Munich.

Soltwedel, Rüdiger (1988), Employment Problems in West Germany – The Role of Institutions, Labor Law, and Government Intervention, in: *Stabilization Policies and Labor Markets, Carnegie-Rochester Conference Series on Public Policy*, Vol. 28 (1988), pp. 153-219.

Visser, Jelle (1986), Die Mitgliederentwicklung der westeuropäischen Gewerkschaften – Trends und Konjunkturen 1920-1983, in: *Journal für Sozialforschung*, Vol. 26 (1986), pp. 3-33.

--, (1989a), *European Trade Unions in Figures*, Deventer, Boston.

--, (1989b), Westeuropäische Gewerkschaften im Umbruch, in: *Gewerkschaftliche Monatshefte*, Vol. 39 (1989), pp. 28-41.

Labour Market Contracts and Institutions
J. Hartog and J. Theeuwes (Editors)
1993 Elsevier Science Publishers B.V.

CHAPTER 8

THE SWEDISH MODEL:
Labour Market Institutions and Contracts*

Christian Nilsson**

A. Introduction

A.1 The Swedish Model

For a long time during the post-war period the most important objective of economic policy in Sweden was full employment: Between 1950 and 1992 unemployment has never been higher than 4 percent. Until the middle of the 1970s, this successful full-employment policy was usually seen as a consequence of what has been called the Swedish Model. This approach was regarded as a guarantee for economic balance; and in addition as something successful and progressive concerning the economic and social development.[1] However, in 1974-1976, Sweden was afflicted with a wage cost crisis and talk began about the end of the Swedish Model. Today it is a common opinion among Swedish economists that the Swedish Model collapsed in the 1970s. Despite the collapse of the Swedish Model, and the cost crisis, unemployment has, until recently, remained low. It is often maintained that the cost crisis is a result of the accommodation policy used to fulfil the full employment goal. During the period 1983-1988 the yearly unemployment rate was on the average 2.2 percent in Sweden, whereas the corresponding figure was 7.6 percent for Sweden's most important trading partners.[2]

To understand the Swedish labour relations system and wage negotiation institutions today, it is useful to start with a resume of the rise and fall of the Swedish Model.

---

* This is a revised version of a paper presented at the Conference on Comparative Labour Market Institutions and Contracts, Netherlands Institute for Advanced Study in Humanities and Social Sciences, Wassenaar, The Netherlands, January 24-26, 1991. I am indebted to Villy Bergström, Nils Elvander and Henry Ohlsson for comments on previous drafts. Financial support has been given from the Bank of Sweden Tencentenary Foundation.

** Department of Economics, Uppsala University and Trade Union Institute for Economic Research (FIEF).

1. Lundberg (1985), p. 1.

2. A weighted average of the unemployment ratios for fifteen of Sweden's most important trading partners, with the actual trade shares as weights.

The first important building stone in the so called Swedish Model was the co-operative spirit underlying the "Saltsjöbaden Agreement" in 1938 (which was called the Basic Agreement), between the Swedish Trade Union Confederation (LO) and the Swedish Employers' Federation (SAF). This co-operative spirit between the labour market parties ("the Social Partners") was regarded as necessary to keep the wage negotiation system free from government intervention. In 1938 the institutional frame for this co-operation consisted of three law-blocks: the Act on Mediation in Industrial Disputes, from 1920; the Collective Agreements Act and the Labour Court Act, from 1928; and finally the Act on the Right of Association and Collective Bargaining from 1936.[3] The right to organize ("the right of association") had for the blue-collar workers been accepted by the employers in an agreement between SAF and LO in 1906.[4]

The Mediation Act made the state responsible for making conciliation officers (*i.e.*, mediators) available for the disputing parties. Mediation became an accepted practice in situations where agreements could not be reached through the normal negotiation process.[5] The Collective Agreements Act (KAL), passed the parliament in 1928 over the protest of the unions. In the KAL a "peace obligation" was prescribed for those parties signing the collective agreement. The Labour Court was set up in 1929 as a result of the Collective Agreements Act and the Labour Court Act of 1928. The purpose of the court was to interpret the provisions of collective agreements, and to handle disputes about the peace obligations included at the Collective Agreements Act.[6]

However, the government were worried about the frequent labour market conflicts. During the unemployment crisis of 1931-1933, the number of industrial actions increased markedly. In 1930 around 1 million working days were lost, this increased to more than 3 million working days lost in 1933 and in 1934.[7] The government tried to find ways to regulate the right to strike, and create rules to protect persons and institutions outside labour market conflicts. Regulations of that nature were desired neither by the unions nor by the employers' organizations. In order to prevent this kind of legislation, and also introducing a procedure for dealing with labour market conflicts that could be interpreted as dangerous to society as a whole, the SAF and the LO (in 1938 in Saltsjöbaden) concluded what has been called the Basic Agreement.[8]

---

3. Elvander (1969), p. 103.
4. Saltsjöbadsavtalet 50 år (1989), p. 40.
5. Schmidt (1977), p. 203.
6. Schmidt (1977), p. 68, and Saltsjöbadsavtalet 50 år (1989), pp. 38-64.
7. Saltsjöbadsavtalet 50 år (1989), p. 29 and p. 50.
8. Schmidt (1989), p. 14, and Saltsjöbadsavtalet 50 år (1989), p. 37.

A.2 The Basic Agreement

The Basic Agreement primarily dealt with the procedural aspects of the bargaining process. The Collective Agreements Act and the Labour Court Act from 1928 did not change the power relationship between the LO and the SAF. On the LO-side the new laws were initially interpreted as a threat against union activities, but the laws did not prevent a very fast growth of union strength. However, through the Basic Agreement of 1938, the LO succeeded in moving its position one step forward. In exchange for a series of rules designed to protect third parties from the consequences of labour market conflicts, there were some improvements for employees in the handling of lay-offs and temporary dismissals.[9]

There are four constitutional rules in the Basic Agreement:[10]
1. When it comes to disputes, the agreement compel the two parties to negotiate according to a given procedure. It prescribes a negotiation procedure, and is an essential part of a system designed to promote peaceful industrial relations.
2. Beyond the peace obligation rules laid down by the Collective Agreements Act, *i.e.*, peace obligation when an agreement has been reached but not during the pre-agreement negotiations, some extensions were made. The agreement mentions limitations of economic sanctions and gives protection to third parties and essential public services. Furthermore industrial action may not be taken with the aim to persecuting persons on religious or political grounds. Another provision prohibits retaliatory industrial action against anyone who has been involved in a conflict, once the conflict has ceased.
3. The Basic Agreement designs a procedure to be followed when employment contracts are being terminated, and when there are lay-offs, reengaging personnel, etc. The employer was given the right to dismiss workers at will (§ 23 (§ 32) in SAF's constitution), but the employer could no longer refuse to give his reasons.
4. The Labour Market Council was established to function as a "negotiating panel", when disputes arose concerning the rules for lay-offs and temporary dismissals on the one hand, and industrial conflicts that affect functions vital for society on the other. In addition, the Council – as an "arbitration panel" – had to handle disputes about the application of the limitations of economic actions in the agreement. The Council had three representatives each from the SAF and the LO, with a neutral chairman when functioning as an arbitration panel.

With the Basic Agreement the LO and the SAF were provided with a procedural agreement, and this was followed by central agreements about industrial councils,

9. Schmidt (1989), p. 12 and p. 109.
10. Johnston (1962), p. 174, and Saltsjöbadsavtalet 50 år (1989), pp. 55-68.

job time-studies and group life insurances.[11] Afterwards, there has been an amendment and enlargement of this frame, and it was also followed by similar agreements between the SAF and the Union of Clerical-Technical Employees in Industry (SIF) 1957; between the SAF and the Union of Supervisors (SALF) 1959; and finally for the public employees in 1965. The Basic Agreement also gave the labour market parties a system of self-government for their common affairs, *i.e.*, freedom from government intervention.[12] The freedom for labour market parties *vis-à-vis* the government is greater in Sweden than in most other countries. The official doctrine concerning the labour market freedom forbids direct government intervention in the wage negotiation process. The ambition to preserve the freedom from state intervention is given very high priority by both employers and union representatives. This freedom has been accepted by the Swedish society as an essential component of the institutional framework. An implicit condition for this freedom has been that the two parties attempt to avoid wage increases, which would worsen the competitive situation of the economy. In other words: the government has delegated the right to establish an "incomes policy" to the parties in the labour market because of its reliance on the willingness of these parties to accept the responsibility for maintaining a macro economic balance.[13] Another consequence was a centralization process, within both the SAF and the LO, which in turn led to central agreements on wages: in 1952 the first Central Agreement between the SAF and the LO about wages was signed. The so called Rehn-Meidner model from the beginning of the 1950s and the EFO-approach from the end of the 1960s are examples of policy models involving a union movement that is aware of its responsibility for the economic balance.

A.3 The Rehn-Meidner Model

The Rehn-Meidner model prescribes a stabilization policy program, a program for structural change and economic growth, and a program for a fair income distribution. The model relies on three means to reach the goals of full employment, low inflation, and economic growth. The indicated means are a fiscal and monetary policy, sufficiently restrictive to suppress inflationary pressure; a solidarity wage policy designed to accelerate the structural change; and finally, an active labour market policy, e.g., vocational training, to support the movement of manpower to the expanding sectors.

The theoretical underpinning of the solidarity wage policy was developed at the end of the 1940s by two economists working for the LO, Gösta Rehn and Rudolf Meidner.

---

11. Saltsjöbadsavtalet 50 år (1989), p. 260.
12. Schmidt (1989), p. 13 and p. 26, and Seth (1987).
13. Edgren *et al.* (1973), p. 29 , Barbash (1972), p. 36, and Elvander (1980), p. 265.

Their idea was that instead of letting the market form the wage structure in the short run, a centralized wage bargaining system would create a wage structure based on the nature and the requirements of different jobs. That wage structure has been characterized as 'rational', and could be said to correspond to the long run equilibrium solution of a competitive labour market.[14]

A.4 The EFO-model

The wage negotiation system in Sweden during the post war period can be characterized as a highly centralized collective bargaining system. Whether the centralization in the private sector of the labour market was caused by the LO's ambition to achieve a genuine wage equalization policy, or if the wage equalization policy resulted from a growing influence of the low wage unions through the centralization, is an open question.[15] There was, however, a connection over time between the growth of a more centralized wage negotiation system, and a gradually stronger emphasis on the equalization of wages and salaries – particularly during the 1960s and the first part of the 1970s. (Compare Figure 1.)

Figure 1: Dispersion of Wages Between Industries, Blue-collar Workers; "the Wage-Cornet"

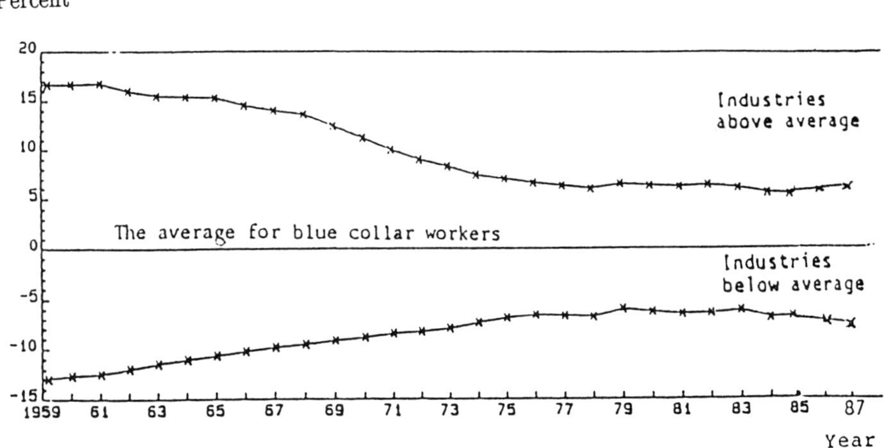

Source: LO

14. See e.g., Hansen (1961), p. 107.

15. Hadenius (1976), p. 90.

The EFO-model was intended to provide a wage setting norm for centralized negotiations. It is an expression of the consensus between the employers association, the SAF, and the two most important employee associations, the LO and the TCO (Central Organization for Salaried Employees); and it was formulated by the chief economists of these three labour market top-organizations (Gösta *E*dgren, Karl-Olof *F*axén and Clas-Erik *O*hdner): "The strength of the Swedish labour market organizations forces them to take a stand on the problems of stabilization in quite a different way from the labour market parties in most other countries."[16]

In the EFO-model the Swedish economy was divided in a tradable sector and a sheltered sector. The room for wage cost increases was defined as the sum of the price increases in world market, and the productivity growth within the tradable sector. The normative implication was that the tradable sector should be wage-leading, and therefore conclude their agreements before the sheltered sector. In addition the wage cost increases in the sheltered sector should – according to the solidarity wage policy – be the same as in the tradable sector.

In reality, however, the central parties in the Swedish wage negotiation system have never had full control over the wage formation process. Negotiations were carried through on three levels: centralized bargaining, industry-wide bargaining, and local negotiation at the individual plants. Even if the EFO-norm was accepted at the first two levels, the central parties have never been able to control the local wage negotiation process. The wage negotiation system therefore caused "wage drift" at the plant level. During the period 1971-1980, the average wage drift per year in the mining and manufacturing industry was about 42 percent of the total wage increases for blue-collar workers, and about 21 for white-collar workers. During the period 1981-1990 the average wage drift was about 50 percent for both blue-collar and white-collar workers.

A.5 The Collapse of the Swedish Model

The unit labour costs for blue-collar workers in the Swedish mining and manufacturing industry increased with 19.1 percent in 1974-1976, relative to the unit labour costs for a weighted average of fifteen of Sweden's most important competitors in the world market. Sweden experienced the beginning of a cost crisis. The unemployment resulting from the cost crisis was accommodated by programs originating within the National Labour Market Board (AMS) – e.g., labour market training programs and relief works; company training subsidy schemes – by an expanding

16. Edgren *et al.* (1973), p. 188.

public sector;[17] and finally by devaluations. Lundberg (1985, p. 23) points out five factors that, taken together, may explain the fall of the Swedish Model: the position of the Social Democrats was weakened, the full employment concept became more inclusive, the growth target became more dubious, the egalitarian spirit in the solidarity wage policy tended to be strengthened, and the EFO-norm was abandoned.

A growing opinion against the policy for economic growth – that included migration from the north of Sweden to the south – forced the government and the Parliament to abandon the growth-oriented policy doctrine in favour of a more job security oriented policy at the beginning of the 1970s. The aim of the new policy became job security. A number of new laws designed to promote job security and economic democracy came into effect. At the same time, these laws indicated something new in the trade union attitude to government intervention in labour market relations. Until the beginning of the 1970s only a few laws had regulated the relations between the parties in the labour market. Now the unions' attitude to labour relations legislation changed. That was probably a consequence of a rising demand from the "left-wing movement" for democracy at the work-place, in combination with the fact that the Social Democrats was in a very strong political position at the end of the 1960s. The party had a majority of the members of Parliament. LO urged the Social Democratic government to introduce new labour relations related laws. The new legislation, which will be discussed below, altered the power balance between the labour market parties in a remarkable sense. This was also a main reason for the legislation.[18] During the period a bitter political debate about the creation of collective wage earner funds also took place. The funds were thought capable of promoting economic democracy, and in addition they would be a complement to the solidarity wage policy through reducing the room for wage drift in the most profitable firms. The fund system was introduced through the Wage Earner Fund Act in 1983, and the funds were financed by a combination of charges on "excess" profits and a general payroll tax.[19] The actual fund system was a very modest version of the original proposals, and seem to have played an insignificant role both to create economic democracy and to dampen the wage drift. From 1990 the funds receive no new money, and in 1991 the new Conservative-Liberal-Center government decided to abolish the funds.

The years 1974-1977 were characterized by new laws dealing with the industrial relations system at plant and company levels. The position of the union factory clubs (the local union bargaining agency) was confirmed and made stronger. The most important new laws were the Employment Security Act (LAS) in 1974; the Act on

17. The public sector share of the total number of employees was in 1970 29.5 percent, in 1980 39.0 and in 1990 41.7. (The Swedish Labour Force Surveys.)

18. Schmidt (1989), p. 15, and Skogh (1984), p. 157.

19. Lundberg (1985), p. 30, and Meidner (1980), p. 363.

Union Representatives (FML) in 1974; the Act on Board Representation for Employees in Limited Companies and Co-operative Associations in 1973; and the Act on Co-determination in Working Life (MBL) in 1977. The new labour market laws, particularly the MBL, are intended to give the union factory club, through its representatives, the possibility to co-operate with the employer in certain aspects of the management of the company. Further, the union representatives will have the right to do union work during their ordinary working time. The central negotiation systems were, however, not changed by these new laws.[20]

The central agreement in 1969, through the introduction of pronounced low wage provisions that meant higher increases at the bottom of the wage distribution than elsewhere, clearly indicates that the LO changed its wage equalization goal. In this central agreement there is a very strong ambition to reduce the wages differential between different jobs, and as well as between skilled and unskilled labour. It is possible to maintain that LO's wage policy during the 1960s and 1970s changed from "market-conforming" to "market-steering". Low wage provisions were designed to establish a wage structure different from what would be the long run solution of the free market. The emphasis on low wage adjustments shows that the wage policy to a lesser degree was guided by the efficiency goal, which was explicit in the Rehn-Meidner model, and to a higher degree by the egalitarian goal.

During the 1970s the EFO-model became less applicable for the actors in the labour market. This was because of increased uncertainty about the development of world market prices and productivity growth. The government tried to win the co-operation of employees' organizations in holding down nominal wage increases, by assuring them that policies will be introduced that will make real wage increases possible. The incomes policy program has taken the form of promises to the central labour market parties that if wage increases are kept low, tax reductions will be possible, or "agreements" about wage increase frames (wage controls). Also, price controls have been used in several years with the same aim.

The conclusion is that the Swedish industrial relations system, with its long tradition of consensus, co-operation, and stability, did not work particularly well. Simultaneously, with the trend towards a growing centralization of the wage bargaining in the 1970s, industrial conflicts in the labour market became more frequent. Swedish industrial relations were for a long time characterized by relatively low incidence of strikes and lockouts; until the end of the 1960s the number of industrial conflicts was relatively small. During the period 1956-1969, on the average, 18 industrial conflicts were registered yearly, representing 46 000 working days lost. At the beginning of the 1970s there was a remarkable increase in the number of industrial conflicts. During the period 1970-1990, on the average, 131 industrial conflicts were

20. Schmidt (1989), p. 97.

registered yearly, representing 449 000 working days lost. One also can discern an increased tendency on the employee side to initiate such actions as blockades of new appointments and overtime work.[21] Finally, the highly centralized negotiation system has been challenged. The LO and the TCO have lost much of their influence over the wage policy.

B. The Institutional and Legal Environment

B.1 The Bargaining Structure

The institutional framework for wage-negotiation in the private sector of the Swedish labour market was established in the 1950s, when the SAF and the LO were completely dominant. This framework has three levels: central agreements, industry-wide agreements for each separate union; and local wage contracts at plant level (normally there are no negotiations at company level). The central agreement has the character of a recommendation; the top organizations (e.g., the SAF and the LO) have agreed to work for the acceptance of the recommendation in the industry-wide negotiations.

The wage negotiation system for employees in the private sector has been very centralized. During the period 1956-1990, nineteen central agreements between the SAF and the LO were concluded. Since 1974 the SAF and the PTK (the Federation of Salaried Employees, *i.e.*, a negotiating organization for white-collar workers in the private sector) have also concluded central agreements. Two-year agreements have been the most common between the SAF and the LO. Sometimes three-year agreements were concluded, and in 1970 the white-collar workers signed a 5-year agreement. However, when the economic situation is uncertain, parties usually prefer one-year agreements.

The wage increases reached in the central agreements typically include the following components ("kitties"): a general wage increase; low wage provisions; compensation for those groups of workers that have lacked wage drift; compensation for price increases over some chosen norm; and finally compensation for shortened working time.

When the central agreement is concluded it has to be transformed to a nation-wide agreement between each national union and employers' association. Until 1983 peace obligation was imposed for these negotiations, and they were not allowed to give wage increases above the Central Agreement; they should only decide the allocation of the kitties between the plants. The nation-wide agreements differ between the

---

21. SOU 1984:19, p. 17, and SOS Statistisk årsbok.

various industries and between white-collar and blue-collar workers, as a consequence of the chosen wage systems.

The central agreements give the national organizations great freedom when it comes to deciding how the available room for wage increases should be allocated. However, the freedom is limited through "no-agreement clauses", which stipulate how the kitties are defined and how they should be allocated if the national organizations cannot agree. Therefore it is always possible for either of the parties in the negotiation to demand an allocation according to the no-agreement clause. In most central agreements between 1969 and 1983, the no-agreement clause had the following form: Each individual who earns less than x öre an hour will receive y percent of the difference between the actual hourly earnings and x.

After the industry-wide agreement has been reached, local negotiations follow between the individual plant and each union club represented there. For blue-collar workers it is possible to notice a significant difference between wage equalization ambitions in the central agreements, and the actual outcome of the wage equalization intentions.[22] One reason might be that ambitions have deteriorated in the industry-wide negotiations.[23] Another reason is that the market creates wage drift so that much of the intended wage equalization featured in the central agreement is lost.

The Central Agreements between the SAF and the PTK usually include the same type of components as the SAF/LO-agreement, though the emphasis on low wage kitties has been less pronounced. On the other hand, an important component of the SAF/PTK-agreements has been the emphasis on earnings development guaranties *vis-à-vis* the blue-collar workers' wage drift. The most important difference between blue-collar and white-collar workers' wage negotiations concern the local negotiations. White-collar workers have individual agreements with the employer, which makes wage setting much freer and more individualistic.

In 1965 there was a wage negotiation reform in the public sector, and in 1966 public employees received the full right to negotiate their wages and to strike (the Central and Local Government Employees Acts). Before 1966 public employers could – formally and unilaterally – decide wage conditions. In reality, however, a wage

22. Nilsson (1989), and Hibbs (1990).

23. It is possible that the ambitions to equalize the wage structure in the Central Agreements, when it comes to nation-wide negotiations will be deteriorated. However, this does not mean that the unions are less interested in equalization of the wage structure than the LO. Instead it can be a consequence of the fact that the equalization ambitions in the central agreements aim, particularly at the equalization between individuals with different qualifications within the plant, while the nation-wide agreements aim particularly at the equalization between the same type of jobs at different plants. (Nilsson, 1987, p. 30.)

negotiation practice was gradually developed.[24] The wage system has been rather hierarchic. This means that a certain wage is ascribed to a position in the hierarchy. Wage bargaining has, until the last years of the 1980s, taken place in a highly centralized system. The inflexibility of this system became obvious during the last decade. The system has been changed towards a more decentralized and individualistic wage setting system, similar to the white-collar workers' system in the private sector.[25]

B.2 The Industrial Relations Structure

A principle characteristic of the Swedish labour market has been, as we pointed out above, the high rate of unionization. The number of union members has grown remarkably since the mid 1960s. The development has been similar for blue-collar and white-collar workers. (Table 1.) The rate of unionization for blue-collar workers grew from 77 percent in 1975 to 87 percent in 1986/87. In the Stockholm area the corresponding figures for 1975 and 1986/87 were 72 percent. Among the white-collar workers the rate of unionization grew from 79 percent to 84 percent during the same period.[26] Lately there is a decline in the rate of unionization; the rate of unionization for all employees has gone down from 83.5 in 1987 to 80.8 in 1991.[27] The high rate of unionization is, however, not the same thing as great confidence in the union leaders; opinion polls indicate a rather low confidence.

The Swedish Trade Union Confederation (LO) represents the blue-collar workers. Membership in the LO has increased about 46 percent between 1965 and 1987. After 1987, there has been a decreasing tendency in membership, particularly in Stockholm and some other cities. During the same period, the number of affiliated unions has decreased through mergers, from 38 in 1965 to 23 in 1990. Centralization has been especially remarkable in the public sector. During the period mentioned two unions joined the Swedish Municipal Workers' Union (SKAF). In 1970 the Swedish National Union of State Employees (SF) was organized from eight former unions in the National Federation of Government Employees. We also can notice the large share of the members in the LO, who are employed in the public sector. From a stable share of 20 percent during the 1950s and the first half of the 1960s, the share has grown rapidly, and in 1990 is about twice as high. (See Table 1.)

24. For references see Nilsson (1987), p. 8.

25. Sjölund (1989).

26. LO (1989), p. 78.

27. Labour information 1992:1, p. 14.

Table 1. The Union Confederations at the Swedish Labour Market[1]

Number of affiliated unions, number of members, and the percentage of women. The share of public employees in the LO (Publ. LO), the share of LO-members in the total number of union members (LO total), and the share of members in public unions in the total number of union members (Publ. total) in percent.

	LO			TCO			SACO[2]			Publ. LO	LO total	Publ. total
	unions	members	women	unions	members	women	unions	members	women			
1950	44	1278	19	43	272	36	..	37	..	19	81	26
1955	44	1384	21	42	338	..	72	55	..	19	78	26
1960	44	1486	23	37	394	39	76	73	..	19	76	26
1965	38	1565	25	31	510	40	64	105	..	20	72	28
1970	29	1680	29	23	719	40	64	134	..	24	66	32
1975	25	1918	34	24	951	45	27	165	31	27	63	36
1980	25	2127	40	21	1043	57	26	225	34	34	62	42
1985	24	2263	43	21	1203	57	25	280	38	37	59	44
1990	23	2230	45	20	1276	59	25	330	41	38	58	42

Notes: 1. The figures concern 31/12 each year. Members in thousands.
2. SACO was SACO/SR until 1988.

Sources: SOS: Statistisk årsbok, Kjellberg (1983), LO, TCO and SACO.

Individual blue-collar workers are not members in the LO. Only unions can be members in the LO. The LO cannot conclude agreements on behalf of the unions; the central agreements must first be approved by the member unions.[28] From the time of the establishing of the LO, in 1898, most of the affiliated unions were organized according to the craft principle. But as early as 1912 the LO Congress recommended that the unions should be organized according to the industry principle, and with only one union in each industry. Despite that recommendation, there were still many craft unions in the LO until the 1960s. Not even today has the industry principle been carried through completely. There are, for example, four craft unions representing the building workers; and the public sector unions (the SKAF and the SF) maintain that they shall represent all workers in publicly organized services, and in the government enterprises, e.g., railway transports and telecommunications (the owner principle).[29]

The solidarity wage policy expresses the LO's ambition of wage equalization. It has been motivated by the claim for a fair income distribution. What is meant by a fair income distribution is, however, not fixed once for all. This becomes quite clear if one studies wage policy reports presented to LO Congresses at different times (this was also discussed in sections A.3 and A.5 above). After 1976 one can say that the LO's ambition primarily has not only been to equalize wages within the LO-collective, but for all wage-earners.[30] This ambition, of course, presupposes co-operation with the white-collar unions, which has not been achieved.

The Central Organization for Salaried Employees (TCO) today represents 20 affiliated unions, with together more than 1.2 million white-collar workers. The total number of members in the TCO has doubled since 1965. (Table 1.) About 50 percent of the members are employed in the private sector, and about 50 percent in the public. Of the members employed in the private sector, about 80 percent belong to industrial unions (e.g., the Union of Clerical and Technical Employees in Industry, SIF). The Foremen's and Supervisors' Union (SALF) is an example of a craft union in the private sector. The members of the TCO in the public sector belong to industrial and craft unions in the same proportions.

The TCO has the same ambition as the LO, concerning wage policy programs. The TCO, however, does not conduct wage negotiations, which makes a fundamental difference in comparison with the LO. The unions affiliated to TCO are also affiliated to "negotiation cartels": the TCO-S for the central government employees; the KTK for the local government employees; and the PTK for employees in the private

---

28. Schmidt (1989), p. 25.

29. SOU 1988:50, p. 73.

30. See Nilsson (1989), p. 125, and LO (1981), p. 76.

sector. From 1991 on, the TCO-OF, the negotiation cartel for public employees, substitutes the TCO-S and the KTK. The Federation of Salaried Employees, PTK, was established 1973, but as early as 1969 an agreement for co-operation was reached between the SIF, the SALF, and CF (the Professional Engineers, within the SACO).

The third large confederation of unions is the Swedish Confederation of Professional Associations (SACO), which has about a quarter of a million members with academic degrees. About 75 percent of the SACO members are employed in the public sector. The SACO is a confederation of 25 independent affiliated unions. Like the TCO, the SACO does not conduct wage negotiations. The negotiation cartels, the SACO-S and the SACO-K, conclude agreements for the affiliated unions in the public sector, state and local. Fourteen SACO unions are represented in the PTK cartel.

The negotiation cartel for white-collar workers in the private sector (the PTK) and the SAF have agreed on the need for individual and differentiated wages for white-collar workers, according to the qualifications demanded for the actual job. At the local level one can say that the CF factory clubs and the SIF clubs, more than the SALF clubs, agree with the employers on wage differentiation principles, with the CF clubs standing closest to the employers in this sense.[31] The main objective of the PTK, however, is to guarantee the white-collar workers their proper share of the value added. This means that a relationship between wage increases for white-collar and the blue-collar workers has to be established.

The Act on the Right of Association and Collective Bargaining did not make any specific requirements, *i.e.*, that the union should be of a certain size, should organize the majority of the workers at the plant, or that the union be nation wide. Maybe, this is the reason for two kinds of union boarder line disputes: first, disputes about what national agreement a job should be assigned to; second, disputes between unions about the right to sign a specific national collective agreement.

There are, of course, some border line disputes of the first kind between the unions within the three federations, and between the federations. A trade union has the right to impose industrial action against an employer in order to reach a collective agreement, even if the employer is tied to an agreement with another union.[32] In practice there is a border line between blue-collar and white-collar workers, and there are several agreements of this kind between LO unions and TCO unions. Between the LO and the SACO, conflicts of this kind are rare. Between the TCO and the SACO there are no agreements. LO unions are, in a few cases, also in conflict with independent unions on the right to sign collective agreements, and in competition for memberships. The syndicalistic workers union, Central Organization of Swedish

31. Nilsson (1987), p. 38.

32. SOU 1988:49, p. 82.

Workers (SAC), has 15 500 members, and it signs just one national agreement, and 300 local agreements. In 1973 about half the stevedores formed their union, the Harbour Workers' Union, with about 2000 members, however, the LO affiliated union, the Transport Workers' Union, signs the national agreements.[33] Unions that are not able to sign national collective wage agreements have to sign subsidiary agreements.

Also, on the employer side, there is a high degree of organization, and about 45 000 private companies – with 1.3 million employees, or about one third of the labour force – are associated with the Swedish Employers' Federation, SAF. The SAF negotiates on wages and other terms of employment with both the LO and the PTK. (See Table 2.)

In the 1950s the SAF had a positive attitude to central negotiations. The attitude was based on an ambition to get a more uniform wage development in the different industries, and to avoid "grab-and-scramble meals".[34] In the wage policy debate during the 1960s and 1970s, the SAF played a concealed role. This debate has, since the LO formulated the solidarity wage policy, been conducted on terms determined by the employee organizations. Because of their weak position of power, the SAF was, according to Jonson & Siven (1986, p. 9), concentrating its energies on delaying the development that the LO had staked out. The new labour relations legislation and the political climate in the 1970s contributed to the weakened position of the SAF.[35] Clearly, the SAF's position has deteriorated also as a consequence of the increasing weight of the public sector and through the establishing of the Employers Association for Companies in Joint Ownership (SFO) in 1970. The establishing of the SFO was a direct consequence of a big wild-cat strike among the miners in the state owned iron ore mines in 1969 (the LKAB-conflict).[36]

In the last decade, however, the SAF has tried to improve its positions in the wage policy debate. During the 1980s the SAF's position seems to have been strengthened. The SAF adopted a new program in 1979. In this program it is emphasized, among other things, that fair wages presuppose individual wage setting, and wage forms and wage determination that consider work performance and efficiency. In the 1980s the SAF has pleaded for a more decentralized wage negotiation system, without central agreements.

---

33. SOU 1988:50, p. 78, and Schmidt (1977), p. 17.

34. Elvander (1969), p. 114, Hadenius (1976), p. 67, and Schiller (1988).

35. Skogh (1984), p. 155.

36. SOU 1984:19, p. 17.

Table 2. The Four Largest Central Bargaining Areas in Sweden, 1990
(Numbers in thousands and percent)

		No.	%
The private sector: blue collar workers			
SAF		742	
SFO	LO	64	
KFO		50	
		856	28
The private sector: white collar workers			
SAF		562	
SFO	PTK	43	
KFO		34	
		639	21
The central government sector			
	SF in LO	159	
SAV	TCO-S	258	
	SACO-S	113	
		530	17
The local government sector			
The Association of Local Authorities	SKAF in LO	636	
and the Federation of County Councils	KTK	316	
	SACO-K	71	
		1023	34

Sources: SAF, SFO, KFO, SAV, LO, TCO and SACO.

The SAF emphasizes the responsibility of the individual firm in the wage formation process:[37]
1. The development of wage costs in the firms is of vital importance for their competitive situation.
2. The productivity at the individual plant can, to a high degree, be positively affected by a performance-related wage setting.
3. Differentiation of wages will make it possible to reward individual workers' production result. It is possible for the employee to increase his wage if he improves his performance, becomes more flexible, gets more experience, and by that improves his ability to take on more difficult and responsible jobs.

The National Agency for Government Employers (SAV) negotiates on behalf of the central government employers. The SAV concludes agreements with the restriction that the agreements must be accepted by the government and the parliament. Of

37. Hellström & Lundberg (1985), p. 8.

course the government, in an informal manner, gives the SAV guidelines for the negotiations. For the local governments the Association of Local Authorities and the Federation of County Councils are the central employers' associations.

As a result of the wage negation reform for the public employees in 1965 and the fast increase in the number of public employees, the sector has obtained an increasingly important role in the Swedish wage formation process. The public sector share of the total number of organized employees has grown very fast, from 28 percent in 1965 to 42 percent in 1990. (Table 1.)

A pronounced element in the wage negotiation processes during the last two decades has been the establishing of the large employee negotiation cartels, and the development of co-ordination between these cartels. The analogy of this co-operation among the public employers' associations is a co-ordination that was intended to take place within the "OAS" between the public employers. Between the SAF and the public employers' associations there is a co-operation in technical questions, but no agreements on wage negotiation questions.

B.3 The Legal Structure of Collective Agreements

The legal structure of collective agreements deals with three problems: the process of negotiation; the resolution of disputes about the interpretation of laws or collective agreements; and the freedom of parties to handle disputes concerning matters not regulated by law or collective agreement. If parties cannot reach an agreement about the first two problems (what is called disputes of right) they can refer the matter to the Labour Court (AD). The last problem is called disputes of interest. For disputes of interest no legal rules or norms can be introduced for their solution, and the parties generally are entitled to resort to industrial action. The distinction between these two types of conflicts is fundamental in the Swedish system of industrial relations.[38]

The Act of the Co-determination in Working Life (MBL) came into force in 1977. The MBL regulates matters that concern basic industrial relations. The MBL is applicable to the private sector as well as the public, even if there are some complementary regulations for the public sector (e.g., concerning the right to strike) in the Act on Public Employment (LOA) from 1977. The MBL is a substitute for the Collective Agreements Act of 1928, the Act on the Rights of Association and Collective Bargaining of 1936, and the Act on Mediation in Industrial Conflicts of 1920 (see

---

38. Johnston (1962), p. 138, Seth (1987), p. 195, Schmidt (1977), p. 23 and p. 167, and Elvander (1969), p. 106.

section A.1 above). The MBL was primarily a codification of the actual legislation, with some extensions.

The MBL was intended to strengthen the influence of the union factory clubs over the work-organization and on the management of the company. The right to collective bargaining from 1936 included the unions' right to demand negotiations. With MBL that right was extended to a right to negotiate on any and all aspects of the employer-employee relationship and it became mandatory for management to initiate negotiations with the factory clubs about any major change in the organization or in the working conditions.[39] The union was also given the right to postpone any change in the employer-employee relationship until the negotiation has been finished; if an agreement has not been concluded after the negotiations the rule is that the employer has the right of final decision. The MBL, however, gives the union the right of veto in certain circumstances when the employer wishes to use subcontractors. The intention with that provision is said to prevent evasion of tax and social contributions, and unlawful employment exchange (the Public Employment Service has monopoly on employment exchange). Besides the extended right to negotiate, the MBL gives the unions an extended right to get information: the employees should not be seen as outsiders, but must be given full insight.[40]

The collective agreement in Sweden is by definition, according to the MBL, a written agreement about employment conditions, and other relationships between the two parties. Collective agreements are concluded after negotiations, as we discussed above, at three levels. Employers and employees, as members of the organizations that have concluded a collective agreement, are tied to the content of that agreement. Collective agreements also apply to unorganized workers employed at organized employers, and the employees at many unorganized employers, through subsidiary agreements. The collective agreement regulates the individual employment contract.[41] From the unions point of view the central agreement is a "normal wage" agreement, *i.e.*, determines the frame for wage cost increases within which the parties have the freedom to make agreements; the agreement lacks compulsory

39. "Rather one would characterize the duty of primary negotiations as preliminary consultations. The choice of terminology seems intended to impress the parties with the will of the legislature that real negotiations should take place." (Schmidt & Victorin, 1988, p. 331.)

40. Schmidt (1989), p. 110, Seth (1987), p. 180, Edlund & Nyström (1988), p. 46, and Schmidt & Victorin (1988), p. 328.

41. An employee working within a national agreement will have strong incentives not join the union, because he/she will got the same wage and fringe benefits through the collective agreement as the union members. How can that be consistent with the high rate of unionization? Maybe the paradox is due to the fact that the unions administrate the unemployment fees funds. (Ståhl, 1978, p. 472.)

terms.[42] In the LO, the TCO, the PTK and the SAF the power is at the member organizations, but these organizations have delegated some rights to the central organization. (Compare Table 3.)

Table 3. Voting Arrangements in the Largest Labour Market Organizations[1]

	Goals	Leaders	Collective agreements	Industrial actions
LO	Congress[2]	Congress	Representative Assembly and actual unions	Secretariat[2]
A typical LO union	Congress	Congress	Board	Board
TCO	Congress	Congress	PTK and actual unions	PTK and actual unions
PTK	Representative Assembly[2]	Representative Assembly	Central Board and actual unions	Central Board and actual unions
SAF	Board	Board	Board and actual employer association	General Council[2]

Notes: 1. The voting arrangements in Swedish trade unions are built on the principle of the representative democracy.
2. The Congress = kongressen, the Representative Assembly = representantskap, the Secretariat (executive board) = landsekretariatet, the General Council = fullmäktige.

Sources: The statutes of each organization.

The MBL also regulates the negotiation procedure. As in the Basic Agreement, the MBL says that negotiations primarily should take place between the parties at the local level, but if an agreement could not be reached there, the dispute could be referred to the central level, which here means negotiations between national unions and employer organizations. The MBL obliges parties to negotiate in all kinds of disputes. Before a dispute about the interpretation of a collective agreement or a law is referred to the AD, there have to be negotiations.[43]

---

42. Victorin (1973), p. 88.

43. Schmidt (1989), p. 125.

In the Act on the Union Representatives for employees' in private firms/companies (FML) from 1974 the union representative (the Shop Steward), is entitled to time-off when it is necessary to carry on the factory club activities. The Shop Steward must be employed at the firm; the law does not give national union representatives access to firms in which union members are employed. According to the FML, the union has "priority in the interpretation" over management on most rules according to the FML, also when it comes to collective agreements that have replaced the law.[44] The Act on Board Representation for Employees in Limited Companies and Co-operative Associations, from 1973 (changed in 1976 and 1987) has, as well, contributed to improve the employees (*i.e.*, the union factory club) possibility of co-determination in firms/companies with more than 100 employees, through the right to choose members of the board. The intention of this law is primarily to make it easier for the union representatives to get information. In the normal case the LO club and the SIF club have each chosen one member of the board. One critique against the law has been that the union members of the board will be in a position of double loyalty.[45]

The union represents the employees in almost all situations regarding employment conditions. The only exception to that rule is the "safety delegate" who, according to the Working Environment Act (AML) of 1978, should be appointed directly by the employees when there is no factory club tied to the employer by collective agreements. This may be the case in small firms. At plants with union clubs, the safety delegate is chosen by the unions. The safety representative has the authority to stop work when he judges it to be too dangerous. He is also entitled to leave of absence, with no loss of benefits, for the time required to do his duties.

The prevailing rules about legal proceedings in disputes about collective agreements are to be found in the Act on Litigation in Labour Disputes (1974). As stated previously, the Labour Court (AD) is the highest level of appeal. The AD has seven members: normally two representatives of the employer organizations and two representing the union confederations, and three impartial judges and labour market experts. The parties in a dispute on collective contracts should belong to opposite sides of the labour market.[46] The new labour market laws have led to an increased number of cases coming before the AD; about 150 − 200 cases are decided each year.[47]

Negotiations concerning disputes of interests can be either negotiations to reach a collective agreement, or negotiations that employers are obliged to initiate according

44. Schmidt (1989), p. 103, and Schmidt (1977), p. 82.

45. Schmidt (1989), ch. 6.5, and Schmidt (1977), ch. 6.4.

46. Schmidt (1977), p. 39.

47. Edlund & Nyström (1988), p. 16.

to the MBL. However, the parties are not obliged to reach an agreement. Interest disputes are not regulated by legislation or collective agreements, and the parties generally are entitled to direct industrial actions against each other, *i.e.*, strikes or lockouts. Unions and individual employers or employers' organizations are entitled to resort to industrial action, so called "lawful conflicts", except where a law or a collective agreement provides otherwise. Even sympathetic actions are lawful, as long as they aim to support a party that has resorted to lawful industrial action.[48] The party that will resort to industrial action has, according to the MBL, to give notice to Conciliators' Office at least seven days ahead. In "unlawful conflicts" the employees who take part in the strike can be ordered to pay damages of up to 200 SEK (a symbolic sum).[49]

Arbitration in interest conflicts is rare, although the MBL does allow for that possibility.[50] When there is a risk for major conflicts the government applies a conciliation commission, or a conciliator, on an *ad hoc* basis. Their conclusions, however, are not binding for the parties.

Within the LO it is the boards of the national unions that have the authority to decide on conflict measures. If a union wants more than 3 percent of its members to go on strike, the LO's acceptance is demanded. In the LO the Representative Assembly is the highest authority when it comes to decisions about conflicts. If a union imposes a strike without the LO's permission, then its right to economic support from LO ceases. In that case it is also possible for the LO to exclude the union. Within the PTK the Central Board is given the right to decide about conflict measures. The unions are obliged to co-operate. If a union does not accept the SAF/LO-agreement, it has the right to decide independently on conflict measures.[51]

The authority that has the right to decide on conflict measures within the SAF is the General Council. It has about 90 members chosen by the national employer associations. The General Council can, with a majority of two-thirds, impose a lockout. If employers associations wish to impose a lockout, they must begin by conferring with the SAF. The SAF Central Board includes the Director-General and 31 deputies chosen by associations with 15 000 employees or more. The Board can stop a lockout. The Board also can decide about lockouts, but only if the involved associations give their consent. Finally, if a member company wishes to impose a lockout, it

48. This right to sympathetic actions may explain why the employers' earlier took an interest in a centralized wage bargaining system.

49. Seth (1987), p. 180 and p. 198, and Schmidt (1977), p. 171 and p. 187.

50. Seth (1987), p. 195.

51. SOU 1984:19, p. 12.

must give notice to the board of their association. The SAF decides, after hearing the board of the association, if the lockout should be accepted.[52]

B.4 Observations on the Balance between Private and Public Provisions

By tradition, employment conditions in the private sector have been regulated through agreements between the labour market parties. The new labour market legislation during the 1970s, which was discussed above, has partially broken that tradition. Despite the new labour market legislation and the negotiation reform in the public sector, the public sector is still, to a higher degree than the private sector, subject to statutory regulations. During the 1980s, however, one can observe a clear tendency towards a negotiations procedure, which has become more similar to practices in the private sector, *i.e.*, a greater possibility to regulate employment conditions through collective agreements.[53]

C. Outcomes

C.1 Working Time

The objectives of the Work Environment Act (AML) from 1978 are that work should proceed in a safe and healthy environment. AML is a basic law and requires to be supplemented by statutory instruments of the National Board of Occupational Safety and Health and collective agreements.[54]

The present legislation dealing with working time, the Working Time Act, is from 1983 and concerns, with few exceptions, all employees. The legislation is non-mandatory, *i.e.*, a collective agreement can be substituted for the law. Primarily, it is up to the central parties to make working time agreements. But it is possible for the local parties to agree about shorter periods, e.g., about overtime and night work that deviates from the law.[55]

The Central Agreement in 1966 between the LO and the SAF stated that the standard working week for blue-collar workers during 1967–1969 should be shortened from 45 hours to 42.5. Between 1971 and 1973 the working week was further reduced, by 2.5 hours per week, through legislation. These reductions of the standard

52. SOU 1984:19, p. 9, and Skogh (1984).

53. See Seth (1987), p. 189, and Sjölund (1989), p. 164.

54. Edlund & Nyström (1988), p. 69.

55. SOU 1989:53, p. 108.

working week also equalized the working week between blue-collar and white-collar workers.

The standard working week is, according to the law of 1973, not allowed to be more than 40 hours. For blue-collar workers in continuous 3-shifts the working week is 36 hours according to the Central Agreement, and for other shift-workers 38 hours. There are no regulations about the daily norm, except for drivers. For employees younger than 18 years of age there are certain restrictions. Further, the law allows the employer to take out up to 50 hours standby duty during a month. Work at night, between midnight and 5 a.m. is not allowed. The working time regulations are under the supervision of the National Board of Occupational Safety and Health and of a regional authority (the Labour Inspectorate). Exceptions to the laws are made (by the authorities) for several reasons. Such exceptions include process industries, hospitals, communications, restaurants, pharmacies, newspaper printing, etc.

There has been a long-term decline in the weekly working time in Sweden. For employees, the average actual working week is presently about 40 hours for men, and 33 hours for women. The development of the average number of working hours is also influenced by variations in the less than full time working week, overtime work, and absenteeism.

The regulations of the standard working week via legislation and central agreements refer to full time employees; it is possible for an employee to agree with the employer on a shorter working week. This has become more common during the 1970s, because of the abolishing of the family taxation system; and the rapidly growing female labour force participation. This development has resulted in an increasing share of the labour force with part-time employment, and consequently the average weekly working time has decreased in relation to the standard working week.

It is, of course possible for the employees to influence their working time by overtime work, or by taking an extra job. The working week regulation also gives firms the right to order employees to work overtime, on the one hand in emergency situations, and on the other to do what is called general, or extra, overtime work. The employer decides when there should be overtime work. The maximum overtime the employer can order is 150 hours per employee per year. It is always possible for the National Board of Occupational Safety and Health to grant exceptions from the maximum overtime rule. The potential room for variation of actual weekly working time that the employer has, through the statutory right to order overtime, represents nearly 10 percent of the yearly standard working time. In reality the potential room for overtime is limited by the unwillingness of the employees to accept overtime work, which among other things may be a consequence of the high Swedish marginal income tax rates. The actual amount of overtime work has not been higher than 3 percent, even during extreme booms in the manufacturing industry. This also may be a consequence of the fact that overtime work is expensive for the employers. The extra costs for overtime work by a blue-collar worker in the engineering industry is (according to the national agreement 1989/90), on an ordinary working day, about 50 percent; on Saturdays, Sundays and religious holidays about 85 percent. The premium varies between the national agreements.

Table 4. Working Time Regulations by Law in Sweden

	Weekly working time	Holidays with pay	Retirement age	Paid leave for care of children
1914			67 years	
1920	48 h			
1931		4 days		
1938		2 weeks		
1939				Protection from dismissal, 12 weeks
1945				-"-, 6 months
1951		3 weeks		
1955				Maternity leave, 3 months
1958	47 h			
1959	46 h			-"-, 6 months
1960	45h			
1963		4 weeks		
1967	44 h 10 m			
1968	43 h 20 m			
1969	42 h 30 m			
1971	41 h 15 m			
1973	40 h			
1974				Parental leave, 6 months
1975				-"-, 7 months
1976			65 years	
1978		5 weeks		-"-, 7+1[1] months
1980				-"-, 9+3[1] months
1989		5 w + 2		-"-, 12+3[1] months
1990		days		-"-, 15 months[2]
1991				-"-, 18 months[2]

Notes: 1. Only the basic benefit allowance.
2. Postponed.
Source: SOU 1989:53, p. 123.

Absenteeism has often been discussed in Sweden. One can observe a rising rate of absence. In 1970 about 9 percent of the potential labour force was absent (for any reason) from their jobs during the whole observation week. In 1988 the figure was about 14 percent.[56] One also can observe a pro cyclical fluctuation.[57]

The falling trend in working time can primarily be explained by longer holidays and extended paid maternity leave. All employees are by law entitled to holiday leave of at least five weeks and two days. It is possible to save the fifth week for up to five years. The same tendency is also valid for parents' right to parental leave. Job-absenteeism because of sickness has also increased during the same period.

Retirement age in Sweden, for state pension and general supplementary old age pension (ATP), is 65 since 1976. It is possible for the employee to choose early pension (*i.e.*, before 65), that will be accompanied by reduced pension – minus 0.5 percent per month. At 60 years the reduction thus will be 30 percent. It is also possible to delay retirement, but there are two obstacles to that: the high marginal taxes make it less remunerative, and after 65 the employment security laws are not valid.[58] The working time regulation by law is summarized in Table 4.

C.2 Wages

Wages in Sweden are regulated through collective agreements. There are no minimum wage laws. There are, however, some regulations that have implications for wage setting. Sweden has adopted the ILO Convention against discrimination on ethnic grounds, and the Swedish constitution forbids discrimination by sex. Finally, in 1980, the Act on Equality between Men and Women at Work was introduced.

The wage cost increases can be separated into contractual change, wage drift, and employers' contribution to social security fees, payroll taxes and insurance fees negotiated by the parties. The high wage drift, about 45 percent of total wage increases, indicates that the central parties do not have full control of over the wage formation process.

Payroll taxes (employers' compulsory contributions) are earmarked taxes levied on the wage sum. The contributions were in total, 38.1 percent of the wage sum in 1991, for blue-collar workers as well as for white-collar workers. Employers' contributions according to collective agreements are 6.3 percent for blue-collar workers, and 7.6 for white-collar workers.

---

56. Söderström (1990), p. 45.

57. Nilsson (1978), p. 84.

58. SOU 1989:53, p. 111. It is possible that employment security laws in 1992 will be extended to 67. From 1991 the marginal taxes have been decreased.

During the 1950s and the major part of the 1960s, the payroll tax, and the average income tax, increased at the same rate, or about 3 percent yearly. Since the end of the 1960s payroll taxes, including employers' social security contributions, have grown much faster, from 11.1 percent in 1968 to 40.8 in 1978, or, on the average, about 14 percent yearly, and represent a significant part of the wage cost increases for blue-collar workers. According to the EFO-model the "room for wage increases" should be reduced by payroll tax increases. Before the wage negotiations in 1974 and 1975-76 this approach was decided upon in an agreement between the Swedish government and the employees' and employers' organizations.[59]

One consequence of tax increases is that the wedge between the product real wage and the consumption real wage has grown; for blue-collar workers the wedge grew with over 30 percent between 1970 and 1990. Of course one can ask what consequences this development may have for the wage formation process. The short run wedge effect on product real wage has been estimated to approximately 0.5, which means that the payroll tax increase in short run has a wage cost increasing effect of half the tax increase. In the long run between 90 and 100 percent of the tax increase is carried by the wage earners.[60]

In the EFO-model it is assumed that wage increases in the tradable sector spill over to the sheltered business sector and the public sector. This assumption is consistent with the solidarity wage policy. In the last two decades the average yearly total wage increase in the sheltered sector has been about the same as the total wage increase in the tradable sector. We know that in the tradable sector the wage drift has been about 40 percent of the total wage increases. In the sheltered sector the corresponding figure is about 20 percent. The workers in this sector have been compensated afterwards, in the yearly wage negotiations. This compensation is to a great extent formalized in the wage agreements of the past year, as "earnings development guarantees". Econometric wage equations confirm that wage increases in the business sector spill over to the public sector.[61]

The LO's attitude to pure piece rate wage systems became more negative at the end of the 1960s. Between 1970 and 1989 the pure piece rate system for blue-collar workers in manufacturing industry has diminished, from about one third of the total number of working hours to below 10 percent. For performance-related wages in total, one observes another tendency. In 1970 about 60 percent of working hours could be counted in this category, and until 1980 the trend was downward, but after 1980 there has been no further fall. During the 1970s the companies have success-

---

59. LO (1976), p. 197.

60. Holmlund (1990), Calmfors & Forslund (1990), and SNEPQ (1991).

61. Holmlund & Ohlsson (1990).

ively replaced the former pure piece rates systems with performance-related wage systems on a group basis. (Compare Figure 2.) Group-related payment-by-result systems represented less than 50 percent of the total working time associated with performance-related wage systems in 1970, while, in 1983 the figure was about 70 percent. Among white-collar workers, fixed wages have been the norm, except for managers and salesmen. In total, about one third of the companies in 1985 used some form of performance-related wage-system for at least some categories of the white-collar workers, in 1983 the corresponding figure was one fourth.[62]

Figure 2: Wage Forms, Blue-collar Workers in Manufacturing Industry

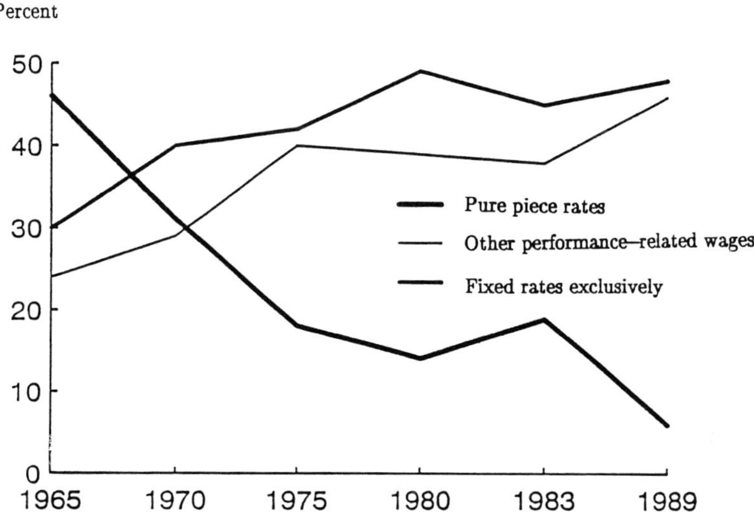

Source: SAF

C.3 Fringe Benefits

In most labour contracts today the employment conditions in several respects go further than what is regulated by law (Table 5). How the statutory regulated holidays with pay, and the paid leave for care of children, have developed over time is seen

62. SAF (1986), and Elvander (1992), p. 48.

in Table 4. Cash benefits from the general system of sickness pay replace about 90 percent of the gross earnings lost because of illness (before 1988 with a one day waiting period). The daily benefit in the general system of child care compensation is the same as for sickness. The general pension replacement rate of gross earnings for single workers is about 70 percent, and for couples about 80 percent. Finally, the average after tax replacement rates for unemployment insurances are between 65 and 75 percent.[63]

Table 5. Labour Contracts which Complement what is Statutory Regulated (different collective agreements)

	Cleaners	Engeneering workers	Central government	Local government	SIF
Holidays			+	+	+
Sickpay	+	+	+	+	+
Child care compensation			+		+
Pension	+	+	+	+	+
Unemployment compensation	+	+	+	+	+

Source: LO (1987, a).

There are many other examples of fringe benefits. There seem to be large differences between firms/companies and between groups of employees within firms. Among 25 of the biggest Swedish companies gave personal discounts on company's products. Other frequent examples are subsidized lunches, localities for sport, daily papers for reading, subsidized dwellings, and holiday houses. There are also conference- and study trips abroad, private insurance for sickness, capital insurance, and arrangements for free train or air travelling, etc.[64] Through the new income tax system, introduced in 1991, the value of these benefits will be reduced.

Many companies offer their employees advantageous loans. These loans may be coupled to personal discounts on the company's products, but also may be used to finance employees' purchase of a dwelling, a car, or shares in the company. Another frequent fringe benefit in Swedish firms seems office cars. About 6 to 7 percent of all cars are company cars. Among newly registered cars the figures are even higher; in 1985 the figure was about 40 percent. Despite less favourable tax rules on com-

63. See Bosworth & Rivlin (1987), p. 197, Björklund & Holmlund (1989), and Edebalk & Wadensjö (1989a and b).

64. LO (1987), p. 42.

pany cars, this benefit still seems economically advantageous for the employees, at least in comparison with owing a new car.[65]

Profit sharing systems on individual basis (as distinguished from the collective wage earners funds) have existed in some firms for a very long time. During the 1980s the system became more frequent, and in 1988 about 10 percent of the wage earners owned profit shares in their company. The individual shares can be withdrawn only after a certain period (generally 5 years). One large Swedish bank in 1986 transferred about 20 000 SEK to a fund of this sort for each full time employee. An individual who has been employed at the bank since 1973 had, in 1987, a share representing a value of about 400 000 SEK (the money is tied until the employee is 60 years old). In total the transfer to profit sharing funds in 1985 was about 400 million SEK. From 1988, and onwards, companies have to pay social security contributions (payroll tax) of about 27 percent on the sum that is disposed to profit shares for their employees. Until 1987 the companies did not have to pay social security contributions on transfers to these funds, if the shares were bound for at least five years. On the other hand the profit shares – from 1988 on – will be counted as income on which the general supplementary pension right (the ATP) is counted.[66]

According to Sköldebrand (1989, p. 73) 247 companies, with more than 200 000 employees, have emitted convertible debentures amounting to more than 16 billions SEK. Another study from 1988 reported that 71 of 96 companies at the Stockholm Stock Exchange had emitted convertibles.[67] In the Metal Workers' union, about 50 percent of the members in factory clubs with more than 150 members have been offered the opportunity to buy convertibles.[68]

C.4 Termination of Labour Contracts

The Act on the Right of Association and Collective Bargaining was intended to protect employees against dismissal on the grounds of membership in a union (*i.e.*, they were granted a positive right of association).

The Employment Security Act (LAS) from 1974, states that employment contracts of indefinite length should be the normal form of employment, and that the employer must have objective causes to dismiss an employee. In the law there is no definition of what is meant by objective causes. However, from the practice of the Labour

65. *Ibid.*

66. LO (1987a), Elvander (1989), and Anell (1989).

67. Anell (1988), p. 47.

68. LO (1987), p. 43.

Court it is possible to make a judgment of what has been considered a valid cause. Two typical cases can be found, namely redundancies and personal relations problems. Redundancies are always an objective cause for a dismissal. Dismissals because of personal problems can in turn be separated into two groups. The first group involves employees who do not do their jobs satisfactory, because of insufficient ability. The second group contains employees who neglect their duties. Insufficient ability because of high age, or ill-health, is not normally regarded as an objective cause for a dismissal. On the contrary repeated neglect of one's work, such as unauthorized absence, refusal to follow orders, intoxication on the job etc., may be grounds for dismissal. But considerations must be taken to the period of employment tenure; a newly employed cannot demand the same degree of employment security as an employee who has been employed in the firm for many years. It can be reasonable for a small firm to dismiss an employee in a case where a larger firm is able to examine other measures before a dismissal. From union representatives the employer has the right to expect more than from the other employees.[69]

In the case of dismissals due to redundancies the firm has to follow strict seniority rules: "last in-first out". There is also a rule that the period of notice is at least one month. This rule is valid both for the employer and the employee. For an employee who wants to quit, the notice is always one month, if the collective agreement does not prescribe anything else. This is the case in some white-collar agreements. Employment security is stronger for older workers than for younger. After at least a six month employment tenure, an employee of 25 years of age or more has a notice of two months; at 30 years of age three months; at 35 years of age four months; at 40 five months; and at 50 six months.

During the period of notice the employee shall have the right to his normal wage and other employment benefits. During that period the employee also has the right to search for a new job. He must, however, be available to his employer. When it is a question of dismissal for crude neglect of one's duties, dismissal has to be written.

The law does not prescribe when the employer can use temporary lay-offs. The rules are found in the collective agreements and in the Labour Courts' practice.[70]

D. Concluding Remarks

One important element of the Swedish model that still remained, in spite of the revolutions of the 1980s, was the full employment ambition. Sweden trusted, on the

---

69. DS A 1981:6, ch. 6.

70. Edebalk & Wadensjö (1989).

one hand, in the "employment principle", as distinguished from the "unemployment benefit principle", and gave on the other hand priority to the full employment goal, when other countries concentrated on achieving price stability.

The institutional background (the labour market laws, the wage negotiation institutions, the labour market policy, the social security system, the tax rates, etc.) probably plays an important role for the performance of the labour market, and accordingly for the possibility to achieve full employment, given the price stability ambition. In the 1970s the Swedish model is said to have collapsed; Sweden experienced a cost crisis (see section A.5). During that period there may have been too much wage equalization, job security, and high marginal tax rates, and as a consequence labour mobility was too low, and wages were too rigid: the balance between efficiency (the market influence) and job security and the strengthening of the union position in the industrial relations system (the political influence) inclined to go too far in the latter direction. But the new policy ambitions, involving more flexible markets, privatization, etc., seem in the short run to cause high costs in terms of unemployment, and there also seems to be a risk for long lasting high unemployment levels (which is, of course, contrary to the ambitions of the new policy). Consequently, with the present lack of sympathy for "planned systems", and a new Conservative-Liberal-Center government, the pendulum might be allowed to swing back so far that the balance instead is inclined to swing in the other direction.

The Rehn-Meidner model was formulated about 40 years ago. The purpose of that model was to solve the conflict between full employment and price stability. Maybe it is time to go back to the Rehn-Meidner model and to a lesser degree emphasize job security and to a higher degree employment security, through mobility subsidies and an active labour market policy. However, it may be right to replace the centralized wage formation system with a wage formation system where the union factory clubs to a higher degree are responsible for wage policy. It will certainly vitalize the clubs, and make it easer to co-ordinate the wage systems for blue- and white-collar workers, or even make a change to a single status system possible.

REFERENCES

Ahlen, Kristina, Swedish Collective Bargaining Under Pressure: Inter-union Rivalry and Incomes Policies, *British Journal of Industrial Relations*, November 1989, 27, 330-346.
Anell, Barbro, *Anställda ägare*, Stockholm: SNS, 1989.
Barbash, Jack, *Trade Unions and National Economic Policy*, London: John Hopkins Press, 1972.
Bosworth, Barry P. and Rivlin, Alice M. (eds.), *The Swedish Economy*, Washington, D.C.: Brookings, 1987.
Björklund, Anders and Holmlund, Bertil, Effects of Extended Unemployment Compensation in Sweden, in: Gustafsson, B.A. and Klevmarken, N.A. (eds.), *The Political Economy of Social Security*, Elsevier Science Publisher B.V., 1989.
Calmfors, Lars and Forslund, Anders, Wage Formation in Sweden, in: Calmfors, Lars (ed.), *Wage Formation and Macroeconomic Policy in the Nordic Countries*, Oxford University Press, 1990.
DS 1989:68, Arbetsmarknadsförsäkringar.
DS A 1981:6, Anställningsskydd.
Edebalk, Per Gunnar and Wadensjö, Eskil, Permitteringsersättning, permitteringar och arbetslöshet, *Ekonomisk Debatt*, 1985, 13, 407-417.
Edebalk, Per Gunnar and Wadensjö, Eskil, Contractually Determined Insurance Schemes for Manual Workers, in: Gustafsson, B.A. and Klevmarken, N. Anders (eds.), *The Political Economy of Social Security*, Elsevier Science Publisher B.V, 1989a.
Edebalk, Per Gunnar and Wadensjö, Eskil, *Arbetsmarknadsförsäkringar*, Stockholm: ESO, 1989b.
Edgren, Gösta, Faxén, Karl-Olof and Odhner, Clas-Erik, *Wage Formation and the Economy*, London: Allen & Unwin, 1973.
Edlund, Sten and Nyström, Birgitta, *Developments in Swedish Labour Law*, The Swedish Institute, 1988.
Elvander, Nils, *Intresseorganisationerna i dagens Sverige*, Lund: Gleerup, 1969.
Elvander, Nils, *Skandinavisk arbetarrörelse*, Stockholm: Liber, 1980.
Elvander, Nils, *Den svenska modellen. Löneförhandlingar och inkomstpolitik 1982-1986*, Stockholm: Allmänna förlaget, 1988.
Elvander, Nils (ed.), *Förhandlingssystem, inkomstpolitik och arbetskonflikter i Norden*, Stockholm: Nordstedts, 1988.
Elvander, Nils, Pay Systems Practices and Labour Flexibility in Sweden, unpublished manuscript for an ILO project, 1989.
Elvander, Nils, *Lokal lönemarknad. Lönebildning i Sverige och Storbritannien*, Stockholm: SNS, 1992.
Faxén, Karl-Olof, Odhner, Clas-Erik and Spånt, Roland, *Lönebildning i 90-talets ekonomi*, Stockholm: Raben & Sjögren, 1989.
Hadenius, Axel, *Facklig organisationsutveckling, En studie av landsorganisationen i Sverige*, Stockholm: Liber, 1976.
Hansen, Bent, *Nationalekonomiska föreningens förhandlingar*, 1961.
Hellström, Tommy and Lundberg, Ulf, *Lönekultur. Individuell lönesättning för tjänstemän*, Stockholm: MGruppen, 1985.
Hibbs, Jr. Douglas A., *Wage Compression Under Solidarity Bargaining in Sweden*, Stockholm: FIEF, 1990.
Holmlund, Bertil, *Svensk lönebildning – teori, emperi, politik*, Bilaga 24 till LU90, 1990.
Holmlund, Bertil and Ohlsson, Henry, "Wage Linkages Between Private and Public Sectors in Sweden", Working Paper , Dep. of Econ. Uppsala University, 1990.
Johnston, T.L., *Collective Bargaining in Sweden: A study of the labour market and its institutions*, London: Allen & Unwin, 1962.
Jonsson, Lennart and Siven Claes-Henric, *Varför löneskillnader?*, Stockholm: SAF, 1986.

Kjellberg, Anders, *Facklig organisering i tolv länder*, Lund: Arkiv, 1983.
Labour information 1992:1, Stockholm: SCB.
LO, *Fackföreningsrörelsen och den fulla sysselsättningen*, 1951.
LO, *Samordnad näringspolitik*, 1961.
LO, *Löner, priser, skatter*, 1976.
LO, *Lönepolitik för 80-talet*, 1981.
LO, *Gemensamt ansvar för arbete*, 1986.
LO, *Lönepolitisk delrapport*, 1987a.
LO, *De centrala överenskommelserna*, 1987b.
LO, *Röster om facket och jobbet*, No. 5, 1989.
Lundberg, Erik, The Rise and the Fall of the Swedish Model, *Journal of Economic Literature*, March 1985, 23, 1-36.
Meidner, Rudolf, Our Concept of the Third Way: Some Remarks on the Socio-political Tenets of the Swedish Labour Movement, *Economic and Industrial Democracy*, 1980, 343-369.
Nilsson, Christian, *Sysselsättning och arbetslöshet*, Uppsala: Almqvist & Wiksell International, 1978.
Nilsson, Christian, Lönebildning och lönestruktur, in: *Seminarium kring arbetsmarknadspolitiken*, Stockholm: EFA, 1985.
Nilsson, Christian, *Lokal lönebildning och löneinflation*, Stockholm: FIEF, 1987.
Nilsson, Christian, *Lönepolitik och regional balans*, Stockholm: FIEF, 1989.
Peterson, Richard B., Swedish Collective Bargaining – A Changing Scene, *British Journal of Industrial Relations*, March 1987, 25, 31-48.
SAF, *Lönformsundersökning 1985*, 1986.
SAF, *Fakta om Sveriges ekonomi*, 1989.
Saltsjöbadsavtalet 50 år, Stockholm: Arbetslivcentrum, 1989.
Schiller, Bernt, *Det förödande 70-talet*, SAF *och medbestämmandet 1965-1982*, Arbetsmiljöfonden, 1982.
Schmidt, Folke, *Law and Industrial Relations in Sweden*, Stockholm: Almqvist & Wiksell International, 1977.
Schmidt, Folke and Victorin, Anders, Labour Law, in: Strömholm, S. (ed.), *An Introduction to Swedish Law*, Stockholm: Norstedts, 1988.
Schmidt, Folke, *Facklig arbetsrätt*, Juristförlaget, 1989.
Seth, Torsten, Labour Relations in the Public Sector Service in Sweden, in: Treu, Tiziano, *et al.*, *Public Service Labour Relations*, Geneva: ILO, 1987.
Sjölund, Maivor, *Statens lönepolitik*, Stockholm: Publica, 1989.
Sköldebrand, Barbro, *Anställd och ägare – konvertibler*, Stockholm: Arbetslivscentrum, 1989.
Skogh, Göran, Employers Association in Sweden, in: Windmuller, J.P. and Gladstone, A. (eds.), *Employers Associations and Industrial Relations*, Oxford: Clarendon Press, 1984.
SNEPQ, A quarterly econometric model for Sweden, unpublished manuscript, Stockholm: FIEF, 1991.
SOU 1984:18, *Arbetsmarknadsstriden I.*
SOU 1984:19, *Arbetsmarknadsstriden II.*
SOU 1988:30, *Arbetsdomstolen.*
SOU 1988:49, *Arbetsmarknadsstriden III.*
SOU 1988:50, *Arbetsmarknadsstriden IV.*
SOU 1989:53, *Arbetstid och välfärd.*
SOU 1991:13, *Spelreglerna på arbetsmarknaden.*
SOS Statistisk årsbok, Stockholm: SCB.
Ståhl, Ingemar, Arbetsmarknadsorganisationerna i stagnationsekonomin, *Ekonomisk Debatt*, 1978, 469-482.
Söderström, Hans Tson (ed.), *I samtidens bakvatten?*, Stockholm: SNS, 1990.
TCO, *Lönepolitik för 90-talet*, 1989.

Turvey, Ralph (ed.), *Wages Policy under Full Employment*, London: William Hodge, 1952.
Victorin, Anders, *Lönenormering genom kollektivavtal*, Stockholm: Allmänna förlaget, 1973.
Victorn, Anders, The Implementation of a Wage Policy: Centralized Collective Bargaining in Sweden, in: Schmidt, Folke (ed.), *Scandinavian Studies in Law*, 1975.

ABBREVIATIONS

AD	Arbetsdomstolen (the Labour Court)
AML	Arbetsmiljölagen (the Working Environment Act), 1978
AMS	Arbetsmarknadsstyrelsen (the National Labour Market Board)
CF	Sveriges Civilingenjörsförbund (the Professional Engineers, affiliated to the SACO/SR and the PTK)
EFO	*E*dgren, *F*axén and *O*hdner
FML	Förtroendemannalagen (the Act on Union Representatives for Employees in Private firms/ companies), 1974
FOS	*F*axén, *O*hdner and *S*pånt
KAL	Lagen om kollektivavtal (the Collective Agreements Act), 1928
KF	Kommunförbundet (the Association of Local Authorities)
KFO	Kooperationens Förhandlingsorganisation (The Cooperative Employers' Association)
KTK	Kommunaltjänstemannakartellen (the TCO negotiation cartel for local government employees)
LAS	Lag om anställningsskydd (the Employment Security Act), 1974
LF	Landstingsförbundet (the Federation of County Councils)
LO	Landsorganisationen i Sverige (the Swedish Trade Union Confederation)
LOA	Lagen om offentlig anställning (the Act on Public Employment), 1977
MBL	Lagen om medbestämmande i arbetlivet (the Act on Co-determination in Working Life), 1977
OAS	Offentliga arbetsgivares samarbetsorganistion (Public Employers' Association for Co-operation)
PTK	Privattjänstemannakartellen (the Federation of Salaried Employees, e.g., a negotiation cartel for white-collar workers in the private sector)
SAC	Sveriges Arbetares Centralorganisation (the Central Organization of Swedish Workers)
SACO	Centralorganisationen SACO (the Swedish Confederation of Professional Associations, until 1988 SACO/SR)
SACO-K	the SACO negotiation cartel for local government employees
SACO-S	the SACO negotiation cartel for central government employees
SAF	Svenska Arbetsgivarföreningen (the Swedish Employers' Confederation)
SALF	Sveriges Arbetsledarförbund (the Foremen's and Supervisors' Union, affiliated to the TCO and the PTK)
SAV	Statens avtalsverk (the National Agency for Government Employers)
SF	Statsanställdas förbund (the Swedish National Union of State Employees)
SFO	(the Employers' Association for Companies in Joint Ownership)
SIF	Svenska Industritjänstemannaförbundet (the Union of Clerical-Technical Employees in Industry, affiliated to the TCO and the PTK)
SKAF	Svenska Kommunalarbetarförbundet (the Swedish Municipal Workers' Union, affiliated LO)
TCO	Tjänstemännens Centralorganisation (the Central Organization for Salaried Employees)
TCO-OF	the TCO negotiation cartel for public employees (substitutes TCO-S and KTK from 1991)
TCO-S	the TCO negotiation cartel for central government employees

Labour Market Contracts and Institutions
J. Hartog and J. Theeuwes (Editors)

CHAPTER 9

FRANCE:
Toward Flexibility

Jacques Freyssinet*

A. Introduction

A.1 The Labour Market

In France, as in other Western countries, two distinct employment categories are regulated by different economic and legal mechanisms. On the one hand, employment in the market sector is regulated by the labour code ("Code du travail") (private law). The code covers not only jobs in the private sector, but also those in public companies.[1] On the other hand, the civil service statute ("statut de la fonction publique") regulates state, regional and municipal employees (civil servants), and public hospital workers.

The analysis presented here includes only workers covered by contracts under private law, that is to say, 72 % of all employees in 1989 (see Table 1). However, it should be noted that current policies are moving toward a "modernization of the civil service" through the introduction of mechanisms inspired by the private sector (employee negotiations, career management and training, advances based on merit, etc.).

Under private law, the normal contract is of indefinite term, which means that it can only be terminated by resignation, lay-off or dismissal, or through liquidation of the company. However, the use of fixed term contracts is increasing (see C.4). In 1989, 9 % of contracts under private law were of the latter type.

---

* University of Paris I and Institut de Recherches Economiques et Sociales.

1. Public companies which compete in the marketplace fall completely under the aegis of the labour code. Public monopolies (for instance, the railroads, electric and gas companies,...) are also regulated by the labour code, but their employees benefit from a status which puts them in an intermediate position between private and public law.

A.2 Historical Overview of Labour Laws and Institutions

The germs of protective legislation covering certain worker categories (mainly women and children) began to appear in the mid-nineteenth century. These grew up in the legal context of the supposedly freely negotiated individual contract, which in reality left the balance of power in the hands of the employer. State intervention manifested itself, above all, in control of the work force and repression of social conflicts.

Table 1. Employment Distribution According to the Statute
(expressed in thousands)

State and Municipal Employees:		5,099
- Tenured	3,735	
- Untenured	695	
- Others	689	
Other Employees:		13,299
- Indefinite Term Contracts	12,081	
- Fixed Term Contracts	611	
- Temporaries	234	
- Apprentices	212	
- Trainees	162	
Non-Salaried Workers		3,355
- Self-Employed or Employers	2,706	
- Domestic Help	649	
TOTAL		21,754

Source: INSEE, "Enquête sur l'emploi", March 1989

The situation changed with the development of the union movement, which obtained legal recognition in 1884. However, the level and quality of collective bargaining was mediocre up until the big strikes of 1936, in spite of the laws of 1919 which gave legal status to such negotiations. Only in the rare sectors or periods where the balance of power was with the unions, is collective bargaining imposed on a reluctant management. In fact, bargaining arose only when social conflicts were prolonged or broadened, and frequently only after instigation by State representatives. Collective agreements were primarily end of conflict agreements. In the face of the employers' resolute hostility to bargaining, the union movement very early brought pressure to bear on the State, to obtain through laws what could not be gotten through collective agreement. After the period of State regulated economy following the second World War, a 1950 law established the jurisdiction of collective bargaining over all parts of the labour contract.

Overall, the centralist and interventionist traditions of the State and the employers' long struggle to escape collective bargaining have given a predominant role to legislative and regulatory mechanisms, although recently the orientation has been reversed again.

B. The Institutional and Legal Context

The nature of the bargaining structure (B.3) can only be understood in the light of both the specific system of industrial relations (B.1) and the legislation on collective bargaining (B.2), since it involves not so much a division as a complex interweaving of measures fixed by law or by collective agreement (B.4).

B.1 Industrial Relations

(a) The employers' organizations[2]

The dominant employer organization is the Conseil National du Patronat Français (CNPF). Although there are a number of differing scenarios, employer organizations are formed along classic lines with companies freely choosing to belong to the primary organizations. These are in turn grouped in, on the one hand, national, industrywide organizations, and on the other hand, in regional "interprofessional"[3] unions. At the top, the CNPF unites these two types of structures. Each level, within its jurisdiction, simultaneously performs two functions: defense of its members interests, and representation at the bargaining table. This dual function separates the French situation from that of numerous analogous countries.

However, the employers are divided by the diversity of their interests and ideologies. One of the most obvious examples is the gap between small and large companies. Since the CNPF is controlled in large part by the big companies, the small companies have created an independent organization, the Confédération Générale des Petites et Moyennes Entreprises (CGPME).[4] The two organizations participate side by side in negotiating national interprofessional agreements. The more restrictive

2. See: Bunel and Saglio, 1980; Agnes and Georges-Picot, 1982-83; Sellier, 1984; and Weber, 1986.

3. The term "interprofessionnel" is frequently used in France to designate organizations, or collective agreements and contracts, covering all industrial areas or branches and not the totality of professions (in the sense of a trade, or an individual type of activity). We have respected this global usage, however please note the possible risk of confusion.

4. The CGPME is not, however, completely independent since a high percentage of primary employer organizations adhere simultaneously to the CGPME and the CNPF.

positions of the CGPME have led to their refusal to ratify certain agreements approved by the CNPF.

(b) The union movement

Ideological divisions

Since the 1884 law legalizing the existence of union organization and the founding of the Confédération Générale du Travail (CGT) in 1895, the French union movement has had a complex history which would be impossible to sum up here. To understand the current situation, one must look at the aftermath of the second World War (see Figure 1). At that point, the CGT was the leading organization, but it underwent a schism in 1947. While the CGT remained within the World Federation of Trade Unions (WFTU), a minority fraction created the Confédération Générale du Travail-Force Ouvrière (CGT-FO) which belongs to the International Confederation of Trade Unions (ICFTU).

The Confédération Française des Travailleurs Chrétiens (CFTC), founded in 1919 on a religious basis, began a long internal transition after World War II leading to its transformation in 1964 into the non-religious Confédération Française Démocratique du Travail (CFDT). However, a minority faction decided to maintain the CFTC along its traditional lines. Having left the World Confederation of Labour (WCL) in 1979, the CFDT was replaced by the current CFTC. Today the CFDT is a member of the ICFTU.

Figure 1. French Union Organizations

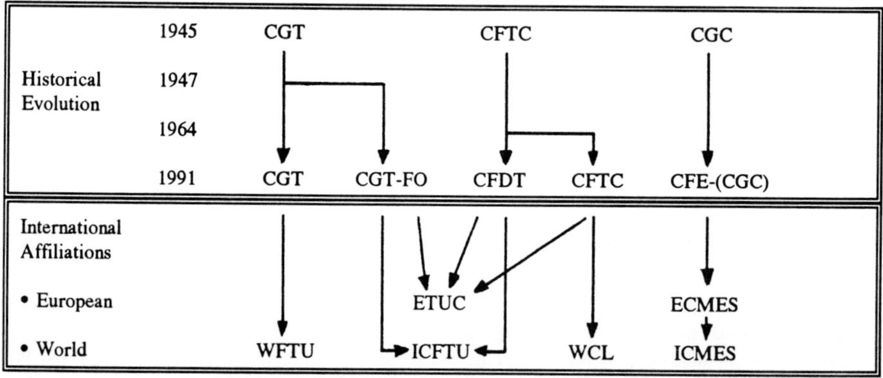

The Confédération Générale des Cadres (CGC) was created in 1944 from a regrouping of a number of professional organizations. Called the Confédération Française de l'Encadrement (CFE-CGC) since 1987, it unites (as its name implies) managerial and white collar workers. It belongs to the International Confederation of Managerial and Executive Staff (ICMES).

At the European level, the CGT-FO, the CFDT and the CFTC all belong to the European Trade Unions Confederation (ETUC). The CGT was rejected by the ETUC, largely because of its membership in the WFTU. For its part, the CFE-CGC has played a major role in creating the European Federation of Managerial and Executive Staff (ECMES).

Internal organization

For the most part, French unions are organized along the principles of industrial unionism. The five confederations thus share analogous internal structures. At the local level, the union unites workers in the same industry. The local union belongs to a Federation based on industrial sector uniting different geographical areas. The local also belongs to a local "interprofessional" union which unites all the locals within a geographic area regardless of industrial sector. The Confederations unite all the Unions, and are structured along the dual lines of the Federations and the Interprofessional Unions.

It is difficult to evaluate how power is divided up between the various levels. On the whole, the French union movement has inherited a strong tradition of decentralisation. As a result, the different elements within the same confederation are fairly autonomous, although the degree varies according to the organization.

(c) The influence of the unions

The divisions between French unions make it difficult to objectively measure the power held by the unions, particularly since such an evaluation is one of the stakes of the competition between unions. The overall influence of French unionism is therefore controversial. Various partial though complementary indicators can be looked at: membership, presence at the plant level and electoral results.

Membership

With the exception of certain special historical periods, the percentage of union membership has always been low in France. The hypotheses given are multiple: the non-existence (excepting a few minor cases) of "closed shop" or "union shop" rules; that collective agreements signed by the unions apply not only to union members, but to all workers; that the unions have, with few exceptions, not created services reserved only for their members; and finally, the plural nature of the unions and interunion conflicts are oft-cited factors in explaining low membership.[5]

Table 2. Rate of Union Membership 1981-1989

	1981	1989
Professional categories:		
- Intermediate professions	36	23
- Employees	22	7
- Workers	25	12
All employees	28	14
Private sector	18	8
Public sector	44	26
Total population (over 18 yrs.)	20	11

Source: SOFRES Study

Table 3. Union Delegates in 1989

Percent of plants with a union delegate by size (# of employees)		Percent of plants where a union organization has a delegate	
50-99 workers	35.9	CGT	30.4
100-199	57.1	CFDT	25.7
200-499	77.7	CFT-FO	19.3
500-999	88.4	CFE-CGC	14.4
1000 or more	92.3	CFTC	7.8
		Others	6.7
Total:	50.7	Total:	50.9

Source: Ministère du Travail, 1991

5. The existence, in France and elsewhere, of an active anti-union policy led by a large number of employers should not be neglected.

The rate of union membership for 1955-1980 has been estimated at 20 % (Visser, 1989; Amadieu, 1989). Several recent studies (Heran, 1988; Haussler, 1988; Gonguet and Perez, 1990) point to a drop by half in the last decade (see Table 2).[6]

Union presence at the plant level

A union's strength lies not only in the number of members or sympathizers. It is also measured by its capacity to implant itself in the workplace and to lead work actions in defense of the workers' interests.

The Labour Code authorizes the creation of a "union section" by representative unions in workplaces with at least 50 employees, and the designation of "union delegates". Table 3 shows the extent, in 1989, of union presence in companies of at least 50 employees. In 51 % of these companies at least one union was present. This figure increases sharply with the size of the company. The rate of presence for the five major union confederations varies between 8 and 30 %.

Electoral results

French workers elect members to the bodies who represent them to the employers. The only statistics available for longer periods are those for the Works Councils ("Comités d'Entreprise") elections.

Table 4. Works Councils. Distribution of Votes 1968-1989

%	1968-69	1978-79	1988-89
CGT	45.2	36.8	25.9
CFDT	18.9	20.5	20.9
CGT-FO	7.4	10.0	12.4
CFE-CGC	5.0	6.3	6.1
CFTC	2.9	2.9	4.2
Other unions	5.6	5.1	5.6
Non-union	15.0	18.5	24.9

Source: Ministère du Travail

Two tendencies emerge from Table 4. First, the relative weight of the different organizations has undergone a clear evolution, even though their ranking has not changed.

6. The relatively high rates for "intermediate professions" can be explained by the increased unionization in the public sector where these categories are predominant.

Second, the percentage of non-union representatives elected has grown considerably,[7] and could be looked upon as a sign of weakening trade-unionism. The correct interpretation is, however, more complex. For a long time the employers only instituted works councils if union pressure was sufficiently strong, and so the representatives had a greater likelihood of being union members. Progressively, companies have come to favour the creation of works councils, either in order to meet various regulations, or because they saw the works councils as a damper on future union organizing. This translates into the fact that the non-union representatives are more numerous in newer councils and much more numerous in small companies than in larger ones. In 1987-88, they gathered 2.2 % of the vote in companies with over 1000 workers and 59.1 % in companies of 50-99 workers.

In sum, certain characteristics can be seen clearly in French unionism which have specific effects on the conditions and content of collective bargaining. The multiple unions engender a permanent climate of competitiveness, in spite of efforts at joint action which are always partial and precarious. The historically low percentage of union membership in France has made union influence very dependent on the given political, economic and social situation, and in particular on the relationship between the unions and the State.[8] The union movement in France has undergone a bigger crisis than in the neighbouring countries, leaving the current bargaining context quite unfavourable. On the other hand, the unions have maintained their predominant position in worker representative bodies. There, they find another mechanism for influencing company personnel management, and thus the functioning of the labour market.

B.2 Legal Framework for Collective Bargaining

(a) The unions' right to represent

The Constitution and the law recognize the principle of freedom to constitute a union. Any person exercising a professional activity can constitute a union, regardless of the number of workers involved. The only restriction is that the statutes and the leaders names must be registered with the administration. The fundamental problem for a union then, is to achieve recognition as a "representative" organization, after which it benefits from a number of legal rights.[9]

---

7. See note 12.

8. It should be recalled that several times in France, particularly in 1936, 1945 and 1968, the mass mobilization of the workers gave, for a short duration, an exceptional impetus to the union movement. Turning these periods to their advantage, the unions were able to obtain major concessions from the employers or the State, on which later action in less favourable contexts could be based.

9. For this question, see Canut and Lenselle, 1989.

A union must meet simultaneously a number of criteria in order to be considered "representative". Some are fixed by law, others have been progressively laid out in the courts. They are: the number of members with respect to the population represented, autonomy from the employer, the payment by members of regular union dues, acquired experience and seniority, activity and influence.

The five union confederations have been recognized as "representative" on a national level. On this basis, all of the organizations they unite (unions, locals, professional federations) are automatically recognized as representative in their geographical and professional areas.[10] Only unions outside of these five confederations have to prove their representative status.

After achieving representative status, a union has a number of rights in three major areas: collective bargaining, collective work conflicts and the running of candidates for bodies representing the workers. For instance, the representative unions have the exclusive right to the bargaining of collective work agreements.[11] Since in France the right to strike is an individual one, the unions have no monopoly over the unleashing of conflicts. However, beyond their concrete responsibility for leading the conflicts, they must intervene when conciliation or mediation proceedings have been established and, above all, for the signing of agreements at the end of the conflict. Finally, the unions have a monopoly over the candidates for the first round of ballots for elections to bodies of worker representation, that is to say, worker delegates (in companies of more than 10 employees), and works councils (companies with 50 or more employees).[12]

---

10. The CFE-CGC has only been recognized as "representative" for white collar and managerial worker categories.

11. Please note that at the company level, the employer can make agreements with other bodies than the unions, for instance with the Worker Delegates or Works Councils. The resulting agreements are based in common law and do not come under the specific regulations regarding contracts or collective agreements.

12. The works councils ("Comités d'entreprise") were created by a 1945 law. The text has been modified many times, notably by a 1982 law reinforcing their rights. A works council must, by law, be elected in every company with 50 or more employees. The election takes place in two rounds. In the first round, only the representative unions may run candidates for election. A second round is held if the unions have not run any candidates or if the number of voters in the first round was not equal to at least 50 % of the registered voters. In the second round, anyone may run.
    The works council has two areas of jurisdiction. On the one hand, it is directly responsible for overseeing the social and cultural activities for the personnel. On the other, the works council has the right to consult on and propose modifications in the areas of economics and technology, all that is job related, training and work conditions. In all these areas the works council has the right to information and to consult with experts, in addition, the employer is obligated to solicit its opinion on many questions, etc.

A union's representative status must be legally recognized before the elections, on the basis of the criteria described above. In any case, elections come into play as a control of representative status, since the different representative unions must be able to mobilize at least half of the voters. If not, they leave the field open for other candidates during the second round. This permits other unions to establish their own representative status for the future.[13]

(b) Collective bargaining

Freedom for the two parties to define both the content of the agreement and its jurisdiction[14] is the general principle. The content of the negotiations is broadly defined by law as the work and employment conditions and the social benefits offered the workers. In this vast framework, the freedom of the negotiators is nonetheless subject to two constraints. First, they are constrained by the hierarchy of legal sources and, second, by the mandatory negotiations required by law for certain areas of the contract.[15]

The two parties are also free to determine the jurisdiction of the contract. The negotiation can be limited to one industrial branch (and would therefore be termed "professional"), or it can include multiple or all industrial sectors (and is then called "interprofessional"). It can apply to the national, regional, local or company level (or to a part of the company, for instance to one plant or workplace). It can apply to a part or all of the professional categories, for instance, there are many agreements applying only to managerial workers. The agreement applies to all the workers concerned, union or non-union, if they work for one of the companies covered under the negotiation. It is negotiated by all the representative unions but to be legally valid it only needs to be approved by one of them. Therefore, the strategies adopted by the employers and the different unions assume enormous importance. The exception to the principle of freedom to determine the jurisdiction of a contract is the procedure for extension and broadening.[16]

Worker delegates ("Délégués du personnel") must be elected in all workplaces with more than 10 workers. The election procedures are the same as for the works councils. Their function is to present the individual and collective demands of the workers. They may call upon the Work Inspection ("Inspection du travail") through complaints in cases of violations of the law or collective contracts.

13. We have shown above the increasing influence of so called "non-union" representatives elected to works councils.

14. For more on this issue, see Chauchard and Nogaret, 1985.

15. See hereinafter, B.4.

16. See hereinafter, B.4.

(c) Regulations regarding work conflicts

The right to strike is recognized by the Constitution as an individual right of all workers. It is forbidden only to certain strictly limited categories of civil servants involved in keeping the public order (army, police, ..). The right to strike as laid out by the Constitution is to be exercised within the framework of regulatory laws. However, no regulatory laws have been passed, except in the case of the civil service where, notably, a warning of five days must be given before the outbreak of a strike. The unions have no desire for such regulations to be adopted. So in practice, on the legal level, the right to strike is regulated solely through the courts.

The contract is suspended by a strike which is only sanctioned in the event of a serious grievance. Both employers and non-strikers can ask the court for damages suffered during a strike, but only if striker conduct can be shown to be at fault. At the end of a conflict an end of strike agreement is frequently signed defining not only the settlement of striker demands but also resolving any strike-related incidents. The employers only have recourse to a lock-out if the strike makes it impossible to continue normal work activity (cut-off of supplies or parts to a plant, proven risk of violence etc.).

It should be underscored that the existing balance of power will determine both the form of a conflict and its outcome. Legal norms are only part of the tools available to the parties, and are used opportunistically. The legal framework of the right to strike is quite flexible, and whether or not the strikers are sanctioned depends more on the final outcome of the conflict than on its causes or the form it takes.

Specific procedures exist to prevent or solve conflicts in the workplace: conciliation, mediation and arbitration. None of them are obligatory, neither before nor during a conflict, unless specified by a collective work agreement. Traditionally, these procedures are little used. The antagonistic conception of labour relations remains steadfast and leaves little room for intervention by a mediator or arbitrator supposedly "outside the conflict".

B.3 The Bargaining Structure

In France, there is no legislative mechanism, historical tradition or consensus between the social players permitting a codification or even a stabilization of a bargaining structure. Except in rare cases, all issues relating to the contract may be negotiated at any level. There is no regular interval for negotiations. Most often, contracts are made for an indefinite term or for a fixed term but include a tacit renewal clause.[17]

---

17. For this reason, it is impossible to measure an average bargaining interval. There are no statistics in this area.

Before we look at the statistical information available in this area, it is indispensable to understand the factors which have brought about such a situation. The answer lies in the respective strategies of the employers, the unions and the State, and in the balance of power which has been established between them.[18]

(a) Complex and changing strategies

As we have indicated earlier (see A.2), the law of 1950 gave collective bargaining jurisdiction over all elements of the labour contract. In keeping with tradition, initially negotiations developed first and foremost at the industrial level. Both employers and unions agreed to this, although for different reasons.

The employers see negotiations at the industry level as a means of equalizing competition among themselves. Above all, employers hope to avoid bargaining at the plant or company level which would facilitate union organizing in the workplace and call into question the authority of the management.

The unions distrust the company's emphasis on individualism and corporatism. They see industrywide bargaining as a way to bring about worker solidarity across company and trade barriers. In fact, the union tactics are more complicated, often taking advantage of strength in one company, or of its prosperity, to negotiate specific gains. These are legitimized through a strategy of "social gains" which, obtained locally, are then spread through industrywide negotiations.

This remained the dominant practice for twenty years. However, the appearance of two other tendencies has progressively made the situation more complex and contradictory. The first tendency has been an increase in so-called "interprofessional" bargaining, which reached full development at the end of the 1960's, notably as a result of the social upheavals of May-June 1968.

From the standpoint of the nature of the agreements, a distinction should be drawn between "content agreements" and "method agreements". The former create new mechanisms, and often establish jointly operated institutions for carrying them out (for instance, the creation in 1959 of the unemployment insurance system). The latter spell out overall objectives and set procedures, looking to industrywide agreements for their concrete implementation (for example, the 1988 agreement on technological changes).

---

18. The bibliography treats this theme extensively. For example: Bunel and Saglio, 1980; Sellier, 1984; Chaigneau *et al.*, 1988; and Supiot, 1985.

From the point of view of function, these agreements are the outcome of a compromise between two strategies. The unions use the bargaining table for creating a base of social rights to halt the widening of sectorial disparities. Direct wages are not dealt with at these negotiations, the emphasis is on indirect wages (complementary retirement plans, unemployment benefits, etc.) and on job guarantees (right to on-going vocational training, protection in the event of economic lay-offs or the introduction of new technologies, etc.).

For the employers, it is a question of gaining control over social policy by demonstrating that bargaining can effectively replace the law and create an area of social consensus. The next step is to encourage mechanisms for flexibility and mobility, which must necessarily span all industrial sectors. It should not be overlooked that these agreements are, for both employer and union confederations, a means of legitimizing or reinforcing their intervention in the social arena.

The second tendency one can observe is that the context of the 1980's provoked a reversal in employers strategies with regard to bargaining at the company level. Previously regarded distrustfully, progressively the employers gave greater weight to this orientation, for a number of reasons. First and foremost, this strategy forms part of an ideological whole seeking to give greater importance to the company in the market. Company level bargaining can be used as a tool for mobilizing workers around company goals and to involve them in performance. In addition, restructuring, modernization and flexibility all require systems tailored to the concrete situation within each company (introduction of new technologies, changes in work scheduling, individualized pay scales, human resource management). Finally, in the context of a weakening union movement, it seemed easier to lead concessions negotiations at the company, or even plant level, while threatening with job cuts or relocations.[19]

It should be noted that certain unions have not been hostile to this evolution. The immediate, concrete gains which company level negotiations offer could, according to these unions, be a means of revitalizing union intervention at its core. The 1982 law requiring bargaining within the company on certain issues (see B.4) emerged from this perspective.

As a whole, the collective bargaining structure today is particularly entangled. It has been sometimes used as an illustration of the articulation between negotiations held at different levels. This kind of intellectual construction is more of a rationalization after the fact then a description of reality.[20]

---

19. It should be remembered that valid agreements can be ratified by minority unions, given the system for according the unions "representative" status (see B.2.a). In fact, agreements are also ratified outside of the unions, by workers representative bodies.

20. Lozier, 1990.

(b) Elements of an assessment[21]

The number of agreements signed annually and the percent of the wage earners covered under agreements are two basic, yet unsatisfactory, indicators measuring the extent of collective bargaining in France.

Table 5. Percent of Employees Covered by Agreements 1981-1985

1. By size of workplace:

Size of plant (# workers)	% of Workers covered by:				Distribution of covered workers by type of coverage (1985)		
	A collective agreement		A company agreement		Industry only	Company only	Company & Industry
	1981	1985	1981	1985	(percentage)		
10-46	72.7	79.0	8.0	15.4	82.27	3.62	14.11
50-199	80.0	85.9	15.7	27.8	70.28	4.80	24.90
200-499	85.7	90.1	29.1	46.0	52.06	4.76	43.17
500 or more	86.1	95.8	51.5	68.7	30.18	1.11	68.71
All sizes	80.1	86.4	24.2	35.4	62.00	3.60	34.40

2. By industrial sector

Sector:	Percentage of Employees covered by:			
	A collective agreement		A company agreement	
	1981	1985	1981	1985
Industry	90.4	92.5	30.7	44.3
Construction, Civil Engineering	64.8	61.8	6.4	15.8
Service	71.9	86.4	21.2	30.2
All Sectors	80.1	86.4	24.2	35.4

Source: Bilan annuel de la négotiation collective, 1985

21. The main source is the "Bilans de la négotiation collective" put out annually by the Ministère du Travail. A synthesis may be found in Chaigneau *et al.*, 1988.

Around 1980, the number of "interprofessional" and industrywide agreements ratified annually dropped sharply, marking the breakpoint for a decline from an annual average of about 1500 at the beginning of the 1970s, falling to under 1000 by the end of the 1980s.[22]

In terms of negotiations at the company level, no statistics are available until after 1980. These show a marked rise from 1600 agreements in 1980 to 6500 in 1990. Two major factors, whose respective impact is however impossible to measure, are the employer strategy favouring company level negotiations, and the legal obligation to negotiate at the company level introduced in 1984 (see B.4). It should be underscored that the number of agreements alone tells us nothing of their quality. This question demands a closer analysis than is possible here.

Table 5 gives figures relative to the percentage of the labour force covered by agreements (in 1990, 18 % of employees were not covered by any kind of agreement). A number of tendencies, growth across the period of coverage in all areas, a positive link to plant size, which determines the differences by work sector, and a clear dominance of industrywide agreements over company agreements, can be seen. The latter should be corrected by a general observation on the effective coverage. Industrywide agreements frequently set the minimums at levels that can be born by the weakest companies. Many companies, whether covered by an agreement or not, actually pay higher scales (notably for wages) than those specified by the industrywide agreements. Thus, the coverage given by the agreements is at least partly illusory.

B.4 Balance Between Public and Private Measures

In analyzing the labour market, the distinction between freely negotiated elements of the employment contract and those imposed by legal texts is a central one. Unfortunately, this distinction is difficult to establish in the French case. Certainly, in principle a separation exists between the structures required by the labour code and those freely adopted in individual employment contracts. On the other hand, the relationship between the law and the collective bargaining agreement is much more complex. This can be illustrated by five structures which have played an important role in the dynamics of contemporary social relations.

22. During this period, agreements dealing with wage levels account for between 70 and 80 % of all trade level agreements.

(a) The hierarchy of legal sources

The general working principle is that lower level texts can only modify a higher level text if the change constitutes an amelioration of the rights granted to the workers. Thus, a collective agreement can only increase the benefits mandated by law. The same is true for a regional agreement with respect to an industrywide agreement.

However, this principle has been called into question by the explicit introduction by law of dispensatory agreements ("accords d'entreprise dérogatoires"), that is to say company agreements departing from legal or contractual (national collective agreement) requirements. The two major examples concern the duration of work (dispensation from legal requirements) and wage increases (dispensation from obligations set out in national industrywide agreements). Unions may annul such agreements, at the moment of their creation, if they had obtained the support of more than half of the voters registered at the previous elections for works councils (or worker delegates).[23] Some legal experts see the possibility of these agreements as the beginnings of a radical challenge to the French structure of social rights (Supiot, 1989).

(b) The obligation to negotiate

The law requires negotiations for certain issues. Since 1982, annual wage negotiations are mandated at the industrywide level and, in several areas, they are mandated at the company level. These include the actual wages, the hours worked and the organization of the work day (1982), ongoing vocational training (if there are no industry level negotiations and if the company employs more than 50 workers-1984) and, on the employees' right to meet in the workplace over job-related issues (if the company has more than 200 workers-1982).

The value of these procedures should not be overestimated. There is no obligation to reach an agreement, and there are no established criteria for verifying that all parties have really tried to conclude one. These measures then serve only as a kind of stimulation by the authorities towards negotiations.[24]

---

23. This structure exists because, as we have seen, a union belonging to any of the five big confederations automatically has representative status in all bargaining. Each union, even if in the minority, therefore has the capacity to sign agreements applying to all workers covered by company negotiations. When the majority unions oppose a dispensatory agreement, it is considered never to have existed.

24. A study by the Work Inspection on the obligation to negotiate at the company level in 1989, showed the following results for a sample of 2100 companies: 65 % of the companies respected the requirement, in 7 out of 10 cases an agreement was reached, and in more than 9 out of 10 cases bargaining took place with no work stoppages.

(c) Extension and broadening of collective agreements by the labour ministry

These procedures do not apply to company agreements. They presuppose an agreement which has been signed by a group of employers. In the case of extension, this agreement becomes binding, within its geographical and industrial jurisdiction, for all companies, even if they do not belong to the employer organization which signed the agreement. Broadening, which is quite rare in practice, makes the agreement binding even outside of its original geographical or industrial jurisdiction.[25]

(d) The articulation of the law and interprofessional agreements

We have already discussed the important role played by national interprofessional agreements since the end of the 1960's. These agreements do not simply complement the existing legislation, but are intertwined with it in a complex relationship. For example, in the areas of unemployment insurance, ongoing vocational training or in some types of contracts (temporary or fixed term, for example), one sees a permanent give-and-take between negotiations, which are often stimulated or provoked by the State, and the law. The latter often takes part or all of the content of the agreements, generalizing them and giving them a binding legal basis.

(e) Implementing labour policy

With the intensification of industrial restructuring, ever since the 1960's, new types of labour policy implementation have made their appearance. Proceeding less and less through uniform, mandatory measures, new mechanisms have been set in motion which are based on a negotiated agreement between the State and a company or industry. This is the case, for example, for measures regarding early retirement seeking to reduce the number of lay-offs in the event of job cuts, or again, for the ongoing vocational training programs, or for ameliorating work conditions, etc.

The government grants funding if it approves the content of measures proposed by the company or industry. These agreements are first submitted to the works councils when they are made at the company level. When an agreement is reached at the industry level, it is submitted to the tripartite commissions of the Ministry of Labour.

---

25. The extension procedure is brought into play on the initiative either of one of the signing organizations, or of the Ministry of Labour ("Ministère du Travail"). The process of broadening is implemented by the Ministry of Labour in the event that there is no union organization in a trade branch or geographic area, or when no collective agreement has been signed for at least five years. In all cases, the final decision, which is made by the Ministry of Labour, is based in large part on the opinion of the national interprofessional commission on collective bargaining which unites both the unions and the employer organizations.

These different mechanisms breed hybrid results. For instance, a legal standard might have contractual origins, but later acquire a mandatory status for companies which were not part of the agreement (see points c and d above). A regulation originating from the State could be modified or have its implementation conditioned by an agreement (see a and e above).

The central problem today is not to trace a dividing line between public and private, but to analyze the process by which these two sources of legal precedent are becoming more and more closely intertwined.

C. Outcomes

As in other market economies, in the 1970's and 80's the functioning of the labour market in France was transformed by slower economic growth and by economic recessions linked to the two oil crises. But given the importance in France of the State's role in this area, the impact of the shifts in political majorities and leadership in 1981, '86 and '88 should also be mentioned. In this light, 1982 is a turning point for the regulations governing the labour market. In 1981, a left coalition came to power after twenty-five years of right wing governments. The new government put together a package of social legislation. At the same time, they launched a plan to boost the economy, which contrasted with the austerity plans being carried out in other countries. For this reason, 1982 reveals two kinds of partially contradictory transformations.

In the first place, a series of legislative measures favourable to the workers and the unions were passed, including increased power to the works councils, mandatory negotiations, a shortened work week (from 40 to 39 hours) and longer paid vacation (from 4 to 5 weeks), measures limiting temporary employment, etc.

In the second place, the failure of the plan for economic recovery forced the government to focus on fighting inflation and increasing competitiveness. In 1982, this can be seen by a halt in wage increases, and in the following years by a succession of measures increasing labour market flexibility.

The return of a right majority in parliament between 1986 and 1988 reinforced this tendency. It was then attenuated, yet maintained, after the left won the elections in 1988.

C.1 Working Hours

Since 1936, the duration of the workday, or week, was fairly closely regulated, with a uniform duration imposed by law, a maximum on overtime hours, fixed work hours, and with all exceptions submitted to the Ministry of Labour. The shortened work week was a union demand which sought to improve living and working conditions.

At the end of the 1970's, new defining elements and issues appeared.[26] Certain governments, mainly from 1981 to 1984, and some unions, wanted to use the reduction in hours worked as a means to create jobs (or at least to slow job cuts). Meanwhile, the employers, with more or less support from the government according to the period, used the adjustment in the work hours as a key point in the campaign for increased flexibility. Finally, the shortened work week was proposed as a compensation for the introduction of rotating shifts (important to employers as a way of maximizing the utilization of machines and facilities).

(a) Legal standards

These have undergone numerous modifications since 1981. Currently, the main texts are a 1987 law regarding the duration and scheduling of work, and a 1989 national "interprofessional" agreement (ratified on the union side by only the CFDT and the CFE-CGC). The choice to favour adjustment of working hours, together with the articulation between the law and negotiations, have made the system particularly complex. Some of the main characteristics are summarized below.

Legal working hours have been fixed, since 1982, at 39 hours per week with 5 weeks of annual paid vacation. Overtime is limited (but the maximum number of hours varies with the way that working hours are set) and is paid at an increased wage rate, in addition to compensatory time off. Overtime premium depends on the number of overtime hours and on their distribution over time. Generally it is between 25 % and 50 %. It is also possible to adjust the duration of work, even on an annual basis, by industrywide or company agreements. Possibilities for the use of part-time employees have also increased. With the passage from a mainly legislative regime to one largely based on contractual agreements, the evolution towards flexibility has been considerable.

---

26. For more on this question, see: Taddei, 1986; Boulin, Taddei, 1989; Afsa, Marchand, 1990; Bloch-London, Marchand, 1990; as well as the "Bilans annuels de la négotiation collective".

(b) Diversification of working hours

Most of the measures have been adopted too recently to be able to evaluate their effectiveness. However, some tentative conclusions can be attempted.

The length of the average work week diminished between 1982 and 1989, from 40.6 to 39.2 hours on the average (from 39.6 to 38.7 for blue collar workers). Table 6 shows the distribution for blue collar workers in 1989. Part time work has increased, from 12 % of the labour force in 1989 as compared to 7 % in 1980. This affects mainly women, for instance 21 % of female workers in private companies worked part time in 1989, as against 17 % in 1982.

Negotiations around changing working hours have been, up until now, more common at the company than the industry level. Whereas, it is precisely at the company level that the balance of power is least favourable to the workers, due to uneven union presence, the possibility of agreements ratified by minority unions (see B.2.a) and threats of lay-offs in the event of non-ratification.

Table 6. Length of Work Week (Blue-collar), January 1, 1989

Length	%
- less than 39 hours	25.3
- 39 hours	55.7
- more than 39 & less than 44 hours	17.2
- 44 or more hours	1.4

Source: ACEMO Study, Ministère du Travail
Sample: Fulltime employees in plants of 10 or more workers

The most significant negotiations are around maximizing the use of machines or facilities through various systems of rotating shifts. These sometimes, but not always, lead to a shortened work day or week and to new jobs.

C.2 Wages and Salaries

In principle, wages and salaries come under the individual work contract and collective bargaining. How it will be calculated is open: by piece or by the hour, with various bonuses and different ways of personalizing wages or linking them to company performance, etc.

Setting aside measures which do not call for comment, such as those against discrimination for equal work (notably on the basis of gender), mandatory scale for paid overtime, etc, the State only intervenes in three major areas. These are: wage indexing, minimum wage, and formulas for profit sharing. In these three areas of pay structuring, the State exercises significant influence by preventing wage indexing on price fluctuations, limiting wage disparities and developing new, flexible kinds of remuneration.

(a) Wage indexing

Between the first and second oil crises, the rigidity of the system for determining wage and salary rates came under fire as the reason for the recession's depth and duration. The negative consequences were said to be multiple, including the reduction of profits resulting in falling investments, job cuts set off by increased labour costs, and an acceleration of the inflationary cycle. Recent studies show that in the early 1980's wage indexing was interrupted.[27] From 1982 on, the government promulgated a wage policy which would tie increases to inflation estimates set in advance by the government, as opposed to increases tied to inflation rates in a prior period. Comparing the parameters of the evolution of respective actual wage levels over two periods, 1970-82 an 1983-88, gives clear results (Ralle, Toujas-Bernate, 1990).

Before 1982, the indexation of wages on prices was complete (that is to say, with a coefficient not significantly different from 1) and rapid (with an average delay in adjustment of one quarter). From 1983 on, indexation is limited (72 %) and the average delay in adjustment increases to two quarters. Thus, the annual rise in hourly wages fell from over 18 % in the beginning of 1982 to less than 4 % after 1986. Two other studies (Blanchard and Sevestre, 1989; Boyer, 1989) show similar results, with the break intervening in 1982 or 1983.

However, in spite of diminishing real labour costs and a rise in real interest rates, the tendency toward substitution of capital for labour was only slowed mildly. The analysis of the sensitivity of the productive forces to variation in the relative costs of labour and capital remains inconclusive (Henry, Leroux and Muet, 1988). Some studies show a weak or insignificant elasticity, while others feel that the delay in adjustment only allows this elasticity to be felt over the medium-term. The time series are too brief, since 1982, for this debate to be definitively resolved.

---

27. Automatic indexation clauses tying indexation to general economic indicators (such as overall price or wage increases, or the minimum wage level) have been forbidden since 1959. The only admissible clauses are those which are directly tied to the company or industrial branch. On the other hand, nothing prevents the parties from taking general indicators into consideration during salary negotiations.

(b) Challenging the reduction of wage disparities

Analyses over the long term have brought to light a tendency, since the end of the 1960's, toward reducing the individual wage differentials[28] (Concialdi and Madinier, 1990). This is globally true, but is also true for isolated criteria such as professional category, industrial sector or geographical locale. Interpreting this concomitant reduction is complicated. It may express an egalitarian tendency, engendered by government action or collective bargaining. In this case the wages reflect less and less the differences in productivity, thus losing their effectiveness in stimulating productivity. It could also be the result of greater worker mobility and a reduced diversity in the workforce.[29]

One finds an argument in favour of the egalitarian thesis just by looking at the role of the minimum wage ("SMIC").[30] The public authorities' policy toward low wages has led to a flattening of the wage scale for blue and white collar workers (See "Bilan annuel de la négotiation collective", 1989). An important debate has sprung up, criticizing the role of the minimum wage, both for the aforementioned reason, and because it shuts less productive workers out of the market, effectively stopping hiring or the creation of jobs. Naturally, the unions have vigorously defended the minimum wage as a guarantee to the worker of a minimum buying power. The government has refused to call the principle of the minimum wage into question, but has in two ways incorporated the criticisms. First, in the last few years it has limited increases to near the legal minimum, and second, the government has lowered the labour costs in other ways (mainly by exempting employers from social charges) for sectors of the workforce faced with unemployment.

---

28. Only wages and salaries are concerned here. Another debate exists over increased inequities in overall income and property ownership, for this period, across the entire population.

29. The Taylor-Ford model was based on polarized qualifications, separating on the one hand conceptual or managerial work, and on the other hand the work of executing tasks. New ways of organizing work, combined with longer schooling (the abundance of diplomas in the labour market), have reduced the gaps between trade and professional categories.

30. The minimum wage ("Salaire Minimum Interprofessionel de Croissance" - SMIC) has been set by the State, since 1950. No effective pay rate can be inferior to this figure. Until 1969, the minimum wage periodically underwent a revision, based only on an index of consumer price increases. Since that time, a second index has been added so that the most disadvantaged workers could benefit from overall economic development. The annual revision is therefore based on a government evaluation, and must increase buying power by a percentage equal to at least half of that of the average salary.

(c) The blossoming of flexible pay schemes

The decade of the '80's saw an intensification of employer discourse extolling a return to more flexible ways of setting wages and salaries. The translation of this discourse into effective wage policy is still limited, often marginal. One must distinguish two elements in this movement, one which bears on the individualization of wages, and another which would have them vary in function of company performance (Faugère, 1989).

In the former area, many companies have shown a strong infatuation with methods of individualized raises (as opposed to general raises uniformly applied over large categories of, or all, workers). A thorough survey done in 1985 (Grandjean, 1987) showed that two major factors had encouraged this practice, reduced inflation,[31] and the weakening of the unions. In any case, a certain disenchantment exists with respect to these schemes, which are faced with a dilemma. Either the hierarchical evaluations are discretionary and the overall climate in the company is in danger of being upset by a growing individual sense of injustice, or the process is formalized and becomes very costly. In the investigation just cited, two thirds of the companies did not use a written evaluation form.

Table 7. "Intéressement" and Profit Sharing

Year	Intéressement		Profit sharing	
	Number of agreements in force	Number of workers affected (millions)	Number of agreements in force	Number of workers affected (millions)
1977	344	0.1	9936	4.8
1983	918	0.3	10408	4.8
1988	4600	1.0	10111	4.5

Source: Ministère du Travail

While the movement toward salary individualization has come up against considerable resistance, certain formulas which vary remuneration in function of company performance seem to be blossoming (Avenal *et al.*, 1990; Girard, 1990). The tendency is clear for "intéressement",[32] where the number of workers covered by agree-

31. Lower inflation has reduced the percentage of overall wage increases which is absorbed by maintenance of the real wage value. Therefore companies have greater liberty to individualize raises.

32. "Intéressement" is frequently translated by "profit sharing", however, we have chosen to leave it untranslated in order to distinguish it from "participation" which is defined below. Instituted by law in 1959 and modified several times since, "intéressement" by workers in company perform-

ments has increased by nearly tenfold in one decade (see Table 7). In 62 % of the cases, in 1988, the "intéressement" was based on company financial results, and in 13 % of cases it was based on productivity (the balance are combinations or other systems). "Intéressement" represents 4.1 % of the total salary costs in the affected companies, and 68 % of the total amount of money involved is distributed by companies with over 500 workers. On the other hand, the number of workers affected by profit sharing[33] has stagnated. In 1986, the profit sharing reserve amounted to 3.4 % of total wages in the companies involved (see Table 7).

These are illustrations of the "share economy" as it is envisaged by Martin Weizman or James Meade. In total, they still represent only a minimal percentage of the total workforce. However, encouraged as they are both by certain employers and by the public authorities, they represent a potential factor for increased flexibility in labour costs.

C.3 Social Security and Fringe Benefits

The French system of social protection[34] is extremely complex since it is made up of the sum, over a historical period, of superimposed systems which lack an overarching rationale. In simplified terms, the system is composed of three levels.

First, are legal regimes covering three areas: old age, health (illness, disability and work-related accidents), and the family (maternity benefits and family allowances). To these should be added unemployment benefits paid by the State to workers who do not qualify for or who have exhausted their benefits under the "interprofessional" unemployment insurance system.[35]

---

ance is optional and presupposes a company agreement. It can be based on quite a diverse array of indicators (financial results, volume of sales, productivity, product quality, etc.).

33. Instituted by a 1967 law and modified in 1986, profit sharing ("participation") is mandatory for employees in companies of over 100 workers, and optional for others, and is based exclusively on the sharing of profits. The company agreement defines the method of calculation and conditions for investing funds which are only distributed to workers after a delay of three to five years. Thus, profit sharing is a kind of forced savings plan seeking to encourage financial investment, and, even beyond that, to modify worker behaviour by giving them an active financial stake in the company.

34. See Andreani *et al.*, 1983; Dupeyroux, 1988; and, Durin and Pollina, 1990.

35. Unemployment benefits are assured through two systems in France. First, a system created in 1958 by a national "interprofessional" agreement and operated jointly by the employers' organizations and the union confederations. It pays an indemnity whose duration varies from 8 to 60 months, depending on the length of time a worker has contributed and their age. This benefit is initially based on the worker's previous salary level, and then becomes a fixed amount. Second, a system created by the State which pays a fixed amount, under certain conditions, to unemployed

Secondly, the union and employer organizations, through national "interprofessional" agreements, have created social protection systems. These mainly cover complementary retirement plans and unemployment insurance.

Finally, the social protection mechanisms having a limited field of application constitute a third level. The origins of these systems are varied and include: worker initiatives creating worker-managed health insurance plans with voluntary membership, company financed initiatives creating specific benefits for the workers which are underwritten by the company, and collective agreements, company or industrywide, creating benefits for covered workers.

The breadth of the mandatory social protection systems explains the low percentage represented by optional fringe benefits (averaging less than 10 % of wages). The relative importance of the latter is linked to two main factors.[36] One the one hand, they form part of company strategies (such as "perks") aimed at increasing employee loyalty and retention (for certain categories of workers), and, for this reason, are correlated to the capital intensity of the mode of production as a kind of "human capital". On the other hand, they fall within the domain of collective bargaining at the company level and are therefore linked to the degree of union organization among the workers, and so to company size. For these two reasons, fringe benefits tend to widen the gap between the base wages across different sectors, according to company size and professional category.

C.4 Terminating Employment Contracts

During the 1970's and '80's, the guarantees with regard to the stability of the labour contract were the subject of permanent confrontation between the employers and the unions. Conflicts and negotiations multiplied, and frequent modifications were made in the regulations. At issue were the relaxation of regulations for lay-off and dismissal under indefinite term contracts, and the increase in types of temporary employment.[37] From these stemmed changes in the number of and forms of mobility of the workers.

---

workers who have not contributed long enough to benefit from the first system or who have exhausted their other benefits.

36. See: Coutrot and Madinier, 1986; Madinier, 1990; and, Abecassis *et al.*, 1990.

37. See: Thelot, 1986; Belloc and Lacroix, 1989; Marchand, 1989; and, Lacroix, 1989.

(a) The contract of indefinite term

Unless specifically specified to the contrary, the employment contract is of indefinite term. In 1989, 91 % of all employment contracts were of this type (see Table 1). The worker may terminate the contract by resigning, provided s/he respects the time period for giving notice. The employer may terminate it by discharge only for a "real and serious motive" and according to two distinct modes.

The discharge for "personal reasons", or dismissal (for instance, for inaptitude or for "professional misconduct"), is subject both to specific procedures (prior interview or notification of the reason), and to supervision by the courts.[38]

The discharge for "economic reasons", or lay-off, is the result of job cuts. It is here that the transformations have been the most profound and controversial. Since World War II, mass lay-offs were subject to authorization by the Ministry of Labour. The work inspector checked the validity of the economic reason given and the quality of the measures adopted by the employer to encourage the reclassification of laid-off workers. This regulation came under increasing criticism from the employers, who saw it as both a factor of rigidity in personnel management and as discouraging the creation of jobs in contexts of economic uncertainty. The law was abolished in 1986.

Since that time, the Work Inspection has only checked the regularity of the lay-off procedures. If it is a mass lay-off, the employer must respect the notice period and the procedures for informing and consulting the employee representatives (this varies with the number of jobs involved). The employer must also present a social plan,[39] spelling out specific measures taken to limit the number of lay-offs (for instance, internal reclassification, shortening the work day or week) or to encourage worker reclassification (for instance, job training, aid toward external employment). Finally, the employer must offer each laid-off worker a conversion agreement allowing him/her access to various benefits (professional evaluation, career orientation, training) available through the public employment service. Thus, the lay-off system has come back under the aegis of private law, under the condition of respecting the legally mandated procedures.

(b) Types of temporary employment

The desire for increased flexibility in personnel management has given the employers greater recourse, over the last decade, to legal procedures allowing the

38. The courts verify that the reason given by the employer is a real one, and that the gravity of the sanction is justified by the motive.

39. Except for lay-offs of less than 10 workers in companies with fewer than 50 workers.

termination of a contract without firings or lay-offs. Two basic types are used: the temporary employment contract whose term is fixed at the point of signature, yet with possibilities for renewal; and the use of "temp help" or interim workers employed by temporary employment agencies, to accomplish specific, limited tasks (see Table 8).

From 1982 until today, a succession of regulations and collective agreements have modified, over and over, the legal status of these types of temporary employment. The unions have tried hard, at one and the same time, to reduce the use of these contracts and to achieve better protection for temporary workers. From their side, the employers demand free recourse to them and conditions ensuring their low cost.

Parallel to this are systems of on-the-job training and vocational training courses developed by the State as part of its employment plan to encourage hiring of youth and the rehiring (in a new sector) of unemployed workers. In the case of training courses, the participants remain classified as inactive, whereas when the training consists mainly or entirely of a work activity, the participants are classified as employed even though there is no employment contract (see Table 8). Some industrial sectors make wide use of these quasi-free, temporary workers. They constitute a new tool for flexibility for management in controlling the number of employees.

Table 8. Types of Temporary Employment
(by thousands)

	1982	1989
Fixed term contracts	306	611
Interim workers	128	234
Trainees *	74	330

* Some trainees are paid by the State or Municipalities. These figure under "others" in Table 1

Source: INSEE, Employment Study

In France, therefore, the last decade has been marked by major structural transformations in the functioning of the labour market. These have resulted from the wider margins of flexibility in personnel management gained by the employers.

D. Conclusion: Evaluation

Without going into the full theoretical debate on the concept of economic efficiency, it should be recalled that once one has set aside the Pareto abstractions on the optimum, one no longer has one single definition of efficiency. When applied to market functioning, this concept of efficiency refers to at least three approaches.

The efficiency of a market could be defined by its functioning, measured by its capacity to absorb any tensions and imbalances, within the shortest time span and at the lowest cost. The indexes gathered measure its flexibility. From this point of view, over the 1980's France has seen a major evolution toward flexibility: abolition of Ministry of Labour authorization for lay-offs and diversification of "special forms" of employment, a work week of varying length, the removal of indexed pay increases and the development of types of remuneration linked to job or company performance. The margins of freedom that a company has to manage their labour force have, therefore, noticeably increased. Whether one can conclude from this that the use of productive resources is more efficient is a question which remains to be answered.

A second conception of economic efficiency rests on criteria of performance. It is measured by productivity indexes. Like other OECD countries, since 1973 France has experienced a slowdown in work productivity, but has recently maintained a growth rate slightly above the OECD average. At the same time, there has been almost no growth in employment. Companies have put the priority on productive investments and have taken advantage of increased job destabilization to eliminate "redundancies". Thus they have eliminated workers judged to be insufficiently productive, moving them to the ranks of the unemployed, where their productivity is non-existent but the costs are transferred onto the community. In this instance, microeconomic efficiency and macroeconomic efficiency do not coincide.

Finally, the market could be considered efficient if it operates systems allowing it to render the behaviour of the opposed players compatible or convergent. Within systems where the fundamental mechanism of social integration is through paid employment, the conditions for social equilibrium, always imperfect and unstable, are determined in the labour market. The market therefore represents one of the determining arenas for social regulation. Two tendencies are at work right now in France. On the one hand, regulation from the public sector is retreating, leaving the field open to regulations originating in contractual agreements, and on the other hand, centralized contractual regulations (interprofessional or industrywide) are regressing, while decentralized regulations (company or plant level) advance. The precise nature of decentralized contractual regulation must be examined. The change in the balance of power has unbalanced negotiations. Taking opportunistic advantage of the weakened and divided unions, the employers are attempting to legitimize their personnel policies through collective agreements. In other cases, they apply them unilaterally.

In conclusion, any evaluation of labour market efficiency must take into account contradictory elements. Over the 1980's one can observe an intensification of the mechanisms of the competitive market: an increase in flexibility in employment and salaries, the decentralization of negotiations and greater liberty in company management. This movement is coupled with a reduction in the number and scope of social conflicts. At the same time, performance indicators dropped. There has been an increase in unemployment and in "mismatches" in the labour market and the growth rate for labour productivity has dropped. Thus it is clear that labour market efficiency depends not only on the contracts and institutions which form its structure, but also in large part on macro-economic contexts and on overall economic priorities and policies.

REFERENCES

Abecassis, Denis, apRoberts, Lucy, and Kartchevsky, Andrée (1990), *La protection sociale complémentaire dans l'entreprise: une étude comparative de secteurs*, Ed. Européennes Erasme, Paris, 198 p.

Afsa, Cédric and Marchand, Olivier (1990), Temps de travail: uniformisation ou éclatement?, *Economie et Statistique*, April, pp. 7-18.

Agnes, Martine and Georges-Picot, Martine (1982, 1983), *Organisations patronales*, Liaisons sociales, n° 8883, Nov. 1982, 41 p. et n° 8938, Feb. 1983, 42 p.

Amadieu, Jean-François (1989), Une interprétation de la crise du syndicalisme. Les enseignements de la comparaison internationale, *Travail et Emploi*, n° 42, April, pp. 46-59.

Andreani, Edgar *et al.* (1983), *La protection sociale*, IRES, Paris, 220 p.

Avenel, Irène, Kairier, Jocelyne, Madelin, Béatrice, Martin, Huber and Beranger, Daniel (1990), Participation, *Dossiers Statistiques du Travail et de l'Emploi*, n° 54, January, 71 p.

Blanchard, Pierre and Sevestre, Patrick (1989), L'indexation des salaires: quelle rupture en 1982?, *Economie et Prévision*, 1989-1, pp. 67-74.

Bloch-London, Catherine and Marchand, Olivier (1990), Les enjeux de la durée du travail, *Economie et Statistique*, April, pp. 19-32.

Boulin, Jean-Yves and Taddei, Dominique (1989), Les accords de réduction et de réorganisation du temps de travail: négociations et conséquences économiques, *Travail et Emploi*, n° 40, pp. 33-50.

Boyer, Robert (under the direction of) (1986), *La flexibilité du travail en Europe*, Ed. La Découverte, Paris, 331 p.

Boyer, Robert (1989), The Transformations of the Capital-Labor Relation and Wage Formation in Eight OECD Countries during the Eighties, Paper prepared to the International Symposium on "Making Economics more Efficient and Equitable-Factors Determining Income Distribution", Tokyo, Nov., mimeo, 59 p.

Brunhes, Bernard (1989), La flexibilité de la main-d'oeuvre dans les entreprises: étude comparée de quatre pays européens, in: OCDE, *La flexibilité du marché du travail: tendances dans l'entreprise*, pp. 11-38.

Bunel, Jean and Saglio, Jean (1980), La redéfinition de la politique sociale du patronat français, *Droit Social*, December, pp. 489-498.

Canut, François and Lanselle, Suzanne (1989), *Le statut juridique des syndicats. Le syndicat dans l'entreprise*, Liaisons Sociales, n° 10393, Paris, 146 p.

Chaigneau, Yves, Ferec, Germain and Loos, Jocelyne (1988), *Négociation collective: quels enjeux?*, La Documentation Française, Paris, 347 p.

Chauchard, Jean-Pierre (1988), Conventions et accords collectifs de travail, *Répertoire DALLOZ de Droit du Travail*, Janvier 1988, 21 p. et Aug. 1988, 27 p.

Concialdi, Pierre and Madinier, Philippe (1990), Formation, mobilité et disparités de salaires depuis quarante ans, *CERC - Notes et Graphiques*, n° 10, January, reprod. in: *Problèmes Economiques*, n° 2174, May 10 1990, pp. 3-7.

Cotis, Jean-Philippe and Loufir, Abderrahim (1990), Formation des salaires, chômage d'équilibre et incidence des cotisations sur le coût du travail, *Economie et Prévision*, n° 92-93, pp. 97-110.

Coutrot, Thomas and Madinier, Philippe (1986), *Les compléments du salaire*, Documents du CERC, n° 83, 120 p.

Dupeyroux, Jean-Jacques (1988), *Droit de la sécurité sociale*, Ed. Dalloz, 11° édition, Paris, 1087 p.

Durin, François, Pollina, Lucien and Seys, Baudouin (1990), Le système de protection sociale, in: INSEE, *Données Sociales*, pp. 412-418.

Faugere, Jean-Pierre (1988), *Les politiques salariales en France*, Notes et Etudes Documentaires, n° 4859, Paris, 144 p.

Fleurbaey, Marc (1989). La productivité en France de 1970 à 1987, *INSEE Première*, n° 8, février, 4 p.
George-Picot, Martine and Agnes, Martine (1987), *Les organisations syndicales*, Liaison Sociales, n° 10071, 215 p.
Girard, Philippe (1990), La participation des salaires aux résultats de l'entreprise. Une étude fondée sur la centrale de bilans (1982-1987), *Economie et Prévision*, n° 92-93, pp. 171-176.
Gonguet, Jean-Pierre and Perez, Sylvie (1986, 1990), 1981-1989: 50 % de syndiqués en moins, *Espace Social Européen*, February 16, 1986, and February 23, 1990, pp. 10-16.
Grandjean, Caroline (1987), L'individualisation des salaires. La stratégie des entreprises, *Travail et Emploi*, June, pp. 17-30.
Grandjean, Caroline (1989), Modalités nouvelles de la rémunération à l'ancienneté, *Travail et Emploi*, n° 41, pp. 7-18.
Haeusler, Laurence (1988), Evolution du monde associatif de 1978 à 1986, *Consommation et modes de vie*, n° 34, December.
Henry, Jérôme, Leroux, Véronique and Muet, Pierre-Alain (1988), Coût relatif capital-travail et substitution: existe-t-il encore un lien?, *Observations et Diagnostics Economiques*, July, pp. 163-182.
Heran, François (1988), Un monde sélectif: les associations, *Economie et Statistique*, n° 208, March, pp. 17-32.
Lacroix, Thierry (1990), Le marché du travail dans les années 1980, in: INSEE, *Données Sociales*, pp. 36-49.
Lozier, Françoise (1990), Une approche sectorielle des accords d'entreprise (1950-1980), *Sociologie du Travail*, n° 1, pp. 1-22.
Madinier, François (1990), Les compléments du salaire, in: INSEE, *Données Sociales*, pp. 126-128.
Marchand, Olivier (1989), L'ajustement douloureux de l'emploi, in: INSEE, *Les entreprises à l'épreuve des années 1980*, pp. 105-119.
Ministère du Travail (1990), Les élections aux comités d'entreprise en 1988, *Dossiers Statistiques du Travail et de l'Emploi*, n° 55, February, 107 p.
Ministère du Travail (1991), Elections aux Comités d'Entreprise en 1989. Délégués Syndicaux en 1989, *Dossiers Statistiques du Travail et de l'Emploi*, n° 68, April, 88 p.
Ministère du Travail, *Bilan de la négociation collective*, publication annuelle, La Documentation Française.
Muet, Piere-Alain (1981), Croissance, emploi et chômage dans les années quatre-vingt, *Observations et Diagnostics Economiques*, n° 35, January, pp. 21-56.
Ralle, Pierre and Toujas-Bernate, Joël (1990), Indexation des salaires: la rupture de 1983, *Economie et Prévision*, n° 92-93, pp. 187-194.
Reynaud, Bénédict (1990), Les modes de rémunération et le rapport salarial, Dynamiques sectorielles et modes de rémunération ouvriers dans la crise: le cas français, *Economie et Prévision*, n° 92-93, pp. 1-14, and 177-186.
Sellier, François (1984), *La confrontation sociale en France*, PUF, Paris, 240 p.
Supiot, Alain (1989), Déréglementation de relations de travail et autoréglementation de l'entreprise, *Droit Social*, March, pp. 195-205.
Taddei, Dominique (1986), *Des machines et des hommes. Pour l'emploi, par une meilleure utilisation des équipements*, La Documentation Française, 358 p.
Thelot, Claude (under the direction of) (1986), Emploi et chômage: l'éclatement, *Economie et Statistique*, Nov.-Dec., pp. 1-134.
Vernaz, Cendra and Moran, Marie-Françoise (1988). *Le Salaire*, Liaisons Sociales, n° 10254, 122 p.
Visser, Jelle (1989), *European Trade Unions in Figures*, Deventer, Kluwer Law and Taxations Publishers, 254 p.
Weber, Henri (1986), *Le parti des patrons. Le CNPF (1946-1986)*, Ed. du Seuil, Paris, 443 p.

Labour Market Contracts and Institutions
J. Hartog and J. Theeuwes (Editors)

CHAPTER 10

SPANISH LABOUR MARKETS:
Institutions and Outcomes*

Juan F. Jimeno** and Luis Toharia***

A. Introduction

During the last twenty years, the legal environment of the labour market and the industrial relations structure in Spain has changed from an authoritarian system with strong government intervention and no recognition of basic workers rights to a democratic system with extensive public provisions and a relatively well-developed collective bargaining system which determines employment conditions.

Simultaneously, in these twenty years, employment has experienced quite dramatic shifts. After the moderate yet continuous increase in the 1960-75 period, in the next ten years the Spanish economy suffered an employment crisis unknown in other Western European countries.[1] In the last five years, this trend has reversed itself, leading to an unprecedented employment growth, which has proceeded at the astonishing annual rate of nearly 3 %. The changes in the legal regulation of Spanish labour markets have decisively modified their operating framework and have very likely affected the evolution of employment.

In this paper, we describe the legal and institutional environment of Spanish labour markets and pose some questions on its economic rationale. The main characteristics of this system turn out to be the predominance of public provisions over collective bargaining provisions, mainly because of the moderate scope and depth of the latter. We emphasize the degree of flexibility and centralization of collective bargaining

* We wish to thank the participants at the Workshop and the editors for helpful comments. This paper was partly written while Professor Toharia was visiting The Institute for Employment Research (University of Warwick) under the support of a grant from the Spanish Ministry of Education (grant number BE90-287).

** London School of Economics.

*** Universidad de Alcalá de Henares.

1. The annual rate of change of employment in the 1975-85 period was -1.7 %. This experience is in sharp contrast to what happened elsewhere in Europe where unemployment soared because employment remained stagnant, or decreased slightly, in the face of a continuously rising labour force.

and the move towards "flexibilization" taken by the Spanish government in 1984 as the key issues in the recent evolution of the labour markets.

The structure of the paper is as follows. We complete this introduction with a brief review of the structure of the Spanish labour market, the historical background of the current system of labour relations, and the Social Security system. In section B, we analyze the legal and institutional environment and, in section C, we present the outcomes of this system in terms of some labour market variables and employment arrangements. Finally, section D contains comments on its efficiency.

A.1 The Structure of the Spanish Labour Market

At present (1991, fourth quarter), total employment in Spain amounts to 12.5 million people. Wage and salary earners account for almost 75 percent of this figure (9.4 million), a proportion which tended to stabilize during the recession period of 1975-85 but which has recovered its past upward trend since the latter date. The still important weight of agriculture in employment (11 per cent) is partly the reason explaining the high proportion of self-employed workers.[2] On the other hand, public sector employees account for 22.6 percent of total employees (or, equivalently, 16.8 percent of total employment). Finally, in terms of the industrial breakdown of employment, the service sector provides the majority of jobs in Spain: 55 percent, followed by manufacturing, (24 percent), agriculture (12 percent) and construction (9 percent).[3] During the recent recovery, construction has been the most dynamic sector, with an overall increase in the 1985-90 period of 35 percent, followed by the service sector, whose employment has also increased at a very rapid pace; manufacturing employment has recovered mildly while agriculture has followed its long-term decline (which even took place during the 1975-85 crisis).

A.2 Historical Background

The Spanish union movement was born at the end of the nineteenth century. This movement reached its peak in the 1930s, when the two largest confederations, the Unión General de Trabajadores (UGT, socialist) and the Confederación Nacional del Trabajo (C.N.T., anarcho-syndicalist) reached very radical standpoints, to the extent that during the Spanish Civil War (1936-39) the latter played an important role in setting up a system of workers' collective firms in important parts of Spain. Nevertheless, the Franco dictatorship that emerged from the war outlawed unions and wiped out most of their achievements. The legal environment of the labour market

2. Agricultural employment represents only 5 percent in the case of employees.

3. The figures corresponding to employees are 57, 28, 5, and 10 percent, respectively.

that the new regime implemented was characterized by a paternalistic legislation, a very high degree of government intervention, and the lack of any structured system of labour relations, in the modern meaning of that concept. Employers and workers were integrated in the same organization (a "vertical union"). Affiliation was compulsory and the degree of representation almost nil. Although collective bargaining was formally established in 1958, the lack of truly representative unions – and employers organizations simply non-existent – and the continuous government intervention in all the stages of the process made this system very different to that prevalent at that time in other Western European countries. Wages were unilaterally determined by employers or by government regulations. It is argued that the counterpart for the workers was the existence of a highly restrictive legal regulation of firings and workers' dismissal. These characteristics have led some authors to label the system as "highly wage-flexible but excessively employment-rigid" (Bentolila and Blanchard, 1990). In fact, firings were possible (mostly for political and repressive reasons) and there were no significant economic recessions to test how the system would have reacted to the necessity of significantly reducing employment.

Despite the repressive nature of the system, the illegal trade unions made a headway in the official organization and started to push for substantial wage increases. The whole system began to crumble in the early 1970s, when the government was forced to impose controls on wage inflation set in terms of past inflation plus a certain number of percentage points, controls which were the target of illegal unions actions. The death of Franco in 1975 paved the way for even more radical demands in 1975-77, when the political reform was being undertaken. The combination of international economic crisis and of political reform constituted the environment in which the "Moncloa Pacts" between the government and all parliamentary political parties were signed, with the support of the trade unions (legalized in April 1977). These Pacts were followed by the approval of the main piece of legislation regarding the labour market, namely, the Workers' Charter (Ley del Estatuto de los Trabajadores, hereafter quoted as LET) approved in 1980.

This law was the object of an important reform in 1984, when the use of fixed-term contracts was permitted under quite general circumstances and without the constraints existing theretofore. These reforms effectively implied the constitution of a "two-tier" employment relationship system, in which permanent workers are entitled to receive a severance payment in the case of firing, whereas temporary workers receive lower severance payments or none at all (see section C.3.). Before 1984, the latter type of contracts was subject to more limitations, although they had always been permitted (even under Franco) when the characteristics of the economic activity of the firm justified them (for instance, the realization of temporary jobs and seasonal tasks). After these reforms, any firm may use temporary labour contracts to hire workers with only minor restrictions. As a result, temporary employment has increased from about 10 % of total employment in 1984 up to over 31 % in early 1991.

A.3 The Social Security System

The current system of Social Security is a reformed version of the Francoist system, finally designed in 1974.[4] This system institutes (transitory and permanent) sickness and unemployment benefits, pensions and family protection measures. Affiliation is compulsory. Some of the reforms of the Social Security system arose from negotiations between employer associations, unions and the government within the national agreements that we describe in section B. Besides this system, some collective bargaining agreements include provisions in the case of sickness and death but, rarely, in the case of unemployment.[5]

The Spanish Social Security system is a "pay-as-you-go" system. The government fixes minimum and maximum effective wage bases and the rate at which employers and workers contribute. The bounds for the wage bases are revised annually. These bases are used to determine the amount of the pension which the worker gets upon retirement. More specifically, the pension is established as a percentage of the "pension base"[6], which may go up to 100 percent when the number of years contributed reaches 35. At any rate, the effective amount of the pensions paid is rather low: in 1990, the average pension awarded to retiring workers was 65.300 pts., equivalent to roughly 40 percent of the average wage and only 20 percent above the minimum wage. The contribution rate is 28.8 percent of the wage base (24 percent paid nominally by the employer and 4.8 percent by the worker). The social security contributions cover health and sickness protection, as well as unemployment benefits.

B. The Institutional and Legal Environment

In this section we discuss the main institutions involved in employment arrangements. The legal environment of Spanish labour markets (as implied by the LET) is characterized by full recognition of workers' rights and collective bargaining as the main process of determination of employment conditions. There are two different

---

4. The General Social Security Act was passed by the Francoist regime in 1974. This law has been maintained as the central piece of the system, but several aspects of it have been modified.

5. This assertion is based on casual observation by the authors, as no statistics exist on this issue.

6. The formula to calculate this "pension base" is as follows: divide by 112 the sum of the wage base used to contribute during the 96 months before retirement; the bases corresponding to the last 24 months are taken at nominal value while earlier ones are upgraded by the consumer price index.

legal frameworks affecting private economy workers, on the one hand, and Public Administration workers, on the other, the latter representing some 12 percent of all employees (workers in public enterprises are regulated by the same rules as private-sector workers). We will focus on the legal environment and industrial relations system regarding private economy workers. Unfortunately, the lack of statistics on the characteristics of the industrial relations structure will not allow a very precise analysis.

B.1 The Legal Framework of Collective Agreements

Collective bargaining is a legally-established (in the LET) right of all dependent workers and is widely accepted by employers as the method of determining employment conditions. The basic rules for collective bargaining in Spain are the following:

i) Bargaining takes place between worker representatives elected by direct vote and the employer or the "most representative" employer association(s). The initiative for the collective bargaining process may be taken by any of the parties.

ii) The bargaining unit can be the establishment, the firm or an economic sector. In addition, the LET considers the possibility of wider, so-called "inter-pr-fessional", agreements which can establish the structure of collective bargaining, the rules to solve conflicts between different collective agreements and the principles of complementarity between various bargaining units. There has been an effort to centralize establishment-level agreements into firm level agreements, but the former are still possible although unusual.

iii) The bargaining parties can freely determine the contents of the agreements, the only restrictions being the minimum standards imposed by the law and, when applicable, by wider (sectoral or nationwide) agreements.

iv) Collective bargaining agreements have to be registered with the Ministry of Labour (or the equivalent regional authority), whose only role is to see that they are legal and to publish them, after which they are legally enforceable and apply to all workers within their scope, the industry to which they apply or, alternatively, the signing firm, independently of the personal characteristics of the workers and their employment relationship with the firm.

v) Worker representatives elections take place every four years. The numbers to be elected depend on the size of the firm. Within a given period set out by the government (usually three months), elections can take place in any firm. The unions themselves are responsible for the electoral process. The electoral documents are sent to a public notary and to the Ministry of Labour, which is responsible for the final publication of the results. Workers vote to the different lists (usually one per union, but occasionally "independent" lists also turn up) which have to contain as many persons as delegates to be elected, in a process similar to political elections whereby people vote to parties rather than individuals. The finally elected delegates are then picked from the different lists in a more or less proportionate way . This means that winning the election in one firm – or industry – does not mean becoming the representing union in that firm – or industry – but rather obtaining the largest number of delegates; this implies, in turn, that no single union has a monopoly right of representation. Elected union representatives have the right not to work (and still get paid by their employer) for a certain number of hours, this number increasing with the size of the firm and reaching 40 per month in the case of firms with more than 750 employees. This whole electoral system has created substantial frictions between the two largest union confederations, especially in small firms, where monitoring the fairness of the process is very difficult. Another source of problems has been – and still is – the lack of an adequate and updated census of firms.

In the case of firms with 50 employees or more, the workers representatives constitute a "works council" (*comité de empresa*) which is then the bargaining agent in that firm, should a bargaining process be initiated in it. In the case of sectoral agreements, the bargaining table is composed of the "most representative" unions and employers. While there are ways of determining on objective grounds who they are in the case of unions (on the basis of the union elections, hence the importance of their global results and, in particular, of the way the process is carried out in small firms), things are much less clear in the case of employers.

vi) Under certain conditions, the government can extend by decree the application field of collective bargaining agreements. When a firm has no collective bargaining agreement in effect and there is also a lack of agreements of higher level which may affect it, the collective agreement of a firm under similar economic circumstances might be extended to apply to it. This extension procedure must be initiated by the employer or the worker representatives affected.

vii) Binding arbitration by the state existed prior to 1981 and played a substantial role in the last few years of the Franco dictatorship. At that time, it was declared unconstitutional. There has been a traditional lack of means to handle conflicts through collective bargaining. Although the establishment of such means has been sometimes attempted, especially during the negotiations of economy-wide agreements, they have not led to an operational system of conflict handling. By law, the parties can appoint a mediator during contract negotiations, but they do not have to commit themselves to his/her proposals.

viii) Most conflicts, as a result, are handled by the judiciary system. There are two types of labour courts, conciliatory courts and judiciary courts. In most types of conflicts, a conciliatory trial is compulsory. In case of disagreement, the conflict is solved by a judge. Conflicts arising during collective bargaining periods usually result in strikes.

ix) Strikes and lock-outs are still regulated by a decree passed in 1977 (i.e. before the approval of the LET, which validated its content relating to these issues). From time to time there have been discussions as to whether a strike law is necessary, and it appears that such a law will be passed in 1992. An advance notice of 5 days is required, except in the case of public services, in which the delay is 10 days. In addition, in the case of services deemed essential to the community, government can establish "minimum services" to be provided in any case by striking workers. These minimum services have been often the subject of disputes between government and the unions (who tend to think that they are excessive). On the other hand, in the case of strikes thought to be particularly damaging to the national economy, government may appoint an impartial arbitrator whose settlement is compulsory for the parties.

B.2 The Industrial Relations Structure

(a) Unions

As already mentioned, trade unions were legalized in 1977, when they were fully restored to the industrial relations structure. At that moment, not only unions were allowed to organize the labour force, they also started to gain institutional recognition and even financial help from the state. The two main trade union confederations are Unión General de Trabajadores (UGT) (socialist)- and Comisiones Obreras (CC.OO.) (communist). Together they hold some 70 percent of union delegates elected, the differences in share of the vote between them being relatively minor. There are also several nationalistic trade unions which are important in some regions (such as Galicia and the Basque Country) and other, smaller, sometimes professionally-based or firm-based unions whose importance lies in their relatively high strength in specific parts of the economy (e.g. the bus drivers in Madrid or nurses in hospitals).

Union density is low. There are no good statistics available on this issue. Some estimations suggest that it is around 10-15 percent of wage-earners. However, the labour relations system in Spain is not a "closed shop" system. As already mentioned, all workers have the right to elect representatives and these may belong to different unions (or to none). In fact, however, the majority of worker representatives belong to well-established union confederations. Table 1 shows the union status of worker representatives at collective bargaining. The socialist and communist unions (UGT and CC.OO.) participate in about 90 % of all collective agreements signed and about 70 % of all workers representatives are trade unionists affiliated with them. Only about 15 % of worker representatives are non-union members. The figures in Table 1 also indicate that the presence of trade unions is more important in sectoral agreements than in firm-level agreements (the proportion of non-union representatives reaches 20 percent in this latter case) and that their influence seems to be more important in larger firms: whereas the average number of workers affected by firm-level agreements was 346 in 1990, it rose to 570 in the case of agreements where CC.OO. representatives were present, 529 in the case of UGT, and to 836 in the case of other unions, as opposed to 176 only in the case of agreements where non-union delegates were present. Thus, although the actual union membership is low, it can be argued that the "effective unionization rate" (i.e. the proportion of workers whose collective bargaining rights are defended by trade unions) is high.

Table 1. Worker Representatives at Bargaining Tables, 1990

	Union status of representatives				
	CC.OO.	UGT	Other unions	Non-union	Total
Number of agreements in which union representatives participated					
- Firm-level	1,568	1,706	786	1,227	3,137
- Other levels	1,008	1,086	388	62	1,297
- Total	2,576	2,792	1,174	1,289	4,434
Workers affected (000s) by these agreements					
- Firm-level	894	903	657	216	1,034
- Other levels	5,546	5,675	1,680	195	5,968
- Total	6,440	6,578	2,337	411	7,051
Number of Representatives					
- Firm-level	5,798	5,760	2,815	3,514	17,887
- Other levels	3,293	3,644	1,228	251	8,416
- Total	9,091	9,404	4,043	3,765	26,303

Notes: CC.OO.: Comisiones Obreras; UGT: Unión General de Trabajadores.
"Other levels" refer mostly to industry-level provincial agreements.
In the case of the number of agreements and the number of workers affected the different union statuses sum up to more than the total because several unions can be present at the same bargaining table.
The agreements covered in this table refer to those registered up to May, 1991. There may thus be some differences between the numbers in this table and others appearing in later tables and whose coverage might be more updated. At any rate, these differences are likely to be inconsequential.

Source: Ministerio de Trabajo y Seguridad Social, *Estadística de convenios colectivos, 1989-1990 Avance*, Madrid, 1991.

Generally, unions have a federal structure by industrial sectors and geographical regions. Coordination within unions is high but coordination among unions is problematic, precisely because they compete for worker representation every four years. In the years prior to 1986, both UGT and CC.OO. followed different strategies, as UGT was more willing to cooperate with the Socialist government elected in 1982. The 1986 union elections marked a turning point, as UGT lost ground particularly in large firms (those "freeing" more human resources paid by employers for union activities, as already discussed). Over the following 3 or 4 years, there has been some convergence between these two unions, mostly opposing what they saw as a "too liberal" economic policy being adopted by government. The most visible sign of this was the common organization of a general strike on the 14th of December of 1988 and the subsequent elaboration of a common platform of demands. This convergence was seriously damaged by the union elections of late 1990.

Even though their membership rates are quite low, Spanish unions enjoy high political influence. Most regulations on the labour market are consulted with unions before the government implements them. Only in two instances, however, does the law establish formally such consultations: the determination of minimum wages and the regulation of the maximum workweek.

The strength of unions at the shop level is, however, questionable, especially in small firms. As we will see in the next section, neither the scope nor the depth of collective bargaining is particularly impressive. The economic crisis of the 1975-85 period and the high unemployment rate might constitute an explanation for the lack of bargaining power which they show at the firm level.

(b) Employer organizations

There are two major employer organizations, Confederación Española de Organizaciones Empresariales (CEOE) – Spanish Confederation of Employers – and the Confederación Española de Pequeñas y Medianas Empresas (CEPYME) – Spanish Confederation of Small and Medium-Sized Firms. They have a federal structure and affiliation is voluntary. There are no precise statistics available on the number of employers who belong to these organizations but the overall impression is that their coverage is high. As in the case of unions, they enjoy political influence (they have to be consulted in the same instances as unions) and there is some divergence between this political status and their influence in employers bargaining at industry and firm levels.

B.3 The Scope and Depth of Collective Bargaining

As a general comment, it could be said that neither the scope nor the depth of collective bargaining in Spain is particularly high and that there is excessive fragmentation in the collective bargaining structure (in the sense that there are too many bargaining units). We turn to justify these two assertions in the following two subsections.

(a) The scope of collective bargaining

Table 2 presents data on the scope of collective bargaining in the last decade. These statistics should be taken with caution since the number of workers affected by collective bargaining agreements is overestimated because of the following reasons. First, there is double-counting between collective bargaining agreements at the industrial and at the firm levels. Additionally, the number of workers affected by industrial collective bargaining agreements is also excessive since it reflects the estimations of the bargaining table, which may be far from accurate and usually are too high. On the other hand, there is an opposite bias since the workers affected by the extension of collective agreements through the process explained above, and some collective agreements are not included in the statistics (those collective agreements in which no wage increase is included and those in effect from the preceding year which do not suffer any alterations are not included). Taking into account these remarks, a more realistic estimation is that about 75 percent of eligible workers are covered by collective bargaining (see Spanish Ministry of Labour, 1988). Thus, roughly one of every four Spanish private sector wage-earner workers is not covered by collective bargaining. This means that the contents of their employment contracts are only restricted by the minimum standards established by law. The sectors were the coverage of collective bargaining agreements appears to be lower are Agriculture and Fishing, Food Industry, Transportation, Personal Services, and Hotels and Restaurants.

(b) Bargaining structure

As already mentioned, the bargaining structure is not constrained by legal regulations and is determined by agreement between the social partners at the relevant levels. In practice, bargaining in recent years has been accomplished at three levels: national economy-wide bargaining, usually tripartite among government, the employer organizations and unions; industry-level bargaining between representative employer associations and workers associations which results in sectoral agreements whose geographical scope might be the whole nation but more usually is the province (Spain has 50 provinces); and firm-level bargaining between employer and worker representatives.

Table 2. Scope of Collective Bargaining

	1981-85	1986	1987	1988	1989	1990
Number of employees (000S)	7,042.7	7,051.0	7,365.9	7,723.5	8,213.0	8,564.4
Workers affected by collective bargaining (000s)	5,847.5	6,045.8	6,867.7	6,993.8	6,993.8	7,426.5
Percentage	83.03	85.70	93.23	88.90	86.71	85.15

Note: The number of employees used in this calculation excludes those working in Public Administration. As mentioned in the text, these figures have to be taken with care, especially since the number of workers affected appears to be upwardly biased.

Source: Ministerio de Trabajo y Seguridad Social, *Boletín de Estadísticas Laborales*, various issues.

Bargaining at the national economy-wide level has not been carried out on a regular basis. It started as a follow-up of the Moncloa Pacts of 1977 and went on until 1985-86. Since that time, "social partnership" (*concertación social*), as it is called, has been – and still is – a hotly debated issue but no general agreement has been reached.

The typical national economy-wide agreement contained two parts:

i) A government statement on its economic policy objectives and macroeconomic forecasts as well as tripartite agreements on incomes policies, social security, unemployment protection, general employment conditions, training and wage increases for Public Administration employees, and

ii) An "interprofessional" agreement between the employer associations and the unions, whose main element was the wage increase range to be followed in collective bargaining at lower levels, but which also contained agreements on other employment conditions, such as productivity increases and worker absenteeism, bargaining structures and conflict handling methods. In practice, however, the non-wage aspects have been of much lower practical significance (for example, the productivity clause included in the 1985-86 agreement which, at the time, received a lot of attention in the press, was a word-for-word replication of the clause contained in the 1980 agreement).

Spanish governments, sometimes in a weak position (in the 1978-82 period), sometimes for political convenience (the case of the socialist government in 1984), and always under pressure because of the unemployment problem, have accepted to negotiate issues in point i) with unions and employers. As a condition, they have promoted economy-wide agreements with the contents in point ii). Their interest in these agreements was to reduce the likely industrial unrest associated with the creation of a new system of labour relations.

Over the period 1978-86, a variety of agreements were signed, with differing participation of government, unions and employers associations. There were two relative exceptions: 1978 and 1984 when no agreement was reached, although there were intensive negotiations on the wage increase range which in fact established a non-agreed framework for collective bargaining. Secondly, even though not all unions – and most notably CC.OO. – signed all agreements, this reflected more a political gesture or a final minute disagreement rather than full opposition.

One criticism often made to this type of agreements refers to the "microeconomic rigidity" that they implied. Given the high coverage of the signing parties and the setting of a usually narrow wage rates range to be applied economy-wide, these agreements did not allow for specific arrangements in firms under special conditions. In other words, the adjustment of wages to firm-specific shocks was not possible under these circumstances.

Table 3. Wage Rate Increases Agreed in Collective Bargaining and their Dispersion by Industry, 1983-1990

	1983	1984	1985	1986	1987	1988	1989	1990
All agreements (44 industries):								
Wage increase	11.4	7.81	7.90	8.23	6.51	6.38	7.77	8.11
Standard deviation	0.9	0.87	0.58	0.47	0.94	0.75	0.74	0.73
Variation coefficient (%)	7.9	11.1	7.3	5.7	14.4	11.8	9.5	9.0
Firm-level (43 industries):								
Wage increase	11.66	7.02	7.75	8.23	6.33	5.69	7.34	7.51
Standard deviation	0.94	0.79	0.78	0.42	0.51	0.95	0.60	0.71
Variation coefficient (%)	8.1	11.3	10.1	5.1	8.1	16.7	8.2	9.4
Other levels (38 industries):								
Wage increase	11.39	7.97	7.93	8.23	6.55	6.5	7.84	8.22
Standard deviation	1.3	9.83	0.8	0.71	1.21	0.95	0.76	0.94
Variation coefficient (%)	11.4	10.4	10.1	8.6	18.5	14.6	9.7	11.4

Note: The number of sectors is not always the same due to the different sectoral coverage of firm-level and industry-level agreements.
Standard deviation is unweighted.

Source: Calculated from data in Ministerio de Trabajo y Seguridad Social, *Boletín de Estadísticas Laborales*, various issues.

As Table 3 shows, and not surprisingly, the dispersion of wage increases across sectors has been rather low. It is more remarkable that in years when no national economy-wide agreement was in effect, this dispersion has not been significantly larger. The reason for this seems to be that this type of agreements have created some kind of inertia in the behaviour of the bargaining parties in the sense that expected inflation, the key variable in the setting of wage increases in economy-wide agreements, is also the main determinant factor of wage increases by collective bargaining at the industry and firm level. So even though it has not existed in recent years, "social partnership" is still an important element in Spanish industrial relations and could be revived at any moment.

The second level of the bargaining structure is the industry level, where the bargaining outcomes are binding for all firms and workers in the industry. At this level, as already mentioned, bargaining takes place between the "most representative" unions and employers associations. The geographical scope of industrial collective bargaining agreements can be the whole nation, a region or, most usually, a province.

The majority of this type of agreements, specifically the industrial collective bargaining agreements whose geographical scope is the province, are usually limited to set minimum wages and maximum working hours for all workers in the industry. In addition, the real application of these agreements is doubtful, as the lack of control by government officials and of information by workers (especially in small firms where the union support is difficult to get) can make it difficult. At any rate, these industrial collective agreements should affect parties engaged in collective bargaining at the firm level since their contents determine their reservation payoffs, that is, the employment conditions should a firm-level collective agreement not be signed.

Finally, bargaining at the firm level is carried out between each employer and the workers representatives (or the works council, when there is one). Usually, this type of agreements offers "over-award" increases on the outcomes of economy-wide and industrial collective bargaining agreements. As a general rule, only large firms have their own collective bargaining agreements (the average of workers affected by each firm collective bargaining agreement is over 350). Nevertheless, as already mentioned, nothing prevents small firms from signing their own agreement. Available statistics do not allow to distinguish between bargaining at plant level and bargaining at the company-wide (firm) level.

Table 4 presents data on the bargaining structure. In principle, these data suggest an excessive balkanization of collective bargaining. About 4,000 collective agreements are signed every year. Approximately 30 % of all agreements are negotiated at the industry level. The proportion of industrial collective bargaining agreements whose geographical scope is the province is near 90 %. With the limitations already commented about on the accuracy of the data on workers affected, about 80 % of workers affected by collective bargaining are affected by industry agreements. In this sense, bargaining at the industrial level is dominant. Given the characteristics of this type of agreements regarding their contents and effectiveness, we can conclude that neither the scope nor the depth of collective bargaining is high.

Table 4A. Bargaining by Level: Number of Agreements

	1981-85	1986	1987	1988	1989	1990
Total agreements	3,473	3,790	4,112	4,096	4,302	4,458
Firm Level	2,294	2,588	2,817	2,826	3,016	3,149
Percentage	66.05	68.28	68.51	68.99	70.26	70.64
Other Levels	1,179	1,202	1,295	1,270	1,286	1,309
Percentage	33.95	31.72	31.49	31.01	29.73	29.36

Table 4B. Bargaining by level: Workers Affected (thousands)

	1981-85	1986	1987	1988	1989	1990
Total agreements	5,847.5	6,275.1	6,867.7	6,864.7	6,993.7	7,426.5
Firm Level	1,022.4	1,092.8	1,106.5	1,070.4	1,061.9	1,099.7
Percentage	17.49	17.41	16.11	15.34	15.18	14.81
Other Levels	4,825.0	5,182.3	5,749.2	5,794.3	5,931.8	6,326.8
Percentage	82.51	82.69	83.71	84.48	84.82	85.19

Table 4C. Bargaining by Level: Average Number of Workers Affected by Each Agreement

	1981-85	1986	1987	1988	1989	1990
Total	1,683.7	1,655.7	1,670.2	1,676.0	1,625.7	1,665.9
Firm Level	445.7	422.3	392.8	378.8	352.1	349.2
Other Levels	4,092.5	4,311.4	4,541.2	4,620.7	4,612.6	4,833.3

Note: 1981-85 stands for the average of the 1981-1985 period.

Source: Ministerio de Trabajo y Seguridad Social, *Boletín de Estadísticas Laborales*, various issues.

Finally, the typical length of collective bargaining agreements is either one or two years and synchronization is low, namely, collective agreements are signed throughout the year, although there is some concentration of collective bargaining between the months of March and July of each year.

B.4 Final Remarks: Private versus Public Provisions

Since the scope and depth of collective bargaining in Spain are limited, it is not surprising that the most important determining factors of the contents of most employment arrangements are the restrictions imposed by public provisions in the form of legal regulations. In practice, most collective bargaining agreements are limited to the setting of wages and working hours where other aspects of the employment relationships are left to be regulated by law. On the other hand, purely private arrangements may exist in those cases in which no collective agreement exists. The importance of this type of arrangements is limited and information on them almost non-existent.

We have already emphasized the role that economy-wide agreements played as fundamental developments in the construction of a new institutional environment. Many legal regulations regarding the labour market were consulted with worker and employer associations during the negotiation of these agreements. Even during years when no economy-wide agreement was being negotiated, government, employer associations and unions held meetings to discuss new and already existing regulations affecting the labour market. In fact, this type of discussions has created some inertia in the sense that both employer associations and unions use their political influence to propose changes in the legislation instead of referring some non-regulated issues to discussion during collective bargaining negotiations. As a result, public provisions dominate.

C. Outcomes

C.1 Working Hours

Working hours are usually contained in collective bargaining agreements at the industry and firm level. There is a legal restriction, though. The maximum number of working hours per week is set, by law, at 40 hours. Overtime pay is usually established in collective agreements. The law establishes that there should be a premium of at least 75 % over ordinary hours. Also by law, the maximum number of overtime hours is restricted at 80 hours per year per worker; similarly, nightly working hours have to be paid at a premium of at least 25 %. Holidays must be at least 12 days per year and paid vacations no less than 30 days. Also by legal restriction, daily working hours cannot exceed nine and between full work spells there should be a minimum gap of twelve hours.

Beyond the maximum working hours and the pay premia which the law imposes, there is considerable flexibility on the organization of working hours. Bargaining parties do, in fact, use this flexibility and this issue is frequently present in collective bargaining agreements. Table 5 presents working hours in collective bargaining agreements in the last few years. There is a decreasing trend in the number of hours agreed and this number is usually lower in collective bargaining agreements at the firm level.

Table 5. Yearly Working Hours

	1982	1985	1988	1990
Statutory Maximum Working Hours	42/week	1,824	1,824	1,824
Hours agreed in collective bargaining:				
All Agreements	1,877.3	1,793.1	1,778.8	1,769.9
Firm Level	1,842.8	1,781.4	1,755.6	1,739.7
Other Levels	1,883.5	1,795.5	1,783.1	1,775.1

Source: Ministerio de Trabajo y Seguridad Social, *Boletín de Estadísticas Laborales*, various issues.

C.2 Wages

(a) Minimum wage policy

The current minimum wage policy consists of a statutory minimum fixed by the Government after consultation with unions and employer associations. This policy was introduced in 1963. This statutory minimum is fixed annually and usually discriminates between workers aged 16-17 years and workers aged over 18 years. Unions are opposed to this discrimination on the basis of age but the government justifies it as necessary and widely extended across other EEC countries.

This minimum is binding for all workers of the economy with no distinctions of occupations, professional status or contractual relationships with the employer (for instance, between temporary and permanent workers). According to the LET, the government must take into account when fixing the minimum wage the following variables:

i) cost-of-living index,
ii) the evolution of productivity,

iii) the share of workers compensations on national income, and
iv) the current economic situation.

In practice, expected inflation is the most important determining factor. There is no pre-established formula on how these variables affect the minimum wage, so the government enjoys a great deal of discretion on this matter.

Additionally, a mid-year revision of the minimum wage when the government forecast of inflation proves to be wrong is imposed by the law (the LET). In practice, no revision has been put forward in recent years even though the trend has been towards a decrease of the minimum wage in real terms.

There are no reliable data on the coverage of the minimum wage. Some estimations suggest that it is between 2-6 % of all wage-earners, but these figures are mere educated guesses as no worker-based wages survey exist in Spain. Indirectly, the minimum wage also affects the income of unemployed workers earning complementary unemployment benefits, workers not covered by collective bargaining (about 25 % of wage workers) and self-employed workers, for whom the minimum wage establishes the minimum base for their social security contributions.

The monthly minimum wage for 1991 has been fixed at 53,250 pesetas (1,775 pts/daily) for workers aged over 18 and at 35,160 pesetas (1,172 pts/daily) for workers aged 16-18. The evolution over the past decade (with the exception of the revision for 1991) has been a decrease in real terms of the minimum wage. Thus, while the consumer price index has gone up 70 percent between 1983 and 1990, the (monthly) minimum wage has increased by 55 percent only. The government forecast of inflation for 1991 is 5.8 %. The minimum wage has increased by 6.5 % from 1990 to 1991. In 1990, the minimum wage represented about one-third of average wages[7].

Thus, the importance of the minimum wage has currently more to do with the fact that its increase establishes a first reference (since the decree is passed very early in the year or even at the very end of the preceding year) as to the rate of inflation expected (or targeted) by government, rather than because of any possible direct effects on wages.

7. The average wage figure comes from the Wages Survey, whose coverage excluded Agriculture, Personal Services and Public Administration. This average figure may thus be somewhat upwardly biased. At any rate, even if one corrects downwards this figure, the minimum wage is likely to remain well below half of it.

(b) Wage components

There are few sources of information about the components of wages. The overall impression is that piece rates or profit-related schemes are not very extended. Table 6 presents some data on the labour cost structure of large firms (more than 200 workers) according to an annual survey conducted by the Spanish Ministry of Economy. According to these data, less than 12 % of total labour costs are bonuses related to worker and firm performance. The base wage accounts for 45 % of the total.

Table 6. Components of Total Yearly Labour Costs per Person, 1986-87

	1986		1987	
	000 Ptas.	%	000 Ptas.	%
Fixed Compensations	1,156	61.9	1,681	62.2
- Base wage	1,141	45.2	1,227	45.4
- Fixed Allowances	288	11.4	307	11.4
- Seniority Allowances	135	5.3	146	5.4
Variable Compensation	299	11.8	315	11.7
- Productivity Bonus	157	6.2	168	6.2
- Non-absenteeism Bonus	26	1.0	26	1.0
- Other Bonuses	116	4.6	121	4.5
Other Components	661	26.2	703	26.1
- Social Compensations	101	4.0	108	4.0
- Overtime	28	1.1	29	1.1
- Social Security Contrib.	532	21.1	566	21.0
TOTAL	2,527	100.0	2,701	100.0

Source: Ministerio de Economía y Hacienda, *La negociación colectiva en las grandes empresas*, Madrid, various issues (yearly publication).

C.3 Firing Procedures

Workers dismissals are generally subject to severance payments imposed by law. Nevertheless, these payments and the procedures to carry firings differ widely depending on the type of contract ruling the employment relationship. As in most Western European countries, the usual employment contract establishes a full-time permanent relationship between employer and employees. However, since 1977, with the Moncloa Pacts, the successive governments have introduced measures aimed at easing the use of "atypical" employment contracts. The Workers' Charter already recognized the possible use of "fixed-term contracts" even for non-temporary tasks.

However, the most sweeping reform was carried in 1984, when, in an attempt at curbing unemployment, by then about 20 % of the labour force, the Workers' Charter was reformed by Parliament. As a result of these reforms and regarding firing procedures, four different employment contracts can be now distinguished:

i) The usual, long-term employment contract: workers under these contracts can be fired after a severance payment of 20 days wages per year of seniority (with a maximum of 12 months-wages). In the case of collective dismissals, an administrative office approval is necessary. Workers fired can sue the employer and after a conciliatory trial, if an agreement with the employer is not reached, the court can declare the firing "fair" or "unfair". In the latter case, severance payments are increased to 45 days-wages per year of seniority (with a maximum of 42 months-wages). It is also possible to fire workers for disciplinary reasons. In this case, the court can also declare the firing "nil" and order the readmission of the worker affected.

ii) Contracts for temporary jobs and tasks: these contracts are subject to no limits in terms of minimum or maximum time and carry no severance payments or social security contributions subsidies. This type of contract always existed in Spain (even in the Francoist legislation). The 1984 reforms only clarified their regulation.

iii) Fixed-term contracts: these contracts can be used for any employer with the only limitation of not having experienced redundancies in the preceding 12 months. The minimum duration of these contracts is six months[8] and they can be extended for a maximum of three years, period after which the worker must be hired under a permanent contract. The regulation of these contracts establishes a severance payment of 12 days-wages per year of seniority at the moment at which this employment relation ends. Additionally, the worker cannot sue the employer and, therefore, the cost of firing workers under these contracts is much lower than in the case of workers under permanent contracts.

iv) Finally, training and practice contracts for youngsters. These contracts are limited in terms of tenure (minimum of three months, maximum of three years), in terms of age (only in the case of training contracts: 20 years) and in terms of level of education (only in the case of practice contracts: workers ought to have finished formal education within the past four years). Training contracts are entitled to state aids for the training provided.

Two comments have to be added. Part-time workers have, by law, the same rights (proportionate to the number of hours worked) than full-time workers, including minimum wage. Secondly, private employment agencies are not regulated by law,

---

8. Very recently – in April 1992 – the government has increased to 1 year the minimum length of this type of contract, in a decree-law which has also reduced unemployment benefits and made more stringent entitlement to them.

although there is a presumption that they are illegal. As a matter of fact, they do exist, but their significance in terms of temporary employment is unknown.

No data exist on the distribution of the employment stock by detailed type of contract. Since 1987, the Labour Force Survey (Encuesta de Población Activa, EPA) includes a question aimed at distinguishing between training, seasonal and "other" temporary workers. The evolution of the last four years shows a large increase of workers under temporary contracts (in a large proportion of workers under "other" temporary contracts): whereas in the second quarter of 1987 the proportion of temporary employment (workers under contract of types ii) to iv) above) was 15.6 %, in the fourth quarter of 1991 it stood at over 33 % of total employees. Other sources suggest that this figure was around 10 % in 1984. The magnitudes of both levels and rates of growth are much higher than in other Western European countries.

C.4 Retirement and Early Retirement Provisions

The Spanish law allows workers to retire when they turn 65 and receive a state pension whose amount depends on the number of years worked. As a matter of fact, this is the standard age for retirement and it is even compulsory in the case of public employees. In addition, several policy measures have been adopted in the early 1980s to promote early retirement especially in sectors under economic distress. On the other hand, collective bargaining agreements have regulated early retirement (e.g. in banking). Finally, private pension schemes were almost nonexistent until a few years ago when they were promoted and regulated by the state.

C.5 Special Clauses on Collective Bargaining Agreements

Besides wages and working hours, there are some issues collectively bargained. These issues include productivity (in about 25 % of all agreements), absenteeism (in another 25 %), union rights at the workplace (in about 60 % of all agreements) and cost-of-living allowances (in about 30 %), but rarely level of employment or manning ratios.

D. Concluding Remarks

We conclude with some comments on three issues that we believe are crucial for the understanding of the recent evolution of Spanish labour markets: the flexibility and degree of centralization of collective bargaining and the availability and widespread use of fixed-term employment contracts.

D.1 A Flexible Collective Bargaining System

As described in section B.1, the structure and contents of collective bargaining is not significantly restricted by the law. In principle, employers and employees are free to choose when, at what level and on what to bargain with the only restrictions of the minimum standards imposed by the law on some of the outcomes (as minimum wages and maximum working hours). One of the consequences of this "flexibility" is the number of bargaining units existing, which is generally considered in Spain to be too large, as already commented on in section B, although it is obvious that this is a judgment whose validity is debatable. This is in contrast with some collective bargaining rules in other countries where some issues are restricted from bargaining by law (for instance, the U.S. where some aspects of the employment relation are subject to collective bargaining only when the employer accepts negotiations over them).

D.2 The Degree of Centralization of Collective Bargaining

The degree of centralization of collective bargaining has important implications for labour relations, in general, and for wage setting, in particular. Specifically, some studies (Crouch (1985), Bruno and Sachs (1985), Newell and Symons (1987), Calmfors and Driffill (1988), Freeman (1988), Dell'Aringa (1989)) support the view that countries with centralized collective bargaining perform economically better and have lower equilibrium unemployment rates. (There is some debate about whether the relationship is "U-shaped", with highly decentralized countries also outperforming less decentralized, but not highly centralized countries, in the second half of the past decade). Additionally, not only the equilibrium unemployment rate is lower when centralization is high, but also the difference between actual unemployment and equilibrium unemployment after adverse supply shocks or in disinflationary periods (Jimeno, 1991). On the other hand, centralization implies "microeconomic rigidities", as already commented in section B.3. However, on balance, it seems that "centralization is best". To what degree is Spanish collective bargaining centralized? In principle, there are too many bargaining units but this does not imply by itself a high degree of decentralization. As the data presented in table 1 shows, most of the worker representatives involved in collective bargaining belong to the two major union confederations (UGT and CC.OO.). Hence, coordination among them could prevent the negative effects of the excessive fragmentation of collective bargaining. However, this coordination is sometimes difficult for reasons regarding the industrial relations structure. Since most worker representatives belong to the two major union confederations (UGT and CC.OO.) and these organizations compete every four years in election for worker representatives, strategic behaviour is likely to affect the prospects for coordination among them. Consequently, and contrary to what the occasional existence of nation-wide collective agreements, the political influence of unions and employers confederations and the importance of "social partnership" might indicate, it is not surprising that the degree of centralization of collective bargaining is rather low.

D.3 The Implications of New Contractual Forms: Permanent versus Fixed-Term Employment

Significant firing costs have been pointed out as one of the most important sources of rigidity in Spanish labour markets. Theoretically, severance payments might be a component of an optimal labour contract when there is asymmetric information in the employment relationship (see Hall and Lazear (1984) and Parsons (1986)). Regarding their macroeconomic effects, as any adjustment costs, firing costs reduce the variability of employment over the business cycle but their effects on average employment are uncertain. Bentolila and Bertola (1990) present a model where firing costs have a negative but not very significant effect on the firm's hiring decision. Conversely, Saint-Paul (1990) shows that when workers' quit rates are procyclical, firing costs can create a "high unemployment trap".

The presumed negative effect of firing costs on employment was the reason why the Spanish Government introduced some reforms in 1984 allowing a wide use of temporary employment contracts. Does this move towards "flexibilization" of the labour market increase its efficiency?. In principle, the answer to this question is not clear since reducing severance payments is not necessarily optimal. Concretely, not very much is known about the characteristics of optimal labour contracts when there is asymmetric information in the employment relationship and there are also adverse selection/moral hazard problems which might be affected by the magnitude of severance payments in the sense that the productivity of a fixed-term worker might depend on the probability of his/her contract being renewed. Jimeno and Toharia (1991) argue that if the probability of rehiring temporary workers is low, then the adverse selection/moral hazard problem is worsened by the non-existence of severance payments and, thus, labour productivity of temporary workers is likely to be lower than that of permanent workers. Similar arguments also apply to investment in firm-specific training. Hence, it is not obvious that "flexibilization", in this sense, always increases the efficiency of the labour market. Additionally, when no wage rate discrimination is possible, as happens in Spain, there are also perverse wage effects of temporary employment since the existence of temporary workers decreases the probability of firing of permanent workers after excessive wage increases which results in higher wage rates. In this case, as in the case of most labour market institutions, more research is needed to help our understanding of their efficiency effects.

REFERENCES

Bentolila, S. and O. Blanchard (1990), Spanish Unemployment, *Economic Policy, A European Forum*, 10: 233-265.

Bentolila, S. and G. Bertola (1990), Firing Costs and Labour Demand: How Bad is Eurosclerosis?, *Review of Economic Studies*, 57: 381-402.

Bruno, M. and J. Sachs (1985), *The Economics of Worldwide Stagflation*, Oxford: Basil Blackwell.

Calmfors, L. and J. Driffill (1988), Bargaining Structure, Corporatism and Macroeconomic Performance, *Economic Policy, A European Forum*, 6: 13-61.

Crouch, C. (1985), Conditions for Trade Union Wage Restraint, in: L. Lindberg and C.S. Mail (eds.), *The Politics of Economic Stagflation*, Washington: Brookings Institution.

Dell'Aringa, C. (1989), Industrial Relations and Economic Performance, Universitá Cattolica di Milano, mimeo.

Freeman, R. (1988), The Impact of Labour Market Institutions and Constraints on Economic Performance, *Economic Policy, A European Forum*, 6: 64-78.

Hall, R. and E. Lazear (1984), The Excess Sensitivity of Layoffs and Quits to Demand, *Journal of Labour Economics*, 2, 233-257.

Jimeno, J.F. (1991), The Degree of Centralization of Collective Bargaining, the Inflation-Unemployment Trade-off and Microeconomic Efficiency Revisited, L.S.E., mimeo.

Jimeno, J.F. and L. Toharia (1991), Productivity and Wage Effects of Temporary Employment: Evidence from Spain, mimeo.

Jimeno, J.F. and L. Toharia (1992), *Unemployment and Labour Market Flexibility: Spain*. International Labour Office.

Newell, A. and J. Symons (1987), Corporatism, Laissez-faire and the Rise in Unemployment, *European Economic Review*, 31:567-601.

Parsons, D. (1986), The Employment Relationship: Job Attachment, Work Effort and the Nature of Contracts, chapter 14 in: O.C. Ashenfelter and R. Layard, *Handbook of Labour Economics*, North-Holland: Amsterdam.

Saint-Paul, G. (1990), The High Unemployment Trap, M.I.T., mimeo.

Spanish Ministry of Economy (1988), *La Negociación Colectiva en las Grandes Empresas en 1987*, Madrid: Ministerio de Economía.

Spanish Ministry of Labour (1988), *Estructura y Contenidos Básicos de la Negociación Colectiva en España. Datos de 1986*. Madrid: Ministerio de Trabajo y Seguridad Social.

Labour Market Contracts and Institutions
J. Hartog and J. Theeuwes (Editors)
1993 Elsevier Science Publishers B.V.

CHAPTER 11

ITALY:
Labour Relations

Tiziano Treu, Gianni Geroldi and Marco Maiello*

A. Introduction. The Economic and Social Context

Certain features of the economic and social context exert a particular influence on the industrial relations system in Italy. It is worth underlining above all the heterogeneous nature of Italy's productive system which is characterized by its relatively late start in the industrialization process and by its even later expansion of the tertiary sector.

The current "tertiarization" of the Italian economy may well be a significant factor, but for the time being it does not seem destined to belittle the importance (even quantitatively) of the industrial sector. The industrial relations system and the logic of its main protagonists are still almost exclusively based on the industrial sector, while it has proved to be especially difficult to establish appropriate types of employment relationships for the different world of the tertiary sector, both in State and in private enterprises.

The economic structure of the labour market is markedly fragmented owing to the high percentage of small and very small firms (more than 50 % of the employment is concentrated in enterprises with less than 20 employees and 70 % in enterprise with less than 99 employee; see Table 1). This traditional aspect of the Italian system has received further confirmation from the trends towards decentralization and "miniaturization" of firms, not only in the tertiary sector but in the industrial sector as well.

An increase in the number of small firms does not necessarily imply that the economic system is fragile, it undoubtedly represents a critical factor (not only for Italy) for the industrial relations system and for labour law, both of which have traditionally taken large-scale industry as their reference point.

The decrease of the average size of the firm below the minimum required for the enforcement of State labour law or of collective labour law has resulted in the law

* Fondazione Regionale Pietro Seveso, Milan, Italy.

regulating an ever smaller percentage of employment relationships in private industry, although it was originally supposed to cover all employment relationships.

This discrepancy is further aggravated by two trends in employment: the spreading of autonomous employment relationships (i.e. self-employment) which are more common in Italy than in most other countries and which, according to some experts, create an anomalous situation – in fact the relationship is often of a precarious nature and of doubtful social utility as it is often either partly or wholly "submerged" (black economy) – and the differentiation of employment forms with respect to the traditional full-time contract of indefinite duration (part-time work, short-term contracts, vocational training contracts, job in self-managed activities, cooperatives, as well as occasional jobs and all those forms of employment relating to the black economy).

Table 1. Employment Shares by Enterprise Size, Total Economy

Country	Year	< 20	12-99	100-499	500+
United States	1982	45.7		13.0	41.3
Japan	1985	37.8[1]	17.9[2]	17.3	27.0
France	1985	25.8	20.4	18.3	35.5
Germany, Fed. Rep.	1970	17.2[3]	24.3[4]	18.3	40.3
Norway	1985	47.2[5]	10.2[6]	10.0[7]	32.6[8]
Switzerland	1985	46.3[9]		27.1[10]	26.5
Italy	1981	53.2	16.1	12.2	18.5

Notes: [1] 1-29 employees; [2] 30-99 employees; [3] 1-10 employees; [4] 10-100 employees; [5] 0-49 employees; [6] 50-99 employees; [7] 100-199 employees; [8] 200+ employees; [9] 1-49 employees; [10] 50-499 employees

Source: IILS Research Report Series.

These trends reveal the inadequacy of the traditional rules governing industrial relations; but for the time being no lasting alternative model has been found (even for the regulation of individual employment relationships). Indeed, the trends are part of a wider transformation process in the quantitative and qualitative make-up of the workforce, a phenomenon common to most developed countries besides Italy. These transformations include the above-mentioned "tertiarization" of the economy, with parallel changes taking place in the labour market, changes in job classifications brought about (also) by the introduction of new technology, the shift in the ratio between male and female workers, between different age groups, and between employed and unemployed, and the ensuing phenomenon of a labour supply which is irregular and not entirely determined by demand.

To these heterogeneous elements we must add other dualisms which have a marked influence on the regulation of employment relationships. The disparities between North and South (see Table 2) continue to represent the major factor of national imbalance; statistics relating to unemployment, which is still predominantly concentrated in the South, are merely the most striking way of highlighting one of a number of disparities.

Table 2. Unemployment Rate Accoring to Sex and Geographical Area

	1987			1988		
	M	F	T	M	F	T
Italy	8.15	18.66	11.97	8.14	18.78	2.03
North	4.81	12.69	7.84	4.08	11.30	6.86
Middle	6.22	15.73	9.73	6.20	16.21	9.90
South	13.63	30.69	19.23	14.55	32.73	20.61

Source: Istat. Rilevazione delle forze di lavoro.

The dualism between the private sector and the public sector in labour relations is, on other hand, common to all countries, even if it has tended to become less marked in recent years. Nevertheless, in the Italian system, it assumes special importance for the sheer size of the public sector. In an international perspective, the percentage of employees working in public employment rates as medium-high. In addition, workers employed in State controlled industries governed by the provisions of private labour law have traditionally played a particular role, sometimes conflicting with the private sector industrial relations system. In the last few years the difference between employment relationships in the public sector and those in the private sector has become the mark of a growing contradiction that affects other countries besides Italy. Actually it has enabled the survival of rigid and formalistic rules in the way public manpower is regulated, regardless of efficiency criteria. This phenomenon is common in the private tertiary sector as well (e.g. in banks and insurance companies).

If difficulties are present in the economic context, the socio-political environment is equally fraught with problems. The fragility of the foundations upon which the Italian industrial relations system rests – firstly the trade unions and collective bargaining – the traditionally high degree of conflictuality of the system (diminished in recent years, see Table 3) and the low degree of institutional regulation of the system are also the overcome of the country's marked ideologico-political polarization, not just between the centre and the left parties, but also within the left wing (given the historical presence of the largest Communist Party of the western countries). This political polarization is strongly reflected in the trade union movement and has recently flared up despite decades of practice of trade union unity.

From the political standpoint, the outstanding feature is what might be termed as the political party dependence of the Italian unions. In spite of the relative strengthening of trade union autonomy and therefore of unity in the period of pluralistic growth, Italy has never witnessed anything approaching an egalitarian relationship between political party and trade union of the type commonly found in other parts of Europe with a long tradition of reformist political representation of workers' interests.

Table 3. Conflicts in Italy: 1975-1988

	N. of conflicts	N. of workers involved (thousands)	Total amount of working days (thousands)
1975	3,568	10,717	22,673
1976	2,667	6,974	16,464
1977	3,259	6,434	9,846
1978	2,465	4,347	6,129
1979	1,979	10,521	20,614
1980	2,224	7,428	9,402
1981	2,176	3,567	5,350
1982	1,741	7,490	14,361
1983	1,550	4,625	10,328
1984	1,759	3,540	3,973
1985	1,336	1,224	1,380
1986	1,462	2,940	4,593
1987	1,146	1,473	2,518
1988	1,767	1,609	2,136
1989[1]	868	1,700	1,514

[1] January-August 1989.

B. The Institutional and Legal Environment

The institution framework presents a traditional contrast between collective and individual labour relations. The former is still among the least regulated by law of all EC countries in the post war period. Both trade unions and collective bargaining developed outside the bounds of legislative guidelines.

This legislative abstentionism in industrial relations, subsequently followed by an attitude of promotion without regulation of trade union activity, reflects the state of balance between unions and political parties in Italy. Such a state of balance prevented, in the first decade after the Second World War, the introduction of restrictive legislation (which in any case was not necessary given the substantial weakness of industrial relations in Italy). At a later stage (1969) it required a strengthening of the trade unions both in their dealings with the employers as well as with the "rank and file", in an economic context of fast growth and high political tension. The factors mentioned in the introduction, including Italy's late arrival on the industrial scene, help to account for the low degree of institutionalization of the industrial relations system. Italy has been slow in developing those "rules of game" – not only legal but also derived from collective bargaining, or from customs and practices – which in other countries supported industrial relations in a multi-party pluralistic setting, serving to lessen instability and conflict.

The lack of legal rules persists notwithstanding the fact that the Italian trade unions, like other unions in developed countries, have been subject to "special" provisions which differentiate them from other types of private associations, ranging from the provisions in support of trade unions activities within the firm, contained in the Workers' Statute (Act No. 300 of 1970); to the provisions – already present in the prefascist era but much more notably so after World War II – awarding to the most representative unions the power to designate members of public boards, to perform various types of duties, mainly of an administrative nature (social security institutions, public placement offices).

Since 1976 relations between employers, unions and the Central Government have intensified, giving rise to various episodes of trilateral agreements, at the national level, aimed in particular at reducing the high inflation rate of the mid-70s. Such agreements included measures aimed at controlling labour costs (in particular the wage indexation system) and therefore the collective autonomy of the parties concerned.

Italian legislation has been traditionally directed to protect the employee, considered as weak party on the labour market, promoting highly restrictive norms to regulate the various aspects of labour relations: from hiring procedures, controlled by a centralized public service, to the various causes of suspension or termination of the labour contract.

In fact the Italian system has adopted a wide ranging set of measures aimed at protecting job security:[1]

1. advance notice in case of dismissals, and indemnities in case of termination of employment;

---

1. More information on these measures in Treu, T. (1990), *Employment protection and labour relations in Italy*, paper for the Conference of WBZ Berlin, 16 May 1990; for general information on Italian labour law and industrial relation, see Treu, T. (1986), "Italy" in: R. Blanpain (ed.), *International Encyclopedia for labour law and industrial relations*, Deventer, Kluwer; Treu, T. (1991), *European Employment and Industrial Relations Glossary: Italy*, Luxembourg, Office for Official Publications of the European Communities.

Table 4. Unionism in Italy: 1980-1988

Total amount of unionized workers

	CGIL[1]	%	CISL	%	UIL	%	TOTAL	%
1980	4,559.050	–	3,059.845	–	1,346.900	–	9,005.795	–
1981	4,595.011	−0.1	2,988.813	−2.3	1,357.290	0.8	8,941.114	−0.7
1982	4,576.020	−0.4	2,976.880	−0.4	1,358.004	0.1	8,910.904	−0.3
1983	4,556.052	−0.4	2,953.411	−0.8	1,351.514	−0.5	8,860.977	−0.6
1984	4,546.335	−0.2	3,097.231	4.9	1,344.460	−0.5	8,988.026	1.4
1985	4,952.014	1.0	2,953.095	−4.7	1,306.250	−2.8	8,851.359	−1.5
1986	4,647.038	1.2	2,975.482	0.8	1,305.682	0.0	8,928.202	0.9
1987	4,743.036	2.1	3,080.019	3.5	1,343.716	2.9	9,166.771	1.8
1988	4,867.406	2.6	3,288.279	6.8	1,398.071	4.0	9,553.756	1.8
1980-88	268.356	5.8	228.434	7.5	51.171	3.8	547.961	6.1

Active workers[2]

	CGIL[1]	%	CISL	%	UIL	%	TOTAL	%
1980	3,495.537	–	2,611.710	–	1,268.823	–	7,376.070	–
1981	3,398.404	−2.8	2,479.342	−5.1	1,269.763	0.1	7,147.509	−3.1
1982	3,277.981	−3.5	2,406.378	−2.9	1,255.065	−1.2	6,939.424	−2.9
1983	3,145.820	−4.0	2,356.922	−2.1	1,232.669	−1.8	6,735.411	−2.9
1984	3,042.423	−3.3	2,414.304	2.4	1,212.129	−1.7	6,668.856	−1.0
1985	2,951.342	−3.0	2,204.060	−8.7	1,159.519	−4.3	6,314.921	−5.3
1986	2,837.975	−3.8	2,124.542	−3.6	1,144.895	−1.3	6,107.412	−3.3
1987	2,782.119	−2.0	2,114.899	−0.5	1,163.475	1.6	6,060.493	−0.8
1988	2,747.013	−1.3	2,192.865	3.7	1,194.298	2.6	6,134.176	1.2
1980-88	−748.524	−21.4	−418.845	−16.0	−74.525	−5.9	−1,241.894	−16.8

Employees

	CGIL1	%	CISL	%	UIL	%	TOTAL	%	Unioniz.
1980	3,484.004	–	2,507.641	–	1,145.910	–	7,137.555	–	48.6
1981	3,387.040	−2.8	2,371.471	−5.4	1,142.756	−0.3	6,901.267	−3.3	47.0
1982	3,266.816	−3.5	2,286.728	−3.6	1,134.376	−0.7	6,687.920	−3.1	45.6
1983	3,134.011	−4.1	2,224.112	−2.7	1,121.054	−1.2	6,479.177	−3.1	44.5
1984	3,030.232	−3.3	2,261.668	1.7	1,114.040	−0.6	6,405.940	−1.1	44.3
1985	2,939.370	−3.0	2,055.663	−9.1	1,064.110	−4,5	6,059.143	−5.4	41.4
1986	2,825.273	−3.9	1,967.105	−4.3	1,046.086	−1.7	5,838.464	−3.6	39.7
1987	2,768.384	−2.0	1,951.994	−0.8	1,069.024	2.2	5,789.402	−0.8	39.4
1988	2,733.017	−1.3	2,018.463	3.4	1,099.727	2.9	5,851.207	1.1	39.1
1980-88	−750.987	−21.6	−489.178	−19.5	−46.183	−4.0	−1,286.348	−18.0	

Legenda: CGIL – Confederazione Generale Italiana del Lavoro (General Confederation of Italian Workers); CISL – Confederazione Italiana Sindacati dei Lavoratori (Italian Confederation of Workers' Union; UIL – Unione Italiana Lavoratori (Union of Italian Workers).

Note: The difference between "total amount" and "active workers" is due to the number of unionized pensioners.

Source: CESOS, Le relazioni sindacali in Italia, Rapporto 1988/89.

2. procedural and substantive requirements (just cause) directed to prohibit the arbitrary use of employer power to discharge employees (see below);
3. wage compensation to employees in case of lay-off and short-time work paid by a special social security fund (Cassa Integrazione Guadagni – Wage Guarantee Fund).[2]

B.1 The Actors: Unions and Employers

After decades of weakness, beginning in the late 60s and with the support of Act No. 300/1970, trade unions have grown strong, reaching a peak in the late 70s (over 45 % of unionization). In the 80s unionization declined but was still considerable (see Table 4).

Union structure is based on a combination of "vertical" structures, industry federations, and "horizontal" structures (so-called chambers of labour) operating on a territorial basis and culmination in Confederations at the national level. The splitting-up of the unitary trade union occurred in 1948 and gave birth to the formation of the three major Italian confederations: CGIL – Confederazione Generale Italiana del Lavoro (General Confederation of Italian Workers) – the trade union of socialist and communist origin; CISL – Confederazione Italiana Sindacati dei Lavoratori (Italian Confederation of Workers' Union – the catholic trade union; UIL – Unione Italiana Lavoratori (Union of Italian Workers) – the liberal/republican and socialist trade union.[3]

The existence of strong horizontal structures is no longer a sign of weakness, as, for example, in the case of the French system, but it does have a function – in the pursuance of initiatives aimed at influencing economic policy and in controlling sectorial bargaining.

Trade union representation at the place of work, traditionally weak in Italy, became strong during the late 60s, especially in the industrial sector, with the spread of union delegates and Workers' Councils. Their organizational model is of the "single

---

2. More precisely, The Cassa Integrazione Guadagni (Wages Guarantee Fund) is a special public fund used to protect workers' income, financed by companies and the state, and administered by the National Institute of Insurance (INPS). In cases laid down by law, the fund makes up the pay of employees affected by lay-offs or short time working, up to 80 % of the lost pay.

3. Regarding the horizontal structure, since the split in the union movement, only the CGIL still uses the term "Chamber of Labour", The CISL set up a structure called the "Union of Trade Unions", and the UIL the "Trade Union Chamber", but their functions, tasks and organization are virtually identical. These structures operate at "comprensorio" level, roughly corresponding to a group of municipalities, uniting within this geographical area the industry-wide structures of the same level and the agricultural and construction unions.

union channel" type (i.e, only one representative body at the enterprise level controlled by the unions) which may be compared with the British system of shop-stewards. The major changes that have taken place in recent years, as a result of changes in the composition of the workforce and of the difficulties in the relationships between the various trade unions, have drastically weakened these unitary representative organizations.

At the present prospects look uncertain. It hardly seems plausible that we shall see the formal development in Italy of a double representative structure, as in France, West Germany or Spain, nor the total disappearance of an elective system for all workers, such as delegates for Workers' Councils.

The difficulties of the Workers' Councils reflect a general crisis in the worker representation system throughout the trade union movement. There has been a drop in the number of members in the traditionally strongly-unionized areas of manual workers in medium-large industries, affected by reorganization. There has been no compensatory increase in those areas where the unions have traditionally been weak (middle class white-collar workers, male and female workers in the service industries, and those employed in small firms); all areas which, unlike medium-large industry, are expanding. In the service industries the representativeness of the major confederations is threatened by the diffusion of small unions outside the control of traditional trade-unions. The latter are strongly linked to sectorial interests and to specific trades (a feature that is practically non-existent in Italy's history) and express the demand for the solution of immediate issues while accusing the traditional unions of being "excessively mediatory" with respect to "general" interests.

The difficulty of providing effective answers to these socio-productive transformations is common to the trade unions of all the developed countries. In Italy's case it is aggravated by the political divisions between the three largest confederations, which in turn means uncertainty, a lack of strategic flexibility, as well as a certain tardiness in taking action.

Employer organization are historically based on the labour union model (not only in Italy).[4] This has meant the same dual organization i.e. vertical and horizontal struc-

4. In Italy there are many of these associations not because of ideological reasons, similar to those relating to trade unions, but because of type of ownership (public or private), size of the member companies, and sector (industry, services, artisanal production, agriculture or commerce). Despite this diversification, the most powerful association in Italy is Confindustria (General Confederation of Italian Industry), which groups together private companies of various size in all industrial sectors, including construction, and some service sectors. At the end of 1985, Confindustria had 111,441 member companies (employing over three million workers), 94 % of them being companies with fewer than 100 employees. Confapi (Italian Confederation of Small and Medium sized Enterprises) represents smaller private companies. It has about 30,000 member companies

tures. The horizontal structures have traditionally played a major role, more so than its equivalent in the trade unions, though for different reasons. Only a few of the industrial federations belonging to Confindustria (Federmeccanica, Federchimici, Federtessile) exert any autonomous activity, and even in these cases under the control of the Confederation.

Generally speaking, it is worth noting the low level of compactness of the employer organizations. Their control over affiliated firms is often loose; their capacity to take the initiative in industrial relations is traditionally weak. All this reflects to a large extent the (already mentioned) dualisms in the economic composition of the country and the divergent interests between the various sectors of the economy.

A typically Italian feature is that the employers' associations are not only divided on the basis of economic sectors and company size (Confindustria, Confcommercio, Confagricoltura, Confapi, Confederazione dell'Artigianato and of the Coltivatori Diretti), but they are also distinguished by the nature of ownership following the split in 1957 between private enterprise representation (represented by Confindustria) and State-owned enterprise representation, with the setting up of Intersind and Asap. These associations played an especially important role in the 60s, when they helped in promoting an industrial relations system that was more open to collective bargaining than it had been until that time.

The recent revival of protagonism among employers in the field of industrial relations, to a large extent reflecting the crisis of trade union representativeness, is more the work of individual employers rather than of employers' associations. As a result such activism often lacks uniform guidelines, apart from the general aim of achieving greater flexibility in the management of human resources, corresponding to the requirements of growing international competition.

---

with almost 900,000 employees. Public sector industrial and service enterprises (state-owned and controlled) belong to two separate associations: the first is Intersind, set up in 1958 after the disaffiliation of these enterprises from Confindustria and grouping together the enterprise (274 with 420,000 employees which make up the IRI (Istituto per la Ricostruzione Industriale – the major state holding in Italy) and EFIM (body for financing and shareholding in manufacturing industry); the second is Asap (Petrochemicals Industry Employers' Association), formed in 1960 with the enterprises (89, employing about 100,000 workers) of ENI (National Hydrocarbon Corporation). Artisanal enterprises, for both goods and services, belong to their own association reflecting their political affiliations: centre (Confartigianato, the General Italian Confederation of Artisans) and left (CNA, National Confederation of Artisans). The larger agricultural enterprises belong to Confagricoltura (General Confederation of Italian Agriculture), which represents the large agricultural capitalist entrepreneurs, as well as individual and associated small farmers (1,380.000 members representing 672,000 enterprises in 1984). Most small farmers, however, are organized on a political base: Coldiretti (National Small Farmers' Confederation), traditionally allied with the Christian Democratic Party; Confcoltivatori, left oriented. Commercial and tourism enterprises are also organized on political lines: Confcommercio (centre), Confesercenti (left).

The possibility of establishing employment relationships without trade unions is considered realistic in certain sectors of small industry and in high-tech firms. Elsewhere management policy seems to waver between attempts to involve the unions in forms of worker participation (emblematically expressed in the so-called "IRI protocol"[5]) and attempts to restrict, in an "opportunist" way, the influence of the unions and the area covered by collective industrial relations.

B.2 The Bargaining Structure

Bargaining goes on at various levels – interconfederal, industry-wide, plant and, sometimes, local levels – a peculiar feature of the Italian system. The importance of the various levels and their interrelationships have varied considerably over the years. The role of interconfederal bargaining was particularly important in the period of post-war reconstruction, and then again in the 1975-'85 period, coinciding with high inflation rates. Thus, this level of bargaining would appear to be characteristic of "crisis" phases; in fact its main function has been that of guaranteeing minimum working conditions or minimum rights for large sectors of the economy (e.g. in the immediate post-war period agreements on collective dismissals and on individual dismissals, on internal commissions and, later, on the temporary redundancy payment scheme and on the wage indexation system). Its role has often tended to spill over into forms of political bargaining with the State, as occurred in those episodes of social concertation mentioned earlier.

Industry-wide national agreements have been the fulcrum of the system since the 50s and still are. Bargaining by occupation is practically non existent (apart from a few cases in the public service). The content of industry wide agreements concerns standard wages and working conditions which may be supplemented by plant-level agreements.

During the 70s the scope of these national agreements was widened so as to include qualitative aspects in the handling of the employment relationship (working environment, work-loads, the organization of work, job mobility, overtime) and in manage-

---

5. IRI Protocol is an agreement signed in 1984, after almost two years of negotiation, between the IRI group (see footnote 2) and the three major trade unions (CGIL, CISL, UIL); it was renewed and clarified in July 1986. In general, the agreement was the result of a convergence of opinions on the importance of: the industrial policy objectives of the IRI group; the consolidation and development of key sectors and the restructuring of the other sectors; the contributions of the employees to these objective, with wider opportunities for them to apply their occupational skill at enterprise level; an active labour policy directed at the rational allocation of resources; guidelines of conduct, including bargaining mechanisms, to favour the solution of these problems. This form of participation was developed by "Joint Consultative Committees" at various level: group, territory, sector and company.

ment policy (unions rights to information and to control over investments, plant restructuring, etc.).

Plant-level bargaining proved to be of decisive importance in the rapid expansion and innovations of the system in the 1968-'75 period. It was decisive in bargaining over wages and working conditions above the standards laid down in national agreements, correlated to the specific production situations and to the capacity to pay of individual firms. Attempts at establishing the objectives and ways of such bargaining by inserting clauses in national agreements have traditionally met with little success because of resistance or opposition from trade unions. Only recently there has been renewed interest and consensus on improving coordination among the various bargaining levels.

As can be seen, one characteristic of the Italian system is the trend towards bipolarism in the bargaining structure, i.e. the presence of two basic levels: in the period of growth (1968-'75) the two dominant levels were national and plant-level bargaining, while during the following decade the interconfederal level has tended to substitute national-level bargaining in line with the progressive centralization of the entire system.

In the last few years (since 1985) the trend has been towards a (further) decentralization of bargaining which has lowered the importance of interconfederal bargaining and, according to some observers, might even affect the role of national industry-wide bargaining. This decentralization reflects a general economic trend encouraged by new technologies with flexible forms of production. In fact it often appears to be stimulated by initiatives on the part of employers, the opposite of what happened during the years 1968-'75 when employers tried to fight against the decentralization of bargaining by restricting the issues that could be raised.

However, the trend towards decentralization has been controlled by the centre. Even the employers' associations have recognized the persisting importance of the national collective agreement as an element of stability for the system, particularly for small firms, which account for the major portion of Italy's economic structure and for which national bargaining remains realistically the only feasible form of bargaining.

The relative importance of the levels of bargaining has changed considerably over time. From 1975 to 1983 the escalator clause, providing an indexation system, bargained at the top confederal level, was the major determinant of wage dynamics. Wage bargaining at enterprise and plant level was almost unified in this period.

In the last years the importance of enterprise bargaining has increased, as shown by wage differentials by size of enterprise. In small firms with less than 30-50 employees, in sectors and geographical areas where this bargaining level is absent and only the national tariffs are applicable, wages are 30-40 % lower than in large firms.

The bargaining rounds *de facto* follow a rather standard frequency: at a national level they occur every 3 years (with a tendency to shift to every 4 years); at an enterprise level in between the national rounds (but formal agreement is followed by a continuous informal activity to apply, adapt, supplement the agreement itself).

The multiplicity of bargaining levels and, above all, the lack of any precise co-ordination between them – which is understandable in periods of growth – have now become factors of instability. Employers and unions (at the confederal level) are currently trying to find a way of distributing the scope of the various bargaining levels in a more rational manner and of controlling plant-level bargaining without suffocating it completely.

B.3 Legal Nature and Effects of Collective Agreements

Labour unions and collective agreements – in the private sector – are in general regulated by the principles of private law. Consequently labour unions do not have in principle any "monopoly" right of representation. However those unions which are considered as "representative" in accordance with a set of loose criteria (membership – not necessarily elections –, diffusion of organization, traditional activities, etc.) are entitled to special legal support, according to Act No. 300/1970 (rights to hold meetings at the workplace; time off-work for unions representatives; specific protection against transfer, dismissal and unfair labour practices).

This "legal advantage" has given the three major unions CGIL, CISL, and UIL a *de facto* control of collective bargaining. In the public sector, on the contrary, collective labour relations are regulated in greater detail (Act No. 93/1983), and the representative unions are the "sole" recognized bargaining actors. This privilege has not protected the large confederations from the challenge of aggressive "independent" unions and small rank-and-file organizations: this is also due to the looseness of the "criteria" applied to verify the representativeness, the "fragmentation" of public organizations and the "weaknesses" of the public employer.

The structure of unions and of collective bargaining in public service is much more "shaky" than in the private sector, and indeed out of control: significantly enough the public guidelines set by government to keep wage bargaining in line with economic indicators are often bypassed due to unrestrained competition among confederal and independent unions and to the weak resistance from the government itself.

Political parties and experts are discussing proposals to reshape the system: a) by requiring more precise criteria of representativeness, e.g. through resort to elections; b) by deregulating the rigid collective bargaining procedures in the public service, and making then more "responsive" to efficiency criteria. But the outcomes are quite uncertain.

In the private sector, collective agreements are binding only for the participating employers' and their organizations – a unique case in Europe.

The legal fragility of collective bargaining, and the absence of *erga omnes* effects, due to the failure to put into practice Article 39 of the Constitution,[6] has been compensated by the exceptional development of unionization during the 60s and 70s through which the general application of collective agreements became feasible in actual fact.

But the issue of generally binding collective agreements, has become critical again over the past few years with the economic crisis and the erosion of trade union representativeness; thus there is once again a pressing need for legislation guaranteeing if not the enforceability *erga omnes* of collective agreements (which would necessitate a revision of Article 39 of the Constitution) or, at least, of basic minimum wage rates for those areas of employment not covered by collective bargaining (especially in small firms and marginal sectors of the economy). The profound changes in the employment relationships have also weakened the prescriptive nature of collective agreements since the content of such agreements does not always imply an improvement but often an adaptation and in some cases a worsening of worker's wages and conditions; moreover, they concern areas of the employment relationship which have traditionally fallen within management prerogatives. Precise data on the coverage of (national) agreements, which varies according to sectors, are lacking: according to estimates the coverage ranges between 70-80 % in the major industrial sectors.

The low degree of institutionalization of industrial relations in Italy can be seen just as clearly in the weak development and enforcement of the so-called "obligatory" part of the collective agreement: "no-strike" clauses on the part of the unions and clauses coordinating the various contractual levels. Only recently have there been signs of a reversal in this trend with renewed attention being paid to contractual clauses which lay down basic rules of the game (e.g. cooling-off periods, prevention of disputes). A major example is the procedure set by the IRI protocol which has been adopted in several national collective agreements.

In each dispute concerning major technological and organizational innovations, the parties promise to suspend any form of direct action (strikes by the trade unions and

---

6. The Article 39 of Italian Constitution establishes that there are no limits to trade unions organization and rules with *erga omnes* force the collective agreements, concluded by the representative bodies of registered unions. The collective agreement is applicable to all workers, whether members or not of the signing association (in fact the literal meaning of the Latin term *erga omnes* is "in relation to everyone).

modifications in the status quo on the part of the employers) until the conciliation procedures drafted in the agreement have been tried out. The agreement also provides for a "quasi-arbitration" entrusted to a group of experts (three appointed by the trade unions, three by IRI management) to whom the parties may resort over any dispute concerning the protocol. If a state of deadlock is reached among the experts it is then possible to resort to a committee of three "superexperts" (all ex-presidents of the Constitutional Court). The decision of the experts is only binding within the sphere of the system set up by the protocol itself and is not justiciable in courts; this in itself reflects the caution applied in this first attempt at entrusting a third party with the task of solving a dispute.

Recently, Act No. 146/1990 has required that in case of strike in the essential services a minimum level of service be guaranteed though collective agreements; and it has empowered a Commission of experts to mediate in case of impasse and judge over the adequacy of these minima.

C. Outcomes. General Trends

Major changes have occurred during the 80s both in the context and in the content of labour relations. The major focus, in Italy as elsewhere, has been on flexibilization of the labour market. This objective has required some innovations in industrial relations practice and in the balance between private and public regulations of the labour market.

A major innovation concerns the reduction of the area regulated by restrictive norms and the widening of the areas subject to flexible regulations: e.g. increased favour (or reduced disfavour) for part-time work; wider possibility to use fixed term contract employment, firstly for young people; partial liberalization of the hiring system; flexibilization in the use of female work (particularly night work and heavy work).

A specific aspect of this flexibilization is worthy of notice. While the need for greater flexibility of labour is recognized, this doesn't imply that the employer is allowed total discretion in these aspects of the use of manpower. The implementation of flexibility is still regulated by collective bargaining, usually coupled with public control by the body competent for labour market regulation (labour offices, tripartite labour commissions). This behaviour corresponds to a wider policy option of the Italian system, which is far from laissez-faire or full market liberalization, impracticable in the political and social conditions of the country. Instead it has promoted a concerted flexibilization of the labour market. Tripartism at the macro economic level is parallelled by some form of tripartism on concertation at the micro (enterprise) or territorial level addressed to improve labour mobility and productivity (i.e. Wage Guarantee Fund).

The opportunity for unions to bargain over the conditions of flexibility appears to vary according to the general characteristics of the labour relations at the territorial and enterprise level (level and type of unionization, previous labour management traditions and attitude). These issues reflect dualisms of the Italian scenario: mainly between small and medium large firms; southern and northern areas of the country; manufacturing and service sectors.

Successful collective bargaining and concertation over flexibility is therefore by no means general; cases of non-regulated areas have developed side by side (particularly at the periphery of the system) with collectively regulated enterprises and areas.

On the whole however one can say that a more collaborative-coordinated approach to the flexible use of manpower is gaining ground. For example, flexible forms of work time and wages (particularly productivity bonuses) have become a rather common subject of enterprise bargaining after 1985.

The positive attitude of the unions in this respect is favoured by another peculiar aspect of Italian legislation: namely that the trend toward flexibilization has not touched the traditional protection of employees from unfair or unjustified dismissals. The legal restrictions on employers' power to discharge have resisted all attacks during these years: on the contrary the protection of dismissals has been partially extended also to small units by a 1990 Act.

C.1 Working Time

The general statutory discipline goes back to Act No. 692 of March 1923, which provides that the hours worked by employees must not exceed eight a day or 48 a week. Since 1973 most national collective agreements have introduced the 40 hour (and five day) week.

The 1983 trilateral agreement indicated that a substantial reduction of working time was a major means to combat growing unemployment. But the results of the subsequent national round were rather disappointing for the unions: a reduction in annual working time ranging from 20 to 40 hours depending on sectors and previous regimes. In public service the standard working week is now 36 hours.

In the 1987 agreements, textile workers and metalworkers obtained a further reduction of 16 hours yearly for regular workers (12 for shiftworkers). In the banking sector the reduction was of 25 minutes a week which brings the weekly hours down to less than 38.

Many plant and enterprise agreements have provided for a more substantial reduction in weekly working time, often coupled to a new shift system in order to allow increased productivity and a more intensive use of machinery (for example, textile plants where a 36 hour week in the form of a six hour/six day shift system is widespread). Redistribution of working time on a multi-weekly basis (so called annualization) is provided for in quite a few national agreements.

The issue of working time was still controversial at the end of the 80s. It is the prime target of union action for the immediate future following the examples of other European labour movements starting with the FRG. Unions have declared they are ready to trade-off wage increases for reductions in regular working time, and willing to be more tolerant about overtime. Wage reduction has also been accepted in case of enterprise crisis. The problem remains conflictual given the resistance of employers who claim that the current annual working time in Italy is shorter than for most foreign competitors. In fact the actual working time is much lower than that fixed in collective agreements. If one takes into account annual vacations and holidays, the official number of yearly hours in industry amounts to about 1750.

The daily distribution of working hours is generally decided by management, after consultation with the plant unions representatives. On the other hand, the employer does not have the power to unilaterally reduce an employee's working hours with a proportional reduction in wages. In practice, the possibilities of reducing working hours allowed by Italian law always require the consensus of the unions and of the worker concerned. The transformation of any full-time employment relationship into a part-time relationship is subordinate to a direct agreement between the (individual) parties, ratified by the provincial Labour Office.

From a quantitative point of view part-time work in Italy is much less relevant than in most parts of Europe. An ISTAT research shows that in 1986 in Italy there were only 692,000 part-time contracts on a total amount of about 15 millions of employees (4.6 %). About 50 % of these contract were in agriculture, and about 58 % were relative to temporary works. Nevertheless the situation is slowly changing. In fact (Minister of Labour data) from 1987 to 1990 there have been about 650,000 new part-time contracts (23 % in industry and 76 % in services), in a period of relative stability of the total employment.

The permanent reduction of the working hours normally performed in a given sector, following the stipulation of a solidarity contract,[7] must be agreed upon at plant level by the trade unions belonging to the most representative confederations.

Traditionally overtime has been widely used; with collective agreements making it compulsory (while the law declared it optional). In the 70s most collective agreements begun to explicitly limit the total amount of overtime (usually to 150 hours per year) and to strictly control the observance of this maximum. However this policy has been under heavy attack by employers as contributing to excessive rigidity in the use of manpower. In the last bargaining round these demands were partly accepted by the labour unions. In some agreements a more flexible use of overtime has been granted, at least within certain maximum limits: e.g. the national metal-workers' agreement now provides a maximum of 2 hours a day, 8 a week with an annual total of 150 hours per worker. For firms with less than 200 employees the annual total is set at 200 hours and for maintenance and installation activities it is increased to 210 hours. The employer is usually obliged to inform the local union delegate of overtime in advance at a special meeting (i.e. after bargaining).

Table 5. Percentage Weight of Overtime on Working Hours (Large Firm Workers)

	Textile	Mechanical	Chemical	Manufacturing
1973	4.0	4.7	1.6	4.4
1973	3.6	4.3	1.6	3.9
1973	2.4	2.7	1.1	2.5
1976	2.5	2.8	1.3	2.6
1977	2.6	2.8	1.2	2.6
1978	2.3	2.7	1.4	2.5
1979	2.5	2.8	1.6	2.7
1980	2.5	3.3	1.5	3.0
1981	1.9	2.9	1.3	2.7
1982	2.0	2.7	1.5	2.5
1983	1.8	3.0	1.7	2.7
1984	2.3	3.3	2.0	3.1
1985	2.3	3.6	2.6	3.3
1986	2.1	4.3	2.9	3.9
1987	2.4	4.5	2.9	4.0
1988	2.3	4.9	3.4	4.4

Source: Istat.

7. Solidarity contracts (job-security/job-creation agreement) are company agreements which, in order to avoid collective dismissals, redundancies or lay-offs because of a labour surplus or overstaffing, or in order to permit the hiring of new personnel, provides for a reduction in the working hours and pay of all the company's employees.

Recently the agreements have given management a certain number of hours of overtime at its disposal which it need not make known to trade unions: 32 hours annually for shift workers and for all employees in firms with over 200 employees, 40 hours for firms with less than 200 employees (see Table 5).

C.2 Wages

The Italian wage structure has been rather rigid until 1984-'85, due mainly to the predominant weight of the escalator clause. Here too major innovations in the direction of flexibility have been recently introduced, mostly in the private sector. The indexation system has been slowed down (and in part differentiated) through tripartite agreements and legislation. Currently it offers total protection from cost of living increases up to a wage level of 850.000 lire monthly (580 Ecu approx.); which means roughly 50 % of the average industrial wage (see Tables 6 and 7).

In this respect the Italian escalator clause guarantees a sort of real minimum wage. Its coverage is *de facto* generalized to all employees, at least in the official market. But a legislation on minimum wage in a proper sense would still be useful, particularly for peripheral and atypical workers.

Seniority wage increases have been largely "frozen" by collective agreements and the seniority allowance[8] (due at the end of employment contracts) has been softened.

Occupational wage differentials, which had reached a minimum in the period 1975-'85 as a result of a strong indexation (equal for all employees) began to increase after 1983. This is a result both of a reappraisal of job classification schemes in the major collective agreements and of an increasing role of individual bargaining, particularly for the upper levels of white collars and "cadres" who are hardly represented by traditional labour unions. Wage differentials by sectors have also grown, and even more so by size of enterprise (see above).

In the private sector an increasing interest is being shown for new types of incentives: not so much piece rate as premiums and productivity bonuses. The typology of these bonuses varies according to the indicators adopted (individual and group labour productivity, quantitative and qualitative parameters of production) and to the collective or individual regulation of their distribution (individual premiums are becoming a major instrument of Human Resource Management particularly for upper levels of employees).

---

8. The seniority allowance is a payment made by the employer to the employee whenever an open-ended contract of employment is terminated. This sum is now equal to one month salary per year of service.

Table 6. Average Monthly Earnings and Hours per Head (%)

	Average monthly earnings			Hours of work per head			Average hourly earnings		
	1986	1987	1988	1986	1987	1988	1986	1987	1988
Total industry	7.9	8.1	9.3	3.2	1.6	2.8	4.5	6.4	6.3
Energetic	9.8	3.5	7.7	-0.5	-0.5	-2.7	10.3	4.0	10.6
Textile	5.2	8.1	6.7	0.1	2.6	2.2	5.1	5.3	4.4
Metal	5.5	7.0	6.4	-0.3	1.7	3.8	5.8	5.2	2.5
Electrical	7.4	8.6	9.3	1.8	0.0	3.6	5.6	7.6	5.5
Transport	10.6	11.3	14.3	13.1	3.8	6.1	-2.3	7.2	7.8
Chemical	7.4	7.1	6.7	3.7	2.2	1.2	3.6	4.9	5.5
Others	6.5	8.2	9.2	1.2	2.1	3.9	5.3	5.9	5.1

Source: Istat. Our elaboration.

Table 7. Earnings Structure in Some Sectors

1984	Manufact.	Agricult.	Banking sector	Trading sector	Insurance sector
Basic rate	33.3	32.4	36.6	31.7	39.1
Escalator clause	49.0	56.6	37.7	53.5	35.1
Seniority	5.0	6.8	11.5	6.1	14.0
Other elements	12.7	4.2	14.2	8.7	11.8
Gross earnings (before tax)	100.0	100.0	100.0	100.0	100.0

1988	Manufact.	Agricult.	Banking sector	Trading sector	Insurance sector
Basic rate	28.9	31.8	33.2	30.7	36.3
Escalator clause	45.6	57.8	35.8	54.4	33.2
Seniority	5.8	5.4	10.9	4.8	14.1
Other elements	19.7	5.0	18.1	9.9	16.4
Gross earnings (before tax)	100.0	100.0	100.0	100.0	100.0

Source: Istat.

The percentage of wages linked to indicators of productivity (in the wide sense) remains low: ranging from 5 % to 10 %. But the trend is clearly upwards. In the last bargaining rounds quite a few large enterprises, both private and state controlled, have distributed a large percentage of new wage increases in forms linked to productivity (up to 50 %). A few profit sharing experiments have been introduced by collective and individual bargaining, but their diffusion is limited due to the high risk for employees attached to them.

The wage structure is heavily affected by social security contributions and taxes. The former are among the highest in Europe in spite of the periodic reduction in contributions paid by the employers. The level of taxes is in the European average, but recent researches demonstrate that erosion and evasion are particularly high. At the beginning of 1989 unions obtained the automatic neutralization of fiscal bracket creep, which drastically reduced employees purchasing power and contributed to distorting wage differentials (particularly to the detriment of upper level wage earners).[9]

9. During the 80s the combined effect of fiscal drag and social security tax relief for employers was to transfer a certain amount of resources from wages to profit which facilitated the recovery in investments, Giavazzi & Spaventa (1989), "Italy. The real effects of inflation and disinflation", *Economic Policy*, n. 8; Brunetta, R. & Tronti, L. For a new incomes policy, in: Treu, T. (ed.) (1992), *Participation in public policy making*, Berlin, De Gruyter.

C.3 Fringe Benefits

Fringe benefits are scarcely analyzed by researchers, also due to the fact that they are usually not bargained collectively. They are administered very "discretely" by employers to maximize their "selective" value and to escape taxation. In fact, the courts have decided that most of these fringe benefits have lost their traditional nature of "liberality" and should be considered extra wage. Therefore they should be affected by ordinary social security benefits and taxation. But all kind of efforts are directed to avoid this definition, by disguising them as "reimbursement of expenses" or as "employment tools": e.g. in the case of telephone bills, house rents, free cars, transfer allowance, research allowance, study tours, professional insurance.

All estimates indicate that fringe benefits are expanding, particularly for middle-higher level employees, and have become a major instrument of selective Human Resource Management in addition to wage differentiation. A most important area of fringe benefits relates to supplementary pensions and insurance bargained both on an individual and collective basis. Old age pension plans are being bargained unilaterally by firms, particularly in some sectors (banking, insurance) and for upper level employees, in order to protect the beneficiaries against the shaky conditions of public social security and to improve on public pensions. These however are rather generous, at least on paper: 2 % of wage per year of service up to a maximum of 80 % for 40 years of service.

Supplementary insurance in case of accident, occupational or not, is becoming increasingly common in the same categories as above. So is health insurance, mainly directed to provide specialized medical care and private hospitalization as an alternative to the poor services provided by the National Health System.

The development of these private insurances (both individual and collective) is widely advocated but it is still curbed by their uncertain legal status and rather unfavourable fiscal treatment (no uniform regulation exists on the functioning of voluntary pension funds).

C.4 Termination of Labour Contracts

As indicated above job security is traditionally well taken care of by Italian law. The basic substantive requirements are similar to those common in most countries. Just cause or justified reason are necessary to legally exercise the power to discharge. Control is stricter than in most other countries: Article 18 of Act No. 300/1970 empowers courts to order reinstatement with back pay of unjustly discharged employees. The employer who does not abide by the court order is obliged to pay regular wages until actual reinstatement, particularly in given areas of the country, where the discharged employees cannot easily find another job.

The effectiveness of this provision has been considerable; in some respect greater than expected. First of all it is quite frequent that a judge orders reinstatement; secondly, recent research indicates that over 40 % of court orders are followed by actual reinstatement (particularly in some areas of the country, where the discharged employees cannot easily find another job).

The rigidity of these provisions was however "compensated" by their limited coverage. According to Act No. 300 they don't apply to units occupying less than 16 employees – 6 in agriculture; to firms employing less than 35 employees courts can only grant an indemnity to unjustly discharged employees.

Given the fragmented structure of the Italian economy, this limitation of coverage excludes a considerable percentage of the workforce (over 1/3); an additional confirmation of the dual nature of the Italian labour market. For this reason it has been repeatedly challenged, lately with success. Under the pressure of a referendum to abrogate this limitation, an Act has been passed extending to employees of small units (at least) monetary compensation in case of unjust dismissal (May 11, 1990, No. 108).

This law doesn't consider collective dismissal, which reflects the traditional view that external controls of the grounds for collective dismissals are incompatible with the discretionary powers of the employer in a free enterprise system to assess the economic requirements of the enterprise. However, courts have always held that an individual dismissed following a decision to reduce the workforce is entitled under Act No. 604 and Act No. 300 to appeal to the court, as if his dismissal were an individual dismissal, for an alleged objective reason, to have its justification reviewed, at least after the conciliation procedure established by the agreement has failed.

The legislative and judiciary protection to workers in cases of collective dismissals has been reinforced by the practice of the parties and the administrative authorities who also tend to apply the principle that dismissals should be a measure of last resort.

Labour unions have been always very determined in protecting the volume of employment from reductions even more than in controlling hiring. That is true also in the last years when they have become less strict than before in regulating crew size, overtime etc. A set of defensive measures is usually directed to concentrate protection on the core labour force, to redistribute work among them and to favour a "soft" expulsion from the market of old workers.

Recruitment freeze, overtime reduction and internal transfer are the first and easiest measures adopted, usually through collective bargaining. Rotation in lay-off and work time reduction follow: in particular the second became a major union demand advanced not only in Italy with different aims (in practice it has been more effective in reducing the impact of reduced employment on the existing workforce than in redistributing over a wider area of the workforce).

Early retirement has been also widely used; subsidized both by law Act No. 115 of 1968 and Act No. 683/1984, and by employers. The ordinary retirement age of 60 (women have the option to retire early, up to 55) has been reduced: male workers of 57, female workers of 52 who have been dismissed because of a duly ascertained local or sectoral economic crisis or because of the industrial restructuring and reorganization of the enterprise (such as would authorize extraordinary wage guarantee payments) are entitled to a special indemnity equal to the length of service pension if they have paid contributions for at least 15 years. Extraordinary legislation has been enacted for the steel industry, permitting early retirement for employees over 50 years of age (Act No. 863/1984).

An important measure to prevent collective lay-offs and dismissals is the above mentioned Wage Guarantee Fund. During the 70s the use of the Fund has been progressively extended in most respects: in the conditions of intervention (not only temporary enterprise difficulties, but also sectoral or local economic crisis, industrial restructuring, reorganization or reconversion in case of a crisis having particular social importance, even though of definitive nature); beneficiaries (originally limited to blue collar workers in industry, the Fund has been partially extended to white collars and other sectors); compensation (which has been unified at 80 % of the gross pay for the hours not worked); duration (originally limited to 13 weeks, it has been prolonged to nine months, and in the case of enterprise reorganization, for an indefinite period of time, e.g. as long as the reorganization lasts), under authorization of the competent ministerial authority. Authorizations have been granted rather automatically, with the consent and under the pressure of both social parties. In fact they usually found recourse to the Fund the easiest solution, in so far as it allows the enterprise flexibility in the amount of workforce employed, at practically no cost for the enterprise itself and the employees concerned.

Following this legal extension and the rather lenient practice, during the 70s the Fund became the major instrument of public protection for workers' income *vis-à-vis* the industrial crisis and, indirectly, for job security. In each case of termination moreover employees receive a seniority allowance now equal to one month salary per year of service. This mechanism has been criticized but well accepted by both employees and employers (who use the funds as a source of self financing).

In case of dismissal for economic sectorial crisis employees receive, instead of the ordinary unemployment benefits which are very low (20 % of regular wage), an extraordinary benefit equal to 80 % of the wage for 6 months.

D. Conclusions

Flexibility is the focal point around which we can begin to draw some conclusions, and it stands out as the foremost issue for future research. The 1980s[10] were characterized by an effort at dismantling the excessive guaranteeism in the mechanisms regulating the labour market. Greater flexibility in manpower management, both at the macro-economic level and at the single company level, has been the leitmotif of recent labour legislation. This chapter argues that the changes in the legislative picture have affected labour relations by leading to an increase in market transactions over regulated and coordinated ones.

There are at least three reasons why it is difficult to measure the social effects of these changes using a traditional Paretian welfare function:

- first of all because the changes are accompanied by massive redistribution;[11]
- second of all because the new types of contract increasingly contain implicit clauses which make it problematic to assign costs and benefits both individually and socially;
- lastly because the flexibilization process is taking place in a dynamic and evolving context, so that the identification of winners and losers and the determination of adjustment costs is not absolute but needs to be reformulated at every step of the transformation.

Consequently, one way to make a tentative evaluation of this process could be to adopt an institutionalist approach, comparing the advantages and costs of an administered mechanism to the advantages and costs of a pure market one. This comparison can be effected at two levels: at the macro level focusing on the labour market and at the micro-economic level focusing on corporate competitiveness.

At the macro level the issue can be examined from three angles:

1) Economic dualism, especially manifest in Italy as a regional gap. From the macro-economic standpoint, flexibilization has increased the dualism between North and South and between areas of rapid economic growth and marginal

---

10. For a general overview on labour policies in Italy during the 1980s see Neri, F. (ed.) (1989), *Le politiche del lavoro negli anni '80*, Milano, Angeli.

11. Rossi, N. 1990, "Benessere disuguaglianza e povertà nell'Italia del secondo miracolo economico (1973-1987)", *Politica ed Economia*, VI, n. 1, April.

ones: unemployment has increased in traditional problem areas and decreased in traditionally strong ones.[12]

2) The other face of economic dualism is the segmentation of the labour market.[13] Most likely only the stronger segment of the labour market has benefited from the flexibilization process. Flexibilization, in fact, does not appear to open communication channels between the various segments of the labour market. Furthermore, a correct evaluation should take into account segregation by sex, skill, and race. Among other things, the most evident problems of segregation (women, workers in small firms) have been addressed through the re-introduction of ad hoc regulatory mechanisms.
Finally it must be pointed out that, generally speaking, flexibilization does not improve the long-term effects of unemployment which continue to be self-reinforcing.[14]
3) It is hard to say whether or not deregulation has improved the traditionally low capacity of the Italian system to respond to external shocks – especially in terms of import-export balance – or whether the current picture is due to a long period of favourable economic conditions which is coming to a close.

At the micro-economic level, the 1980s were characterized by a rebound in company profits and productivity.[15] Labour surplus turned out to be less than expected and an overall stock adjustment was effected. Costs deriving from irrevocable or uncorrectable choices dropped (less sunk costs), bringing many advantages in terms of competitiveness, an especially gratifying effect in view of European unification.

But this process should be measured not counting the distortion caused by the favourable economic expansion. In fact at the first signs of slowdown the economy shows a labour surplus which clearly underlines the limits of the flexibilization process and, consequently, the need to reactivate the usual dumper measures, as:

---

12. Wolleb, E. & Wolleb, G. (1990), *Divari regionali e dualismo economico*, Bologna, il Mulino; M. D'Antonio, Sviluppo economico e rididstribuzione: il caso del Mezzogiorno, in: Cimoli, M. & Musu, I. (ed.) (1990), *Cambiamento strutturale e asimmetrie nell'economia italiana*, Milano, Angeli.

13. Tronti, L. (1990), "Protezione dell'occupazione e segmentazione del mercato del lavoro: i 30 anni della Cassa Integrazione Guadagni", *Economia & Lavoro*, n. 3.

14. OECD (1988), *Measures to Assist Long-Term Unemployed: Recent Experiences in Some OECD Countries*, Paris, OECD; Ricciardi, L. (1991), "La disoccupazione di lunga durata in Italia, una analisi dell'evidenza empirica nel periodo 1977-1989", *Economia & Lavoro*, n. 2.

15. Abbate, C. & Piacentini, P. (1990), "Costi e margini nell'industria italiana degli anni '80", *Economia & Lavoro*, n. 3; Filippi, E. & Varetto, F. (1989), "Fattori nominali e fattori reali nella dinamica dei profitti industriali negli anni '80", *Finanza, imprese e mercati*, n. 2; Signorini, L.F. (1991), *Grandi e piccole imprese negli anni '80: la ristrutturazione dell'industria in un'analisi dei dati di bilancio*, Banca d'Italia, "Temi di discussione", n. 157, August.

- direct state intervention to reallocate redundant workers;
- widening the field of application of early retirement;
- increased use of the Wages Guarantee Fund);
- renewed risk of using public employment as a welfare mechanism.

Labour Market Contracts and Institutions
J. Hartog and J. Theeuwes (Editors)

CHAPTER 12

THE U.K.:
Labour Market Institutions, Law and Performance

John T. Addison* and W. Stanley Siebert**

A. Introduction

The British industrial relations system stresses 'voluntary' collective bargaining: "In no major country in the world has the law played a less significant role in the shaping of industrial relations than in Great Britain" (Kahn-Freund, cited in Salamon, 1987, p. 219). Thus, for example, with the exception of a brief interval following the 1971 Industrial Relations Act, collective agreements have never been legally enforceable in Britain. There is therefore no labour court apparatus; and no codetermination law enforcing works councils or workplace consultation. Similarly, there is no system providing for union recognition.

Nevertheless, Britain has a strong and well established system of trade unionism and for most of the present century approximately one-half of the workforce has been organized into unions. In addition to their workplace strength, unions have also sponsored Members of Parliament and have been the major source of funds for the Labour Party. They have therefore been able to influence the legal framework defining individual contracts (e.g. dismissal rules and minimum wages) as well as determining collective contracts through the bargaining process.

In what follows, we preface discussion of the nature of collective bargaining and the legal framework with information on the organization of employees and employers. Our discussion of the legal framework incorporates the major changes in the law relating to strikes, union democracy, the closed shop, and union recognition that have occurred since 1979. The focus then shifts from institutions to 'outcomes', along the dimensions of working time, wages, and fringes, and termination of labour. A concluding section addresses the controversial issue of changes in union power during the Thatcher period and productivity performance.

* University of South Carolina and Universität Münster.

** University of Birmingham.

B. The Institutional and Legal Environment

B.1 Collective Bargaining Structure

(a) Trade union membership

The dominant features of the time series of union membership in the post-war period, are, first, an increase in density during the 1970s over an interval that corresponds to the Labour government's "social contract" with the unions and, second, a steep fall in density since 1980. Union density among employees according to the Labour Force Survey of 1990 is 38 % (Employment Gazette, 1992, 188); the comparable 1979 figure, at the height of union strength, would have been about 56 %. Carruth and Disney (1988) have analyzed the determinants of union membership over the sample period 1896-1984 using a fairly conventional business cycle model. They report that union density is negatively related to real wage growth and the rate of unemployment. In addition, they find a moderate political party effect: a Labour rather than a Conservative government is associated with an increase in density of 2.5 percentage points per administration.

An altogether stronger 'political' effect is reported by Freeman and Pelletier (1990) in their analysis of union density over just the post-war (1945-85) period. The authors develop a subjective index of industrial relations laws – coded 5 when the laws were most favourable to unions down to 1 when they were least favourable – which variable dominates cyclical and structural arguments (*inter alia*) as a determinant of union density. Specifically, the cumulative effect of changes in the law between 1980 and 1986 is to reduce union density by 9.4 percentage points, or practically the entire fall in density observed over this interval. Left unanswered in this treatment, however, is the question of whether the laws themselves are exogenous. Also, of course, the weight to be placed on a subjective index, though certainly more innovative than the usual political regime dummy, is an issue of great controversy and one heightened by the fragility of conventional models of union determination (Hirsch and Addison, 1986, Chapter 3).

We note that neither study includes a measure of foreign competition. With the abolition of exchange controls in 1979, the effects of foreign competition would have been sharpened. Unions frankly do not do well in competitive environments, some broad indication of which is provided by their resistance to privatization schemes. In other words, enhanced competition may be expected to have contributed in part to the decline of union density in the 1980s.

Union membership by various demographic characteristics is documented in Table 1. The main body of the table refers to the private sector, but the final column gives overall density measures for the U.K., that is, also including the public sector.

Table 1. Percentage of Private Sector Wage and Salary Employees Belonging to Labour Union, 1983

	Blue collar	White collar	Total inclusive of government
All employees	48	22	49
Sex:			
Male	53	26	56
Female	39	19	40
Race:			
Non-white	63	19	63
White	48	22	49
Age:			
under 25	32	19	36
25-44	51	21	50
45-54	58	25	56
55 or over	56	14	56
Education:			
Less than high school graduate	50	21	51
High school, no post school	46	21	45
Some post high school education	52	27	53
Region:			
North	56	27	57
Midlands & S.W.	49	23	47
Wales & Scotland	54	27	59
London & S.E.	38	17	40
Industry:			
Agriculture	12	5	13
Mining	69	17	89
Construction	28	9	33
Manufacturing	68	31	57
Transportation & communication	48	30	74
Wholesale & retail trade	25	15	20
Finance and insurance	38	29	32
Service	10	22	58

Source: General Household Survey, 1983

The pattern of union density can be explained in terms of the fact that unions organize where it is economically profitable to do so, given the law. For example, it is rarely profitable to organize in small firms because such firms face higher competition, and also have higher labour turnover. Thus the U.K. has a strong union density gradient by firm size. The fact that women and young workers typically are under-represented in the bigger firms in part explains their lower levels of organization. Note that all categories of worker in Britain, including managerial workers, are protected by the system of trade union immunities [see section B.3]. This explains the relatively high levels of white-collar unionization and also why it is that less educated workers are not more highly unionized than highly educated workers.

(b) Union structure

Currently, Britain has about 300 organizations that are required to file their accounts with the Trade Union Certification Officer. Some 230 unions have 'certificates of independence', indicating an absence of 'employer domination' in the eyes of the Certification Officer. Each year the number decreases as unions amalgamate; 20 years ago there were twice as many unions as today. Most union members are located in a few large general unions. The top 6 unions between them have over 5 million members, approximately one-half of all union membership (Employment Gazette, 1992, 186).

Because British trade unions have developed uninterrupted over a long period of time, there is no 'order' to the movement. The large unions are represented in every industry. At the same time there are some pure industrial unions (such as the National Union of Mineworkers), as well as many small occupational and craft unions. Consequently, many firms, especially if they are large, recognize and negotiate with several unions. This problem of 'multi-unionism' was analyzed at length by the Donovan Commission (1968, paras lll ff., and 1074 ff.).

The extent of multi-unionism can be gauged from the 1990 Workplace Industrial Relations Survey (WIRS). Of those firms recognising manual (non-manual) unions some 34 (55) percent recognized more than one union (Millward *et al.*, 1992, pp. 48, 79). A 1979-80 Confederation of British Industry (1988, p.27) study reported that 63 percent of manufacturing firms recognized two or more unions, and that plants with over 1,000 employees averaged 4.6 unions per plant. The 1990 WIRS gives a similar figure a decade later, so the problem continues. The Donovan Commission (1968, para. 113) calculated that 80 percent of manual worker trade unionists worked in a multi-union establishment, and that up to one in six of these workers were in occupations in which two or more unions competed for members.

Two difficulties of multi-unionism were identified by the Commission. First, small groups of workers scattered over many factories meant that union officials had difficulty keeping in touch with their members. This strengthened workplace organization (the shop stewards) at the expense of the centre, and made unofficial strikes more likely. Second, demarcation issues were elevated in importance as unions defended their recruiting areas. This served to reduce flexibility. Typically production workers are not allowed to do maintenance jobs and one type of craftsman is not allowed to do the work of another type – though these restrictions do seem to have decreased in the 1980s (ACAS, 1989, 19). It was also argued that unions would be tempted to out-do each other in militancy (1968, para. 673). A third problem, not diagnosed by the Commission but important, is that multi-unionism makes negotiations and communications between management and workers more difficult. This factor might explain why strikes have been found to be more likely in multi-union workplaces, other things being equal (Millward and Stevens, 1986, pp. 71, 73). We note parenthetically that the multi-unionism phenomenon in Britain is to be distinguished from that in France and Belgium, for example, where it is defined along political/ideological lines. This bifurcation weakens the union movement and rules out the closed shop.

Multi-unionism lies at the root of recent firm initiatives to conclude single union deals. As yet such arrangements do not cover many workers; only 25,000 according to a recent estimate (Gennard, 1989, p. 249). However, the deals have caused great controversy amongst unions, leading to the expulsion of a major union – the Electrical, Electronic, Plumbing and Telecommunications Union (EEPTU) – from the Trades Union Congress in 1988. The first single union deal seems to have been struck between Toshiba and the EEPTU in April 1981 (Bassett, 1986, p. 125), but since then most of the major Japanese companies have been involved as well as companies from the U.S., Sweden, and Norway. The difficulty for unions in such deals is that the single union recognized in the agreement is forced to organize jobs which have traditionally been the property of other unions, a practice termed "cannibalism" by its opponents in the union movement.

Single union agreements also offer an opportunity for Japanese-style consensus management. The package usually includes a no-strike clause (substituting final offer arbitration), reduced differentiation between salaried and hourly paid employees, a system of employee communication and consultation via an enterprise council with representatives from all sections, and labour flexibility backed up by effective training and re-training (see Fox, 1987).

However, the Japanese consensus approach – which logically extends to company-based unions – is quite alien to the British industrial relations tradition. In keeping with this tradition, as noted, a union has to be officially certified by the Trade Union Certification Officer as independent of employer influence. Only independent trade unions have legal privileges including the right to call strikes, and the right not to have their members victimized. The Certification Officer also administers monies paid to trade unions to finance their strike and other ballots.

(c) Employers' Associations

About 15 percent of British firms currently belong to employers' associations, down from 30 percent 10 years ago (Millward *et al.*, 1992, p. 46). The proportions range from about 30 percent of firms in engineering to 10-15 percent in services, and thus broadly parallel the level (and decline) of union density in the various industries. In 1986 the Trade Union Certification Officer had about 300 employers' associations on his list, with 314,000 member companies.

In the British context, the employers' association fulfils two roles: first, to represent the management side in collective bargaining (see next section) and, second, to give advice in the resolution of disputes between the employer and the union. In fact, the role of the employers' association in the disputes procedure is older than the collective bargaining aspect; for example, the "Provision for the Avoidance of Disputes" in engineering dates from 1898. A traditional aspect of disputes procedures is to have arbitration by the employers' association as the final step. In practice, however, the official arbitration and conciliation machinery [see B.3(e)] seems to be used twice as often to resolve disputes as the association (Millward and Stevens, 1986, Table 7.6).

Evidence from the Workplace Industrial Relations Survey (WIRS) indicates a trend towards more formal procedures in recent years, even among non-union firms (Millward and Stevens, 1986, Chapter 7). This greater formalization presumably reflects heightened legal intervention in the employment field, particularly in the dismissals area (9 percent of firms in the 1990 WIRS had an industrial tribunal case over dismissals in the previous year) (Millward *et al.*, 1992, p. 202). Greater formalization could give a residual role to employers' associations, in provision of legal advice (the Engineering Employers' Federation, for example, has a consultative group made up of the personnel directors of its members). Consultation of an employers' associations has declined, however, over the last decade and their place seems increasingly to have been taken by lawyers (Millward *et al.*, 1992, p. 47).

B.2 The Nature of Collective Bargaining

(a) National collective bargaining

National wage agreements are quite widespread in Britain (though coverage is declining – see below). Whether national agreements are a good or bad thing has been much debated. The government has noted that "national pay rates tend to be set in the light of labour market conditions in the prosperous South-East", and has sought "greater regional pay differentiation" (Financial Times, 12 November 1986). Others have called for more national bargaining, and even for its extension to Swedish-type corporatism (Metcalf, 1986, p. 13) with centralized wage bargaining, no ratification of wage agreements at local level (thereby limiting the independence of shop stewards), and tight organization of employers. The Donovan Commission also seemed to call for such corporatism. It identified two systems of industrial relations, one formal and the other informal. The formal system was that established by industry-wide bargaining; the informal system resulted from that "bargaining which takes place within factories (and) is largely outside the control of employers' associations and trade unions" (1968, para. 1010). In the latter system it saw "a tendency of extreme decentralization and self government to degenerate into indecision and anarchy ..." (para. 1018). The Commission wished to extend the formal system.

The debate as to whether a competitive or a corporatist bargaining structure would be better has continued. Arguably a corporatist solution was attempted by the Labour government under the 1974-79 Social Contract experiment, whereby unions agreed to practise incomes restraint in return for pro-union legislation and an increase in welfare benefits, the so-called "social wage". Eventually, incomes restraint failed, ushering in a period in which competitive rather than collectivist solutions have been put forward.

It can certainly be argued that unemployment differences between regions are so large that the same (or approximately the same) wage should *not* pertain in all regions. A simple correlation between the unemployment rate by region (10 regions with an unemployment rate spread of 8.6 to 16.3 percent) and regional male manual standard weekly wage rates for 1986 yields a correlation coefficient of approximately zero (−.025). When we include overtime pay, the market is seen to have more effect: the coefficient increases (in absolute value) to −.37. However recent work by Elliott and Hemmings shows that pay for (unskilled male) manual workers who are covered by national wage agreements is no more unresponsive to local unemployment than is pay for uncovered workers (Elliott and Hemmings, 1991, 67). Thus while it might be thought that if competition were encouraged, wages would fall in areas of higher unemployment, thereby bidding workers back into employment, the situation is more complex than that. However at least for women, those who are not covered by national wage agreements have pay which is significantly more responsive to local labour market conditions than those who are covered, which is more as expected (*ibid.*, 68).

Figures on the extent of national bargaining are contained in Tables 2 and 3. Looking first at Table 2 (relating to establishments), it is evident that national level bargaining is much more prevalent for the public sector, as might be expected. Since the public sector (central and local government, plus public utilities) employs about 30 percent of the workforce, it would seem that the problem of national bargaining, if problem it is, lies mainly in that sector.

Table 2. Basis for Most Recent Pay Increases, 1980 and 1990

Type of Agreement	(Proportion of establishments in each sector) Public Sector				Private Sector			
	Manual		Non-Manual		Manual		Non-Manual	
	1980[a]	1990[b]	1980[c]	1990[b]	1980[a]	1990[b]	1980[a]	1990[b]
National	58	61	79	69	23	14	9	7
Company	18	15	15	14	10	13	9	13
Plant	–	1	–	–	15	12	8	6
No collective bargaining	23	22	6	16	51	62	73	74

Sources: a Daniel and Millward (1983), p. 181;
b Millward *et al.* (1992), pp. 221, 228, 232;
c These are estimates based on Millward *et al.* (1992), assuming that public sector establishments constituted the same proportion of the total in each category in 1980 as 1990.

There seems to have been a decline in the extent of national bargaining in the 1980s. Some data are given in Table 3. The central column shows that by 1990 between 27-30 % of the workforce were covered by national agreements only, a 10 to 13 point decline from the 1985 figure. A major fall has been in the private sector – in particular the large national agreement negotiated for engineering, which covered about one million workers directly or indirectly was suspended in November 1989. The CBI has also found, for a matched sample of large private firms, that over 70 % of the sample negotiated pay at the establishment level in 1986, compared with only 58 % in 1979 (CBI, 1988, Table 57). National bargaining seems to have remained extensive in the public sector however – though with ending of collective bargaining for nurses (1984) and teachers (1989), the trend has been downward here, too (see particularly non-manual workers in Table 2).

Nevertheless, there is still a considerable degree of centralization in wage determination. The top twenty national agreements in the public and private sectors cover nearly 4 million workers, increasing to 6.5 million or one-quarter of the workforce when the eight principal wages councils are included. [Wages councils are discussed in C(d)]. Decentralization clearly has some way to go. By potentially increasing the responsiveness of wages to their underlying economic determinants, the move toward decentralization is broadly to be welcomed despite the allegation that it has increased the 'insularity' of insiders (Brown and Wadhwani, 1990, p. 67).

Table 3. Summary of Collective Agreement Coverage
(Coverage of Male and Female, Manual and Non-Manual taken together)

Percentage affected by:	National and company agreement	National agreement only	Company agreement only	No collective bargaining
1990	?	27-30[a]	?	36+6[b]
1985	13	40	11	36
1978	20	39	10	30
1973	22	42	10	28

Notes: [a] these figures taken from estimates of national agreement coverage as reported in *Times Rates of Pay and Hours of Work*
[b] this figure is approximate, and is obtained by allocating half of the 10-13 point decline in the 'national agreement only' category to the 'no collective bargaining category. Taking a weighted average of public and private, manual and non-manual from Millward *et al.* (1992, Tables 4.3, 7.6, 7.9) we also obtain 42 % as the estimated 1990 figure for no collective bargaining; their figure for national agreement coverage is 30 %, and the remaining 24 % pertains to plant/company agreements.

Source: Figures for 1973-1985 taken from *New Earnings Survey*

(b) Frequency of contract negotiations

Of the agreements monitored by the Confederation of British Industry (C.B.I.) pay databank, approximately 5 percent of post-1980 agreements have been of greater than one year's duration. In 1987, for example, some 7 percent of collective agreements in manufacturing industry extended beyond one year (Confederation of British Industry, 1987, p. 4). According to the 1990 WIRS, 95 % of collective bargains run for 12 months (Millward *et al.*, 1992, p. 241).

The C.B.I. has conducted a survey of long-term agreements in 35 companies employing 350,000 workers, and also in a number of employer associations (representing firms employing about 50,000 workers). The survey found that most of these agreements were of 2 years' duration and in the majority of cases held for the agreed length of time. (It must be remembered that British law does not recognize collective agreements as legally enforceable, so there is nothing to stop bargaining re-opening before the contract is due to expire.) There seems some trend for long-term contracts to be increasing in frequency, particularly where removal of restrictive practices and/or more flexible working arrangements are negotiated, so that a period of industrial relations stability is required. Not unnaturally there is also some evidence of union resistance to elimination of the annual pay round (Confederation of British Industry, 1987, pp. 12, 18).

(c) Content of collective bargains

National agreements are usually thought of as establishing minima which are to be supplemented at company level (Incomes Data Services, 1989b, p. 5). This is true particularly of the largest agreement, that for engineering. But there are also more comprehensive agreements. An example is that for manual workers in civil engineering construction. Here, firms agree to apply nationally agreed pay rates, particularly on large 'nominated' projects, and also bonuses, hours, holidays, sick pay, risk allowances, safety procedures, and apprenticeships schemes. Regional committees can vary the national agreement (Incomes Data Services, 1989b, pp. 4, 18).

Table 4. The Effectiveness of Multi-Employer Agreements in Private Manufacturing, 1979

Component	Percentage covered by multi-employer bargaining	Percentage for which actual terms and conditions within ± percent of agreement
Basic pay	47	20
Incentive pay	22	7
Overtime	52	49
Shift pay	44	42
Sick pay	19	9
Hours	53	52
Holidays	52	50

Source: Confederation of British Industry (1988), Table 17.

A question thus arises as to how loosely or closely national agreements are adhered to. A recent survey of manufacturing concluded that the effectiveness of multi-employer agreements is quite low, particularly among larger firms (Confederation of British Industry, 1988, p. 18). Some results are contained in Table 4. Thus, 47 percent of employees in firms in the sample had basic pay determined by a multi-employer agreement; but for only 20 percent of employees was their pay equal to or within 10 percent of the agreed terms. Even for hours and holidays, only about one-half of employees whose terms were determined by a multi-employer agreement actually stuck closely to that agreement. On the other hand, the low correlation between manual worker wage rates and unemployment at the regional level indicate that multi-employer agreements do matter. The lack of responsiveness of pay to economic determinants can only be produced if there is some force such as the national agreement overriding local conditions.

(d) The extent of negotiations over non-wage issues

Data from the Workplace Industrial Relations Surveys on bargaining over (some) non-wage conditions are summarized in Table 5, again based on management responses. The data do not identify the full extent of bargaining, but rather refer to the extent to which there is bargaining at some time over the issues. The most interesting aspect of the material, therefore, is the pattern of changes in the extent of bargaining over the issues identified between 1980 and 1990. Apparently there has been a decline in bargaining over non-wage issues, particularly redundancy and recruitment issues.

Table 5. Changes in Joint Regulation of Working Conditions and Employment, 1980-1990

(Proportion of establishments negotiating in each sector)				
Subject for Negotiation	Public Sector		Private Sector	
	1980	1990	1980	1990
Physical working conditions	95	86	87	70
Redeployment in establishment	90	65	70	56
Manning levels	82	74	65	35
Redundancy	93	35	83	55
Recruitment	73	38	58	21

Notes: Figures relate to establishments with recognized trade unions and refer to management's opinions of negotiations with the largest relevant bargaining unit. Responses for negotiations with manual and non-manual unions are averaged together.

Sources: Millward and Stevens (1986), pp. 248, 250; Millward *et al.* (1992), pp. 251, 252.

There is also industry bargaining over issues such as pensions and training. There are about 30 industry-wide pension schemes. Training agreements setting trainee wage rates and performance standards are to be found in printing, electrical contracting, and building. It is generally considered that such agreements, by setting too high a level of trainee wages, have contributed to the poor training record of the U.K. (Siebert, 1990; Prais and Wagner, 1988).

National procedural agreements backing up the terms and conditions negotiated at industry level are of course an integral part of the industry-wide arrangement. Any dispute over the interpretation of the agreement is referred to national officials of the unions and employers' associations concerned. For example, in the chemical industry (where the agreement covers about 350,000 workers) a Headquarters Conference is called if the dispute is not solved at local level. The procedure then calls for a 21-day cooling off period, after which interval the parties have the option to approach the Advisory Conciliation and Arbitration Service (ACAS) [see B.3(e)] for arbitration (Incomes Data Services, 1989b, p.9).

B.3 The Legal Structure of Collective Agreements

(a) Industrial action

There is no right to strike *per se* in Britain. Strikes constitute a breach of the *individual* contract of employment. That said, *trade unions* have, since the 1906 Trade Disputes Act, enjoyed immunities in respect of strikes and collective action undertaken in contemplation or furtherance of a trade dispute in that they cannot be sued for damages.

Following its accession to power in 1979, the Thatcher administration sought to narrow these immunities. The first step took the form of limitations on lawful secondary action. The 1980 Employment Act decreed that, to be legal, secondary action (in contemplation or furtherance of a trade dispute) had to put direct pressure on the employer in dispute. If such action merely damaged the secondary employer alone and did not affect the primary employer (a customer or supplier of the secondary employer), the union lost immunity and could be sued on grounds of breach of a commercial contract. The 1980 Act also addressed one aspect of secondary unionization by removing the immunity of employees at one company to 'black' the goods produced by a second company where the purpose of the action was to compel the second group of workers to join a particular trade union. Finally, the 1980 Act also removed immunity from secondary picketing – a worker is not allowed to picket another plant or site of his own employer let alone the premises of another employer. The immunity initially granted primary picketing under the 1906 Trade Disputes Act still obtains, provided that the picketing is peaceful and (in practice) constitutes no more than six pickets. Currently, as a result of the 1990 Employment Act, peaceful picketing would appear to be the sole form of 'secondary' action enjoying immunity.

In 1982 the government turned its attention to the wider organizational immunity granted trade unions. Under the 1982 Employment Act, in order to attract immunity a trade dispute had now to relate "wholly or mainly to" industrial relations matters rather than merely be "connected" with them. Moreover, the Act also narrowed the definition of a trade dispute itself: disputes between "workers and their employers" alone were to constitute trade disputes afforded immunity under the law. As a result, political strikes, inter-union disputes, and actions lacking a specific employer focus lost immunity. The 1982 Act also provided that unions could be held liable for unlawful acts authorized or endorsed by a "responsible person" within the union. This action represented an important dilution of union immunities but did not address unofficial action *per se*, a loophole closed by the 1990 Employment Act. Unions today can thus be held liable for unofficial industrial action unless they repudiate that action with a written individual notice to all members taking part.

In the next piece of legislation, the 1984 Trade Union Act, the policy focus shifted from the employer-union relation to that between the worker and his union. In the specific context of industrial action, the Act required that prior to official action being initiated (i.e. authorization or endorsement of a strike) a secret ballot of the membership be taken. If industrial action was taken without a ballot or, where a ballot was taken, without a majority voting in favour, the union would immediately lose its immunity in tort. All members who might be involved in the industrial action had to be balloted, the ballot had to be secret, and it had to be made clear on the voting paper that the industrial action being contemplated necessarily involved a breach of the contract of employment. The 1988 Employment Act gave members the right to apply for court orders to end official industrial action where this had been authorized without a secret ballot. A newly created Commissioner for the Rights of Trade Union Members was empowered to assist them in enforcement proceedings against the union in this and other matters (see below). The same Act also prevented unions from disciplining members who had failed to take part in a strike or who had indicated opposition to that action.

Where unions lose their immunity in tort by operating outside the new restricted range of immunities noted above, they become liable to injunctions and actions in damages. For unions with less than 5,000 members the maximum damages that can be awarded are £10,000, rising to £250,000 for unions with 100,000 or more members. Note that these maxima in principle obtain in respect of each affected party that joins the union, so that the scale of damages can well exceed the upper limit of £250,000; for example, in its 1984/84 dispute with the Stockport Messenger newspaper, the National Graphical Association was faced with claims of £3 million, although only £125,000 were actually awarded. Additionally, damages payable to workers held to have been unfairly dismissed for not belonging to a union can exceed £20,000 (see section C.3).

Note, finally, that the fines imposed for contempt of court – that is, where a union fails to obey a court injunction ordering it to desist from unlawful strike action – are not subject to any limits. Repeated disobedience can produce multiple fines and, in the limit, sequestration as happened to the National Union of Mineworkers during its 1984 strike.

(b) Union democracy

An important plank in the Conservative government's reform program has been to strengthen the individual member's rights *vis-à-vis* the union bureaucracy. The Employment Act of 1980 sought to encourage wider use of secret ballots in trade union governance by establishing a voluntary scheme to permit trade unions to request reimbursement from public funds for the cost of holding postal ballots of their members in such areas as union elections, including the election of shop stewards, and proposed strike activity. The 1984 Trade Union Act marked a more fundamental development by requiring direct secret elections of union executives every 5 years, and regular ballots (every 10 years) on whether unions should incur expenditures for political purposes. As we have seen, the Act also removed union immunity in tort where industrial action was taken without the prior approval of the membership.

Yet more fundamental changes were introduced under the 1988 Employment Act. Union members were for the first time given a direct right to inspect their union's accounting records. In addition, unions were not allowed to use their funds to indemnify officials or members in respect of criminal offenses or contempt of court (e.g. failure to observe an injunction pertaining to industrial action or secondary picketing). As regards elections, only postal (not workplace) ballots for the election of a union's principal executive committee were allowed. The balloting requirement was furthermore extended to all members of the union's principal executive committee, not just the voting members, and to the positions of general secretary or president. Unions also had to appoint an independent 'scrutineer' prior to any ballot. In contemplating and pursuing legal action to enforce any of their new statutory rights, members may receive assistance from the Commissioners for the Rights of Trade Union Members in the form of advice, legal representation, or the payment of legal costs.

(c) The closed shop

Closed shops have long been a controversial element of British trade union structure. In the pre-entry variant, a union controls the supply of labour to employers by restricting entry to those who hold the union's membership card prior to their application. Surveying workers themselves, about 1.3 million union members, say they to fall within this category (Employment Gazette, 1990, p. 3). A further 1.3 million workers say they belong to post-entry closed shops, where union membership is not a pre-condition of employment but, rather, is imposed subsequent to gaining employment. Thus, some 2.6 million workers be in some form of closed shop, down from 5 million in 1980. In 1990 only 4 % of establishments had a closed shop, compared to 20 % in 1984 - interestingly, however, in both 1984 and 1990 management in 15 % of establishments "strongly recommend" union membership (Millward *et al.*, 1992, p. 97).

Recent legislation has sought incrementally to erode the enforceability of the closed shop. First, in 1980 the Employment Act widened the grounds on which an individual was protected against dismissal under existing legislation and decreed that future union membership agreements would have to be approved by a ballot (requiring 80 percent support among those entitled to vote) to permit fair dismissals. Remedies were established for those unreasonably excluded from a union in closed shop situations. The 1982 Employment Act further increased the protection for non-unionists in a closed shop by making dismissals for non-membership automatically unfair had the union membership agreement not been approved by ballot within 5 years of the date of dismissal; and introduced a special system of remedies in respect of dismissals for non-membership, while extending the circumstances in which a union could be sued before an industrial tribunal.

Further curbs were placed on the closed shop under the 1988 Employment Act: first it became unlawful to take any form of industrial action to establish or maintain a closed shop; and, second, it was now automatically unfair to dismiss an employee for non-membership irrespective of whether or not the closed shop had been supported in a ballot. As a result, even though the closed shop is not illegal *per se* any action taken to enforce a union membership agreement is automatically unfair and hence actionable.

Finally, the 1990 Employment Act tackled the pre-entry closed shop, making it unlawful to refuse a person *access to* employment on the grounds of non-membership (or membership) of a union or his or her unwillingness to take steps to become a member (or disaffiliate) or to make payments in lieu of membership.

That said, the questions of whether the laws will do other than drive the closed shop underground is moot given that it is a matter of survival for many craft unions.

(d) Union recognition

The union recognition process in Britain has a basis not in law but rather in the ability of the union to organize labour at the place of work and ultimately to apply the sanction of industrial action. During the 1970s, however, a statutory procedure existed – first under the 1971 Industrial Relations Act and then via the 1975

Employment Protection Act – whereby a union could petition the Advisory, Conciliation and Arbitration Service (ACAS) that it be granted recognition from the employer. This procedure was repealed under the 1980 Employment Act. The same legislation also repealed another ACAS procedure whereby unions could petition for an extension of "recognized" terms and conditions achieved under collective bargaining to comparable workers (see below).

Analogously, the 1982 Employment Act forbad employers (e.g. local authorities) from requiring that contractors recognize, consult, or negotiate with trade unions or operate closed shops. The legislation thus sought to render void the keeping of "fair lists" (i.e. restricting the range of potential contractors to those firms operating closed shops or union firms more generally) and (union) "labour only" clauses. Today, therefore, a system of 'compulsory competitive tendering' obtains in Britain, at least in theory.

(e) Conciliation/Arbitration

The voluntary system of conciliation and arbitration in Britain dates from the 1896 Conciliation Act. During war-time intervals and their aftermath the voluntary system has, however, given way to compulsory arbitration. Thus, for example, formal compulsory arbitration machinery was in place from 1940 to 1959 and vestiges of this system persisted until 1980. First, under the Terms and Conditions of Employment Act 1959, appeal could be made to the Industrial Court (a standing arbitration body set up in 1919) in circumstances where employers were observing terms and conditions less favourable than those established by agreement or award for the relevant industry. Awards made by the Industrial Court became implied terms of the contract of employment for the workers concerned. Then, under the Employment Protection Act 1975, which replaced the previous system, this form of unilateral arbitration was extended to include claims based on the "general level of terms and conditions" for comparable employees of other employers in similar circumstances in the same industry and district.

As we have seen, this procedure was revoked under the 1980 Employment Act. Also as we have seen, the same Act repealed a parallel unilateral arbitration procedure whereby unions could seek recognition on the basis of a degree of employee support. And in 1983 the Fair Wages Resolution – legislation dating back to 1891 – requiring government contractors to observe terms and conditions not less favourable than those established under collective bargaining was abolished.

Today, therefore, one observes a purely voluntary conciliation and arbitration system, operated by the Advisory Conciliation and Arbitration Service (ACAS) which is formally independent of government. Its role is basically two-fold. First, it has the remit to upgrade industrial relations practice; for example, by issuing codes of conduct (e.g. the ACAS Code on Disciplinary Practices). Second, it is charged with the duty to help resolve disputes through conciliation or by providing a secretariat for arbitration, mediation, or committees of investigation.

Millward *et al.* (1992, pp. 194-196) have documented the ACAS role in industrial relations procedures. In terms of discipline and dismissals, they report that 15 percent of establishments with procedures for third-party intervention specified an ACAS route in 1990. This is about half the figure for 1980. (ACAS still has an important role in dismissals, however, since it conciliates all cases of unfair dismissal taken to Industrial Tribunals - see below.) With respect of disputes over pay and conditions, 31 percent of procedures calling for third-party intervention recognized an ACAS role. This is similar to the 1980 figure (35 %). This it seems that ACAS has remained important in disputes over pay, but not in dismissals. Dismissals procedures are becoming more formal in most companies, and management might see this as a better protection in an Industrial Tribunal hearing than conciliation.

C. Outcomes

C.1 Working Time

(a) Hours and holidays

In Britain there is no statutorily determined standard or maximum working week, unlike other EC countries (with the exception of Denmark) which provide for either a 40 or 48-hour week. Among principal collective bargaining agreements, agreed hours fall within the range of 35 to 40 hours per week (Incomes Data Services, 1989d, p. 5). The 1988 New Earnings Survey reveals that full-time adult males work 40.6 hours per week on average. Overtime amounts to roughly 3 hours, producing an average standard hours value of 38. A similar standard week obtains in respect of full-time adult females.

Likewise, these is no statutory entitlement to annual leave in Britain. This situation is again in sharp contrast with most other EC countries which have a statutory entitlement to 3 or 4 weeks. The main collective agreements allow 4 to 6 weeks annual holiday (Incomes Data Services, 1989e, p. 5). That said, such provisions would not apply to workers in small firms, or non-union firms, or part-time workers, most of whom would have no holiday entitlement. Since 20 percent of the British workforce is part-time and 40 percent in small firms with less than 100 employees (Siebert and Addison, 1990), the lack of a statutory holiday entitlement in principle allows employers greater flexibility.

(b) Restrictions on working time

No general statutory provisions apply in the areas of daily and weekly rest periods or night work. Restrictions on the working time *and* the employment of women were loosened under the Sex Discrimination Act of 1986 and the Employment Act of 1989. The latter legislation also lifted all restrictions on the hours of work of young people, including the prohibition on night work (dating from 1920). Such restrictions as remain in respect of both groups are those regulated on health and safety grounds. Note, more generally, that health and safety legislation ensures against excessive hours. The UK generally seems to have more flexible working hours than other EC countries. Thus 30 % (10 %) of UK male (female) full-time employees work more than 46 hours a week; the corresponding figure for the EC is 16 % (7 %) (Eurostat, 1991, Table 50).

Perhaps because of legal restrictions, shift working has in the past been much more important for men than women. According to the 1988 New Earnings Survey, 22 percent of males in manual occupations received shift premia, compared with only 12 percent of females. However, since most of male shift workers are in continuous process industries (e.g. chemicals, oil, and security services), while female shift workers are in different occupations (e.g. catering and nursing), it is doubtful whether relaxation of the law introduced under the 1989 Act will have much impact.

C.2 Wage and Fringes

(a) Wage components

According to the Survey of Labour Costs in 1984 (Employment Gazette, 1986, p. 213), gross wages and salaries contributed some 80 percent of total labour costs in manufacturing, construction, and distribution, and 75 percent of labour costs in the financial sector. The residual 20 to 25 percent mainly comprised statutory payroll taxes (namely National Insurance contributions), accounting for approximately 7 percent of total costs; pension and sick pay contributions, varying in magnitude from 5 to 14 percent of total costs in the manufacturing and financial sectors, respectively; and subsidized services such as canteens, housing, and transportation.

There has been a tendency for the wage and salary component of total labour costs to fall over time. In production industries (for which we have a time series), the share fell from 92 percent in 1964 to 84 percent in 1984. Part of this movement reflects a doubling in the burden of payroll taxes. (We note parenthetically that because such taxes do not apply to those earning less than a certain level of earnings, currently £45 a week, the rise in payroll taxes also accounts in part for the growth in part-time employees who avoid the tax by earning below the threshold value.) Part of the decline in the share of wages and salaries reflects an expansion in occupational pension schemes; amounting to 3 percent of total costs in 1964 but in excess of 5 percent in 1984.

Sick pay provision has also increased over time. A survey by the Department of Health and Social Security reveals that 90 percent of employees were covered by a sick pay scheme in 1988 as compared with 80 percent in 1974. Those most commonly excluded are part-timers working less than 30 hours per week. Small firms are also less likely to be covered: 50 percent of establishments employing fewer than 10 employees have no such scheme (Incomes Data Services, 1989a, p. 6). The typical arrangement tops up statutory sick pay – a scheme dating from 1983, whereby the state pays sick pay at levels similar to unemployment benefits – to normal earnings. Currently, 65 (53) percent of non-manual (manual) employees receive full pay during sickness. It appears that growth in coverage noted earlier was not caused by the introduction of the statutory scheme but was instead a device to attract staff.

Unemployment benefits last for 1 year in the UK, and are then replaced by social welfare payments (income support) which continue indefinitely. Benefits are payable after 3 waiting days if the job was lost involuntarily, but if the adjudication officer believes the job was "left voluntarily without just cause", or if the cause of dismissal was misconduct, a disqualification period of up to 26 weeks can be imposed. After 6 months of unemployment, a "Restart" interview will be scheduled (these began in 1986) and the individual will be questioned about job seeking activities, and possibly offered a place on a training scheme. Unemployment benefit is not payable while on strike, nor is it payable to part-timers if they earn more than £54 a week, nor is it payable to married women if they elect to pay reduced national insurance contributions (see LRD, 1992, 3-10). In general those under 18 would not be eligible either, since entitlement depends on national insurance contributions made over 2 years. The replacement ratio for a single person (gross benefits as % of "most relevant wage") is given by Layard *et al.* as 36 % – the lowest of all OECD countries apart from Italy (Layard *et al.*, 1991, 514). However, under the income support scheme, all of an individual's rent (or his/her mortgage interest if a house owner) is also payable (unless the individual has savings of over £3,000; also account is taken of pension and/or redundancy payments). This obviously increases the replacement ratio. In fact Layard *et al.* ascribe much of the increase in equilibrium unemployment in the UK in the 70s and 80s to the increased generosity of the unemployment benefit system, in particular the indefinite duration of benefit payments (*ibid.*, 448).

(b) Piece rates

About 40 percent of manual males and 30 percent of manual females receive some of their pay on a payments-by-result basis, according to the 1988 New Earnings

Survey (Department of Employment, 1988). These piece rate payments constitute between 10 and 15 percent of total pay (time-based pay constituting the next). The fraction of white-collar workers paid by such incentive schemes is less than one half that of blue-collar groups but, where operated, they contribute the same proportion of pay. The fraction of workers on piece rates has been falling steadily in recent years (Incomes Data Services, 1987a, 1989d).

(c) Profit sharing

There is little systematic evidence on the extent of profit sharing in the UK. Millward *et al.* (1992, pp. 262-266) information on profit sharing and *share-ownership* schemes. They report for 1984 that the proportion of British workplaces in industry and commerce where the parent company operated a profit sharing scheme had risen to 43 percent (from 18 percent in 1984). Actual participation in share-ownership averaged only 34 percent in 1990, higher than the 32 percent figure of 1984.

Share ownership is considered as a form of profit sharing and may indeed involve profit sharing in the mechanical sense. The following types of profit sharing may be identified. First, *cash-based profit sharing* in which a proportion of calculated profits is set aside and distributed to employees as a cash bonus have in the past not enjoyed tax concessions and therefore have been subject to PAYE (pay-as-you-earn tax deductions at source) and National Insurance deductions. However, as a result of the 1987 Finance Act, analogous schemes may be approved by the Inland Revenue to qualify for tax relief; so called "profit-related-pay" (PRP) in which a set proportion of pay is made to vary with profits. Under qualifying PRP schemes, for pay formally linked (in both directions) to the profits of the business, up to 10 percent of an employee's total pay or £2,000, whichever is the lower, can be free from tax in any one year.

Second, *executive (discretionary) share option schemes* have been somewhat more widespread in Britain than their broader based counterparts (on which more below). Since the 1984 Finance Act, such schemes have been exempt from tax if the share option is exercised between 3 and 10 years following its introduction.

Third, *savings-related share options schemes* (popularly known as SAYE or save-as-you-earn) were established under the 1980 Finance Act. Under qualifying schemes, employees save a monthly amount with a designated savings institution and simultaneously the company grants them an option to buy shares (generally at a 10 percent discount on the option price) at the end of the savings period. The lump-sum bonus (the value of the contribution after 5 years) may then be used to buy the shares or received in cash. Employees do not have to pay tax on any bonus or interest received, or capital gains on any increase in the value of the shares between the given option date and execution of the option.

Fourth, *approved deferred share trust (ADST) schemes* were the earliest form of profit sharing arrangement to enjoy tax advantages. Since the 1978 Finance Act, a company has been able to allocate profit to a trust fund which acquires shares in the company on behalf of employees who generally may not sell the shares during the first two years that they are held by the trust. Employees may then sell the shares. Their tax liability is reduced in line with the number of years that the shares are held, with zero liability after five years. Note that under so-called *mixed schemes* the employee is given a choice between taking the 'bonus' in cash or shares. No tax concessions attach to the former route.

Other profit sharing schemes are the *company share option*, whereby employees are given the option of purchasing shares typically at a marked discount, and *incentive schemes* based on added value or sales rather than productivity based measures. No tax advantages attach to either instrument.

Note that there has been little development of American-style employee stock ownership plans (ESOPs) in Britain: Incomes Data Services (1989c) report that just 14 firms have adopted this route to employee ownership, mostly in circumstances following management buy-outs. The lack of a statutory definition of an ESOP for tax purposes has in the past discouraged their adoption.

Baddon *et al.* (1987) report that of the 356 companies they examined almost two-thirds operated one of the variants discussed above. The incidence of the main profit sharing and employee share ownership schemes was as follows: cash-based, 31.0 %; executive share option, 22.9 %; SAYE, 21.9 %; incentives based on sales, 10.1 %; and ADST, 6.6 %. The schemes varied in coverage: cash-based profit sharing and ADST involved a much larger proportion of employees than did SAYEs. Larger companies (≥ 1,000 employees) were significantly more likely to operate share ownership than smaller companies although cash-based and incentive-based schemes were broadly distributed across all company size intervals. The authors report that, although 21 percent of the cases of profit sharing (n = 137) yielded a bonus amounting to more than 10 percent of pay, over 60 percent of the cases involved a bonus that made up less than 6 percent of pay. Similarly, the proportion of share capital owned by employees was small: in no less than 55 percent of the cases (n = 108) less than one percent of total shares issued belonged to employees. In no Inland Revenue approved schemes did this ownership level exceed 10 percent. Finally, the study reveals that profit sharing and employee share ownership are the most popular forms of employee 'participation' although there is seldom bargaining over these schemes (see also Smith, 1986, and Poole, 1989).

Evidence on the performance effects of profit sharing is mixed. Blanchflower and Oswald (1988), using data from the 1980 and 1984 Workplace Industrial Relations Surveys, find no evidence of positive effects on firm financial performance, holding constant firm size, stability of product demand, wage costs, and unionism, *inter alia* The authors also report little indication of any correlation between employment behaviour and profit sharing.

Rather more positive findings are reported in two studies of a sample of 52 British engineering firms, 1978-82. Estrin and Wilson (1986) find the effect of profit sharing is to *reduce* wages by some 3.8 percent. Positive *shifts* in employment are also found among profit sharing firms: employment is some 12.4 percent higher, other things being equal. Furthermore, using the same sample and time frame, Cable and Wilson (1984) regress a value-added measure of output on capital, labour, organizational characteristics, and profit sharing. They find profit sharing adds between 3.1 and 8.2 percent to value added, ceteris paribus.

Unfortunately, endogeneity of profit sharing is *not* modeled in these studies. We do not know whether the productivity and employment gains associated with profit sharing (where observed) are causal or simply the result of, say, retaining its correlation with superior management. Another contentious issue is the role of wider employee participation in mediating performance outcomes. Unexamined is the role of *particular* profit sharing schemes on performance and the manner of their selection by firms. The safest conclusion would appear to be that policy favouring 'profit sharing' through tax concessions does not offer certain results (see also Addison, 1991; Wadhwani and Wall, 1990).

(d) Minimum wages

Although wages and conditions of employment are typically fixed by voluntary agreement in Britain, in certain trades and industries minimum pay and (until 1986) holidays and holiday pay are determined by statutory wage fixing machinery in the form of Wages Councils. These bodies were initially set up under the Trade Boards Act of 1909 as a means of dealing with the problems of "sweated labour".

Wages Councils consist of equal numbers of employer and employee representatives and (after 1986) up to five 'independents', one of whom is chairman. Determinations made by the Councils, or Wage Orders, are enforceable as implied terms of the contract of employment. Their implementation is monitored by a Wages Inspectorate. The minimum in 1989 ranged from £78 in made-up textiles to £98 in retail bespoke tailoring, which values can be compared with per capita GDP at factor cost of £150 per week. Roughly one-third of workers earn the minimum for their industry or trade.

In 1984 there were 26 Wages Councils covering 2.7 million workers, the bulk of them being in catering, retail distribution and hairdressing. In 1968 there were 57 Wages Councils covering 3.5 million workers. Today just over two million workers are covered. To these must be added the 300,000 workers covered by separate wage fixing machinery under the Agricultural Wages Council.

Consistent with its deregulatory goals the Conservative government made significant changes to the operation of the statutory wage fixing machinery under the 1986 Wages Act. First, the power of the Councils to determine rates for those workers under the age of 21 was removed entirely. This goes some way towards explaining the fall in coverage noted earlier. Second, only one minimum hourly rate and one overtime rate could be set. Hitherto, the relevant Wages Councils could set a range of minima to reflect skill differentials. Third, the power to determine holidays, holiday pay, weekend pay, unsocial hours pay, and shift premia was abolished. Fourth, the constitution of Wages Councils was revised to allow for greater representation of independents (up from 3 to 5 members). Moreover, small business representation on the employer side was strengthened and Councils were required to recognize the effect of their wage orders on employment in setting minima.

It appeared that this surgical approach would be followed by outright abolition. But opposition from larger firms and the suggestion that their elimination might increase the pressure for a national minimum wage (on the separate impact of which, see Bazen, 1990) would seem to have blunted any such move.

(e) Measures against wage discrimination

The United Kingdom passed the Equal Pay Act in 1970, and the Sex Discrimination Act in 1975. In 1984 it amended the Equal Pay Act, after a ruling by the European Court of Justice, to allow equal pay for work of equal value (comparable worth). A statutory body, the Equal Opportunities Commission, hears claims under the Acts, conciliates, and if necessary supports prosecutions.

With the passing of the Equal Pay Act in 1970, which was phased in over 5 years, there has been an increase in the female/male pay ratio. Prior to 1975 the ratio fluctuated around 65 percent, since then it has been about 75 percent. Female relative employment has not apparently suffered, but equal pay might have been a factor behind the increase in part-time work among women.

In addition to equal pay, there have been measures to end discrimination in statutory entitlements and pensions. The 1989 Employment Act removed the difference whereby men could receive statutory redundancy payments up to age 65 and women only up to age 60. The Sex Discrimination Act of 1986 removed the right of employers to set different retirement ages. This latter Act (and the Social Security Act of 1980), was again a result of European Community pressure against discrimination by sex in sickness, invalidity, and pension schemes.

C.3 Termination of Labour Contracts

(a) Individual dismissals

Prior to statutory intervention in the form of the 1971 Industrial Relations Act the legal position of employees at common law was that as long as proper notice of termination had been given, an employer was free to terminate at will. In the event that no notice was given, or a fixed term contract was prematurely terminated, the only remedy available to the employee was to file a wrongful dismissal suit through the ordinary courts, a course of action for which the sole remedy was damages usually limited to pay for the notice period (see Anderman, 1986, for a survey).

The statutory right not to be "unfairly" dismissed initially established under the 1971 Act is now covered by the 1978 Employment Protection Consolidation Act (EPCA). The Act extends to *qualified* employees the right to complain to an industrial tribunal that the dismissal is unfair. To qualify, employees must now have at least two years' continuous service, or five years in the case of part-timers working between 8 and 16 hours per week. (We note parenthetically that the qualification period was just six months in 1975.) In addition to the employment continuity requirement, those claiming unfair dismissal must not be aged over the "normal retirement age" for the relevant work or in any case not above 65, and present their application to a tribunal within three months of the termination.

The first step in presenting a case before an industrial tribunal is to establish that there has indeed been a dismissal. The EPCA lays down that a worker is dismissed if his or her employment contract is terminated (with or without notice); if a fixed term contract is not renewed; and in circumstances of "constructive dismissal", namely, where the employee quits but claims this was brought about by the employer's conduct. In addition, redundancy and the failure to reemploy after transfer of a business (see next subsection) constitute additional sources of dismissal, as does the failure to permit a woman to return to work after confinement.

In determining whether a dismissal is fair, a two-stage test is applied by an industrial tribunal: first, has the employer established a fair reason; and, second, did he act reasonably? Capability, conduct, redundancy, the occurrence of a strike or lockout, compliance with some other statutory duty or restriction, or "some other substantial reason" all constitute grounds for fair dismissal. Note that although redundancy normally constitutes fair dismissal, it may be unfair if the reason for selection for redundancy is on grounds of union membership or non-membership. Similarly, although tribunals are normally excluded from considering claims from those on strike (since this constitutes a breach of contract), if the complainant can show that *at the time of his dismissal* some workers were not dismissed or, in circumstances where all strikers were dismissed, that some were re-engaged *within* three months of the dismissals, then a case for unfair dismissal may be heard by the tribunal. Victimization in the form of selective dismissal or re-engagement is, then, prima facie unfair except in those circumstances where the worker was taking part in unofficial action at the time of dismissal.

The next stage requires the industrial tribunal to test whether the employer's action was reasonable in the circumstances and in accordance with equity and the substantial merits of the case. In this endeavour the tribunal receives guidance from the ACAS Code on Disciplinary Practice and Procedures in Employment, referred to above, and case law.

Not all cases are subject to this two-stage procedure. Some dismissals are automatically unfair. Specifically, dismissals on the grounds of trade union membership or non-membership (distinct from dismissals in connection with industrial action), unfair selection for redundancy, and pregnancy are unfair irrespective of the reasons put forward by the employer to justify them. In addition, there are some other special cases including dismissals arising out of the transfer of an undertaking (see below), constructive dismissals (a common law test is applied here), and denial of a woman's right to return to work after her confinement.

Action before an industrial tribunal is initiated by the employee, and the employer has 14 days to reply to the application. However, full hearings may be attendant upon a pre-hearing assessment, to prevent unmeritorious applications by advising applicants with weak evidential cases that a (transaction) costs award might be made against them. Under the 1989 Employment Act a deposit of up to £150 can be required in cases having no reasonable prospects of success. An important role is reserved for ACAS in conciliating cases, and approximately one-third of all applications are resolved via this route.

If the dismissal is adjudged unfair, the industrial tribunal may make an order for reinstatement; a remedy that occurs in just 3 percent of successful cases. Noncompliance with a reinstatement order may trigger an *additional award* amounting to between 13 and 26 weeks pay (26 to 52 weeks in cases of racial or gender discrimination). The vast majority of actual determinations in such cases thus involve monetary awards. These consist of two main elements: a *basic award* and a *compensatory award*. The former is a function of the employee's length of service and age prior to dismissal. For those aged under 22 the basic award is one-half a week's pay for each year worked. This rises to one week's pay (up to a current maximum of

£184) for each year worked between the ages of 22 and 41, and tops out at one and one-half weeks' pay for each year worked between the ages of 41 and 65. The ceiling on the basic award is fixed at £5,520 (the basic award is reduced by one-twelfth for every month beyond the age of 64). The maximum compensatory award stands at £8,925, although as in the case of the basic award may again be reduced to the extent that the employee contributed to his dismissal. Any social security benefits are offset against payment.

For those dismissed by reason of trade union membership/non-membership a *special award* is payable. This remedy is set at a minimum value of £12,550 and a maximum of £25,040. These special awards are payable in addition to the basic and compensatory awards and are automatically triggered by a request for reinstatement on the part of the applicant. Since the 1982 Employment Act, the tribunal may order that compensation be paid by the union instead of the employer in cases of dismissal for non-membership of a union.

In 1986-87 the total number of applications received by industrial tribunals was 29,392, of which about one third were successfully conciliated by ACAS and one-third were withdrawn. Of the remaining 10,067 applications, 3,129 were successfully pursued at a tribunal hearing. The median award in simple dismissal cases – those not covering unfair dismissal on grounds of trade union membership, pregnancy, or refusal of right to return to work after pregnancy, and as a result of a strike or lockout situation – was £1,805. Some 37.9 percent of awards fell below £1,000, 36.2 percent exceeded £1,000 but amounted to less than £3,000, 15.8 percent were in the range £3,000 to £5,000, and just 10 percent exceeded £6,000 (Employment Gazette, 1987).

(b) Mass dismissals

A system of legal rights again applies in the case of redundancies, defined by the 1978 Employment Protection Consolidation Act as dismissals consequent on the cessation or diminution of a business. Employers are required to consult "at the earliest opportunity" with recognized trade unions over any proposals to make workers redundant, and also to inform the Department of Employment. Where the employer proposes to make 100 or more employees redundant in one establishment within a period of 90 days, the consultation process has to begin at least 90 days prior to the scheduled termination date, but this period is reduced to 30 days if between 10 and 99 workers are to be made redundant over a period of 30 days. The employer has also to provide unions with the reasons for the redundancies, the number and types of workers involved, the method of selection to be used, and the implementation procedure but is under no obligation to bargain. Failure of management to inform and consult may result in the payment of a *protective award* of up to 90 days pay (or 30 days, as appropriate) to each employee involved.

The duty to consult does not displace the right of the individual worker to proper notice. Legal minima established by the Employment Protection Consolidation Act amount to one week for those with less than 2 years' service and one week for each year of continuous service up to a maximum of 12 weeks. Again, the employer may offer payment in lieu of notice.

The law also lays down statutory redundancy pay. To qualify, employees must have been continuously employed for two years (five years for part-timers working less than 16 hours per week) prior to the point of dismissal. Those aged less than 20 years or over the normal retirement age (generally 65) are not covered. Employees are disqualified if they have been offered suitable alternative employment, are guilty of misconduct, have been working under fixed term contracts and have waived their redundancy rights, and in those situations where strike action has preceded the issuance of the redundancy notice. Of these latter exclusions the most problematic has been the offer of suitable alternative employment. Any such offer has to be made prior to the end of the old contract and must begin within 4 weeks of its expiry. Where the terms of the new job differ from those of the old, workers have the right to a trial period of 4 weeks in the new job and to receive a written copy of the agreement documenting its terms and conditions and the termination of the trial period. The right to redundancy pay is maintained intact during this trial period.

The number of claims before industrial tribunals are small relative to the number of declared redundancies (e.g. 5,389 in respect of the 144,135 to 238,001 declared redundancies in 1986-87). It would appear that collective agreements generally exceed the statutory minima (Incomes Data Services, 1988) and that the legislation has stimulated management planning of redundancies and the negotiation of redundancy agreements.

Workers whose employer is insolvent may recover the redundancy monies due to them via a redundancy fund. Other debts which can be recovered from this fund include arrears of pay for up to 8 weeks, holiday pay for up to 6 weeks, notice pay, and unfair dismissal basic awards.

Turning finally to the implications of a change in the identity of the employer, the normal common law position is that a change in ownership terminates the contract of employment, so that qualified workers can claim redundancy payments from their old employer unless the contract is renewed by the new employer. In the latter event, if the employee rejects the offer, his entitlement to redundancy pay from the old employer hinges on the suitability of the offer and whether he has unreasonably rejected it. If he accepts the offer, then he is not regarded as having been dismissed from the old employer and has no claim for a redundancy payment. Continuity of employment is thereby preserved for most *statutory* purposes (see Hepple, 1982).

The Transfer of Undertakings (Protection of Employment) Regulations 1981 reverses the normal common law position that a change in ownership automatically terminates the contract of employment. The new regulations state expressly that there is an automatic transfer of employment contracts (and of union recognition, but not pension schemes) when there has been a change of business. Accordingly, the change in the identity of the employer does not give the worker the right to resign and claim redundancy pay. Note that the regulations only apply to the transfer of a business or a self-contained part of a business as a going concern. Transfers of share capital, the main form of takeover in Britain, are excluded, as are dispositions of physical assets. In such cases continuity of employment for statutory purposes hinges upon an arcane distinction between "transfers of business" and "transfers of assets".

As noted earlier a dismissal prior to or after the transfer of a business is automatically unfair if the transfer is the reason for that dismissal. Yet in practice it appears that the dismissal can be fair if it is for an economic, technical or organizational reason involving changes in the workforce. The qualification falls within the "some other substantial reason" gateway, although the obligation to show reasonableness then applies. Dismissal for such reasons in effect means dismissal for redundancy, and hence entitlement to redundancy pay alone for qualified workers.

D. Conclusion/Evaluation

Any attempt to analyze the impact of British institutions on labour market behaviour and economic performance must recognize that the institutions are themselves endogenous. Nevertheless, in the context of changes in the law, the following observations seem warranted.

First, there is good reason to suppose that changes in the law over the past decade have had a major impact on union membership/density [B.1(a)].

Second, although union bargaining power would appear demonstrably to have been reduced, there are few *obvious* signs in the economic aggregates that changes in the law have impacted economic performance, leading some observers to conclude that the negative impact of unions must have been exaggerated by the proponents of union reform. Brown and Wadhwani (1990) in particular have argued that little could be expected of legislation. They ascribe those changes in behaviour that are observed (e.g. alterations in working practices and organizational change) to enhanced product market competition which forced employers to put their own house in order but do not identify the sources of this increased competition.

Our interpretation of the facts of the case would be rather different. Broadly speaking, we find much to commend the interpretation of Oulton (1990, p. 56) who argues that much of the improvement in labour productivity during the 1980s was due to a decline in the "disadvantages of unionization." Oulton examines unionization in the context of the so-called 'shock thesis' which is that the dislocation of the 1980-81 recession, and its associated employment losses, forced firms and workers to adapt or die. The shock effect should be greater in heavily unionized industries if the Thatcher administration's sequence of Employment Acts broke union power. For a similar reason, the shock effect should be greater in industries with large plants (since these tend to be the most densely organized).

Oulton analyses the acceleration in productivity growth between 1982-85 and 1976-79 for 94 manufacturing industries. The shock variable is the reduction in employment between 1979 and 1981. Union variables comprise the proportions of the industry workforce covered by both national and supplementary agreements, by a manual agreement only, and by a company agreement only. It is found that a reduction of 10 percent in the labour force (the shock) produces an increase in productivity growth of 2.5 percentage points. Union and firm size variables are found to be positively and significantly associated with the acceleration of productivity growth (at least for one of the productivity measures employed) suggesting that the more highly unionized industries improved their performance the most after 1979 – presumably because of the Thatcher programme of union reform.

Oulton also deploys a panel regression model of employment and productivity, following each industry over the period 1972-86. The upshot of this detailed procedure remains that the most highly organized industries improved their performance most after 1979. It also emerges that unionization is associated with *reduced* productivity growth over the *entire* sample period, 1972-86 (though with a lesser reduction in the 1980s). More precisely, of the 4 percentage point average improvement in the growth rate of productivity in the 1980s, exclusive of shock effects *inter alia*, Oulton estimates that between one-quarter and one-half is due to unionization affecting productivity growth by a lesser adverse extent than it once did.

It is notable, however, that much of the improvement in productivity growth modeled by Oulton is 'explained' by time period dummies. A related issue is the imprecision of our understanding of reduced union bargaining power that presumably underpins the reduction in the "disadvantages of unionization". For example, if union power fell, why did the union premium apparently not fall during the 1980s? (We note parenthetically that we would not expect to observe any impact of reduced bargaining power on strike activity since strikes are not related to union power but, rather, to information asymmetries.)

A number of observers have focused on the productivity growth findings to argue that these provide sufficient evidence in and of themselves for a shift in the balance of power in favour of employers. Wadhwani (1989) interprets evidence of a greater organizational change in union workplaces (defined from answers by managers to a question on "substantial changes in work organization or working practices not involving new plant or equipment") observed in the 1984 Workplace Industrial Relations Survey (WIRS), as indicative of a weakening of union power in the face of major changes in the law. He also allows for the possibility that the relaxation of restrictive practices was prompted in part by high unemployment, although Oulton's panel regression model suggests that effect may have been exaggerated.

Also using data from the 1984 WIRS, Blanchflower, Millward, and Oswald (1990) contend that unions have served to depress the rate of employment growth and increase the extent of employment decline. (In the 1990 WIRS there is again a relationship between unionization and firm decline - Millward *et al.*, 1992, p. 64.) Blanchflower (1990) further reports that union wages are not responsive to perceived chance of redundancy, unlike wages in the non-union sector which display a high unemployment elasticity of pay. Although these findings may suggest the relevance of 'insider' forces in union pay determination and offer some clue as to the persistence of the union wage premium in the 1980s, the broader and more important reason could well be the bargaining away of restrictive practices at this time.

Returning to the role of legislation in all of this, a dissenting note is entered by Nickell, Wadhwani, and Wall (1989) who argue that if anti-union legislation was of significance in promoting growth in the 1980s then pro-union legislation in the 1970s should have retarded growth, whereas their estimates point to insignificantly negative effects of unions on total factor productivity growth 1975-78. However, as Oulton has pointed out, the Nickell *et al.* results are obtained from a unbalanced sample of firms, with many fewer firms after 1982 (their sample period is 1972-86). Oulton notes that when they restrict their firm sample to be a balanced panel, unionization *significantly reduces* productivity growth in the 1970s.

Finally, we know of no study that seeks to identify the impact of *reduced* employment protection legislation upon labour market performance. But given that U.K. job protection legislation even prior to the accession of the Conservative administration in 1979 was amongst the least 'coercive' in Europe (Addison, 1989) the current emphasis upon the union dimension as a source of labour market inflexibility and poor performance seems warranted. (For a review of union impact on economic performance, see Metcalf, 1990.)

REFERENCES

ACAS, *Labour Flexibility in Britain : the 1987 ACAS Survey*, Occasional Paper 41, London: Advisory, Conciliation and Arbitration Service, 1987.

Addison, John T., The Absence of Job Protection Legislation: A Source of Competitive Advantage for the U.S.?, in: Gary D. Libecap (ed.), *Advances in the Study of Entrepreneurship, Innovation, and Economic Growth*, Vol. III, Greenwich, Connecticut: JAI Press, 1989, pp. 159-218.

Addison, John T., Paying for Productivity. A Review, *Journal of Comparative Economics*, Vol. 15, No. 3 (September 1991), pp. 505-511.

Anderman, Steven, Unfair Dismissals and Redundancy, in: Roy Lewis (ed.), *Labour Law in Britain*, Oxford: Basil Blackwell, 1986, pp. 415-45.

Baddon, Lesley, *et al.*, *Developments in Profit Sharing and Employee Share Ownership – Survey Report*, University of Glasgow Centre for Research in Industrial Democracy and Participation, July 1987.

Bassett, Phillip, *Strike Free*, London: Macmillan, 1986.

Bazen, Stephen, On the Employment Effects of Introducing a National Minimum Wage in the U.K., *British Journal of Industrial Relations*, Vol. 28, No. 2 (July 1990), 215-26.

Blanchflower, David G., Fear, Unemployment and Pay Flexibility, unpublished paper, Dartmouth College, April 1990.

Blanchflower, David G., and Andrew J. Oswald, Profit Related Pay: Prose Discovered?, *Economic Journal*, Vol. 98, No. 392 (September 1988), 720-30.

Blanchflower, David G., Neil Millward, and Andrew J. Oswald, Unionisation and Employment Behaviour, unpublished paper, Dartmouth College, March 1990.

Brown, William, and Sushil Wadhwani, The Economic Effects of Industrial Relations Legislation Since 1979, *National Institute Economic Review*, No. 131 (February 1990), 57-70.

Cable, John, and Nicholas Wilson, Profit Sharing and Productivity: An Analysis of U.K. Engineering Firms, *Economic Journal*, Vol. 99, No. 396 (June 1989), 366-75.

Carruth, Alan, and Richard Disney, Where Have Two Million Trade Union Members Gone?, *Economica*, Vol. 55, No. 217 (February 1988), 1-19.

Confederation of British Industry, *Long Term Agreements: A C.B.I. Study*, London: C.B.I., 1987.

Confederation of British Industry, *The Structure and Process of Pay Determination in the Private Sector 1979-1986*, London: C.B.I., 1988.

Daniel, Wayne W., and Neil Millward, *Workplace Industrial Relations in Britain: The DE/PSI/SSRC Survey*, London: Heinemann, 1983.

Department of Employment, *New Earnings Survey 1988*, London: H.M.S.O., 1989.

Donovan Commission, *Royal Commission on Trade Unions and Employers' Associations*, Cmnd. 3623, London: H.M.S.O., 1968.

Elliott, Robert F. and Peter J. Hemmings, Are National Wage Agreements a Source of National Wage Rigidity in the Depressed Regions of Britain, *Regional Studies*, Vol. 25, No. 1 (March 1991), 63-69.

Employment Gazette, Labour Costs in 1984, *Department of Employment Gazette*, Vol. 94, No. 5 (June 1986), 212-18.

Employment Gazette, Industrial Tribunal Statistics, *Department of Employment Gazette*, Vol. 95, No. 10 (October 1987), 498-502.

Employment Gazette, New Employment Bill to Ban Pre-entry Closed Shop, *Department of Employment Gazette*, Vol. 98, No. 1 (January 1990), 3.

Employment Gazette, Membership of Trade Unions in 1990, *Department of Employment Gazette*, Vol. 100, No. 4 (April 1992), 185-90.

Estrin, Saul, and Nicholas Wilson, The Micro-Economic Effects of Profit-Sharing: The British Experience, *Discussion Paper No. 247*, Centre for Labour Economics, July 1986.

Eurostat, *Labour Force Survey – Results 1989*, Luxembourg: Office of Official Publications of the European Community, 1991.

Financial Times, Battle Looms Over National Pay Bargaining, London: Financial Times, 12 November 1986.

Fox, Jonathan, Reaching a Single Union Agreement, *Employment Gazette*, Vol. 95, No. 12 (December 1987), 611-16.

Freeman, Richard B., and Jeffrey Pelletier, The Impact of Industrial Relations Legislation on British Union Density, *British Journal of Industrial Relations*, Vol. 28, No. 2 (July 1990), 141-64.

Gennard, John, Motives for and Incidence of Seeking Single Union Agreements, in Brian Towers (ed.), *Handbook of Industrial Relations Practice*, London: Kogan Page, 1989, pp. 248-64.

Hepple, Bob, The Transfer of Undertakings (Protection of Employment) Regulations, *Industrial Law Journal*, Vol. 11, No. 1 (March 1982), 29-40.

Hirsch, Barry T., and John T. Addison, *The Economic Analysis of Unions--New Approaches and Evidence*, London and Boston: Allen and Unwin, 1986.

Incomes Data Services, Incentive Bonus Schemes, *IDS Study 389*, London: Incomes Data Services Ltd., July 1987.

Incomes Data Services, Redundancy Terms, *IDS Study 422*, London: Incomes Data Services Ltd., December 1988.

Incomes Data Services, Sick Pay Schemes, *IDS Study 430*, London: Incomes Data Services Ltd., March 1989a.

Incomes Data Services, Negotiating at Industry Level, *IDS Study 434*, London: Incomes Data Services Ltd., May 1989b.

Incomes Data Services, Employee Share Ownership Plans, *IDS Study 438*, London: Incomes Data Services Ltd., July 1989c.

Incomes Data Services, Incentive Bonus Schemes, *IDS Study 443*, London: Incomes Data Services Ltd., October 1989d.

Incomes Data Services, Hours and Holidays, *IDS Study 444*, London: Incomes Data Services Ltd., October 1989e.

L.R.D., *State Benefits*, London: Labour Research Department, 1992.

Layard, Richard, Stephen Nickell and Richard Jackman, *Unemployment*, Oxford: Oxford University Press, 1991.

Metcalf, David, Labour Market Flexibility and Jobs: A Survey of Evidence from OECD Countries, *Discussion Paper 254*, Centre for Labour Economics, 1986.

Metcalf, David, Union Presence and Productivity Levels, Productivity Growth and Investment in British Manufacturing Industry, *Working Paper No. 1203*, Centre for Labour Economics, January 1990.

Millward, Neil and Mark Stevens, *British Workplace Industrial Relations 1980-1984 – The DE/ESR/PSI/ACAS Surveys*, London: Gower, 1986.

Millward, Neil, Mark Stevens, David Smart and W.R. Hawes, *Workplace Industrial Relations in Transition*, London: Dartmouth, 1992.

Nickell, Stephen J., Sushil Wadhwani, and Martin Wall, Unions and Productivity Growth in Britain 1974-86: Evidence from UK Company Accounts Data, *Working Paper No. 353*, Centre for Labour Economics, August 1989.

Oulton, Nicholas, Labour Productivity in UK Manufacturing in the 1970s and in the 1980s, *National Institute Economic Review*, No. 132 (May 1990), 71-91.

Poole, M., *The Origins of Economic Democracy – Profit Sharing and Employee Shareholding Schemes*, London and New York: Routledge, 1989.

Prais, S.G., and Karin Wagner, Productivity and Management: the Training of Foremen in Britain and Germany, *National Institute Economic Review*, No. 123 (February 1988), 34-47.

Salamon, Michael, *Industrial Relations*, Hemel Hempstead: Prentice Hall, 1987.

Siebert, W. Stanley, Collective Bargaining Coverage in the U.K. 1973-1990, *mimeo*, University of Birmingham, September 1991.
Siebert, W. Stanley, Notes on Industrial Training in Britain, *Quarterly Economic Bulletin*, Vol. 11, No. 2 (June 1990), 46-48.
Siebert, W. Stanley, and John T. Addison, Internal Labour Markets: Causes and Consequences, *Oxford Review of Economic Policy*, Vol. 7, No. 1 (Spring 1991), pp. 76-92.
Smith, Willian R., Profit Sharing and Employee Share Ownership in Britain, *Employment Gazette*, Vol. 94, No. 8 (September 1986), 380-85.
Wadhwani, Sushil, The Effects of Unions on Productivity Growth, Investment and Employment: A Report on Some Recent Work, *Working Paper No. 356*, Centre for Labour Economics, April 1989.
Wadhwani, Sushil, and Martin Wall, The Effect of Profit Sharing on Employment, Wages, Share Returns, and Productivity: Evidence from U.K. Micro-Data, *Economic Journal*, Vol. 100, No. 399 (March 1990), 1-17.

Labour Market Contracts and Institutions
J. Hartog and J. Theeuwes (Editors)

CHAPTER 13

THE NETHERLANDS:
Labour Market, Labour Contracts and Collective Bargaining

Ton Korver*

A. Introduction

Collective bargaining is an essential part of Dutch labour relations. Depending on definitions used and on inclusion or exclusion of the public sector, the coverage of collective bargaining agreements is roughly between 70 and 80 % of all employees. This percentage, in spite of many changes in the postwar Dutch economy and in Dutch society at large, has shown a remarkable continuity over time.

The continuity of collective bargaining has transformed it from an instrument into an institution, something valued as such and for its own sake. For many years after the Second World War, up to the early eighties, the central government intervened quite regularly into the process and/or the results of collective bargaining. At times, especially during the first two postwar decades, collective bargaining may have looked like an empty shell, rather than like a mechanism to establish wages and conditions. By statute and otherwise the government pre-empted the large majority of the decisions of the bargaining process. Nevertheless, the number of collective bargaining agreements and the number of workers covered, grew steadily. During the eighties, with a much more liberal bargaining climate, collective bargaining proved its attractiveness for employers and unions. Although union density shrank rather drastically, neither unions nor employers contemplated a goodbye to collective bargaining. The reverse, in fact, seems to hold. The number of agreements, and the number of covered workers, keeps on growing. Also, the number of items concluded under the umbrella of collective bargaining, is growing. The traditional item list of wages, hours and conditions is being extended and may include by now agreements on employment opportunities, recruitment, and vocational education and training.

Governmental influence is still dominant in the public sector, and in what in the Netherlands is called the sector financed through government subsidies or through premiums (for short: the semi-public sector). But here too we observe major steps in the direction of establishing normal bargaining relationships. The unilateral and

* Faculty of Social Sciences; Department of Personnel Sciences Catholic University Brabant.

centralized setting of wages and conditions for public and semi-public employees is swiftly becoming a thing of the past. Governmental and quasi-governmental bodies, in their role as employers, have been and are being organized as employers' associations in order to negotiate with the unions. Centralized directives as to how personnel policies are to be conducted, are withdrawn and so on. Collective bargaining in the full sense of the word is taking over the terrain formerly occupied by governmental rules and regulations. The labour market in the Netherlands, in summary, is best approached through the spectre of collective bargaining.

A.1 The Labour Market in the Eighties; Selected Data

The employment record of the Netherlands during the 80's is mixed. Employment fell during the first half of the decade, especially in the period 1981-1984. The second half showed a remarkable growth in employment:

Table 1. Change in Employment, 1968-1990, in persons

Period	Number of years	Yearly change (%)	Total change	
			persons	%
1968-1971	4	1.28	192,000	5.2
1972-1977	6	0.22	68,000	1.3
1978-1980	3	1.40	210,000	4.2
1981-1984	4	-0.19	-39,000	-0.8
1985-1989	5	2.04	583,000	10.6

Source: Rapportage Arbeidsmarkt 1989, p. 26

Comparatively, the record is not unfavourable:

Table 2. International Comparison of Employment Growth (persons)

	average % of changes per year		
	1978-1980	1981-1984	1985-1989
Netherlands	1.3	−0.2	2.0
EC	0.3	−0.6	0.9
US	2.6	1.4	2.2
Japan	1.5	1.0	1.0
OECD	1.3	0.5	1.2

Source: Rapportage Arbeidsmarkt 1989, p. 27

The overall gain in employment was not sufficient to solve or to avoid growth of unemployment. Despite a comparatively modest increase in the total working population (Rapportage Arbeidsmarkt, 1990, p. 37, Table 3.14) unemployment was high during the eighties:

Table 3. Standardized Unemployment Percentages

	1984	1986	1988	1989
Netherlands	11.8	9.9	9.2	8.3
West Germany	7.1	6.4	6.2	5.5
Great Britain	11.7	11.2	8.5	6.9
France	9.7	10.4	10.0	9.6
Italy	9.4	10.5	11.0	10.9
Japan	2.7	2.8	2.5	2.3
United States	7.4	6.9	5.4	5.2
EC	10.7	10.8	9.8	8.9
OECD	7.9	7.7	6.7	6.2

Source: Rapportage Arbeidsmarkt 1990, p. 34

There is a substantial amount of long term unemployment in the Netherlands. Long term unemployment (one year and over) accounts today for over half of total unemployment (Statistical Yearbook 1990, p. 85, Table 6). Next to the effect of negative duration dependence, the probability of long term unemployment is positively correlated with age, and negatively with skill (Rapportage Arbeidsmarkt 1989, p. 19). Unemployment in the categories of women, of older workers (40 years and over), of first and second generation guest-workers, is comparatively high. Relatively, their chances of getting employed have diminished during the past few years (Rapportage Arbeidsmarkt 1990, p. 103, Table H; Teulings, 1990).

The unemployment picture is softened by several influences which in themselves are at best a mixed blessing. For example, programs for early retirement and worker disability have been used extensively in the Netherlands (DCA 1990, p. 13; Rapportage Arbeidsmarkt 1990, pp. 25, 40). Also, the percentage of part-time (35 hours per week or less) employment in the Netherlands is quite high and shows unparalleled growth rates (Rapportage Arbeidsmarkt 1990, pp. 38-39). About one fourth of employment in the Netherlands consists of part-time jobs, the large majority of which are held by women. The growth of employment, when measured in persons, is therefore higher than the growth measured in labour years (Rapportage Arbeidsmarkt 1990, pp. 11-12, figure 1.4).

As for the employment side proper, the eighties witnessed the continuation of the structural trend towards a strengthening of the tertiary sector and a concomitant weakening of the secondary sector. The relatively small primary sector also lost some ground, due to a further shrinking of employment in agriculture and fishing. Within the secondary sector manufacturing and construction did poorly for most of the period; employment in public utilities remained constant. In the tertiary sector transport lagged during the first half of the eighties, then revived. The trend for 'other services' (government included) was more stable, notwithstanding the slowing down of the growth rate relative to the decade of the seventies (Rapportage Arbeidsmarkt 1989, p. 54).

A.2 Social Security

Time and again one finds the suggestion that the Dutch social security system is at least partly to blame for the tenacity of unemployment. Two arguments stand out. One is that the generosity of Dutch social security has raised the reservation wage to too high a level. The second is that the costs of wage related social security are too high. This, in turn, has led to too high wage costs, especially in labour intensive sectors. The first argument, thus, concerns compensation, the second contribution.

It cannot be denied that Dutch social security is generous. Starting from a rather low level immediately after the Second World War, Dutch social security has developed into a complex, encompassing and huge system, geared to the guaranteeing of financial security rather than to labour market participation. The 'active' component in social transfers is low, the total transfer level is high (Rapportage Arbeidsmarkt 1990, p. 80). In particular in social transfer benefits Holland is generous (de Kam *et al.*, 1988, p. 189, Table 2). The generosity of the Dutch system derives from the fact that the floor in financial security (welfare) is connected to the statutory net minimum wage. The rise in the latter is connected to the overall rise in contract wages. Also, the lowest incomes in the Netherlands are entitled to several subsidies (for example rent subsidies), which they might lose in the case of higher employment income. The net income effect of paid employment at the lowest level is therefore quite small and may even be negative. The high level of minimum income, plus the entitlement to government subsidies, leads to a high level of the reservation wage. Hence, one would expect this to have a positive effect on unemployment duration (Groot/Jehoel-Gijsbers, 1989).

Recent empirical research gives a qualified support to this argument (Rapportage Arbeidsmarkt 1990, p. 71). Reservation wages indeed are high in the Netherlands; yet those people that did find employment accepted lower wages than their reservation wage predicted. It might be that the kind of employment (tenure possibilities, career perspectives and the like) and therefore income prospects over a long term, are more important than the reservation wage. For example, unemployed workers tend to accept the trouble of long commuting and they tend to accept a requirement of further or new training. What they tend to reject, however, is working on purely temporary assignments and having to change residence (Groot/Jehoel-Gijsbers, 1989, p. 53). Also, the fact that 'pull factors' (expected wages in the case of employment) are stronger than 'push factors' (level of income from social security) is noteworthy (Groot/Jehoel Gijsbers, 1989, pp. 49-51).

The second point is related to the influence of social security contributions on wage costs. Since contributions for social insurance (welfare is financed through taxes) depend on payrolls, it is evident that, ceteris paribus, labour-intensive industries carry a heavier burden. This, however, is an argument on a mechanism of financing social security, and not on its level. In the recent past several proposals have been put forward to change the base of financing social insurance. As yet, these proposals did not lead to definite results. On the issue of the level of wage costs in the Netherlands it should be noted that these are quite competitive in international terms (Rapportage Arbeidsmarkt 1990, p. 32, Table 3.7), and also tending to behave in the mode of the EC as a whole (Rapportage Arbeidsmarkt, 1990, p. 33, Tables 3.8, 3.9).

A.3 Employment Relationship, the Law, the Institutional Setting

In Dutch law a labour contract is sharply differentiated from a service contract. The distinguishing criterion is authority: present and defining in a labour contract, absent and immaterial in a service contract. The worker in a labour contract, the employment relationship therefore as contrasted with the service relationship, is dependent. The dependent position of the worker is reflected in a series of protective laws (on industrial accidents insurance, sickness insurance, pension insurance, unemployment insurance), dating mainly (unemployment insurance excepted) from before the Second World War – as in most countries (Flora/Alber, 1987, p. 59, Table 2.4). After the Second World War worker protection was enhanced by strong prescriptions in the case of dismissals. Job security ranks high in the Netherlands (Metcalf, 1987). Over 80 % of all employees in the Netherlands has a contract of unspecified duration. Given such a contract the employer has to quote acceptable reasons, checked by independent outsiders, before dismissal is possible. This holds in the individual case and (since 1976) also in the collective case (Bakels/Opheikens, 1982, pp. 84 ff.). Before termination of the contract an advance notice period is required. The law states a period as long as the period between one payment date and the next. In many contracts, however, a longer period is stipulated. Severance pay is not required, although when termination has been irregular it may occur. In case of collective dismissal the trade union of course may try and bargain for severance pay.

The dependency relationship is also reflected in the series of specific demands made on the employer and the employee. On the employee's side of the contract we note:

(1) an obligation to perform and to appear in person
(2) an obligation to obey 'reasonable' instructions of the employer
(3) an obligation to work 'to the best of one's capacities'. In some cases, limited mainly to craft and professional workers, a fourth obligation exists:
(4) a prohibition of competition in the case of exit. Specific skills, know-how, or good-will, acquired while being employed, can not be used during a specified time and in a specified area to compete with the former employer. Recently this clause has been specified to the effect that the prohibition is valid only when employer and employee have agreed to it in writing.

The employer's side of the contract stipulates:
(1) an obligation to pay wages, including the guaranteeing of minimum wages where appropriate (since 1968) and equal payment for men and women in the same occupation (since 1975)
(2) an obligation to grant the employee a certain minimum period for holidays, and the obligation to continue wage payment during that period (since 1966)
(3) an obligation to prevent damage to the 'person or goods' of the worker
(4) an obligation to provide the worker, on exit, with a certificate as to the work performed and the period of employment – if so requested by the worker
(5) an obligation to behave like a 'good employer'
(6) an obligation (since 1980) to treat men and women alike in alike situations (conclusion of a labour contract, provision of education, wages and benefits, promotions, and exit)

The newer clauses have somewhat improved the position of women. Much remains to be done, however (DCA, 1988, pp. 28-29; Kok/Schoneveld, 1987, pp. 58-68). Partly the low pace of emancipation is due to the newness of the subject itself; partly it is due to the simple fact that much work of men and women is not comparable (both because of the heavy concentration of women in a few occupations only, and because of the over-representation of women in part-time and temporary jobs); partly to the rather lukewarm attempts, expressing intentions rather than concrete projects and procedures, to push the subject by means of collective bargaining.

Collective agreements substantiate the individual labour contract; they do not replace it. Since 1927 we find an Act on Collective Labour Agreements in the Netherlands, the first article of which states that collective agreements may specify the conditions on wages and benefits, to be respected in individual labour contracts of all employees, irrespective of their membership of one of the organizations party to the agreement. The same article lays down that collective agreements can be concluded only by one or more employers or their representatives and representative unions of employees. The representation applies exclusively to legally recognized subjects of law, whether as natural persons (employer, employers) or otherwise (representatives of employers, representatives of employees).

Collective agreements are of overwhelming importance in the Netherlands. Once concluded they are legally binding and ultimately enforceable by law for the period convened. In practice, it means that employers and employee representatives meet regularly at the company level to check the execution of the provisions of the collective agreement. The strength of the institution of collective bargaining is enhanced by the Act of 1927 and by the Act of 1937 – the latter creating the possibility of mandatory extension of the provisions of a collective agreement over employers and employees not party to the conclusion of the agreement. One recent estimate, for the year 1987, is that about 80 % of all employees covered are directly involved in a collective agreement, and 20 % through mandatory extension (DCA, 1988, p. 13). For 1990 the estimate is 90 and 10 % respectively (van Kooten/Stolk, 1990, p. 43). The highly developed circuit of negotiation and consultation in the Netherlands has worked to the same effect. Both at the national and at the sectoral level employers' and employees' representatives regularly convene, eagerly watched or actually accompanied by government officials, politicians and independent experts. The most renown central institutions are the Social and Economic Council (a publicly established and acknowledged advisory board of 15 employee representatives, 15 employer representatives, and 15 independent experts) and the Labour Foundation (a privately established and publicly acknowledged board of employer and employee representatives). Quite telling, for Dutch labour relations, is the fact that although the Acts of 1927 and 1937 by now have reached a very respectable age, none of the parties interested in labour relations contemplates any serious departure from them (Sociaal Maandblad Arbeid, 1987).

A.4 Public or Private?

Dutch labour relations are, at least in their legal cloth, both prescriptive and detailed. Labour and employment laws usually lay down in some detail what has to be done or refrained from. The same prescriptive thread characterizes much of post war collective bargaining. The prescriptive detail echoes a rather strong governmental influence on labour relations, relative to autonomous societal influence. We should distinguish two developments. The first is the role of government in actively influencing economic developments, for example in terms of full employment. Here, the Dutch record in the eighties has been one of withdrawal, rather than direct intervention to accomplish such objectives of economic development. The second is the role of government in regulating its relations with employers and employees, defining the space for social action independent from governmental approval and interference. For collective bargaining this is, obviously, a crucial matter.

A small open economy and a strong governmental influence on the economy, often go together (Katzenstein, 1985). Yet, the difference between a strong and a strongly prescriptive government should not be slighted. The policy gap separating the Netherlands from a country like Sweden may serve as an illustration. Both countries have a postwar history of central negotiations between peak federations of employers and employees. But the Dutch negotiating history, much more so than in the case of Sweden, has been characterized by many governmental interventions, especially in wage formation. The Dutch government never left much room for private endeavours, or for developments too far removed from the mean. On the other hand, precisely the eighties have indicated some shifts in emphasis. We will quote the two most prominent renewals. The first is the Working Conditions Act of 1980: still prescriptive, but no longer detailed. The Act integrates previous legislation on occupational health and safety and adds an important clause on the quality of work. Implementation and precise specification of the Act, however, has been delegated to the co-operative efforts of employer and employees. The second is the brand-new Labour Provision Act. This Act replaces the old Act on the provision of labour, and with it the public monopoly on such provision. The public monopoly had been eroded since the sixties, but the new Act is far more than a recognition of that situation. Its explicit aim is to improve the quality of the employment service by establishing a tripartite governing structure, consisting of government, employer representatives and employee representatives. Also, through a variety of measures, the prescriptive role of government is reduced. By the same token, the position of employers and employees is strengthened. Decentralized decision-making is favoured; several checks and balances guarantee that only decisions that command a very large and qualified support from all the represented interests, will be taken at the central level.

Dutch labour relations today are in flux. The old emphasis on the law is diminishing somewhat, as is the character of labour and employment law. The role of government, therefore, is becoming both less pronounced and more indirect; the emphasis on collective bargaining and collective agreements between employer and employee representatives is enhanced. Private arrangements between employer and employee, on the other hand, have hardly come to the fore as a prominent influence in their own right.

B. The Institutional and Legal Environments

B.1 The Structure of Bargaining

(a) General

A relatively comprehensive survey of the number and types of collective bargaining agreements since 1911 may be found in Table 4.

Table 4 documents general agreements only, i.e. agreements on wages, working time and the like. Next to general agreements we find specific ones. Their number has risen significantly during the last decade. In 1974 2 specific agreements were signed, in 1980 there were 74 of them, in 1986 one counts 158 specific agreements, in 1987 168, in 1988 178, and in 1989 they number 185. Specific agreements are one-item agreements. The majority of them are about early retirement schemes, and funds for training and education.

Table 4. Number of Collective Bargaining Agreements (general agreements only)

Year	Industry-wide		Company-wide	Total	Employees covered
	nationwide	regional			
1911				87	23,000
1920				984	274,000
1930				1554	386,000
1940	31	354	1159	1544	352,000
1947	7	91	54	152	?
1951	48	77	239	364	900,000
1956	149	118	322	589	1,749,000
1960	170	118	398	686	2,073,000
1966	205	96	432	733	2,381,000
1970	196	66	484	746	2,310,000
1975	161	23	450	634	2,355,000
1980	162	23	543	728	2,762,000
1985	177	15	627	819	2,772,000
1986	179	12	590	781	2,708,000
1987	197		606	803	2,950,000
1988	200		649	849	3,113,000
1989	198		694	892	3,253,000

Sources: Sociaal Maandblad Arbeid, 1987, p. 709; DCA, 1988, p. 143; DCA, 1989, p. 10; DCA, 1990, p. 59

The number of regional agreements (during the fifties still quite large, especially in agriculture) has shrunk considerably during the post war period. Regional agreements today are of marginal significance only. Usually, they were first consolidated at a national level, and later directly concluded at the national level.

Pre-war data are scanty; much of the relevant statistical material was lost during World War II. The period after the war usually is broken down into smaller periods, the punctuation deriving from the slow waning of the governmental controls over wages. The periods are:

(1) *1945-1963*. During the period the number of collective agreements and the number of employees covered is steadily growing. Yet wages are controlled centrally. Wage-issues in collective bargaining are standardized through governmental 'general prescriptions', deviations from which are not allowed. Also, a host of 'mandatory wage regulations' are issued by the government. The prewar habit of concluding minimal agreements and adjusting them upwards if need be, is rejected. Collective agreements therefore are factually restricted to non-wage issues. Both in regard to procedure and outcome collective bargaining is limited through active governmental intervention.

(2) *1964-1973*. Mandatory regulations all but disappear. Nevertheless, many of the old controls still exist, albeit in a somewhat adapted form; eventually they are renewed by a 1970 Act on wage formation. The Act proclaims procedurally free bargaining. Its importance can be gauged by observing that the collective agreement loses its standard and uniform character, to the favour of the re-establishment of a 'minimum agreement'. The minimum agreement allows, depending on specific circumstances, for upward adjustment of the clauses in the collective agreement. Factually, also, employers and employees strengthen their hand in the collective arena, especially at the national level. The predominant characteristic of the period is a very tight labour market with (frictional) unemployment vacillating around 1 to 2 percent only.

(3) *1974-1981*. The government, reacting to the first oil crisis, assumes responsibility for all incomes through the so-called Authorization Act. Its practical result is a new series of controls on wage formation. When the Authorization Act expires (in 1975) it is not renewed. Instead, the Act of 1970 is re-activated. Although the procedure of free collective bargaining occurs more often than before, the government regularly intervenes to forestall unwanted outcomes. Towards the end of the period unemployment is rising in an accelerating pace.

(4) *1982-present*. Against the background of soaring unemployment, the government in the early eighties withdraws from active intervention in the domain of wages. The formal recognition of this new situation is codified in 1986. In that year the 1970 Act is changed, such that the only remaining legitimate reason for governmental intervention in the formation of wages is a national emergency, caused by 'external factors'. Central, and especially sectoral, negotiations have finally come into their own, procedurally as well as regarding outcomes. The influence of the government has been transformed from intervention into persuasion. The national Labour Foundation fills in the gap created by the relative retreat of the government.

Despite the intensive governmental involvement in wages, up to 1982, the growth in collective bargaining never was impeded. It is the growth of the working population which is reflected in the spread of collective bargaining. Since the fifties about 75 %

of the wage-dependent population is covered by a collective agreement. If we include government employees the percentage goes up to around 80 % (Sociaal Maandblad Arbeid, 1987, p. 711, Table 3).

(b) Bargaining: Sectoral and occupational aspects

The predominant levels of bargaining in the Netherlands are the sector and the industry. Company bargaining is growing in importance (see par. B.1.3 below). In contrast, occupational bargaining and occupational agreements are very rare occurrences in the Netherlands and are of marginal importance only. This reflects, of course, the marginal existence in the Netherlands of occupationally delimited trade unions (Albeda/Dercksen, 1989, p. 41). So-called occupational federations (a conference of trade unions organizing specific occupations or ranks) do figure strongly in the public services (for instance in the public utilities and in education), in the private sector they are not prominent. Their existence is strongly correlated with the presence of only one employer (the government) determining directly or indirectly the terms of collective bargaining or its functional equivalents, or with the presence of a few employers controlling the market.

Granted that the extent of collective bargaining and collective agreements reflect the growth of the active working population, it should be expected that the change in sectoral weight in the total distribution of economic activities will return in the number of employees under collective agreements per economic sector. This is shown in the following table:

Table 5. Distribution of the Number of Employees under Collective Agreements According to Economic Activity

Year	agriculture	%	industry	%	services	%	Total	%
1911	–	–	22,000	96	1,000	4	23,000	100
1920	12,000	4	253,000	92	9,000	4	274,000	100
1930	27,000	7	316,000	82	43,000	11	380,000	100
1940	101,000	29	221,000	63	30,000	8	352,000	100
1960	112,000	5	1,360,000	65	628,000	30	2,100,000	100
1970	72,000	3	1,408,000	61	830,000	36	2,310,000	100
1980	64,000	3	1,418,000	51	1,280,000	46	2,762,000	100
1986	70,000	3	1,186,000	44	1,451,000	53	2,708,000	100

Source: Sociaal Maandblad Arbeid, 1987, p. 713; DCA 1988, p. 111

Recently a start has been made with observations on economic activity, number of employed workers, and degree of coverage by collective bargaining agreements. A first result is shown in Table 6. Coverage of workers is rather even over the sectors, especially if we bear in mind that the high percentage for construction is somewhat artificial. In terms of numbers, manufacturing still ranks first. Recent research suggests, however, that the dominant position of manufacturing is disappearing, while trade etc., banking etc., and construction are becoming more important numerically. The change in the pattern of collective bargaining, in short, reflects the change in the distribution of employment (van Kooten/Stolk, 1992, pp. 39-40).

Table 6. Economic Activity (SBI-code), Employed Workers, and Coverage by Collective Bargaining Agreement

SBI		Employed workers (1987)	Workers under coll. agreement (1988)	Percentage of workers covered
0	Agriculture and fishing	98,000	71,900	73%
1	Mining	11,000	7,200	65%
2/3	Manufacturing	1,076,000	840,000	78%
4	Public utilities	51,000	20,600	40%
5	Construction	345,000	349,100	101%
6	Trade, repair, hotels, restaurants, etc.	860,000	595,000	69%
7	Transport, storage, and communication	338,000	233,200	69%
8	Banking, insurance, business services	479,000	299,000	62%
9	Other services	1,023,000	659,000	64%
	Total	4,346,000	3,110,000	72%

Note: Several collective bargaining agreements in construction overlap agreements in other economic activities.
Source: DCA, 1990, p. 52

(c) Bargaining levels: Industry and company

Since 1974 yearly data are available on the distribution of collective agreements at the industry- and the company-level.

Company bargaining is growing at a faster rate than industry-level bargaining. As Table 4 already indicated, the number of contracts is growing faster at the company-level. Now, in this table, we note that the number of workers under company contracts also is growing at a much faster rate than the number of workers under industry contracts. This underscores the recent trend towards less uniform bargaining in Dutch industrial relations. That, however, is not the only recent trend. Next to decentralization we find the tendency to include ever more items in the collective agreement, both at the industry- and at the company-level.

Table 7. General Collective Agreements since 1974

Year	General collective agreements					
	Industry		Company		Total	
	number of agreements	workers	number of agreements	workers	number of agreements	workers
1974	192	1,940,945	441	327,006	633	2,267,510
1975	184	2,010,865	450	344,311	634	2,355,176
1976	184	2,117,506	462	348,259	646	2,465,765
1977	186	2,161,883	479	371,264	664	2,533,147
1978	192	2,311,934	510	383,869	702	2,695,803
1979	185	2,326,736	533	406,562	718	2,733,298
1980	185	2,349,796	543	412,259	728	2,762,055
1981	184	2,407,065	560	416,276	744	2,823,341
1982	180	2,373,241	607	414,127	787	2,787,548
1983	190	2,395,212	593	406,686	783	2,801,898
1984	192	2,419,000	607	410,600	799	2,829,600
1985	192	2,351,700	627	420,600	819	2,772,300
1986	191	2,284,800	590	422,900	781	2,707,700
1987	197	2,516,500	606	433,800	803	2,950,300
1988	200	2,568,600	649	544,300	849	3,112,900
1989	198	2,687,400	694	565,500	892	3,252,900

Source: Sociaal Maandblad Arbeid 1987, p. 710; DCA 1988, p. 13; DCA 1989, p. 10; DCA 1990, p. 10

B.2 Industrial Relations

(a) The parties: Employers' associations, trade unions

Dutch industrial relations are strongly institutionalized. The parties involved have a stake not merely in the results of negotiations but also in the maintenance of the process of negotiating itself. The parties concerned, employers' associations and trade unions, have a monopoly of representation in many of the relevant fields of consensus formation, decision making, and implementation (see par. B.2.2).

(1) Employers' associations

Employers in the Netherlands are densely organized (Van Voorden, 1984). Most employers are member of several associations. The current estimate is that there are about 1500 employers' associations (Albeda/Dercksen, 1989; de Vroom, 1990). Many of these have been organized into a few peak federations; again, many employers join or are represented in more than one peak organization. Seven peak organizations exist, two for the larger employers in trade, industry, and services, two for the medium and small enterprises, and three for the agricultural sector. The fact that there are two or more peak federations in existence for the several categories of employers mentioned, is due to the still present influence of "pillarization" (bloc formation along denominational lines) in Dutch society. The peak organizations (those in agriculture excepted) do not conclude collective bargains themselves. Instead they construe, publish, and check guidelines on the major issues of collective bargaining. The actual bargaining is conducted by the sectoral association, whose importance has grown in the past few decades but whose history largely remains to be written (van Voorden, 1984, p. 213-226). The latter also holds for the General Employers' Association (Algemene Werkgevers Vereniging), an organization that offers expert advice and support in sectoral negotiations. It should be kept in mind that, in contradistinction to the trade unions, no regular official statistics are available as to the membership and organizational impact of employers' associations.

(2) Trade unions

Official data on trade union membership are published regularly. Table 8 is composed from the Statistics on Trade Unions from the Central Bureau of Statistics (CBS, 1987, p. 21, Table 10).

The 80's have been rough years for the unions, both in numbers and in density. Today, the unions are recovering somewhat from the hard blows dealt to them, although their numerical growth is slow and uneven (growth for FNV and MHP, stagnation for CNV). Moreover, density remains low at about 30 %, and even this percentage is quite optimistic because it includes retired workers in the number of union members. A 'net' percentage (without retired union members) does not exceed 25 % (CBS, 1987, *ibid.*; Albeda/Dercksen, 1989, p. 47; Visser, 1990).

As with the employers' associations, Dutch trade unions share a history of pillarization. Until January 1 1976 the FNV did not exist apart from its two component parts, the NVV (the largest federation, social-democratic), and the NKV (the catholic federation). An extended process of integration ended in 1982, when the two federations formally merged. The statistical grouping of these federations under the label of FNV is therefore, at least until 1976, a matter of convenience, rather than of accurate history. The CNV is a federation of protestant origin. Although invited to join the integration of NVV and NKV, the CNV has decided to stick to its own.

Two out of three CNV-members are employees in the (semi-)public sector. Two out of three FNV-members are employees in the private sector. The MHP, on the other hand, is in a different class. It organizes employees of middle and higher rank, and does not claim a religious, ideological or political background or heritage. Two out of three of their members work in the private economy. The MHP appears in the statistics only since 1975 because before that time they were not allowed representation in the Labour Foundation and the Social and Economic Council.

Table 8. Trade Unions; Membership, Density

Year	Name of federation								
	FNV		CNV		MHP		Other		Density
	numbers	%	numbers	%	numbers	%	numbers	%	%
1947	524,900	54.6	119,000	12.4			316,300	32.9	35
1950	678,000	58.4	155,600	13.4			326,700	28.2	39
1955	824,100	67.5	199,700	16.3			197,600	16.2	37
1960	887,100	65.5	219,000	16.2			248,000	18.3	38
1965	933,200	63.8	228,900	15.7			300,000	20.5	37
1970	962,600	63.2	238,500	15.7			323,200	21.2	36
1975	1,044,200	61.1	228,100	13.3	123,300	7.2	314,300	18.4	40
1980	1,077,800	60.2	304,300	17.0	112,100	6.5	289,100	16.2	39
1985	898,500	58.3	300,000	19.5	108,100	7.0	234,300	15.2	29
1987	896,100	57.7	294,100	18.9	110,800	7.1	252,600	16.3	29

Note: FNV = Federatie Nederlandse Vakbeweging/Federation of Dutch Trade Unions; CNV = Christelijk Nationaal Vakverbond/Christian National Trade Union; MHP = Vakcentrale voor Middelbaar en Hoger Personeel/Trade central for Middle and Higher Personnel.

In 1990 a fourth federation has been founded: the General Federation of Employees (about 125.000 members). The core of this foundation is the Centre of Civil Servants. Thcy are part of the large category of 'other' trade unions and federations in the table above, a category of considerable numerical weight, but excluded from the central core institutions of Dutch labour relations, the Labour Foundation and the Social and Economic Council (see par. B.2.(b)).

One way of assessing the position of organized labour in the Netherlands is by relating the number of organized employees and the employing sector:

Table 9. Members of Trade Unions (thousands) and Union Density, per sector

Year	SBI 0		SBI 1-2-3-5		SBI 4-6-7-8-9		unclass.
	numbers	density	numbers	density	numbers	density	numbers
1979	29	48	643	46	920	38	200
1981	27	44	579	44	912	36	219
1983	22	37	495	41	895	33	233
1985	19	33	412	35	849	31	260
1987	20	33	403	34	850	29	281

Note: SBI 0: Agriculture and Fishing; SBI 1-2-3-5: Mining, Manufacturing, Construction; SBI 4-6-7-8-9: Utilities, Trade etc., Transport etc., Banking etc., Other Services
Source: Statistics on Trade Unions, CBS 1987, p. 15

We note substantial losses all over. Especially illuminating is the onmarch of the category of the unclassified, i.e. non-employed, trade union members. Within the private sector losses are heaviest where union density used to be highest: in industry (a 44 % loss in membership between '77 and '87), construction (23 %), and transport (23 %). In contrast, 'other' membership rose by roughly 40 % during this period of time (Source: *ibid.*). In terms of union density the same decline may be observed. Moreover, the trade unions are quite weak in the growth sectors of the economy; in banking, insurance and business services the density is a meagre 8 %, in trade it is even less with 7 % in 1987 (*ibid.*, p. 19, Table 5). It is the governmental sector in the widest sense that nowadays produces the highest union density (Wijmans, 1987). Yet precisely the civil servant has been denied the right of collective bargaining, although in the past decade major strides in homogenizing the collective bargaining positions of the public and the private employee have been made.

Union stagnation combines two trends: the decline in private industry and its traditional absence in private services. The stagnation is compounded by the weak organizational position of the unions among women and the young, reflecting both their relatively weak labour market attachment and the failure of the trade union movement to effectively impose a policy to improve their position – assuming that the unions first have to deliver before potential membership will join.

Table 10. Trade Union Membership and Density by Age and Sex (1987)

	men	women	total
Membership (numbers)			
Below 25 years	116.600	36.500	153.200
25-64 years	1.061.000	198.100	1.259.700
65 years and older	127.900	13.000	140.800
Total	1.306.100	247.600	1.553.700
Density (%)			
Below 25 years	22	7	15
25-64 years	37	20	33
Total	35	16	29

Source: Statistics on Trade Unions, CBS 1987, p. 18

(b) Where they meet; how they negotiate

Within the confines of the law on associations (stipulating for example clauses on internal democracy and external accountability) anyone can start a union. A fixed union recognition procedure does not exist (Bakels/Opheikens, 1982, pp. 156 ff.). Clubs of employee representation, restricted to the employees of one company, can be certified as unions and are in principle capable of becoming party to a collective agreement (a few years ago this occurred in the port of Rotterdam). The true tests of the union consist of two kinds. One is to achieve recognition by the employer as a bargaining partner. The second is to gain a seat in the representative national and sectoral organs of Dutch labour relations. The major condition in the first test of course is organizational density and muscle, although that is no guarantee of recognition. In terms of law such a guarantee does not exist (Bakels/Opheikens, 1982, pp. 164 ff.). In itself this is no more than a logical consequence of the fact that collective bargaining in the Netherlands developed on the base of private law. Therefore within broad limits the bargaining partners are free to create their own law (explaining the diversity in the issues dealt with under collective bargaining), and to freely choose their own bargaining partners. Moreover, since an employer usually bargains with several unions, the possibility exists that an employer negotiates with a series of unions, but concludes an agreement with only one or two of them. In recent years several major companies (Philips, some larger banks) have resorted to this possibility. Being recognized, thus, is not equivalent to having a say in the ultimate agreement. The major conditions in the second test are the joining or creation of a federation and the recognition of that federation. The recognition, and therewith the admission to the representative institutions, is controlled by the organizations already admitted. In the Labour Foundation co-optation is direct. Formally, in the case of the Social and Economic Council, it is the Crown, which nominates. In practice, it is the Council itself.

There are 251 trade unions in the Netherlands. Less than ten percent of these is a member of one of the larger federations (FNV, CNV). Most of the non-affiliated unions are quite small (about half of them counts less than 500 members). Their sphere of influence is, one must assume, usually restricted to one employer in a local setting (data from CBS 1987: Statistics on Trade Unions, p. 20, Table 7). An example is the negotiating situation of the KLM, the Royal Dutch Airlines. This company bargains with seven unions. Three of them are affiliated with FNV, CNV and MHP. The other unions (of cabin assistants, flight engineers, air pilots) are occupational ones; they restrict there sphere of action to the KLM. Their role, accordingly, is limited to the attempt to claim a seat at the bargaining table of the employer; nationally and sectorally they do not play a part.

The major national institutions where employers and employees meet are the Social and Economic Council and the Labour Foundation. It is hard to say which is the more important. The Council was constituted in 1950; its first function was to top a corporatist restructuring of the postwar Dutch economy. The restructuring along government-controlled lines never materialized. The Council, therefore, concentrated on its second function: that of an official advisory board to the government on matters relating, in a broad sense, to social and economic policy. The Council has 45 members (15 representing employer's organizations, 15 representing the trade unions -10 FNV, 4 CNV, 1 MHP-, and 15 independent experts, appointed by the Crown). The Council's influence is directly proportional to the unity of its advice. If unions, employer's associations and the independent experts speak to the government with one voice the government rarely deviates from the path indicated by the Council. The heyday of its influence was the long period, in the fifties and early sixties, of active government intervention in wage formation and labour relations generally. The Council, during that period, secured the required legitimacy for the interventions, in exchange, of course, for some influence on the actual outcomes.

The Labour Foundation predates the Council. It was created in 1944, and is composed of the larger employer's associations and trade union federations (with the exception of the communist-led EVC, which was and remained excluded until its demise in the early sixties). It is officially recognized as the exclusive representative employer-employee institution in the private sector of the Dutch economy. The Foundation has twenty members, 10 representing the employers, 10 the employees (7 FNV, 2 CNV, 1 MHP). Its importance can hardly be overestimated. Nowadays, with free collective bargaining restored, the Foundation (and especially its Wage

Committee) is the major meeting place of employers and employees in which sectoral and company negotiations can be prepared or, as the case may be, pre-empted. Also, it is the major institution that the government refers to in trying to influence developments in wages, and therewith the comparability of income developments in the private and (semi-)public sectors. The Foundation has always been essential in the mechanism of mandatory extension of provisions of collective bargaining agreements. It is only after advice has been given by the Foundation on the desirability of mandatory extension that the Minister of Social Affairs and Employment is allowed to make a decision. As a rule, the advice is followed.

There is no legal prescription as to the duration of a collective bargaining agreement. In practice, the usual length is one year, although a two-year period is not exceptional. Here, we will assume a one year-period. The cycle of bargaining starts in September, when the government publishes its budget for the following year. The statistical data and econometric prognoses, relevant for the bargaining parties, have been prepared mainly by the Central Planning Bureau (CPB), an autonomous division of the Ministry of Economic Affairs. The employer and employee organizations of the Social and Economic Council are represented in the Board of the CPB, the Central Planning Council. This set-up guarantees a wide acceptance of the data and prognoses of the CPB. During the last decade, next to the data supplied by the CPB, yearly reports on the labour market (Rapportage Arbeidsmarkt), prepared by the Ministry of Social Affairs and Employment, have become available as well.

A few weeks after the government presented its budget, the union federations publish their bids for the negotiations. These bids contain the markers, on the basis of which the federations approach the employer members in the Foundation. These markers can be specified in some detail; obviously, for both internal reasons pertaining to the federations themselves and external reasons relating to the process of negotiating with employers and the other federations, they allow for some manoeuvring space. Usually demands about government policy in a large number of fields – ranging from taxation to social benefits and entitlements – are also included.

The possible outcome in the Foundation is a Central Agreement. This is not a collective bargaining agreement. Legally, a Central Agreement is not binding. It constitutes a strong directive for sectoral and company negotiations, which indeed do lead to collective bargaining agreements. In the eighties a few Central Agreements have been concluded, including a.o. strong recommendations on wage restraint in combination with a policy for shortening of hours, and on the necessity of implementing a policy to reduce youth unemployment. It is up to the actual collective bargaining process to materialize these recommendations. So far, the results are equivocal. Some of the recommendations were indeed translated into collective agreements, with varying degrees of commitment and concreteness. Moreover, the initiatives for shorter hours soon petered out. On the whole, the mixed success of the central recommendations should come as no surprise, as employers, federations and unions have been discovering procedurally new terrain since 1982 in a legal setting that is only slowly adapting to the new situation. What the Central Agreements do indicate, however, is the tendency to include in collective agreements clauses on employment, recruitment, equal opportunities, and so on.

Roughly by the end of each calendar year employers and employees have made their respective positions clear on which issues are and which are not negotiable, and with what margins. By that time the unions have published their demands, pertaining to their bargaining partners in industries and companies. The process of negotiating itself, though, usually waits for the results in the Foundation. At the sectoral and company level the actual agreements have to be reached. Formally, the bargaining parties are completely autonomous in their negotiations. This goes far to explain the rather varied pattern in the processes of collective bargaining. In the chemical industry for example company bargaining is the rule. In the metal industries, industry bargaining is the accustomed mode. Despite the formal autonomy, a larger or smaller part of the outcomes in the negotiating arena has been prepared and, given a central agreement, also been pre-empted by the Foundation (sources: Albeda/Dercksen, 1989; van Drimmelen/van Hulst, 1987).

B.3 Below Public, Above Private

Dutch labour relations are reputed for their consensual character. And rightly so: conflicts figure as problems to be solved, rather than as expressions of ultimately antagonistic interests. Even acknowledging Shalev's dictum on lies, damned lies and strike statistics, it cannot be disputed that in the Netherlands strikes are rare, and lockouts are even rarer (Bakels/Opheikens, 1982, p. 203). There is no strike law in the Netherlands, nor a law on the lockout. With Germany and Sweden, the Netherlands rank among the countries with very low strike figures and low amounts of days lost because of strikes. More telling is the proportion of official (i.e. union initiated) compared with unofficial 'wild' strikes. The latter usually outnumber the former. The fact that there is no law on strikes in the Netherlands is not felt to be a disadvantage. The Dutch courts have adopted the European Charter on the subject, which recognizes the right to strike. Moreover, many collective agreements contain a provision on grievance mediation, in the form of arbitration or a binding advice (Bakels/Opheikens, 1982, pp. 129-130). Also, the Foundation has created a mediating provision, in existence since 1985. The right to strike of civil servants is slowly being established. Since 1984 an independent mediating committee for civil servants has been established. By now it commands considerable respect from both the public unions and the government in its role of employer (Albeda/Dercksen, 1989, pp. 167 ff.).

The above underscores the high premium the government, employer's associations and trade unions place on mutual understanding and elaborate procedures of consensus formation. The relative retreat of the government from direct intervention is therefore not a victory of autonomous societal parties on the government. Rather, it is a renewed division of labour, supported by all the major actors, explicitly including the government. Its results, for the time being, have been twofold. On the one hand we find a growing extension of the field of collective bargaining itself. On the other hand, we find a new articulation in the division of tasks and responsibilities between trade unions and company councils. The latter has put the unions – traditionally very underdeveloped on the company-level – on the defensive. Yet, legislation of the late seventies (on company-councils) and the early eighties (on working conditions, including the quality of work) accords a prominent place to the activities of company-councils. These activities have a growing overlap with collective bargaining issues (hours, schedules, promotion, demotion, lay-off schedules, preferential treatment, industrial accidents and so on), so there is no escaping the issue. At present, however, there are no clear union or federation policies discernible in this area. The employer's associations likewise have no clear policy. In some sectors, banking being an example, there exists an outspoken preference for extending the role of company-councils up to and including the realm of collective bargaining proper. Even there this has not led to specific and concrete policy proposals. One fundamental difficulty is caused by the fact that company-councils are not legal subjects and therefore cannot conclude collective agreements. A second major difficulty is that the employers too are not united as to the delimitation of collective bargaining relative to company-specific co-determination.

The former – the extension of the field of collective bargaining – is enhanced by the new Labour Provision Act, and by the presence of free collective bargaining as such. The new act does not specifically single out collective bargaining; yet the emphasis it gives to decentralized negotiations will result in a strengthening of the importance of collective bargaining agreements. The same holds for the rather pivotal position of the Labour Foundation since 1982. If and when the Foundation reaches a Central Agreement, this will only materialize if it gets translated into collective bargaining agreements. We pointed out above the swift expansion in specific agreements since the eighties. But the general agreements as well tend to increase in scope. By now, collective bargaining may encompass, next to traditional issues like wages and hours, clauses on subjects such as employment programs, vocational training and education, pension plans, travel expenditures, technology, emancipation, recruitment and selection, fringe benefits, temporary jobs and workers, and more. Many of these newer provisions are recommendations and intentions, to be specified and detailed later on. They are not free-floating, though. Most instructive, no doubt, is the idea to enlarge the realm of application for the Act on the mandatory extension of one or more of the provisions in a collective agreement. Traditionally, mandatory extension has been limited to the issues of wages and wage-related costs. But the number of requests for mandatory extension for new, non-wage related, subjects has been growing in the eighties. The Minister of Social Affairs and Employment, consequently, has asked, June 1987, the Labour Foundation to advise him on the needs and the possibilities for further extension. The Foundation published its advice in October 1989. The opinions in the Foundation were far from uniform (Duk, 1989, pp. 692-696). We may ascribe that in part to the very complicated nature of the issue under review. Next, the interested parties in the Foundation have predictable difficulties of reaching their conclusions, not the least because a further extension by definition strengthens the formal position of the Minister in the collective bargaining field. In 1990 the Minister filed a demand for advice at the Social and Economic Council. In his demand the Minister indicated that the scope of mandatory extension, in his view, might have to be widened to include agreements on employment and recruitment among others. No final results on the issue have been reached. As an example, though, of the extensive network of relations between the government, the employers and the trade unions, the preparation for a change in the rules of mandatory extension is quite instructive.

C. Outcomes

C.1 Working Time

Working time has many dimensions. Four issues are distinguished:
a. minimum working age
b. work- and restperiods
c. holidays
d. maximum age of participation.

a. Items a. and b. are dealt with in the Labour Act of 1919, which has many times been adapted to new situations (the Act is under review for complete renewal; how drastic the changes are going to turn out is as yet unknown). The minimum age follows the period of compulsory education, and is on average around 15 to 16 years (although exceptions are possible, depending on a decision of the, governmental, Labour Inspection). Between 16 and 18 years of age, working youth has to combine work and vocational training and education (partial compulsory education). Due to more extended schooling all over the rate of participation of the young has declined considerably, also by international standards.

b. As for work- and restperiods the Act specifies a maximum of 8 ½ hours per day and 48 hours per week. Sunday should be a holiday. Exceptions, including overtime, may be allowed. Some branches use overtime structurally (transport being the usual example), other branches hardly at all (banking, services). On the whole, since the fifties, overtime constitutes a small fragment of total working time: between two and four percent.

Employers repeatedly contest the time clauses in the Act. Their point is hardly the maximum number of hours as such, but the limitation of the number per week and even per day. They argue for a more flexible determination of hours, for example by establishing a maximum number per year and detailing these in negotiations with individual employees, unions and/or company councils. Hours are always one of the provisions in a collective agreement, as are free weekends or Sundays, shift work, overtime and overtime payments and the like. The Labour Act functions as a base-line; the actual number of hours is on average much lower than 48. By 1961 a 45 hour week was the rule in the Netherlands. Then, between 1968 and 1974 the number of hours was reduced again, albeit rather slowly, to 40 hours. Also, the 5-day week became practically a general habit. Since 1983 a new round in working time reduction has been started, initiated by the 1982 Central Agreement in the Labour Foundation. Here, working time reduction was pushed as a policy to reduce unemployment. It led, between 1983 and 1985 to a reduction in working time to 38 hours for a considerable number of employees. In contrast to the earlier reductions, however, the phenomenon this time was far more selective. High level employees were almost everywhere excluded from the arrangements; smaller companies – lacking the organizational capacity to cope with the reductions – hardly reduced working time; companies that did agree on reduction insisted on the right to specify their own modes of introduction. In fact, employers and unions were not substantially divided on these measures, since the collective agreements were based on the understanding that the reduction of working time was not to be translated as a reduction of company time. Moreover, the employees, through wage restraint, paid their share of the costs. By 1985, working time reduction had been realized for about 60 % of the employees in the private sector. With the government the coverage was far more complete (CBS: Statistical Yearbook, 1990, p. 89, Table 13). Since 1985 some, rather isolated, reductions in working time have been agreed upon, but the issue has lost much of its acumen. One reason is undoubtedly that its major motive – the redistribution of employment and the reduction of unemployment – has not been a success. In the industrial sector (representing the lion's share in working time reduction) the refilling of vacant hours was zero in 1983, and only 25 % in 1984 (Visser, 1989). Part-time jobs (see Section A) have been far more prominent in reducing the unemployment of the eighties than reductions in working time.

c. Since 1966 an employer is legally obliged to grant his employees a minimum number of holidays consisting at least in part of a consecutive period. Since 1971 the minimum number of vacation days is three times the number of workdays of one week, i.e. 15 days. Payment of wages during the holidays must continue. For workers below eighteen years of age the minimum number of vacation days is larger (at least four times the number of days worked per week, instead of at least three times).

Most collective agreements do not deviate much from these prescriptions although there is an upward tendency, especially for older workers, shift workers, and night workers. Extra pay for holidays is usual in collective bargaining agreements, as it is in the public sector. Before taxes, the extra pay amounts to about one month of salary. After taxes, the harvest is smaller, due to tax rates and social security contributions (DCA 1989, pp. 40-46).

d. Although there is no legal compulsion to retire at 65, the obstacles (including protective employee insurance) to continue working after 65 years of age are huge. Often collective bargaining agreements contain provisions excluding workers from 65 years on, or provisions severely curtailing their rights and entitlements. Also, the right to the statutory minimum wage is lost from 65 years on (Ars Aequi, 1988; Doup (ed.), 1990). The rate of participation, measured in 1987, of workers aged 65 and over is, consequently, just over 4 % for males in the Netherlands, for women it is even less than 1 %; internationally that is quite low (Rapportage Arbeidsmarkt 1989, p. 80, Table 7.9) From the age of 65 years on a state pension (AOW) is paid, the level of which is connected to the minimum wage. In net terms the state pension is at the same level as the net minimum wage (which is about 75 % of the net wages of the average worker). Above that most employees have, through their companies or otherwise, provided for an extra pension. Since the early seventies the Labour Foundation is working on a more systematic approach to extra pensions, in order to ensure for all employees a retirement income guaranteeing a fair proportion (the idea is 75 %) of the last earned wage. The general expectation is that it will take a considerable period of time before the goal is reached. In the public and most of the semi-public sector this had already been realized.

A low participation is also characteristic for the age group between 55 and 64 years, as Table 11 goes to show.

The Netherlands were already low in 1980. In fact, with Belgium and Luxembourg, the Netherlands are low in participation throughout (CBS: Statistical Yearbook 1990, p. 81, Table 1). Since then the drop in participation of the 55-64 age group has been enormous. It should be noted that most of the early retirements are of an involuntary nature, being due to long-term sickness, accidents and disablement. The latter component, though, presumably contains a sizeable amount (between 25 and 50 %) of hidden unemployment (Visser, 1989).

During the eighties the preponderance of voluntary early retirement schemes, as part of a general collective agreement or as a specific collective agreement, has been growing. Early retirement age for a large majority of employees has been set by collective agreement at around the age of 60 years. Of companies with 100 or more employees 91 % had an early retirement scheme in 1988. Roughly two out of three of the workers eligible under such a scheme use it. It does appear, however, that the growth of early retirement schemes has lost its momentum (DCA, 1989, pp. 29-30; CBS: Statistical Yearbook, 1990, p. 89, Table 14).

Table 11. Participation of the Potential Working Population, 15 to 64 years (percentages)

		Men		Women	
		1980	1987	1980	1987
Netherlands	15-24	49.7	48.6	47.6	47.5
	25-54	93.6	91.0	37.2	46.0
	55-64	63.6	40.7	14.3	10.1
Sweden	15-24	71.5	66.1	70.1	66.7
	25-54	95.4	94.7	82.9	90.4
	55-64	78.7	74.9	55.3	64.1
USA	15-24	74.5	72.6	61.7	64.6
	25-54	93.4	92.9	63.8	71.7
	55-64	71.2	67.0	41.0	42.4

Source: Rapportage Arbeidsmarkt 1989, p. 81, Table 7.10

C.2 Wages and Wage-costs

The Netherlands has a statutory minimum wage, the net level of which is, for adult workers, around 75 % of the wages of the average employee. The number of adult workers earning the minimum wage has been declining significantly over the years.

Table 12. Contract Wages of Adult Employees, annual averages, 1980=100

Wages per hour	1980	1985	1986	1987	1988
Government	100	98.2	100.7	102.1	102.4
Private sector	100	121.0	123.3	124.7	126.1
(industry	100	120.1	122.0	123.7	125.3
construction	100	134.2	137.6	137.7	138.8
services	100	117.7	119.9	121.4	122.6)
Total	100	113.7	116.1	117.4	118.5

Source: CBS: Statistical Yearbook 1990, p. 101, Table 31

In the period 1960-1985 the share of wages has been fluctuating between 65 and 75 % of the net income in the private sector of the economy. The fluctuation in the share of wages responds roughly to the changes in the growth rate of production, albeit with some delay and with a smoother pattern (van Drimmelen/van Hulst, 1987, p. 65). Most wages show roughly the same pattern, although as Table 12 shows, diverging developments do exist.

The wage developments of employees under collective bargaining are more modest and restrained than the developments for employees not under a collective bargaining agreement. The differences are ascribed to sectoral effects (non collective bargaining employees are members of faster growing sectors such as banking and insurance) and to more incentive based payments (for employees not under collective agreements). Table 13 compares these developments (all figures are percentages).

Table 13. Average Wage Changes since December 1985

Year	employees under collective agreements collective	employees not under collective agreements	all employees
1986	3.4	3.8	3.5
1987	3.8	4.2	4.0
1988	3.9	4.0	3.9
1989	4.4	5.5	4.8

Source: Loontechnische Dienst, Arbeidsvoorwaardenontwikkeling cao'ers en niet-cao'ers in 1989 in de marktsector, 1991, p. 26

Table 14. Contributions to Social Security to be Paid by Employers and Employees as of January 1, 1992, in percentages of gross annual wage income

	Employers	Employees
National insurances:	–	25.55%
Employee insurances:		
- Sickness	4.00%	1.20%
- Disability	–	13.00%
- Unemployment (public sector employees)	0.35%	0.35%
- Unemployment (private sector employees)	0.85%	0.85%
- Sickness costs	5.15%	1.20%

Note: National insurances (maximum income that is charged for contributions is 43 thousand guilders a year)

Source: De kleine gids voor de Nederlandse sociale zekerheid, 1992, p. 89

Fringe benefits are widespread. Table 14 specifies social security contributions for employees and employers.

In case of sickness and disability many employers make up some or all of the difference between social benefits and net wages. On a smaller scale this also occurs in the case of unemployment (Table 15).

Table 15. Number of Employees with Fringe Benefits (%) and Conditions

	Fringe Benefit	Maximum duration stipulated	Benefits up to net wages	Conditions		
				(a)	(b)	(c)
	(1)	(2)	(3)	(4)	(5)	(6)
Sickness	100.0	100.0	89.1	31.3	22.5	26.1
Disability	82.3	99.1	60.3	–	22.5	20.4
Unemployment	23.1	100.0	100.0	–	4.0	100.0

Notes: (a) = The first or first few days are not covered by the fringe benefit
(b) = benefit dependent on length of tenure
(c) = Other
The figures in rows (2) upto and including row (6) are percentages of the figures in row (1)

Source: Second Chamber of Parliament: Financiele Nota Sociale Zekerheid 1988 (Financial Report Social Security 1988), p. 33

Most wages are tied to the job. Job evaluation schemes are widespread and their scope is widening (Loontechnische Dienst: Functiewaardering in Nederland 1989, 1991, pp. 6-11). Piece-rates, and in general forms of incentive, bonus, and merit-payments, are relatively unimportant in this respect. Most wages are based on working time. As might be expected payments tied to company results (profit sharing, company savings plans and the like) are rare. When measured in 1984 and in 1986 some 6 % of all employees covered by a collective bargaining agreement had part of their income tied to company results (DCA 1988, pp. 37-39).

D. Discussion

The verdict on the efficiency of the labour market in the Netherlands is in reality a mixed verdict; the labour market cannot be considered in isolation from the institutional structure and the political constraints within which it is embedded. Several large problems stand out:

a. pertaining directly to the labour market
- the very high percentage of long-term unemployment
- the level and the distribution of unemployment
- the absorption of new labour supply through part-time jobs and temporary jobs rather than through full-time regular jobs
- the co-existence of unemployment and of unfilled vacancies
- the tendency in the labour market to react to changes mainly through volume adaptation, to the relative neglect of wage adaptation
- the low participation in the labour market of the elderly and of women

b. pertaining to the institutional framework
- the industrial base line of collective bargaining and of labour relations generally is eroding. Services, banking, (semi-)public activities predominate in today's division of labour. This straines the representative claims of the trade unions and their federations under strain
- the overall tendency of upgrading, noticeable within the employed labour force, enhances the problems of representativeness of unions and federations. Unions organize, proportionally, fewer high skilled than low skilled workers
- recent legal developments place a new and outspoken premium on the co-operation and initiative of company councils; this includes some overlap with collective bargaining. Again, this hits the unions in a weak spot
- collective bargaining has not been able to contribute significantly to the alleviation of problems of groups of disadvantaged workers.

c. pertaining to the political environment
- the decade of the eighties has, in terms of employment policy, been lost. Reducing inflation, reduction of government deficit, curbing the tendency to a profit-squeeze of the previous decade have been deemed more urgent tasks than employment policy
- the policy of allowing for more decentralization and free collective bargaining has not been streamlined with the tendency to uniformity emanating from the welfare state. Only in the very recent past some differentiation, for example in relating social security contributions and sectors, is noticeable
- no clear policy is as yet discernible in shifting the weight in transfers from passive to active expenditures, i.e. in integrating policies of guaranteeing income and policies promoting labour market participation.

Institutional laggards are endemic to institutions; to that rule the Netherlands, clearly, forms no exception. One should be careful, though, before concluding that the institutional and political structures and constraints are ineffective. The problems under a. are hardly specific for the Dutch alone, apart maybe the low participation rates and the problem of long-term unemployment. These seem to be matters of degree, however, rather than matters of principle. On the other hand, it cannot be denied that Dutch labour relations are in for some drastic changes. These will be provoked by the coming of 'Europe 92'. But even apart from that it is obvious that neither Dutch politics, nor Dutch institutions, have been very creative in dealing with the new departures and changes in the world and national economies since 1974.

REFERENCES

Albeda, W., and W. Dercksen, *Arbeidsverhoudingen in Nederland*, Alphen aan den Rijn 1989.
Ars Aequi, Ouderenrecht (October 1988).
Bakels, H., and L. Opheikens, *Schets van het Nederlands Arbeidsrecht*, Deventer 1982.
CBS (Central Bureau of Statistics), Statistiek van de Vakbeweging, Den Haag 1987.
CBS, Statistisch Jaarboek (Statistical Yearbook), Den Haag 1990.
DCA (Dienst Collectieve Arbeidsvoorwaarden), DCA-Bevindingen 1987, Den Haag 1988.
DCA, DCA-Bevindingen 1988, Den Haag 1989.
DCA, DCA-Bevindingen 1989, Den Haag 1990.
Doup, A. (ed.), *Leeftijdscriteria in het Arbeidsbestel*, Alphen aan den Rijn 1990.
Drimmelen, W. van, and N. van Hulst, *Loonvorming en Loonpolitiek in Nederland*, Groningen 1987.
Duk, R., De Stichting van de Arbeid en het a.v.v.-beleid, *Sociaal Maandblad Arbeid* (December 1989): 692-696.
Flora, P., and J. Alber, Modernization, Democratization, and the Development of Welfare States in Western Europe, in: P. Flora/A.J. Heidenheimer (eds.), *The Development of Welfare States in Europe and America*. New Brunswick and London 1987.
Groot, W., and G. Jehoel-Gijsbers, De invloed van loon en uitkering op arbeidsmarktgedrag, Den Haag 1989.
Kam, F. de, *et al.*, Economic crisis and its aftermath: the reform of social security in the Netherlands, 1984-1986, in: J.-P. Jallade (ed.), *The Crisis of Redistribution in European Welfare States*, Stoke-on-Trent 1988.
Katzenstein, P.J., *Small States in World Markets; Industrial Policy in Europe*, Ithaca and London 1985.
Kok, L., and E. Schoneveld, Arbeidsvoorwaarden voor deeltijdwerkers in cao's, *Tijdschrift voor Arbeidsvraagstukken* (1987, nr. 3).
Kooten, G. van, and J.S.H. Stolk, *Arbeidsverhoudingen in Balans*, Woerden 1992.
Loontechnische Dienst, Functiewaardering in Nederland 1989, Den Haag 1991.
Loontechnische Dienst, Arbeidsvoorwaardenontwikkeling cao'ers en niet-cao'ers in 1989 in de marktsector, Den Haag 1991.
Metcalf, D., Labour Market Flexibility and Jobs, in: R. Layard/L. Calmfors (eds.), *The Fight Against Unemployment*, Cambridge and London 1987.
Ministerie van Sociale Zaken en Werkgelegenheid, Rapportage Arbeidsmarkt 1989, Den Haag 1989.
Ministerie van Sociale Zaken en Werkgelegenheid, Rapportage Arbeidsmarkt 1990, Den Haag 1990.
Sociaal Maandblad Arbeid (Special Issue on Collective Bargaining), November 1987.
Teulings, C., *Conjunctuur en Kwalifikatie*, Amsterdam 1990.
Visser, J., New Working Time Arrangements in the Netherlands, in: A. Gladstone *et al.* (eds.), *Current Issues in Labour Relations*, Berlin and New York 1989.
Visser, J., De Tropenjaren Zijn Nog Niet Voorbij, in: *Zeggenschap; Tijdschrift voor Vakbewegingsvraagstukken*, Vol. 1, number 1 (1990).
Voorden, W. van, Employers' Associations in the Netherlands, in: J.P. Windmuller/A. Gladstone (eds.), *Employers Associations and Industrial Relations*, Oxford 1984.
Vroom, B. de, *Verenigde Fabrikanten*, Groningen 1990.
Wijmans, L., *Beeld en Betekenis van het Maatschappelijke Midden*, Amsterdam 1987.

Labour Market Contracts and Institutions
J. Hartog and J. Theeuwes (Editors)

CHAPTER 14

INSTITUTIONS AND THE LABOUR MARKET:
Many Questions, Some Answers*

Robert J. Flanagan**
Joop Hartog***
Jules Theeuwes****

A. Introduction

In his recent review article on the role of institutions in economic history Douglas C. North (1991, p. 97) defines institutions as "humanly devised constraints that structure political, economic and social interaction. They consist of both informal constraints (sanctions, taboos, customs, traditions and codes of conduct) and formal rules (constitutions, laws, property rights)". Institutions "raise the benefits of cooperative solutions or the costs of defection" and they "reduce transaction costs and production costs per exchange so that the potential gains from trade are realizable" (p. 98). In the same article he warns against the view that institutions in society will always develop in an optimal direction creating an environment that induces increasing productivity. History is full of examples of "economies that failed to produce a set of economic rules of the game (with enforcement) that induce sustained economic growth" (p. 98). To illustrate this he compares the existence for thousand of years, until today, of the Suq in North Africa and the Middle East with its "inefficient" forms of bargaining and the much more impersonal and efficient market economy of Europe. Sometimes society can get stuck with inefficient institutions.

The theme of the conference and this volume has been labour market institutions and contracts. Drawing up a private contract between an employer and an employee is governed by formal and informal institutions which put constraints on the terms that can be convened. Two basic questions can be asked about labour market institutions: (1) *why* do they originate in the labour market and (2) *what* is their effect on labour market performance? The first question is about the endogeneity of labour market institutions, the last is about efficiency. While summarizing the papers in this volume

* Thanks are due to Karl Heinz Paqué and John Addison and Stanley Siebert for their comments on an earlier draft.

** Stanford University.

*** University of Amsterdam.

**** University of Leiden.

we will deal with endogeneity and efficiency of institutions, but we realize that we are only taking a first step towards an institutional approach of the labour market.

We begin with a discussion as to why the labour market is characterized by so many formal and informal institutions. What is so special about the labour market or more in particular about the employment relation that it needs all this institutional framework? We will try to present that case in the next section (2) of this chapter. In the same section we will try to make clear that all the neoclassical reasons for market failure are applicable and hence there is always a substantial involvement of the government in the labour market.

Not only are there many institutions in one labour market but to complicate matters even further, institutions differ widely across national labour markets. In section 3 we review and compare the various labour market institutions presented in the previous chapters. This review follows the structure of the individual country chapters.

After having presented all the evidence we will face two crucial questions: Can we explain why we encounter different institutions and can we tell which institution is more efficient than others? There will be no definitive answers to these question in this chapter (will there ever be?) but in section 4 we develop a first endeavour at our institutional approach of the labour market to understand and explain what we learned from the country chapters. The questions about the efficiency of labour market institutions also relates to what we discussed in our opening chapter.

B. Why are there so Many Labour Market Institutions?[1]

Many social restrictions and legal regulations govern the employment relation because that relation has a number of special features that other exchange relations do not have. These special features of buying and selling labour services require a completely different set up. There are at least five special characteristics of the employment relation.

a. Personal involvement

When selling labour services a person has to come along for the execution of the contract. When selling carrots, the seller usually does not care who the buyer is or what happens to the carrots afterward. Also the carrots themselves do not care. When selling labour services the working conditions and the working environment become very important to the worker and can influence the wage that a

1. This rationalization of institutions is different from North's who sees them as reducing transaction costs.

worker will accept. Labour compensation has both a pecuniary and a non-pecuniary element.

Directly related to personal involvement is the level of effort that the employee exerts at his or her job. The employee can vary this level and has an interest to do so. The employer on the other hand is interested in a high level of effort but is at the same time unable to control this level to a sufficient degree (there is a problem of asymmetric information). Balancing the desired effort level of both parties requires intricate incentive schemes, performance monitoring arrangements, codes of conduct, mutual trust etc.

b. Long term relationship

An important characteristic of most employment relationships nowadays is their long term character. When employer and employee start off with each other, chances are that they will be together for a large number of years. To illustrate: the number of employees in the same job for 5 years and more, as a percentage of total employment in 1984/5 was in Germany 63 %, France 57 %, Great Britain 62 %, USA 40 % and Japan 67 %.[2]

This long term dimension implies that investing in each other might be very profitable for both parties. At the same time the long term relationship makes them hostage to each other. A worker learning the ropes of the production process of the employer specializes his human capital. This always reduces the attractiveness of outside opportunities, increasingly so as time goes by. The employer spending resources on the training of an employee always runs the risk that this investment will be lost if the employee suddenly decides to quit. As they mutually want to protect their investment in each other and their long-term relationship, labour market institutions develop to do just that. Seniority rules,[3] promotion priorities, dismissal provisions are examples that come to mind.

c. Wage is price is income

The wage is obviously more than just the market price of labour. For most individuals and households labour income is, if not the only, then certainly the most important source of income. Furthermore quite a number of other incomes (e.g. unemployment benefits, pensions) are related to (previous) labour income levels. Hence the price of labour is a crucial determinant of one's income position, and public policies often confound equity and allocational objectives. Anti-poverty policies or broader income distribution policies often try to achieve their goals through altering the price of labour. Minimum wage laws are the obvious case in point.

---

2. Percentages were kindly provided by Günther Schmid.

3. There are also other motivations for seniority, see chapter 2.

But there is more. Participants in the labour market often have a notion about what seems to be the 'fair' or 'just' wage for the kind of work they are doing. Hicks (1955) was among the first to develop this notion in modern labour economics. Recent contributions in the same vein are by Akerlof (1982) and Frank (1985). Also 'just' wage differentials between occupations seem to be important considerations. It would seem to us that there exists no other market where relativities are so important. These considerations might set desirable wage differentials that one will try to protect against market forces.

d. Labour demand is derived demand

The demand for production factors is always labelled "derived demand", implying that the vagaries of product markets determine the fortunes of the factor markets. Prosperous firms have vacancies. Slumps on the product markets create reorganizations, lay-offs and if worse comes to worst even shutdowns. This creates a dependency for employees that is beyond their control. At the same time they seem to be risk averse and are not interested in sharing the uncertainties on the demand side (or there is an asymmetry in the ability of dealing with risks). Employees usually want stable labour income or at most one sided variation: i.e. they will gladly participate in profit sharing but not in loss sharing.

At least that is one possible explanation of the paucity of worker managed firms in Western economies. Also full revenue or profit sharing hardly ever occurs. Even Weitzman (1983) in his enthusiastic book about the "share economy" is realistic enough to suggest that this sharing will only come about if the government provides tax advantages.

The approach of modern "contract theory" in labour economics is based on the same "stylized fact": workers are risk averse and employers are risk neutral. Hence labour contracts will be written in which insurance for workers is an essential element.

e. Power relations

The view that employers bring superior power to the employment relationship provides a foundation for many private and public labour-market institutions. Individual workers are seen as powerless compared to the employer. They are assumed to have less choice in labour markets than the employer. A coalition of workers may redress the power balance. Labour unions (or public policy) may establish a "countervailing power," to use Galbraith's durable term. In this way, labour markets become bilateral monopolies.

This mental picture of the "weak worker" versus the "strong employer" also applies to other areas of the labour market. In many countries labour law is mostly biased in favour of the worker or some subgroups of workers (children, women). In some countries blue collar workers are treated different from white collar. Most of these provisions in labour law were established in times when capitalism was ugly and workers were untrained or uneducated and desperately poor. Some of these provisions would seem to be archaic for well educated high income wage earners.

These special characteristics of the employment relationship can help to understand and even explain existence and importance of formal (legal) and informal labour market institutions. The 'special' character of the employment relationship is underscored even more if we look at the labour market from the viewpoint of market failures. There are several reasons why markets fail to achieve economic efficiency. Market failures are generally accepted as sufficient reason for government intervention. Important examples of market failure are monopoly (or in general non-competitive) situations, public goods and external effects. Governmental intervention and regulation is also accepted for equity reasons and in the case of merit goods.

Monopsony power at the demand side of the labour has been historically offset to some extent by trade union power creating a bilateral monopoly situation. Power relations, certainly when the division is very unequal are often a sufficient reason for government to regulate or control the process of bargaining. Often the relationship between employer and employee is seen as one of unequal power and national labour law often has provisions that favours or protects the weaker party.

Many characteristics of the labour market have a public good property. Working conditions have a (local) public goods aspect. Work councils at the firm or plant level in which employers are consulted on working conditions are institutions that can channel the preferences of employees concerning working conditions. Public goods such as a collective bargaining system that regulates the rhythm and ritual of collective agreements or the presence of official mediators in labour conflicts are institutions which might benefit all parties.

Strikes are an obvious example of a labour market phenomenon which has often negative external effects for third parties. Merit good aspects are present in safety regulations, in restrictions on working time, provisions for holidays etc. Macroeconomic externalities are an argument in corporatist institutions whereby the government consults with representatives of unions and employers' associations on social and economic policy questions.

Besides market failure there are also strong equity arguments for labour market intervention. Society usually has strong ideas about the fairness of wage differentials. The social insurance system does not just provide insurance but is also motivated by the desire to compensate the unemployed, sick and disabled for their bad luck at the labour market. Discrimination and comparable worth legislation is also motivated by equity considerations.

In the next section (3) we will review and compare the content of the 12 country papers stressing special labour market features and institutions. This review section will form the basis of some first steps towards an institutional theory of the labour market which we will take in the final section (4).

C. Institutional Differences across National Labour Markets

This section of the chapter basically follows the common outline of the country chapters. We start with a broad review of similarities and differences in the historical development of national institutions (3.1). In the next subsection (3.2) we discuss and compare the institutional and legal environment stressing trade unions, employers' organizations and bargaining structure. The last subsection (3.3) presents a selection of what we call "outcomes" of the labour market contracts and institutions such as working time, total labour compensation and dismissal provisions.

C.1 Historical Perspective

Public intervention affects contracts in two ways: constraints on the outcomes (minimum and maximum bounds or outright fixing) and regulation of the bargaining structure (e.g representation rights of unions, legal position of collective agreements).

Public intervention started more than a century ago. The industrial revolution changed labour relations, and created a category of individuals dependent on wage labour. In the nineteenth century, it was realized that the balance of power rested with employers rather than employees.[4] Initiatives sprung up to create worker power by uniting in labour unions, and by providing support and protection through legislation. Although union activity made a start in the first half of the nineteenth century,[5] they could only begin to develop some relevant power in the third quarter of that century, when wage earners got political power through the voting process (Heaton, 1963, p. 741). In most countries unions were recognized, *de jure* or *de facto*, before

---

4. "The awakening of Western Europe to a consciousness that certain things were cruel, intolerant and inhuman was one of the most remarkable events of the late eighteenth and early nineteenth century ...", Heaton (1963), p. 722.

5. Unions were illegal in England until 1824 and until forty or more years later on the continent (Heaton, 1963, p. 741).

World War II. With a few exceptions such as Spain, were unions were outlawed during the Franco regime, up to 1975.

During the twentieth century, nations have often travelled different roads, but for some purposes also have taken identical routes. An interesting perspective on the early developments is given by the economic historian Heaton (1963, p. 724): "Great Britain led in dealing with minimum age, maximum hours, and working conditions. Germany was the first to deal with insurance, and Australia led in wages regulation. International imitation was widespread. England dealt with sweating by copying wages boards from Australia and with health insurance by adopting the German method. But she pioneered in unemployment insurance, and Germany copied that scheme from her. Many laws made national and compulsory the conditions voluntarily established by the best employers. Most of the things which reformers advocated were already to be found in the better factories or were urged by employers who wished to adopt them but were prevented by the competition of their rivals".

Regulation and institutionalization of labour markets has proceeded quite differently in the different countries. There is a parallel with changes in the economic structure, from agriculture and small-scale manufacture into larger scale industry, and with political and economic thinking. The period of unconstrained economic and political liberalism approached its end, and socialist ideas caught on, as a promise to some and a threat to others. Without attempting to give a full account of historical developments, it is interesting to follow the lead in a number of country chapters that "historical accidents" have been vital in shaping the specific format of employment relations.

In the US Constitution, the jurisdiction of the federal government over the employment contract is restricted, in favour of state jurisdiction. The chapter on the US relates this to the issue of slavery at the time when the Constitution was written: with a strong federal authority, the Southern states might have been forced to give up slavery. This may be one reason why centralization never developed in the US. The union federation AFL-CIO is even constitutionally constrained in its relation with national unions and in fact these national unions decide over all important matters.

Both in Australia and New Zealand, compulsory arbitration was introduced in the 1890's after a series of major strikes. It provided the starting point for the high degree of centralization and regulation in these countries. In Sweden, the Saltsjobaden Agreement of 1938, that laid the foundation for the "Swedish Model", was an agreement between employees' and employers' organizations fostered by the fear of government regulation after major strikes. Hence, while in New Zealand and Australia strikes provoked government regulation, in Sweden they provoked self-regulation.

In the Netherlands, unions lost a railroad strike in 1903 and after this painful experience decided to prevent disrupting strikes and conflicts as much as possible. Stability of labour relations in the Netherlands is often attributed to the choices made at that time. In Japan, the important labour laws were introduced by the occupation army after World War II, to change Japan into a democratic society. In Austria, the institutional structure was decisively affected by the Works Council Act and the Chambers of Labour Act, both passed during the November Revolution of 1918.

These examples suggest that singular events may have a long lasting effect on the structure of labour relations. Of course, this is a particular reading of history, focussing on incidents rather than on underlying structural forces. But it would indeed seem quite difficult to explain the variety of institutional arrangements from a general deterministic model. We will come back to these issues in the final section of this chapter.

C.2 Institutional and Legal Environment

Apparently no modern society has ever accepted purely individualistic determination of the employment relationship. Labour unions have been a ubiquitous institutional feature of economic growth in all countries, irrespective of ideological orientation or stage of development. The country chapters in this volume nevertheless document that both the scope of collective activity in labour markets and the way in which workers and employers organize themselves for collective action vary substantially across countries. Past attempts to explain this variation tend to be idiosyncratic – rooted in the special circumstances of a country's history. Without denying the importance of "historical accidents" in determining some key employment arrangements, we also wish to consider possibilities for broader categories of explanations.

Union membership and coverage

Developed countries exhibit a striking diversity of arrangements for collective influence on the employment relationship. Unions may exist in all countries, but the scope of union representation varies widely (Table 1, column 1). Union membership (as a percent of nonagricultural employment) is highest in the Scandinavian countries, in the middle range in most large European countries, and lowest in North America and Japan. Within countries, union membership varies substantially by sector – generally higher in goods-producing than service industries, higher among blue-collar than white-collar employees, and higher in the public than the private sector. Some 1988 data on the last regularity, a comparatively recent and not well-explained development in some countries, appears in column 2 of Table 1.

Table 1. Union Membership and Coverage

Country	Membership			Coverage (%)	
	Total	Public/Private[a]	Change	Total	Change
Australia	42	2.1	Declining	85 (awards)	Stable
Austria	60	1.4	Declining	?	?
France	14	3.2	Declining	90	Stable
Germany	35	1.5	Declining	90	Stable
Italy	39	1.7	Declining	39	Declining
Japan	25	2.4	Declining	25+*	Declining
Netherlands	25	2.4	Declining	100	Stable
Spain	10-15	n.a.	–	75	Growing
Sweden	85	1.0	Increasing	?	?
U.K.	49	1.5	Declining	?	?
USA	16	2.8	Declining	20	Declining

[a] Ratio of public sector to market sector membership rates in 1988 (Visser, 1991, Table 4.9).

* In companies where at least 74 percent of employees belong to the union, non-union members also receive working conditions specified in the union contract.

Taken as a group, the country chapters caution against making too much of the membership variations, however. The data on the effective coverage of collective bargaining agreements (Table 1, next-to-the-last column) show how irrelevant union membership figures are for describing the scope of collective determination of private-sector employment arrangements in many countries. Outside of North America and Japan, legal rules frequently extend the reach of collective bargaining far beyond union membership. Indeed, effective coverage is so great in some larger countries of continental Europe that a research issue that preoccupied many North American labour economists for almost 25 years – the magnitude of union-nonunion wage differentials – has no useful meaning. The fact that the coverage of collective bargaining agreements is effectively complete also limits significantly the scope of application of theories of individual (implicit) employment contracting.

In focussing on the arrangements in their individual countries, the authors of the country chapters were not expected to address why workers and particularly legislatures appear to have a bias in favour of the collective determination of employment contracts. The pattern is too widespread to be attributed to country specific historical accidents. Can legal extension of collective bargaining outcomes to workers who did not choose collective representation instead be rationalized as an economically efficient mechanism for the determination of employment arrangements?

Two kinds of efficiency argument might apply, in principle. One is based on allocative efficiency. Collective action may be desirable to the extent that employers have superior bargaining (monopsony) power. The idea that workers have less choice than employers in their employment contracting would seem to be easier to defend for earlier historical periods when high unemployment was a more common phenomenon, however. The other is based on organizational or X efficiency. The questions are whether collective organization into unions improves productive efficiency and, if so, whether such efficiency would carry over into legal extension arrangements. Arguments for the efficiency of labour unions generally rest on purported "voice" mechanisms – the comparative effectiveness of a union in aggregating members' preferences and securing employment arrangements that raise morale and job attachment (Freeman and Medoff (1984)). Even if these voice arguments have validity in a union setting, the same efficiencies might not emerge when unions (or some substitute) are not present.

In the absence of efficiency explanations, one must consider the interests in legal extension of the union and employer groups that bargain over employment arrangements. Institutional arrangements that eliminate competition from a nonunion sector cut two ways for unions. First, by eliminating the possibility of competition from a lower-wage nonunion sector, legal extension arrangements reduce the incentives for employer resistance to unions. Overt and subtle employer resistance to union recognition is a staple of union-management relations in the United States where the nonunion sector comprises over 85 percent of private employment, but is relatively rare in countries with legal extension. Moreover, by eliminating the incentives for consumers to shift purchases toward the nonunion sector, legal extension reduces the elasticity of labour demand in the union sector, thereby increasing union bargaining power. On the other hand, by providing for free what unions charge for, legal extension encourages free riders, undermining the financial strength of unions.

Widespread legal extension most likely could only occur with support from employers as well as workers. Employers often form collective groups (multi-employer bargaining associations, for example) in order to establish a common floor for labour costs. Legal extension achieves the same result, thereby removing the threat of nonunion (if not foreign) competition. Employers also are unlikely to oppose legislative rules that are not (expected to be) binding. Employer acceptance of legal extension arrangements may therefore signal information about the level at which wages and other employment conditions are set in collective bargaining. Legal extension arrangements are most likely to survive where the outcomes of collective bargaining are unlikely to threaten the survival of firms, that is, where the bargained wage binds only the least efficient firms.

Finally, and perhaps most provocatively, the country chapters confirm an almost worldwide decline in private-sector union membership among developed countries

(Table 1, column 3 and Visser (1991)). This development raises a number of issues that we return to at the end of this discussion of institutional influences on the employment relationship.

The organizational structure of unions

The desire for collective determination of employment arrangements assumes diverse organizational forms in different countries (Table 2). There are three dominant organizational bases for unions – craft, enterprise, and industrial – as well as certain hybrids. Craft unions, which organize workers along skill or occupational lines, were the earliest labour unions. Countries with the earliest labour movements historically tend to have important elements of craft unionism (the United Kingdom, the United States, Australia). As craft work gave way to manufacturing in large mass-production industries, industrial unions, which organize workers in a given industry irrespective of their skill became a more suitable basis for organization. Countries with late-developing labour movements, generally avoided the craft basis of organization. Enterprise unions organize workers at a particular workplace and are the dominant form of organization in Japan. (The distinction between organizational basis and bargaining structure is important here. Enterprise bargaining can occur in countries such as the U.K. and the U.S. that have craft and/or industrial bases for organization.)

Table 2. Union Structure

Country	Number of Unions		Altern. Represent. Available	Organizational Basis
	Total	In Barg. Unit		
Australia	299	Multiple	No	Craft
Austria	15	1	Yes	Industry
France	–	Multiple	Yes	Industry
Germany	24	Multiple	Yes	Industry
Italy	–	Multiple	No	Variable
Japan	72,222	1	No	Enterprise
Netherlands	251	Multiple	Yes	Industry
Spain	–	?	Yes	Industry/Enterprise
Sweden	70	2-3	No	Industry/BC/WC
U.K.	230	Multiple	No	Craft/Industrial
USA	120	1+	No	Craft/Industrial

BC = blue collar; WC = white collar

A comparison of the first and last columns of Table 2 shows that the number of unions in an economy is correlated with the basis of organization, with an enterprise basis producing the largest number and an industrial basis producing the smallest number. By itself, the number of unions in an economy has no simple efficiency implication. Bargaining structure is the more important variable, and many bargaining structures can emerge from a given style of organization, as will be discussed below.

The number of unions in a bargaining unit does have efficiency implications, since higher transactions costs generally result from negotiating, implementing, and monitoring compliance with multiple agreements. Yet Table 2 indicates no simple relationship between organizational basis and the number of unions in a bargaining unit. Japan, with an astoundingly high number of contracts nationwide, has only one union per bargaining unit. Countries with 100-300 unions may have from one to several unions per bargaining unit. Given the transactions costs associated with multiple unions in a bargaining unit, one puzzle that emerges from the country chapters in this volume is why the notion of exclusive jurisdiction, which allows only one union per bargaining unit and obliges that union to represent all workers in the unit, is limited to the U.S. and (de facto) Japan.

In several countries, workers who desire active collective representation (as distinct from passively accepting legal extension) have plant-level alternatives or supplements to union membership. Works councils and related legally-required forms of plant-level representation are common in European countries, but again, not in North America and Japan (Table 2, column 3). Representatives are chosen by majority rule of the employees at the plant. The existence of these institutions is very much a function of official union bargaining structures. Central agreements typically address issues, such as wages and hours, that are common to all firms, but ignore many plant-level (often non-wage) issues that are of great concern to workers. Works councils therefore can address gaps in the collective bargaining agreements. As such the councils can compete with the unions (offering valued services ignored by unions) and can threaten employers (because unlike central bargaining structures, their demands often imply plant-specific labour cost differentials). Unions may "capture" some works councils to the extent that union members are the representatives selected in plant-level elections, but this is by no means the normal outcome. In North America and Japan, where most negotiations occur at the company or plant level, such representation would be redundant.

This issue provides a transition to the discussion of bargaining structure, for it poses the question of whether it is efficient to have collective institutions that may produce plant-level variation in outcomes overlaid on a comparatively centralized collective bargaining system. It would seem, for example, that transactions costs would be increased by competition between unions.

Bargaining structure

Collective representation by unions also produces diverse collective bargaining structures (Table 3). Well-known differences in the level of negotiation appear in column 1. More interesting is the extent to which bargaining structures have decentralized in recent years (column 2). Recent decentralization seems more-or-less independent of the initial degree of centralization. (Reports of decentralization range from Sweden to the United States, two countries often cited as opposite poles in bargaining structure.) To the extent that collective bargaining establishes final outcomes, this development should produce a greater variety of employment arrangements than in the past, since decentralized determination is usually more sensitive to plant-level needs. Moreover, employment contracts should be more comprehensive. As a rough rule of thumb, the more centralized the bargaining, the more limited the agreement for reasons discussed above. (This provides a clue into the endogeneity of bargaining structures. Employer demands for different levels of bargaining may be motivated by objectives concerning the scope of the contract.)

Table 3. Bargaining Structure

Country	Level(s) of Negotiation	Changes	Number of Contracts	Wage Drift?***
Australia	Federal/State awds.	Stable	–	25%
Austria	Industry (Fed./State)	Stable	608+	Yes
France	Industry/Enterprise	Decentral.	6,261	Yes
Germany	Industry (reg.)/comp.	Stable	32,000	Yes
Italy	Industry/plant	Decentral.	–	?
Japan	Enterprise	Stable	72,222	No
Netherlands	Industry/company	Decentral.	849*	Yes
Spain	Economy/Ind./Enterprise	?	4,000	Yes
Sweden	Economy/Industry	Decentral.	4**	40-50%
U.K.	Industry/company	Decentral.	–	Decl.
USA	Plant/company multi-employ	Decentral.	120,000+	No

* Plus single-term agreements
** Plus industry-level implementation agreements
*** Numbers express wage drift as a percent of earnings

Table 3 also reminds us of the important distinction between official and effective bargaining structures. The last column on the right provides information on wage drift. Wage drift is virtually unknown in decentralized bargaining systems (e.g., Japan and the United States) but can become an important element of earnings in centralized systems, where official collective bargaining outcomes are inevitably less sensitive to the individual variation in workplace needs. The experience of the United Kingdom since the 1960s confirms that wage drift declines as bargaining decentralizes.

The importance of wage drift cautions that in countries with centralized bargaining, earnings may in fact be generated by some combination of both centralized and decentralized pay determination processes. In the extreme, observable institutional activity may be irrelevant for market outcomes – a kind of veil through which market forces break through. As the decentralization of bargaining continues and collective bargaining gets closer to the plant level, wage drift may become less important, and theories of union behaviour may become more pertinent for actual outcomes, but these outcomes will also be subject to more dispersion and variation.

The decline of union representation

We began this section by noting that the development of labour unions was one of the great institutional constants of economic growth. As noted, we now observe a broad-based decline in private-sector union representation. A key question is whether the decline results from events that were specific to the 1980s or from broader developments characteristic of later stages of economic growth. To sort out these possibilities, we consider five less global hypotheses: (1) Declining unionization is a mechanical consequence of changes in the structure of employment that are part of the process of economic growth. (2) The original bases for collective representation may no longer exist (e.g., less monopsony power). (3) Collective determination of employment arrangements may still be desirable, but effective substitutes for unions have emerged. (4) Increased international competition and deregulation has limited the ability of unions to protect their members. (5) Employer resistance to unions has increased. (6) Specific public policy changes have suppressed unions. Viewed as a whole, material in the country papers in this volume helps us sort out these hypotheses, and it becomes clear that no single hypothesis is equally applicable to each country.

Consider hypothesis 1. Economic growth produces changes in the employment structure away from industries and occupations that are traditional sources of union strength toward sectors where union representation has been low. Aggregate union representation can therefore decline with no change in union strength at the sectoral level. The same might be said with regard to changes in the structure of the labour force (e.g., the increasing participation of women). This is reasonably easy to check with available data, and it appears that this factor accounts for less than half of the decline in union representation (Visser, 1991). Note that this influence is permanent rather than transitory. For the rest, one must find influences common to all sectors.

Turning to hypothesis 2, if unions are interpreted as a mechanism to counter employer bargaining power in labour markets, one might ask whether the degree of monopsony power has decreased. We are aware of no studies on this issue, and the country chapters provided no direct guidance. Several general institutional developments imply reduced monopsony power, however. The spread and integration of European markets has increased the labour market choices available to some workers, for example, and the development of labour market programs in many countries has reduced the costs to workers of acquiring information and training and of relocation. None of these developments is closely correlated with the timing of the decline in union representation, however. Also, the increased average level of general human capital (schooling) and possibly of specific human capital may have lead to more market power for employees reducing their need for unions.

As we have seen, important substitutes for unions have emerged in continental European countries. Legal extension requires union activity somewhere in a sector but often permits up to a majority of employees to free ride on union activity. At the plant level, important alternatives to union representation have emerged. While these institutions do not exist in North America or Japan, federal legislation and state judicial decisions in the United States have increasingly extended working conditions formerly found only in union contracts to all workers (see US paper). While not tied to collective agreements as European legal extension provisions are, these developments effectively provide a kind of general legal extension. As a result, it has become increasingly difficult for unions to differentiate their product. Finally, we note that in countries with centralized bargaining, wage drift comprises a significant element of earnings growth. We must instantly note an anomaly, however. Sweden, where wage drift is greatest, has increasing union membership!

It is often claimed that unions would profit from the monopoly power of their employers on the product market. Marshall already showed that the wage elasticity of labour demand gets smaller if the price elasticity of product demand gets smaller. More (international) competition and deregulation will reduce whatever monopoly power might exist on the product market, increase wage elasticity and hence limit the ability of unions to protect employment of members.

Increased employer resistance to unions, the fifth hypothesis, is a factor mentioned mainly in the United States and (to a lesser extent) the United Kingdom. When confronted with this hypothesis, social scientists who are sceptical of exogenous shifts in preferences must ask, "If it is worth resisting unions now, why not ten and twenty years ago?" One must at least consider the possibility that behaviour attributed to ideological shifts may in fact be a response to shifting incentives. In the case of the United States, shifting incentives stimulated greater employer resistance. A large increase in the union-nonunion wage differential during the 1970s produced increased resistance to union recognition as well as capital-labour substitution and plant relocation to nonunion areas by unionized employers. In a sense, unions became victims of their own success. This mechanism appears to have limited scope on the continent of Europe, where legal extension more-or-less eliminates a nonunion sector.

Finally, the role of public policy directed at union power is mentioned mainly in the chapter on the United Kingdom. Here the decline in unionism is to some extent correlated with statutory actions increasing internal union democracy and limiting protected union actions, but the magnitude of the contribution of these statutes to declining membership is still debated.

Overall, the factors influencing the decline of unions, while quite diverse when viewed across a range of countries, do not seem to be idiosyncrasies of the 1980s. Rather they seem like longer-term institutional developments that are unlikely to be easily reversed.

C.3 Outcomes

Institutions and bargaining power on the labour market determine the content of the employment relationship. In this section we will summarize the country chapters on three items that are important in the employment relationship: working time, total remuneration and termination. The country chapters contain mostly only factual information and this is of course reflected in our summary.

(a) Working time

Lifetime working time can be decomposed along the individual's time axis in labour force participation at any age, part of the year worked (annual leave, holidays), weekly hours (part-time/full-time) and daily hours. At all these levels there is the effect of regulation, of norms and of individual choice. Also, there is a distinction between formal, contractual hours (including overtime) and effective actual hours, as influenced among other things by absenteeism, sickness, participation in training programs, parental leave etc. Some of these are related to institutional arrangements such as health insurance.

Youth

Participation by age or life stage may be regulated at both ends: schooling and retirement. Many countries have restrictions on youth labour. The US has child labour laws by state, Australia does not allow minors in "apprenticable trades", Japan has restrictions on working hours, Germany prescribes lower maximum hours for youth and a higher minimum annual leave. The UK however, recently abolished such restrictions. Most countries have compulsory education up to a certain age, e.g. the Netherlands has compulsory fulltime education up to age 16 and so has France. It would seem then that regulation and restriction of youth labour is quite common, but the specific format can vary between countries.

There are generally two important considerations for restrictions on youth labour. There is first of all statutory, compulsory education, restricting the age at which one can enter the labour market on a full time basis. Compulsory education has generally been increasing over time in most countries, reflecting the increased need for a higher educated work force as a consequence of technological growth. An additional motive to keep youngsters longer in school maybe as a restriction of labour supply, in order to improve the position of adults. Although, as we will discuss later, an opposite policy is also possible. Having elderly workers leave the labour force earlier in order to make room for the youngsters. It would be interesting to research why sometimes labour force participation of youngsters is less important than that of older workers and vice versa. Is it just a matter of relative scarcities, of demand and supply?

The second important motive for regulation of youth work, restricting the amount and type of work they can do, is probably concern for the well-being of youth: protection in the early stages of life, a safeguard to build up a good starting position in the labour market. Remarkably, most of the regulation seems to stem from statutory constraint, with restrictions through collective bargaining virtually absent. The logic of collective bargaining provides some argument if youngsters cannot exert pressure through unions as older workers can. The latter may then try to keep young workers out or make entry difficult e.g. through training requirements. Yet the dominance of statutory constraints would seem to put much weight on the "concern" or "merit good" motive.

Retirement

Retirement behaviour will usually be strongly influenced by the availability of public pensions. The age of entitlement will be the age where a marked income effect on the retirement decision manifests itself. There is variation among countries in the entitlement ages (mostly between 55 and 66) and in the existence of differentiation between men and women (in a number of countries, like the UK, Germany and Italy, female's entitlement starts earlier). Private contracts may include termination at some age (e.g. public sector workers in The Netherlands), not necessarily the age at which the public pension starts, although this would seem to be rational. In the USA mandatory retirement has become unlawful (with only a few exceptions). Retirement ages are often also influenced by the age at which legal job protection ends.

In addition, there are often early retirement plans, in a mixture of government and private provision. Early retirement programs differ from regular retirement programs by differences in eligibility, in benefits and by termination of rights at a particular age (usually the public pension age).

The public pension arrangements probably started mostly out of the distribution (or "concern" motive). Different entitlement ages (and benefit levels) economically should be explained as "tastes" or as the outcome of the political process. The differences in mixture of state provisions and private supplements (and hence in the routes to obtain improvements: statute or collective bargaining) over countries is part of a general problem that also occurs at other instances e.g. fringe benefits. We will come back to it later.

Hours

Moving towards annual hours, there appears to be a great variation in the statutory annual leave. The UK has no regulations at all. Japan has an experience related sliding scale. Other countries prescribe between 18 and 25 days. Japan is a curious exception in that the *actual* annual leave on average is about half the entitlement. However, casual observation suggests that in the Netherlands this might also hold to some extent for high level management and to a larger extent with respect to entitlements following from (privately bargained) worksharing arrangements. In addition to the annual vacation period, there are usually a number of generally observed public holidays. While the availability of such holidays can be considered as exogenous and culturally determined, the earmarking of such days as paid holidays is certainly endogenous. There may be much arbitrariness in the selection, to the extent that the different forms of leisure are more or less perfect substitutes. We will return to this issue below.

With respect to the choice of fulltime or part-time work, or more generally, the weekly hours not surpassing the statutory maximum, there appears to be no constraint at all. Usually there exist many effects from regulation that affect the choice (such as entitlement to social security benefits in the widest sense), but the hours choice itself seems to be constrained neither by statute nor by collective agreement.

Most countries specify a statutory maximum on weekly hours (with special provisions for overtime); only the UK has none. The levels vary from 38 in Australia to 48 in Germany, Italy and the Netherlands. Considering the length of the actual standard week, it is clear that the statute is non-binding in the latter three countries, whereas the statute might certainly be binding in Australia (38 hours), Japan (46 hours plus a plan for future reduction) and France (39 hours). Obviously there must be exemptions for certain workers.

The national mixtures of statute versus collective bargaining appear to be variable over time. The 48 hours week in Germany, Italy, the Netherlands has been established through the statute. Further reductions have come through collective bargaining. In the recent period of high unemployment, work sharing has been debated as an instrument to increase employment, and the French workweek of 39 hours is certainly to be attributed to this policy.

The standard work week, whether fixed by statute or collective bargaining, is the kink point where standard wage rates turn into overtime rates. Some countries have regulation on that. In Japan, there are government guidelines on maximum overtime (450 hours annually), in Germany the unilateral decision by employers is restricted to 30 hours a year, in Sweden to 150 hours. The US and Austria prescribe a minimum overtime premium of 50 %, the minimum is 25 % in Japan.

Thinking about explanations of patterns and differences, it seems best to distinguish between the amount of annual hours worked, and on the distribution within the year. Separability of these elements may not be a correct assumption, but it is certainly justified as a first approximation. Annual hours worked could then be explained within the standard labour supply model, or perhaps within a bargaining model with the union caring about hours. The next thing to explain would be the decomposition: holidays, vacation, length of the work week, length of the day. Relevant considerations would be the public goods character of the decomposition (both nationwide and within a firm), external effects (simultaneous vacations), imperfect substitutability of leisure at different times of the year/week/day, imperfect substitution of labour time at different points in time in production, non-proportionality of wage and social security cost, non-proportionality of wage and income taxes.

But these considerations are not all equally important when it comes to explain international differences. We would speculate that the only serious candidates to explain international differences are the level and structure of social security premiums and benefits and the level and structure of taxes.[6] High marginal tax rates favour leisure over earnings, fixed labour cost and regressive social security contributions make employers favour many hours per employee over many employees. Workers (unions) may try to counter this by a restricted length of the working year, at the same time collecting overtime premium and increasing demand for number of employees. This assumes that public goods considerations, external effects, worker preferences over leisure spacing and labour time substitutability do not grossly differ among countries. It would be interesting to carry this analysis further, collecting first more detailed data on these issues.

6. These levels and structures may very well be endogenous, but they are not necessarily related to preferences on the decomposition of annual hours worked.

Women

With respect to the special position of women on the labour market, interesting developments occur. Historically, there have been many restrictions on female labour supply in many countries, such as a ban on working night shifts, exclusion from heavy physical work, and even complete forbidding work by married women (especially in the public sector). But more recently emancipatory developments have changed this, and equal opportunity legislation serves to counter such regulations. In the US, there are federal equal opportunity laws to this effect, and in the UK, all constraints on differential treatment of females have been abolished. We are not sure where the constraints on female labour came from (statute or bargaining), but the abolishment seems mostly a statutory affair. With unions dominated by males, this is perhaps what one might expect. It is less evident, however, why women did not start unions of their own, to improve their position. Or is the statutory route obviously more effective?

Related to women's position is the provision for parental leave. It seems that such regulations are not present, at the statutory level, in every country. They are explicitly mentioned to exist in New Zealand, Germany and Sweden, and are also available in the Netherlands. Again, it seems mostly a statutory affair, rather than a bargaining affair.

Finally, in this section it is worth mentioning that legal worker protections commonly have exceptions. This suggests the existence of more and less protected groups, or (if one searches for duality) protected and non-protected groups. The borderlines might vary between countries. With the available evidence, it is hard to draw exact lines, but the suggestion is there that the strength of a labour market position may not only derive from bargaining, but conversely, may also carry over into legal protection: those with a strong market position also manage to secure the best legal protection. In the US, the Federal Labour Standards Act (which sets minimum wages, maximum hours, overtime premiums) excludes some sectors, like agriculture. In Australia, the provision by awards of annual and sick leave covers only 30 % of part-time workers. In New Zealand, the five day week and the two day weekend does not apply for retail and services, statutory leave entitlement requires a tenure of at least 12 months. In Sweden, there are exceptions on work time regulations for particular industries such as the process industry, restaurants, hospitals, etc. It seems that in a number of cases groups are excluded which would precisely need the legal protection to make up for their weak bargaining position. A systematic investigation of such exceptions would be most valuable.

Concluding this section we can say that we are able to identify arguments for the various restrictions on working time over the life cycle, over the year, the week or even the day. In addition to private sector arguments (preferences, technology) there are always public considerations (external effects, public good properties, unemployment policies) and consideration of merit (protection of youth, women, special categories of workers) which explain statutory provisions. But as yet we do not have a general theory to explain the national mixtures of private and public determinants and the changing national balances over time.

(b) Composition of total labour compensation

An immediate problem here is the confusion of terms. Terms such as "fringe benefits" and "incentive payment" mean different things in different countries. Distinguishing minor international differences is probably not interesting. What we think is interesting in this context is to make four broad subdivisions of total labour compensation:

1. immediate monetary reward for working time (straight pay or salary);

2. immediate monetary reward (on whatever basis: weekly, monthly, annually) tied to individual or group indices of productivity (piece rates, merit rating) or to profits, revenues or any relevant indicator for the state of business (end-of-year bonuses, profit sharing etc);

3. (legally) required social insurance contributions or premiums (e.g. social security contributions, premiums for health insurance, disability insurance, unemployment insurance plans) whereby the distinction between the employee's and the employer's contribution might be relevant. Also included here are legally required vacation payments;

4. voluntary (i.e. private or collectively agreed upon) pensions and insurance payments (private health plans, private pension schemes). Other private or collectively agreed upon monetary or non-monetary rewards (company car, cheaper rates for loans, company travel etc.).

Each of these broad categories can be further subdivided. The proposed decomposition of total labour compensation is motivated by a number of hypotheses which have been put forward (and in some instance have been tested on individual country data) about each of these categories.

The four subdivisions signal three different kinds of balancing. The first two are about the division of total monetary remuneration into a fixed part and a flexible part. The tension here is between the desire for stability in remuneration if workers are risk averse and the employer's objective to stimulate productivity by providing negative or positive incentives (penalties and rewards) for higher productivity. A second balance is between the last two subdivisions: will fringes, in this case mostly social insurance provisions, be provided publicly (e.g. public health and old age insurance) or privately (e.g. private health plans, private pension schemes)? The third balance has to do with the choice to be made between immediate monetary remuneration (the first two items) and deferred monetary remuneration or non-monetary remuneration (the last two items). This last choice is of course heavily influenced by the existence of a non-linear tax and social insurance premiums system, but this is not really the ultimate explanation. Because one still has to explain why the tax and premium system is such that one is more favourably treated than the other.

A first finding, quite consistent across countries, is that piece rates and commissions as a form of labour compensation play only a minor role in labour income and are furthermore declining. This is confirmed for most countries in our sample. They play a minor role in Germany, Sweden, France, Spain, Italy and the Netherlands. They are said to be declining in the USA and Australia. Although piece rates would provide the obvious empirical counterpart of textbook marginal labour productivity they clearly have a negligible role. Obviously piece rates introduce variability into labour income across individuals, with hardly any possibility for the employee to cover him- or herself against this risk or to diversify. Also piece rate payments are often subject to rate and norm revisions by employers, which not only irritates the workers but introduces extra income variability over time.

There is only scarce information on the importance of merit rating (said to be important for white collar workers in the US and of some importance in the Netherlands). Neither do we have sufficient information across countries on the importance of group incentives (there is some diverging evidence on Sweden where it is said to be increasing and on the Netherlands where it is of minor importance).

In the recent literature there has been a surge in the interest for profit sharing schemes. Also the more conservative mood (free market orientation) that took hold of many countries in the eighties would seem to favour new experiments with profit or equity sharing. This seems to be the case for the USA, Japan, Sweden, France (here it is called "intéressement" although in the paper it is stressed that it is not the same as profit sharing), and the UK. However there is some contrary evidence from Australia, Spain, Italy and the Netherlands.

As far as the first two items on the list in the beginning of this section are concerned it would seem that over time in most countries a shift has taken place towards more stability in monetary remuneration (less piece rates) or towards incentive remuneration that has less effect on the variability of labour incomes (e.g. more profit sharing). This could be caused by increased welfare levels and increasing preference for more stability. No doubt, there will also be a relation to changes in technology which make individual contributions harder to identify.

As to fringe benefits there are two discussions going on in the literature. There is the US based discussion which stresses the significant increase over time in the relative importance of fringes as compared with time payments. The obvious reason is the difference in marginal (US) tax rates on fringes compared with straight pay and salary. This discussion might be relevant for other countries also. Note that in the US most of the fringes are voluntary instead of legally required.

In most European countries, fringe benefits (read: social security and social insurance premiums for disability, health, unemployment and comparable welfare state schemes) are legally required. Over time they have grown into a substantial part of total compensation (20-25 % in the UK, 46 % in the Netherlands in recent years). Hence most European countries worry about the wedge between total labour costs to be borne by the employers and net take home wages (after deduction of wage tax and premiums). There are reports on worries about this "growing wedge" in the German, Swedish, Italian and Dutch country chapter. Those countries worry because the wedge increases total labour cost and hence reduces labour demand. In an open economy these worries are accentuated by the pressure of international competition. The social discussion about the "wedge" signifies a basic tension between the desire for a reduction in the labour costs (stressed by employers) and the wish to hold on to the social protection provided by the welfare state (stressed and defended by unions).

(c) Termination

If an employment contract would be as any other contract between two consenting parties there would be no reason for legal regulation of dismissal. Any well specified contract provides provisions for what constitutes an acceptable end or an unacceptable breach of contract and what compensation is due in the case of breach of contract. So why is there in many countries such an extensive protection of the worker against dismissal by the employee? The presumption must be that the worker is very much the weaker party in an unequal bargaining situation and needs all the protection he or she can get. This argument is weakened by the fact that in some countries differences are made in dismissal protection between white and blue collar workers (only Austria reports on this in this volume, but it is also true for e.g. Belgium).

Legal provisions for terminations can usually be grouped under three headings: regulation of standard (individual) termination, procedures and resolution in the case of conflict and regulation of collective lay-offs. The issues in this context are:

1. Determining just cause for termination by the employee or the employer;

2. Requirements for a fair or legally acceptable termination of the employment contract. Requirements normally consist of a proper notice period. This period is

not always symmetrical between employer and employee and differs between countries. There are exceptions to the requirement of giving notice;

3. The (legal) requirements for collective dismissals or lay-offs. There is usually advance notification and in Europe there is often an additional requirement of notification of a governmental labour market agency and sometimes the submission of social plans and other provisions to prove that the employer has done the utmost to cushion the blow;

4. Compensation (redundancy payments, compensation awards) to be paid. A distinction has to be made between payments in the case of just or fair dismissal and compensation to be given in the case of unacceptable dismissal. In the case of just dismissal, having to give advance notice usually implies one has at least to pay wages for this period. Sometimes there is extra payments on top of that. In the case of unjust dismissal the problem can be solved by paying off the worker. After litigation there are sometimes punitive damages.

5. Provisions for "special" protection of certain groups of workers such as union workers and pregnant women against dismissal.

The more basic results can be summarized as follows. In all countries termination of labour contracts is asymmetrical. Quits can proceed on proper notice whereas lay-offs are legally restricted. This asymmetry relates to the desired legal protection of what is considered the weaker party in the labour market. What remains is that there are basically two reasons why an employer can dismiss for a just cause (taking into account proper notice): 1. misconduct, incompetence or disobedience of the worker; 2. economic reasons. Some countries have notification for economic reasons only. One wonders whether this remarkable consistency in reasons for fair or just dismissal across countries is really surprising? What these reasons imply is that an employer can dismiss only for negative or zero worker productivity, but cannot dismiss a worker because he or she happens to be less productive than an outside worker. Hence legal protection stresses that an employment relations is a long term relation which can only be broken if it's future is hopeless.

Quite a number of countries (Japan, Austria, Germany, France, Spain, the UK and the Netherlands) have substantial requirements in the case of collective lay-off: notification of some governmental labour market agency (sometimes getting their approval), drawing up a social plan taking measures to re-assign workers threatened with lay-off and making redundancy payments. In some countries (USA, Australia) there is only a legal duty to give advance warning of collective dismissal. The reason for this major requirement must be the sizeable external effects on the (regional) labour market in the case of large scale lay-offs or plant closures. What has to be explained however is why some countries (e.g. USA) think that advance notice is enough to take care of these externalities whereas other countries (e.g. the Netherlands) require more elaborate plans and procedures.

Perhaps the most surprising result in the termination of employment contracts is that every country regulates termination legally and that this regulation is quite uniform across countries. There seems to be less variation in this component than in others.

Yet some authors (e.g. Australia) comment on the growth of casual employment contracts or "atypical" contracts, with only straight pay and (almost) no fringes or other (non)-monetary benefits. This is seen as a way to get at more "flexibility" in the labour market. Also Spain has a large sector with only temporary contracts (6 months, renewable during at most 3 years). It is not clear whether this is a broader trend among countries and why countries would go to such a two-tier (or multi-tier) labour market (i.e. protected and unprotected workers) to achieve flexibility. Increased international competitive pressure or maybe more competitive pressure in general (shorter product cycles) would require a more flexible labour force. Employment commitments made to incumbent primary labour force prohibits more flexibility in these parts of the labour market, hence it has to fall on new entrants in the labour market and secondary workers.

D. Toward an Institutional Approach of the Labour Market

Reviewing the country chapters one first of all notices the big differences. But there are also some common developments and there are probably also some structural variables that would be relevant for a general model. During the last century, all these national economies have moved from agriculture to industry, and from there on to services. There is a difference in the size of the economies (e.g. the US versus Austria) and probably in the degree of homogeneity which may be significant for the possibility of centralization. There are differences in political institutions inherited from the past, which may affect crucial choices. But that may not be enough to explain the variation across countries in the organization of the labour market. Rather, a satisfactory theory would seem to require a mixture of general principles and particular incidents.

In the literature (e.g. see Eggertsson (1990)) there are two research programs that can provide these general principles: traditional (neoclassical) micro-economic theory and the neo-institutional economics. Traditional micro-economics would generate explanations and general principles relying on its hard core of stable preferences, rational choice and equilibrium structures. Neo-institutional economics, a modification of neoclassical economics, would stress information and transaction costs and the constraints of property rights (see e.g. Williamson (1974, 1985)).[7]

For instance the emergence of worker protection (income level, income variation, job security, health, safety) has been almost universal in all developed countries. A neo-classical explanation of this general development in worker protection would rely on preferences. Worker protection could be seen as a luxury good with a high income elasticity which would then "explain" the higher levels as the national income levels grew. Not every country exhibited the same growth rate of protection (compare USA with European countries), but the direction was similar. Note however, that the argument can be turned around: increased employee security has promoted economic growth (efficiency wage theory, easier acceptance of structural change and adjustment).

Neo-institutional theory on the other hand would stress the high adjustment cost of institutional change. A particular institutional arrangement may come about by accident: a specific response to strikes, the influence of some charismatic economist or politician, some unique historical combination of factors. Once a choice has been made, institutions have an innate tendency to continuity. There are vested interests and there is high cost (socially, economically, politically) of a move to a new structure, with new organizations and new rules of conduct. A transition will only be made if the gains are so large as to obviously outweigh the losses. Recent movements in most countries to reduce worker protection could be the response to a general perception that the adjustment cost will be overcome by the gains from increased efficiency.

Both the special character of the employment relation and the massing of acceptable reasons for government intervention give rise to a set of institutions which govern (or restrict) the content of the bilateral employment contract between the employer and the employee. According to North's definition quoted in the beginning of this chapter labour market institutions could consist of:

---

7. The following quote from the introduction of John Pencavel, *Labour Markets Under Trade Unionism*, (Basil Blackwell, 1991), is quite revealing: "..., because labour services cannot be disembodied from the worker, because of difficulties in measuring the input of labour services, because labour services possess experience characteristics making experimental exchanges worthwhile through costly, and because specific skills introduce bargaining costs into the exchange, the market for labour is characterized by much greater costs of transacting than is the case in many consumer goods markets. It is prohibitively expensive of time, effort and money to draw up and enforce detailed contracts. An efficient market should be expected to develop means to economize on these transaction costs and it has been suggested that this drive for efficiency accounts for the extent and nature of the rules, procedures, and institutions that have developed to mediate between 'raw' labour and the application of 'effective' labour input in production."

1. legal statutes and jurisprudence: e.g. social labour law, rulings of labour courts etc.;

2. collective agreements: the outcome of collective bargaining at a more aggregate level than the private level between employer and employee;

3. social customs and moral codes.

Across different countries and across time the relative importance of each of these different institutional elements will differ drastically. There exist different institutional mixtures in time and space.

The explanation of why the mixture of formal and informal institutions differs so much between countries cannot be reduced completely to differences in economic resources, technology and preferences. Reviewing the evidence brought together in this volume it would seem that historical accidents such as traumatic strikes or almost revolutionary changes in the political system bring about a particular mixture which is consequently congealed or frozen and only seems to change gradually.

There are two basic related issues that an institutional approach to economic organizations has to deal with. First, the institutional approach has to explain how institutions emerge and how they change. Second, an answer has to be given to the question on whether existing institutions are efficient in the general sense that they "induce sustained economic growth" (North 1991, see also chapter 1).

An economist would hope that these issues are related and that in any economic organisation inefficient institutions are only temporary and there is continuous evolutionary change towards a more efficient set of institutions. For example from a comparison of the Australian and the New Zealand labour market institutions one has the impression that until recently they where very much the same. At this moment New Zealand is changing its institutions drastically, whereas in Australia everything remains as before. From a neo-institutional point of view one should ask: why is only one of them changing and is it a change towards a more efficient set of institutions (implying that the Australian set is less efficient than it could be)?.

D.1 Explaining Institutional Changes

As was made clear before, institutions often emerge suddenly because of historical accidents (e.g. Spain, Australia). Because of continuing marginal changes they also develop slowly into something structurally different over time. There are at least three possible sources of explanations as to why institutions change over time:

1. Costs of change: changing institutions is costly, not only in terms of actual costs of change but also in terms of the loss of value of the knowledge capital that agents have accumulated about the workings of the older institutions. Hence there is bound to be some inertia in the existence of institutions, even of patently inefficient institutions. Institutions will only be changed if the expected efficiency gains of the new institutions are large enough to offset the costs of change.

2. Market forces: if inefficient institutions lead to higher labour costs and hence to higher prices they can only survive in monopolistic situations protected from the forces of competition. If such a protected situation is all of a sudden broken open by international competition say, than that could lead to institutional changes.

3. Public choice: changes in legal institutions will clearly depend on the relative power of pressure groups. Forceful pro-labour pressure groups with strong representation in the legislative body can bring about institutions that protect the workers. Radical political changes can radically change labour market institutions, the clearest example being the UK under Thatcher.

D.2 En Route Towards Efficiency: Two Views

There are two ways of looking at the different institutional mixtures over time and across countries. The first one is to consider each of these different mixtures as (approaching) an equilibrium situation. Over time some sort of social evolutionary mechanism is at work. Non-efficient institutions do not survive. They either have to disappear or have to be adjusted to make them more efficient. There does not necessarily exist a unique efficient set of institutions. It is for instance quite possible that different institutional mixtures lead to the same total labour costs. We would then observe a set of multiple equilibria each of them being a consistent system of checks and balances leading to labour market results which are in some sense optimal or at least satisfactory for society.

The other view is that these systems are nothing more than a colourful patchwork. They might if lucky be efficient at the moment they were initially developed but through sheer inertia (and high cost of change) they become more and more inefficient. Only after they pass a threshold of unacceptable performance will they be changed again. Market forces are not strong enough to weed out the negative aspects. National economies are assumed to have enough protection against foreign competition (devaluation, import restrictions). Both unions and employers benefit from the inefficient system. In good times the partners on the labour market share in the rents that come with boom periods. In bad times the insiders of the labour market can relegate all the necessary and painful adjustment to the bottom part of the labour market or to outsiders, thus creating a two-tier labour market with a cushioned niche for themselves.

A strong argument in favour of treating these different systems as ever so many equilibria is the strength of competitive market forces. Once a country is open to international competition and possibly also to unhindered mobility of people and capital, there is no way an inefficient system of rules and regulations can survive for a long time. Evolution powered by market forces will weed out the inefficient systems. It would be nice to know the extent to which inefficient institutions have been weeded out, but the country chapters in this book lack the historical perspective to do this.

D.3 Institutional equivalences

Broadly defined, there are five components in labour contracts: compensation, working time, termination and job security, working conditions and training/promotion. Such a labour contract translates into unit labour cost, or its inverse, labour productivity.[8] Unit labour cost determines the competitive position in the world market. Hence, different contract outcomes with the same unit labour cost lead to the same international competitive position: they are on an iso-cost line.[9] The decomposition of a contract into its components is now a choice of location on the iso-cost line. Preferences may play a role (on paid leisure versus income, on trade-offs between wages, severance pay, working conditions, etc) as well as predetermined public regulations (e.g marginal tax rates, tax treatment of fringes, of pension rights, etc). At a deeper level, such regulations have to be considered as endogenous, however. Within this approach, with unit labour cost decisive for the international competitive position, there is easy substitution of the various components of the contract, as far as employers are concerned. Generosity of one component can be compensated by restraint on another.

Equivalences across countries are quite natural for the mix of private and public determination of contract clauses. Ex post, there is no difference between a legally enforceable private contract and a public decree at the same level (there may be a difference in cost and cost distribution of enforcement). A well known example is

---

8. Does flexibility of the contract fit in? One may argue that inflexibility implies high labour cost after a change in underlying conditions, relative to more flexible competitors. In that sense, flexibility simply transforms into unit cost. But flexibility in a dynamic situation, with continuous change, may be something else.

9. To verify this hypothesis we would need persuasive cross-country evidence of "compensatory contractual arrangements", i.e. evidence that a country with a costly arrangement in one part of the contract has low-cost arrangements elsewhere.

the equivalence of a legal minimum wage and a collectively agreed wage at the same level. But the same holds for pensions, job security, working conditions, etc. Many, if not all contract outcomes that can be set by public decree can also be set by voluntary agreement between the same parties. Hence, the difference between public and private determination of contract outcomes should be in ex ante differences: the level of the contract outcome (i.e the height of the – minimum – wage), the coverage of the contract (the jurisdiction, or "bargaining area"), the level of transaction cost (the cost of parliamentary and government decision making versus the cost of collective bargaining) and the set of available instruments. For a given set of bargaining parties, with a given jurisdiction, public determination of contract outcomes is like negotiation through a third party, a sort of arbitration (the parties will usually not sit back and let a government decide without any lobbying activity).

More detailed analysis is needed to predict something on conditions for equivalent outcomes and on direction and magnitude of differences. Such analysis should also acknowledge that sometimes public decrees set minimum levels, with private determination of additional employee benefits (suggesting that for given coverage the mixture of public and private determination is not relevant) and that sometimes governments may overshoot (reaching levels that are not supplemented by private benefits and that would not have been reached in private bargaining). And it should analyze why some components of the contract are more intensely regulated than others: compensation and promotion/training practices are often free (except for minimum wages, and for the awards system in Australia), whereas in all countries there is public regulation of working time, job security and working conditions (safety regulation).

Finally, there are questions about the bargaining structure. The bargaining structure can differ in many ways, in the nature of worker representation, unions versus works councils, multi-union/multi-employer versus single union/single plant bargaining, industry or national bargaining. The differences probably will mostly affect dispersion of outcomes, but this is not all certain. It depends on the scope for local variations in outcomes, as is clearly illustrated by the phenomenon of wage drift in case of centralized bargaining. It is even conceivable that in the end, outcomes are identical, but obtained at different cost of transacting.

E. Conclusion

Neoclassical theory used to ignore the institutional details of the labour market. Efficient institutions raise the benefits and reduce the costs of economic transactions. When efficient they oil the economic machine, when inefficient they are sand in the wheels. Formal and informal institutions are prominent in the labour market due to the special characteristics of the employment relation. While comparing labour market institutions in 12 industrial countries across four continents we discovered a wide variety of institutional mixtures. The institutional and legal environment for collective bargaining differs enormously (but at the same time there are many similarities). We found that working time, retirement provisions, contract termination, composition of remuneration etc. can be specified in many different ways. Yet there are also many similarities. These contractual provisions can either be convened in private or collective agreement or made mandatory by public regulation. The private-public mix can be very different, yet produce similar results.

Our cross-national comparison raises the question of how labour market institutions come about and if and why they change over time. Comparing the country papers made clear that different institutional mixtures can quite possibly be efficient in the sense of achieving for instance the same unit labour cost. Different institutional mixtures can increase labour productivity, stimulate economic growth and foster social welfare in very much the same way. But not all institutional mixtures will be efficient all the time. Hence the crucial question remains whether economic forces (e.g. international competition) will over time generate an evolutionary equilibrium in which only efficient institutional mixtures survive or whether the cost of change are so high or interest groups benefitting from the present institutional set-up are so strong that they can frustrate institutional change towards more welfare for all. To these questions we hope to turn in the future.

REFERENCES

Akerlof, G.A. (1982), Labour Contracts as Partial Gift Exchange, *Quarterly Journal of Economics*, pp. 543-569.

Eggertsson, T. (1990), *Economic Behavior and Institutions*, Cambridge University Press, Cambridge.

Frank, R.H. (1985), *Choosing the Right Pond: Human Behavior and the Quest for Status*, Oxford University Press: New York.

Freeman, R.B. and J.L. Medoff (1984), *What Do Unions Do?* Basic Books, New York.

Heaton, H. (1963), *Economic History of Europe*, London: Harper & Row.

Hicks, J.R. (1955), Economic Foundations of Wage Policy, *Economic Journal*, pp. 389-404.

North, D.C. (1991), Institutions, *Journal of Economic Perspectives*, pp. 97-112.

Visser, J. (1991), Trends in Trade Union Membership, in: OECD, *Employment Outlook*, OECD, Paris, Chapter 4.

Weitzman, M.L. (1983), *The Share Economy*, Harvard University Press, Cambridge.

Williamson, O.E. (1974), *Markets and Hierarchies*, The Free Press, New York,

Williamson, O.E. (1985), *The Economic Institutions of Capitalism: Firms, Markets, Relational Contracting*, The Free Press, New York.

BIOGRAPHIES

John T. Addison is currently Professor of Economics at the University of South Carolina (USC). He was educated at the London School of Economics where he received his B.Sc. (Economics), M.Sc. and Ph.D. degrees and specialized in labour economics. He joined USC in January 1981, but has continued to lecture extensively in Europe, most recently as Visiting Professor at the Westfälische Wilhelms-Universität Münster (1991-). During the latter half of 1991 he was selected as Bradley Resident Scholar at the Heritage Foundation in Washington.

Professor Addison has published widely in the major economics and specialist labour journals. He is the author or coauthor of labour texts, the most recent of which is *Job Displacement: Consequences and Implications for Policy* (Wayne State, 1991). His current research focuses on unemployment and earnings development in the wake of job displacement, the effect of unions on economic performance, and mandated benefits with special reference to the EC 'Social Charter'.

Robert J. Flanagan is Professor of Labour Economics in the Graduate School of Business, Stanford University. He was educated at Yale University (B.A.) and the University of California at Berkeley (M.A. and Ph.D.). He has been a faculty member at the Graduate School of Business, University of Chicago and the Department of Economics, University of California, Berkeley (visiting). Professor Flanagan has also been a Senior Fellow at the Brookings Institution (1983-1984), the Research School for the Social Sciences at the Australian National University (1990), and the Netherlands Institute for Advanced Study (1991), and he has served with the Council of Economic Advisers, Executive office of the President (1978-1979) and the Organization for Economic Cooperation and Development (1988).

Jacques Freyssinet, Professor of Economics, University of Paris I; formerly (1981-1987) President of the Board of "Agence Nationale pour l'Emploi" (France); since 1988 Director of the "Institut de Recherches Economiques et Sociales" (Paris). Main areas of research: macro-economics of employment, employment and unemployment policy, labour market. Recent publications are: *Politiques d'emploi des grands groupes français*, P.U.G., 1982; *Le chômage*, Ed. La Découverte, 1984; Pour une prospective des métiers et des qualifications, La Documentation Française, 1991; "Trois années de croissance forte de l'emploi en France", *La Revue de l'IRES*, no. 7, automne 1991.

Gianni Geroldi, Professor of Economics, University of Parma and the Catholic University of Milan. Responsible for Economic Research at the "Fondazione Regionale Pietro Seveso" in Milan. He has participated in international working parties on industrial structure transformation and long-term unemployment. On this topic, he also conducted comparative country studies funded by the European Commission. Presently he is interested in the economic aspects of different social security systems in Europe. He is author of several publications in the field of labour market, industrial and public economics.

Joop Hartog got his first degree in economics from the Netherlands School of Economics (Rotterdam) in 1970. He added an MA degree at Queen's University (Canada) in 1971 and defended his Ph.D. dissertation in 1978 at the Erasmus University Rotterdam. He worked at the Erasmus University from 1972 to 1981, and then became a full professor at the University of Amsterdam. He was advisor to the Social and Cultural Planning Bureau from 1979 to 1981 and worked as a visitor at the University of Wisconsin (Madison), Stanford University, Queen's University, the World Bank and Cornell University. He published on labour economics and economics of education. Jointly with Jules Theeuwes he founded and edits *Labour Economics: An International Journal.*

Juan F. Jimeno is Lecturer of Economics at the London School of Economics. He holds a Ph.D. degree in Economics from the Massachusetts Institute of Technology (M.I.T.) which he received in 1990. His professional interests include macroeconomic and labour market topics. He is the author of *Unemployment and Labour Market Flexibility: Spain*, written jointly with Luis Toharia, to be published by the ILO.

Ferdinand Karlhofer studied political science at the University of Salzburg where he received his doctor's degree in 1982. He is Assistant Professor of Political Science at the University of Innsbruck. He has also lectured at the University of Salzburg and the University of Linz. In the spring semester 1991, he was Visiting Assistant Professor and Lecturer of Political Science at the University of New Orleans. His publications include the book *Wilde Streiks in Österreich* (1983) and a number of articles on industrial relations, and on political theory. At present, he is preparing a habilition thesis on Austrian trade unionism in comparative perspective (to be published in 1993).

Anton Korver is a lecturer in sociology. He holds a degree in economics (1971) and has been employed at the University of Amsterdam. In the fall of 1985 he was visiting associate professor at the University of Oregon (US). Since September 1992 he is employed as lecturer at the University of Brabant, Department of Personnel Sciences. His Ph.D. was completed in 1989 at the University of Wageningen. His research interests include work organizations and (internal) labour markets. He published a book on the labour market in the USA (The Fictitious Commodity, Greenwood, New York, 1990).

Ulrich Ladurner studied political science at the University of Innsbruck. He received a Mag. phil. degree in 1990. At present, he is preparing a doctoral thesis on the ideological and ethnic division of trade unions in South Tyrol. He is co-author of articles on industrial relations.

Marco Maiello, Researcher of "Fondazione Regionale Pietro Seveso" on labour market subjects, with specific interests in long-term unemployment, job creation initiatives and local development. Assistant to the scientific coordination of the National Research Council Project: "Structure and Evolution of Italian Economy" (1983-1988). Consultant of The Labour Agency of Trento and Friuli Venezia Giulia. Italian Consultant of "Eurocounsel", a programme of the European Foundation concerning long-term unemployment.

Richard Mitchell has Masters Degrees in law (the University of Melbourne) and industrial relations (the London School of Economics and Political Science). He has taught labour law and industrial relations in the Department of Business Law at the University of Melbourne since 1975, and in 1990-1991 was Associate Professor at the National Key Centre in Industrial Relations (Monash University). He is joint editor of the *Australian Journal of Labour Law*, and the author of several books and numerous articles on labour law and industrial relations.

Christian Nilsson is senior lecturer at the Department of Economics at Uppsala University. He is also working as researcher at the Trade Union Institute for Economic Research (FIEF) in Stockholm. His research interest is in empirical labour economics. He has written about the Swedish wage formation process on local and central levels and published econometric studies on time series and regional data on wages, inter-regional migration and unemployment. He takes part in the project "An Econometric Model of the Swedish Economy (SNEPQ), a medium sized model intended for policy simulations.

Karl-Heinz Paqué is a senior economist and head of the Department I (Growth and Structural Policy) at the Institute of World Economics in Kiel, Germany. He has studied at the Universities of Saarbrücken, British Columbia (Vancouver, Canada) and Kiel. He received his doctorate in Kiel with a thesis on the economics of philanthropy for which he was awarded two national prizes for research in political economy. He has previously been visiting research fellow at the Center for Study of Public Choice, Blacksburg, Virginia, and lecturer at the University of Kiel. His main research interests are in political economy, labour economics, economic history, and in methodological matters. He is co-author of *The Fading Miracle – Four Decades of Social Market Economy in Germany* (Cambridge University Press, 1992).

Solomon W. Polachek is Professor of Economics at the State University of New York at Binghamton. He has been a Visiting Professor at Erasmus University, the Catholic University of Leuven, and Tel Aviv University, and has held post-doctoral fellowships at the University of Chicago as well as the Hoover Institution at Stanford University. He received his Ph.D. from Columbia University. His work on earnings differences is widely published in learned journals, as is his work relating international relations to country economies. His most recent book is *The Economics of Earnings* (with Stanley Siebert), forthcoming in 1993. He has held numerous fellowships and grants and currently serves on the editorial boards of *Conflict Management and Peace Science* and the *International Studies Quarterly*.

Yoshio Sasajima graduated from Tokyo Metropolitan University (mathematics, B.S.) in 1967. Studied at Brown University (economics, M.A.) between 1971 and 1973. Got a position in the Ministry of Labour in 1967 upon university graduation. Jointly with his position in the Ministry, he worked as an economist for both the Economic Planning Agency (Research Department, 1976-77) and the OECD (Directorate for Manpower, Social Affairs and Education, 1980-83). In the Ministry of Labour, he held various positions mainly as an economist. In 1986, he moved to Meijigakuin University, and currently holds a position as a professor of economics. Current major research interests are related to the changing structure of the labour market and its policy implications.

Peter Scherer has a Masters Degree in Sociology (Australian National University) and a Ph.D. in Economics (Cornell University). He has taught labour economics and comparative industrial relations at Sydney University, and in 1984 was appointed Deputy Director of the Australian Bureau of Labour Market Research. Since 1986 he has been working at the Organisation for Economic Co-operation and Development in Paris, where he is now head of the Social Policies and Industrial Relations Division.

Stanley Siebert graduated in economics from the University of Cape Town, and gained his Ph.D. from the London School of Economics in 1975. His most recent book is *The Economics of Earnings* (with Sol Polachek), forthcoming in 1993. His research is concerned with how free labour markets and informed individual choice can work to increase wages and improve job opportunities.

Jules J.M. Theeuwes, Professor of Economics, Faculty of Law, University of Leiden (1986-). University Lecturer, Faculty of Economics, Free University Amsterdam (1985-1986) and Faculty of Economics, Erasmus University Rotterdam (1976-1985). Research Associate at the Centre for Operations Research and Econometrics (CORE), Leuven, Belgium (1975-1976). Visiting Professor of Economics at the University of British Columbia, Vancouver, Canada (1978-1979) and at the University of Wisconsin, Madison, USA (1988). Fellow at NIAS, Wassenaar (1990-1991). Jointly with Joop Hartog he founded and edits *Labour Economics: An International Journal.*

Luis Toharia is Professor of Economics at the University of Alcalá de Henares (Spain). He holds a Ph.D. in Economics from M.I.T. (1979). He has written many articles and books on the Spanish labour market. He has acted as consultant for the Spanish government as well as for the Commission for the European Communities. His professional interests include all aspects related to the operation of labour markets generally and to the Spanish labour market in particular.

Tiziano Treu (1939), Professor ordinarius of Labour Law at the Catholic University of Milan, Law School. From 1970 to 1988 Professor ordinarius of Labour Law at the University of Pavia. President of the Italian Industrial Relations Research Association from 1980 to 1991; member of the Executive Committee of the International Industrial Relations Association (since 1989). Member of the editorial staff of *Rivista giuridica del lavoro*, of *Rivista di diritto del lavoro* and of *Le nuove leggi civili commentate*; national correspondent for the *International Labour Law Reports* and the *International Encyclopedia of Labor Law and Industrial Relations*; member of the editorial board of the *International Journal of Comparative Labour Law and Industrial Relations.*

Alan Williams is a graduate of the universities of Wales, Auckland and Massey and a senior member of the Department of Human Resource Management at Massey University, where he holds a personal chair in Industrial Relations and Labour Economics. He has held visiting appointments at Missouri, Warwick, and Cambridge, where he is a visiting fellow in Management at Wolfson College. He is a member of the editorial boards of the International Journal of Human Resource Management and Employee Relations. In addition he has worked as a consultant with the UNDP, the ILO and the OECD. Professor Williams has published widely in industrial relations, labour economics, labour law, and human resource management. His contemporary research interests involve a range of topics relation to the theories of labour market deregulation, and to human capital formation. He is presently writing a book on theoretical linkages between labour market flexibility and human resource management, which will be published by Avebury Press in late 1992.

INDEX